Let's Spend the Night Together

Backstage Secrets of Rock Muses and Supergroupies

Pamela Des Barres

CHICAGO
REVIEW
PRESS

An A Cappella Book

Library of Congress Cataloging-in-Publication Data

Des Barres, Pamela.

 Let's spend the night together : backstage secrets of rock muses and supergroupies / Pamela Des Barres.

   p. cm.

 ISBN 978-1-55652-668-8 (cloth)

 ISBN 978-1-55652-789-0 (paper)

 1. Groupies—Biography. 2. Groupies—Interviews. I. Title.

 ML406.D47 2007

 781.66092'2—dc22

 [B]

 2006100148

Cover design: Monica Baziuk

Front cover photo: Pamela Des Barres

Back cover photos: (left) Lori Lightning with Jimmy Page, Lori Mattix collection; (right) Pleasant Gehman with Iggy Pop, Jenny Lens; author photo, Randee St. Nicholas

Interior design: Pamela Juárez

Copyright © 2008 by Pamela Des Barres

All rights reserved

Published by Chicago Review Press, Incorporated

814 North Franklin Street

Chicago, Illinois 60610

ISBN 978-1-55652-789-0

Printed in the United States of America

5 4 3 2 1

Contents

Little Wing is like one of those beautiful girls that come around sometimes ... you play your gig; it's the same thing as the olden days, and these beautiful girls come around ... you do actually fall in love with them because that's the only love you can have. It's not always the physical thing ... "Oh, there's one over there ..." It's not one of those scenes. They actually tell you something. They release different things inside themselves ... Little Wing was a very sweet girl that came around that gave me her whole life and more if I wanted it.

—JIMI HENDRIX

We all started playing guitar for one reason: groupies. Groupies never torture you the way your girlfriend does. They never ask you what sign you are, why don't you call, and other horrific torture devices women have invented through the ages to maximize the amount of hoops the male species has to jump through in order to get to the honey pot. Every rock star knows the truth: while it's a lot of fun being on stage, it's more fun going back to the hotel for the encores.

—GENE SIMMONS

Groupies are beautiful. They come to hear you play, they throw flowers and underpants, they give you kisses and love. They come to bed with you. They're beautiful. We love groupies.

—COUNTRY JOE MCDONALD

Groupies are a better ball, by and large ... they've had more experience and they're willing to try more things. The sex angle is important. But no more important than girls who are also good friends and make you feel like family.

—JIMMY PAGE

You were at school and you were pimply and no one wanted to know you. You get into a group and there are thousands of chicks ... little girls screaming ... man, it's power!

—ERIC CLAPTON

Some nights I look out and want to fuck the whole front row!

—Robert Plant

I got into music for chicks and beer, and fortunately it's working out.

—Mark McGrath

I love 'em, they keep a young man hard. They're like our alter egos. They're doin' the same thing we are.

—Steven Tyler

I went through my crazy period in the '70s. Yes, I *was* Caligula. "Bring me thy drugs and women."

—Peter Frampton

I only love musicians! I can't help it! Bass, drums, guitar— you've just got to play something.

—Ashlee Simpson

Part of rock is dick, part of rock is going to see a gig and wanting to fuck the guy.

—Courtney Love

Appreciation is a wonderful thing; it makes what is excellent in others belong to us as well.

—Voltaire

Extraordinary how potent cheap music is.

—Noel Coward

Acknowledgments

This book is dedicated to all the amazingly forthright women who have graciously told me their stories. I sincerely thank these bold, sassy, unrepentant dolls for taking me (and you) on stage, backstage, into hotel rooms, aboard tour buses, and into bed with them (and their chosen rock gods).

Kisses to the best agent a chick could ask for, Peter McGuigan. I didn't know chivalrous agents like Peter existed. And thanks to the folks at Chicago Review Press, especially my editor, Yuval Taylor—definitely a rebel in his field. Copious hugs to Patti Johnsen, who happily and expertly assisted me as my deadline drew near. Much appreciation goes to my oldest friend, Iva Turner, for focusing her considerable intelligence on this project, editing each chapter as I completed it. I needed an objective viewpoint, and that's exactly what she gave me. To all my gal pals who haven't seen much of me the past two years—we'll have dinner soon, I promise. Thanks to MDB for always offering excellent advice and being the best ex-husband ever. To my boy, Nick, for believing in his hippie-hearted mom. Endless adoration to my darling teacher, Light, for always pointing her laser beam directly at the truth. Thanks to Victor Hayden for just being Victor. To Bob Dylan, a source of eternal inspiration. To all the musicians who have rocked my universe and continue to do so. And to my boyfriend, Mike Stinson, for looking at me the way he does.

Introduction

As a young girl, I was drawn to Jesus. Even though my parents weren't religious and rarely went to church, my sweet, perceptive mother made sure the Good Book was handy, and for my twelfth birthday, my dear Aunt Edna got me my first white leather-bound, gilt-edged Bible, which I still have. I voraciously studied the New Testament, especially the words printed in red ink. The words HE said.

It wasn't long before I hung photos of Elvis next to the huge color portrait of a glittery Jesus that my dad brought home from Mexico. The way I felt about these icons was strangely similar, with one blasphemous exception: the King made me feel giddy and horny, while the King of Kings made me feel guilty about it. When I was about thirteen, and had just started rocking out, the pastor at the Methodist church I'd recently joined stated that dancing was a sin. I was dumbstruck and pored through the pages of my Bible, looking for the verse that made this horrid proclamation. I never found it. But aha! Psalm 150 says, "Praise Him with timbrel and *dancing*." Whew. I had no idea what "timbrel" was, but the passage gave me mighty relief.

Until I left the square churches behind and started calling Laurel Canyon "God's Golden Backyard," I assumed that the oft-mentioned Mary Magdalen was a fallen whore who Christ had redeemed. I thought it was cool that he risked his reputation by defending such a wicked girl, and many other so-called outcasts. If Jesus saved such a tragic wretch, there must be hope for me! But even before I discovered the truth, I suspected there was more to the story than a rehabilitated hooker. After all, Magdalen was the only recorded female disciple, and the first person he appeared to after the stone was rolled away.

As a teenager I read *The Last Temptation of Christ* by Nikos Kazantzakis, and a massive jumble of guilt was suddenly lifted.

It gave me solace that, besides being holy, Jesus was also a *man* who struggled with life just like we all do. I went digging again. Where exactly in the Bible did it say that Magdalen was a whore? Guess what? It doesn't. Seventeen hundred years ago, an early church father (read: pious jackass) turned several shameless women in the Bible into *one* immoral sinner, and Jesus' beloved muse disappeared.

Long before *The Da Vinci Code*, before the books, documentaries, and discussions about what Magdalen's real relationship with Jesus might have been, I went on a quest to discover her true identity. I even took a vacation to Israel and wandered around Magdala, the seaside town where she was born. Shortly after my trip, I discovered an ancient Gnostic text, the Gospel according to Mary Magdalen, confirming my suspicions that she was indeed, the Lord's beloved. The disciple Peter asks, "Did He really speak privately with a woman and not openly to us? Are we to turn about and all listen to her? Did He prefer her to us?" Levi answers, "But if the Savior made her worthy, who are you indeed to reject her? Surely the Savior knows her very well. That is why He loved her more than us."

Since I had personally experienced the cosmic closeness that can evolve between a creative genius and an adoring fan, I began to see the Lord's closest companion as the first genuine groupie muse. In fact, the dedication in my book *Rock Bottom* reads, "To My Soul Sister, Mary Magdalen, the First Groupie." I was also inspired to write a poem:

If I had been Mary Magdalen
I would have kissed the hem
Of his garment
Nothing could have stopped me from
Stroking His immaculate thigh
Baring my quivering soul
To this God made flesh –
This Light dipped in hell
Come to secure my soul

From the clutches
Of the unholy temple
Made holy by his caress

From my newfound revelations and ongoing communica-
tion with the spirit of Magdalen, the idea to write a book about
modern-day muses started swirling 'round my head.

I think Mary Magdalen was so cool, she was like the first
groupie. I mean she was really into Jesus and following
him around and I wish she would've left a diary. I mean
all this stuff about Jesus, how wonderful he was, and how
he's gonna save us. All I'd like to know is if he was a good
lay. That interests me.   —Patti Smith, 1977

According to the Merriam-Webster dictionary, a muse is "a
source of inspiration: a guiding spirit." I believe this describes
the role of the groupie. A brilliant, creative man is often brought
to the height of his genius by the muse. Throughout the ages,
such women have helped revolutionize the arts. The ancient
Greeks brought us the nine Muses through the prodigious loins
of Zeus, and since then, attention and blessings from a muse are
certain to stimulate any mere mortal's creative juices. "Happy he
whomsoever the muses shall have loved," wrote Hesiod. "Sweet
is the sound that flows from his mouth."

When Dante Alighieri first laid eyes on his beloved Beatrice,
they were only nine years old, and even after her untimely death,
his *Paradiso* acknowledges her profound, inescapable influence
on his every word. Salvador Dalí's tempestuous wife Gala was
so roundly recognized as her husband's muse that when a Surre-
alist painter was on a roll, he was said to be "in love with Gala."
And although Zelda's ecstatic miseries tortured F. Scott Fitzger-
ald, she was constant fodder for his art. "I married one of my
heroines," he once said, and admitted to lifting large portions
of Zelda's diaries for *The Beautiful and Damned.* Constanze
Mozart, given little respect by historians, was so adored by her
husband that he couldn't bear being away from her. "I kiss and

squeeze you 1,095,060,437,082 times," he wrote in a letter. To his sister he wrote, "When Constanze heard the fugues, she absolutely fell in love with them . . . she scolded me roundly for not recording some of my compositions in this most artistic and beautiful of all musical forms, and gave me no peace until I wrote down a fugue for her."

After his death at thirty-six in 1791, Constanze spent the next fifty years making sure Mozart would never be forgotten. She obviously loved his music. The music, the music, always the music.

No matter how she is viewed by those who believe she busted up the Fab Four, John Lennon obviously believed that Yoko Ono was his muse. "With us it's a teacher-pupil relationship. That's what people didn't understand. She's the teacher and I'm the pupil. I'm the famous one. I'm supposed to know everything. But she taught me everything I fucking know." Yoko set her sights on John, even waited by his gate before finally drawing him in to one of her art shows. "As usual," he said, paraphrasing the cliché, "there is a great woman behind every idiot."

All creative souls need passionate encouragement from devoted admirers. There have always been dewy-eyed believers standing in the wings, eager to offer themselves up to the source of the enchantment. The phenomenon is nothing new. It's an ancient, enduring practice that will continue as long as artists feel the desire to create. I'm sure Beethoven's masterpieces aroused exquisite longing within audience members, and Mario Lanza's operatics inspired weak-kneed adoration. Sinatra's intrepid bobby-soxers waited by the stage door to get a glimpse of the swingin' crooner. But nothing is sexier than rock and roll. I was a preteen when Ed Sullivan chopped Elvis off at the waist so we couldn't see his hellfire swivel-hips, and I was contaminated right there and then. From that long-ago illicit moment to last night's rowdy MTV Awards, sensuality has oozed through amplifiers, spilled from guitar strings, and dribbled down microphone stands, wreaking riotous havoc.

The word *groupie* started out innocently enough. I remember the first time I heard it spoken at the Continental Hyatt "Riot"

House on the Sunset Strip. I was standing by Led Zeppelin's shiny black limo, smoothing my pink feather boa, reapplying my gooey Yardley Slicker lip gloss, preparing to slide in next to Jimmy Page for a hot night on the town. As the car door slammed, I heard a shrill voice from the gathered throng behind the roped-off area: "Look at *that* girl, she must be a *groupie*."

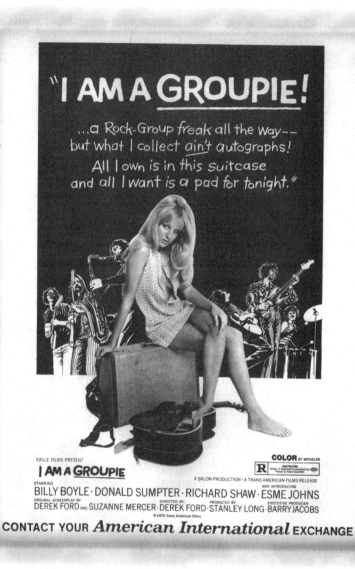

Hmmmm. The word made sense. It's true I spent a lot of time hanging out with *groups*, so I wore the new moniker proudly for a brief spell. It wasn't long before the sparkling, newly minted utterance made it into the dictionary.

Alas, the G word quickly became a scurrilous accusation. Some women, claiming to be forward-thinking, began branding groupies as backward-thinking concubines, when all we were doing was exactly what we wanted to do! To this day, the word *groupie* is usually used as a pointy-fingered put-down, aimed like a poison dart at the girls who make it backstage—dancing in the wings, sitting atop amplifiers, climbing aboard private jets—the ones lavishly draped on the arms of much-desired, seemingly unattainable rock stars. There is only one Robert Plant, after all. One Steven Tyler. One Nikki Sixx. One Eminem. And millions of salivating fans.

What makes a fan take that precarious leap into the center of the regaled and reviled G word? For me, it was *always* the music. The seductive howl of the electric guitar, the throb of the bass, and the sensually moaned promises made my heart beat below my waist. The lyrics! How did they know what was whirling around in my head and pulsing through my veins? Where did it come from? How did they write *that* song that made me feel so wildly alive? I wanted to be in on the cosmic secret. I wanted to get so close to the music that I could taste it—and nothing was going to stop me.

Now it's 2007 and the groupie mentality hasn't changed. Yes, it's more difficult for music devotees to get close to their heroes, but they will always find a way.

While Googling around on the Internet, I came across a perceptive piece by Robert J. Lewis from www.artsand opinion.com. I got in touch with him, and he gave me permission to quote from his "Guitars, Gonads & Groupies Are Wild."

We mock and deride them, dismiss them as tramps
and tarts, in order to disassociate ourselves from the
ethos that compels them to give themselves away to

total strangers . . . When we find ourselves inexplicably
drawn to the gods who created the B Minor Mass and
Abbey Road it is because we are drawn to and want to
participate in the very mystery of creation itself. . . . For
when all is said and done, the groupie, without apology,
is simply and frankly expressing his/her devotion to the
principle of creation. That young women will continue
to give themselves away to lead guitarists in tight
pants, total strangers known only through their music,
confirms the exceptional status of the artist, who by
making exceptional demands on himself, commands the
means (the groupie) to genetically preserve and transmit
his gift. . . . There should be no shame in this; the only
shame is to deny the longing.

In 2003, Virginia Scharff, a professor of history at the University of New Mexico, wrote the book *Twenty Thousand Roads: Women, Movement, and the West* with a chapter entitled "The Long Strange Trip of Pamela Des Barres." It felt a little weird being analyzed in a scholarly text along with an Indian squaw and a civil rights activist, but at least I was in fascinating company. "To find the story of a woman traversing and remaking the landscape of the counterculture in a more or less skilled and knowledgeable fashion," she writes, "we need search no further than the comic and troubling odyssey of self-proclaimed groupie Pamela Miller Des Barres. . . . It was the music that first called Pamela, and literally millions of other girls, out of themselves in quest of a bigger, wider, higher reality." Later in the chapter, Professor Scharff states, "Pamela Des Barres is the Lewis and Clark of wanton women, who prowled the land anew, from sea to shining sea." Yikes.

There are actually professors who teach entire courses on the topic. During the last few years, I've heard from several college students writing term papers on the groupie phenomenon. Here's a paragraph from Jessica Waks's 2005 thesis, "Groupie Slut or Groupie Goddess? The Paradoxical Nature of Groupies and Rock Culture": "Groupies were some of the first sexual warriors, fighting to bag the men they wanted and to fulfill their wildest fantasies. As young women struggling to find their own identities in rock culture, they chose to be with the band rather than stuck under Mick's thumb."

The rabid curiosity about our mythological rock gods, past and present, hasn't abated a smidgen. I hear daily from dolls that desperately want to know how I did it, and how can *they* meet the rock god of their dreams? I've also heard from women who managed to discover for themselves the heady high of being romantically linked, even for a night, with their favorite unruly rocker.

From Elvis's penchant for girls frolicking together in white cotton panties and "Top Forty Fuckers" landing '60s pop idols to the Rolling Stones' array of infamous supergroupies and Winona Ryder's long list of rock conquests (Soul Asylum's Dave Pirner, Paul Westerberg, Beck, Conor Oberst, Pete Yorn, Ryan Adams), the beat goes on. With so many musicians snapped up by models, porn stars, and actresses (Gwyneth and Chris Martin, Drew Barrymore and Fab Moretti, Denise Richards and Richie Sambora, Nicole Kidman and Keith Urban, Pamela Anderson and . . .), the groupie's quest is even more difficult.

Only a handful of girls are fearless enough to cross the precarious line into the rock and roll danger zone. What does it take to make it past the endless barricades, grim-faced roadies, officious publicists, and stern record company execs? What kind of girl makes it her life's passion to meet the rocker of her dreams, consequences be damned?

Some of the dolls I interviewed shared one or two naughty, unforgettable nights with their dreamboats. Others had delicious, long-term flings and ooh-la-la romances with coveted rock gods, becoming the envy of millions of envious fans. Many had their hearts shattered—but not one of them would take back a single glorious, mad night.

The music takes on new meaning for the rock muse. She was with the band and nobody can take it away from her. Once she's shared those special moments with the man who rocks her world, her favorite song will never sound the same to her again.

According to *Rolling Stone*, Frank Zappa saw groupies as "freedom fighters at the avant garde of the sexual revolution."

You don't hear the term "movie gods" very often. There aren't many football gods or political gods either. And television stars are never referred to as "TV gods." But there *are* rock gods roaming the earth. Perhaps by embracing their cherished rock gods, groupies tap into their own divinity.

"The altar was rock 'n' roll," Gail Zappa once said, "the guys were the gods, and the women were the high priestesses."

They still are.

Tura Satana

Miss Japan Beautiful and the King

*W*hen I was barely old enough to discern the dusky difference between the sexes, I dreamed about Elvis. His perfect greasy quiff, smoky cheekbones, and rebellious insouciance defined a generation's desire and made a certain skinny, preteen Valley girl thrill with delight. Years before puberty caught me between the legs, Elvis's unfettered carnal purity gave me a spine-shiver of my destiny. The unsullied wickedness of his wail roused lurking, tamped-down wantonness and created a slippery peephole in immaculate '50s squaredom all over the world. He loosened the screws on the earth's axis, and then greased it up good with pomade.

And the way he danced! Who knew human hips could gyrate like that? I have one of those old-fashioned flip books that shows Elvis revolving across the stage in his gold jacket, his knees at odd angles, his pelvis thrusting forward, arms outstretched, eyes half-closed, sweat glistening danger. Did moving that way just come naturally to the country boy truck driver? I always assumed Elvis came out of the womb with a brand new kind of rhythm. But that was before I met the astonishing Tura Satana—the doll who taught Elvis to dance, onstage and between the sheets.

Miss Japan Beautiful.

Credit: Tura Satana

Back in the '50s when Elvis came into power, the media kept its collective nose out of celeb bedrooms, so we could only imagine what the King got up to under the covers. Years later when word leaked out that he liked to watch two lovelies go at it wearing nothing but white cotton panties, the titillation factor went into high glee. Even at his polyester sideshow Vegas peak, Elvis continued to entrance the masses (and misses), and rumor had it that he dallied with many a fortunate showgirl.

When I decided it was about time music muses got their due and began the search for the formidable damsels featured in this tome, my dream was to begin with Elvis. It *did* begin with Elvis, after all . . .

Ask and ye shall receive, sayeth the Lord. Before I even got the word out that I wanted to meet a babe who had bedded the King, my good pal artist/songwriter Allee Willis invited me to a poolside bash for the cast of Russ Meyer's 1970 cult classic *Beyond the Valley of the Dolls*. Allee always attracts an avant eclectic crew. She's sold millions of records (the Pointer Sisters' "Neutron Dance," and "Boogie Wonderland" by Earth, Wind & Fire), and her uncommon paintings grace the walls of the grooviest L.A. homes. Among the middle-aged campy darlings gathered around the pool in Allee's superbly '50s backyard was the buxom, raven-haired bombshell Tura Satana—the star of another Meyer film, the riotous feminist opus *Faster, Pussycat! Kill! Kill!*

I was enjoying a boisterous chat with the absurdly ample Kitten Natividad when I noticed my ex, Michael, deep in conversation with Tura. He caught my eye, giving me a look that said, "Get your ass over here NOW!" Michael introduced us, announcing that Tura once held the title of "Miss Japan Beautiful" and had been voted by those in the know as "one of America's Ten Best Undressed" along with burlesque legends Lili St. Cyr and Tempest Storm. How could I not be impressed? I figured the lady must be somewhere in her mid-sixties, and I was inspired instantly by her saucy, free-spirited attitude. Slightly more zaftig than in her *Kill* days, she wore her weight well, decked out in a low-cut black ensemble with shiny hair down to her ass. Loads of black eyeliner, glossed frosty lips.

"There's something else you should know about the lovely Ms. Satana," Michael said with a gleam in his baby blues, but just then Allee beckoned us to join the fun at the yum-laden buffet table. Several *Beyond* Dolls were gleefully comparing notes about the size of various actors' members. A showbiz wingding was described in which three Hollywood heroes unzipped and displayed their merchandise on the table for measurement. Since I had often heard one of that evening's participants, Milton Berle, was loaded in that department, I was surprised to discover that a certain A-list film actor came up the winner that night. The Dolls began a rousing competition of their own, shouting out names of the lucky dogs that had shared their various boudoirs. I got into the spirit of things and blurted a couple of my own pertinent headliners. But when Tura slowly licked her lips and growled "Elvis Presley," everybody at the table knew they were licked as well. I looked heavenward through the velvety Valley smog and said a silent *thank you, Jesus.*

Tura was intrigued by my latest project and warmly welcomed my proposed interview. Since she had dallied with the King, I told her she'd have chapter one all to herself. I had thought about finding a gal who'd romanced Sinatra, but even though he was a master crooner, he wasn't a rock star. At this news, Tura grinned wickedly. "Too bad. I could have been chapters one *and* two!" Be still my eternal groupie heart!

As the final kicker, Tura opened a notebook and handed me an eight-by-ten '50s photo of herself as Miss Japan Beautiful. In stark-raving black and white, she leans into the camera, smoldering, sequined pasties poised just so. Her unbelievably steamy, come-hither geisha beauty must have raked thousands of male libidos over the red-hot coals. "I was unique on the burlesque circuit," she purred. "Orientals weren't supposed be busty like I was."

Tura was in L.A. staying with her manager, Siouxzan Perry, for a few days (she handles all the Russ Meyer Dolls and Dandies), and I was invited to her trippy Topanga Canyon pad the following night for bourbon-soaked chicken and a trip down Tura's momentous Memory Lane.

Credit: Tura Satana

After dinner, Siouxzan leads us to a cozy, quiet den where we recline on pillows under a massive *Pussycat* poster of Tura's menacing self as the vampy Varla. We drink a few glasses of red wine in the candlelight, and the conversation flows with the merlot. Tura's story is astounding, dolls, and I advise you to keep a wide-open mind. Just sit back and go with the glow.

I learned that she didn't live on Easy Street as a kid. In fact, a lot of her childhood was spent behind double barbed wire. During World War II, the young Tura did time with her father and brother in Manzanar, a Japanese relocation camp outside Lone Pine, California. She remembers soldiers with dogs paroling the tents and Quonset huts. Each one housed at least ten confused, displaced families, and any food they ate they had to grow themselves. Tura's mother, an American Indian, was left behind. "She came to the fence, but she wasn't allowed to touch it," Tura recalls. "If she did, she wound up with a baton across the knuckles." The humiliation and horror made Tura's father more determined to be recognized as an American citizen. "When we finally got out of there, he refused to speak Japanese. We weren't even taught our own language at home."

Things got tougher back on Chicago's west side. Tura wasn't even ten years old when she was raped by a gang of five guys, one of whom turned out to be the cousin of the cop who came when she crawled out of the alleyway. A judge was paid off, and Tura wound up in reform school "for tempting those boys into raping me. I was classified a juvenile delinquent." After the rape, Tura couldn't stand to be touched by anybody, not even her parents. She assumed a tough stance, soon heading a rowdy girl gang, and found herself fending off "slant-eye" insults with her fists and her wit. "We patrolled the neighborhood to keep that kind of thing from happening to anybody else." Because of her resilient nature, the hideous experience gave Tura an enigmatic edginess that somehow became part of her charm. Despite all these difficulties, her down-deep dream was to sing and dance.

Tura regales me with tales of her circus performer mom, who taught her how to hula to her favorite tune. "The 'Hawaiian War Chant' was really fast; that's how I learned to do some of my shimmies and moves." Tura stands and wriggles her hips around with remarkable grace and aplomb. "Mom loved Hawaiian music, those drums and electric guitars. You automatically want to move to it."

At fourteen Tura looked years older and worked as a cigarette girl at the Trocadero, the Sunset Strip celeb hang where all the "famous personages" wanted to be the first to show her a good time. Every man Tura came in contact with was bowled over, but she still couldn't stand to be touched. With Japanese, Filipino, Chinese, and Cheyenne Indian blood pumping through her, Tura's exoticness made her quite an enticing treat. "Asians just weren't built like I was," she reminds me. By the early '50s, when she sashayed around in her peekaboo skirt, offering "cigars, cigarettes, cigarillos" to the likes of Martin and Lewis, the Troc had become a faded dream, and Tura moved on.

She tried all kinds of entertainment jobs before landing a "legit" Spanish dancer gig (amusing, considering her heritage), which would catapult her into a surprising new realm. When her boss suggested she remove her La Cucaracha clothes for a substantial hike in salary, Tura's career as "Miss Japan Beautiful" began. Back in 1954, $125 a week was a lot of dough. "At first it was scary," she admits, "but when I saw the looks of appreciation on some of the guy's faces in the audience, it made me feel very special."

More wine is poured and I ask what made her act different from others on the circuit. "I made my audience participants in my routine; I talked to them, played with them, made jokes with them. I said 'OK, where have you got your hands right now?'" There must have been a lot of action going on under the tables, because Tura soon became a hothouse staple on the burlesque scene across the country. Although she was still a bit wary, she soon warmed up to her new means of self-expression, because "the men in audience wanted to adore you."

Long before the yucky debacle of crotch-in-the-face lap dancing, strippers left a lot to the rampant imagination. Burlesque was an exquisite art form in the '50s, and Tura's costumes were elaborately beaded, highly embellished Asian rhapsodies, which brought a man's inherent geisha-girl fantasies to the eye-popping surface. She gracefully balanced ornamented headdresses, stroked long Japanese swords, and slowly slipped out of her hand-painted kimonos. Her prop Buddha rested in his velvet-lined case, and his hands burst into flames when she brushed against his upturned palms.

The family atmosphere of the "Burly-Q" circuit helped Tura unlearn the bad habits she picked up in reform school. Her fellow dancers completely accepted her mixed-up heritage, and it soothed her injured soul. It was a good job. She was taken care of, and nobody messed with her. But because of her nightmare childhood experiences, Tura began to drink heavily. "The minute a guy touched me, I'd deck him. My automatic reflex was to go on the defensive and strike out blindly. I took up drinking and I was damn near an alcoholic, downing maybe two or three fifths a day." It took a long time before Tura could be touched without flinching. "People on the circuit cared and made me feel like I was family, so I listened when they told me drinking would make me old and dumb very fast. The gals I worked with helped me face what happened. I did a deep cleansing of my mind, and I was a lot better off." Due to the nurturing Tura received from her newfound family, she gradually began to accept affection from her many suitors, and was free to become even more daring, enthralling men and women alike with her peerless stage presence.

"My audience knew I enjoyed fooling around with them, and there was always one who yelled, 'Oh, I wish you were my mother!' and I'd say, 'Yeah, and you'd still be a breast baby, wouldn't ya?'" Tura's specialty was tassel twirling. She could make those sequined mini-cups that covered paradise spin every which way but loose. "It came to me naturally," she insists with pride. "During my routine, my boobs would automatically move with the rest of my body. I had good muscle control, everything got moving and the tassels started twirling!" Tura was the only person in the universe who could twirl tassels lying flat on her back. And twirl them in opposite directions! She could also stop the whirling tassels, change direction, stop again, and spin 'em the other way! "When I twirled my tassels I'd say, 'Someday I'm gonna fly if I can get enough RPMs!'" It must have been quite a salacious spectacle. The sailors blushed and stammered when she twirled their peaked white hats round and round on her creamy globes. "I had so much fun with those navy men. I'd slide up to the end of the stage on my knees and say, 'OK, who's first?'"

There were those who looked down their highfalutin noses, believing that Tura was nothing but a plaything for men. "It was the other way around," she insists. "Men were *my* playthings."

It was after a wild night of tassel twirling for agog sailors in Biloxi, Mississippi, that Tura made the acquaintance of a certain blossoming rock and roll singer. "I was a big draw that night," she recalls with delight. Oftentimes it took the teenage girl hours to unwind after dishing out damp dreams to horny strangers. On this early morning, she was cooling down by walking along the sand outside the club. "I was unwinding on the beach and this good-looking guy came walking up to me, and I said, 'Nice night, isn't it?' 'Yes it is, ma'am.' 'Ma'am?' I was only sixteen years old and I'd never been called 'ma'am' before. I'd been fibbing about my age, everybody thought I was nineteen. He said, 'What are you doing out here so late at night?' I told him I was trying to unwind, and he said 'You too?'" The young couple walked slowly along the beach, then sat on the sand, talking 'til the sun came up. "He said he did a show up the road apiece, but I didn't know who he was. Once I took a look at those eyes of his, aahhh. . . ." Tura has always had a weakness for blue eyes. "I looked at his eyes and thought, 'Oh God, this one's a keeper.'" Later she realized she'd never even asked his name.

They didn't meet again until nine months later when the twenty-one-year-old arrived backstage at Chicago's Follies Theatre with the owner. "Do you remember me?" Elvis asked. "Biloxi," Tura said, smiling. "I didn't know your name then, but yes, I remember Biloxi." Turned out Elvis did see Tura's show in Biloxi, and he enjoyed her Follies routine as well. When he wondered how she moved the way she did, Tura told him her routine was based on martial arts. "He asked if I could teach him," she recalls with a throaty chuckle. "I told him, 'Martial arts is not only a disciplinary art form, it also teaches you control,' and he said, 'Well, you sure got control!'" He wanted to know how she did the slide and the splits at the same time. How she did the shimmy, how she shook all over. He was quite intrigued. The enamored singer then jokingly asked Miss Japan Beautiful if she could teach him how to twirl the tassels. "I said, 'No, honey. I can't teach you how to spin *two* tassels, but I can teach you how to spin *one!*'" Elvis grinned, "Well, that might be a novelty."

Elvis may have been shaking up the planet, but even back in '56 he had the Colonel's minders watching his every move. Obviously smitten, he wanted to be alone with Tura. He somehow managed to sidestep his two furtive sidekicks and take her to breakfast at an all-night diner. "He had the aura—you knew he was going to go places. I was drawn to him mostly by his smile," Tura says wistfully. "And that Southern drawl could make your knees melt. Back then he was so down to earth, so natural. He had the magnetism; he drew women right and left. He was a natural attraction."

Elvis was able to slip away from his protectors two more nights in a row, but the third evening they parked outside Tura's family home, waiting while Elvis enjoyed his first Japanese meal, cooked by Tura's daddy. "The Colonel and those two guys thought that was the last of it, but anytime he could get away and sneak out of his room, I would meet him at a hotel or at my friend's house."

On the first couple of dates, Elvis gave Tura "wet kisses on the cheek," which she thought was sweet, but when he got to her mouth and gave her a "wet fish" kiss, she felt it was her duty to teach the boy one of life's most important lessons.

"No, no, no, you don't kiss a girl like *that.*"

"None of the girls have complained before."

"Well, maybe they didn't know what they were doing either."

"What do you mean? I don't know how to kiss?"

"That's what I'm tellin' ya, you don't know how to kiss."

And she literally showed him how to do it.

OK. Deep breath. I have heard a few fantastical claims to fame before, but this one takes the entire bakery full of three-tiered cakes. You mean those Love-Me-Tender lips needed assistance?

She assured the bewildered, slightly chagrined Elvis that he didn't have to hold his lips so tight. "I didn't do a French kiss at first, I wanted to show him the beginnings of it. Then when he felt my tongue going around his lips, he went 'Mmmm,' and he opened his mouth and I showed him how to French kiss. 'Oooh, I like that!' And he went on from there. Once I showed him the difference between how *he* was kissing and how *I* kissed, he said, 'Oh God, that feels *so* good.' When I said, 'Yeah, it feels good all over too,' his eyes lit up."

Elvis and the exotic dancer began meeting secretly whenever possible. Tura sneaked into his shows and was very pleasantly surprised to see how he had taken her shakes and shimmies and made them his own. "It was a thrill to see him do the moves on stage, and to know that I was the one to teach 'em to him. Also how to do it in the bedroom—*that* was even better." Tura insisted they keep their affair quiet so the relationship wouldn't damage his upwardly spiraling career. She also didn't expect him to be faithful. "When we were dating I said, 'I know you're going to have women throwing themselves at you and you're not gonna be able to say no.'" He said, "I will, I will, if you stay with me." Tura knew better. "There were guys who could say no, and guys who couldn't, and Elvis didn't know how to say no. He was always afraid of hurting people's feelings. That's why they took advantage of him, especially the Colonel. They walked all over him because he was so giving. He was a down-home country boy who loved his mama."

Tura leans into me conspiratorially, about to divulge some classified info. "He didn't have too much respect for his papa, not until he got older—because his papa was a player and Elvis knew his papa was *cheatin'* on his mama. He didn't like that one bit."

Tura had already lived an unusually untamed life for one so young. She was a spicy seasoned doll with all the finesse that comes with life experience. Her offbeat relationship with the King gathered erotic steam as she continued to play the role of capricious muse to the unpolished Southern boy. "When we first started out, he was kinda like 'wham, bam, thank you, ma'am,' until I showed him what to do. Eventually he became *much* more sophisticated." Does that mean Elvis became a good lover? "Yes, it was worth the effort," Tura says, closing her eyes. "He was *definitely* worth the effort." Remembering that long-ago night,

Tura smiles. "I also showed him how highly sensitive my boobs are."

Elvis was becoming more passionately adept, but there was one very important amorous pleasure he had yet to experience. "Four or five nights later I showed him how to give head." Tura grins. "He hadn't done it yet." Apparently other women had tried to entice Elvis in that direction, but that particular female scent had put him off. "I had just made love to him in the shower, and I said, 'Wait a minute! Before I took you in my mouth, I washed you very well, because I don't know who you've been with. And the same applies to me. I will not make love to anybody until I know I'm clean.'"

It seems Tura instructed Elvis in one of life's finest sensual arts. "When a man wants to give *you* pleasure, that's what makes the difference—'Honey, not so hard there, just nibble, and when you find that little man, nudge him. Several times. But try to do it gently at first . . . then a little harder . . . when you've got him nice and hard, then you start to suck . . .'"

All of a sudden it's very warm in the room. Does anybody have a fan? Can you turn the air conditioning on, please? I'm palpitating here! Hmmm. Should I be crude and ask the obvious size question? Oh, why not, I may never get this opportunity again.

"Elvis was about average in that department, and that was fine with me," Tura laughs wickedly. "It all depended on how excited you got him."

When the Colonel saw Tura's risqué act, he suggested that he manage Miss Japan Beautiful, promising to make her a very big star, indeed. But stripping was Tura's form of rebellion. She was totally in control and holding her own reins, thank you very much. "He said, 'I could make you a big star,' and I said, 'How much of me would you want?' He got 55 percent of Elvis. All he did was act like a big-league bodyguard. He kept Elvis away from everybody, kept him isolated." Her refusal angered the former sideshow huckster, and he went out of his way to break up the lusty lovebirds.

Tura had been lonely on the road for quite a while. "Then Elvis came along and he filled up a big empty hole, so to speak," she laughs. "Literally, too! It was great while we were together. We were both very private people. He didn't like all the hullabaloo about who he was dating." She accepted that the studios made Elvis date his costarlets, but it hurt.

One night after Tura performed in Memphis, a fervent, obsessed fan got into his car, put a double-barrel shotgun in his mouth, and pulled the trigger because she wouldn't date him. When Elvis came to pick Tura up in his pink Cadillac, he came upon the grisly scene. The cops were hassling her, as if she had something to do with the tragic mess. "The shotgun was still in his mouth and his brains were on the backseat," Tura recalls, "and when Elvis got there he said, 'Baby, they ain't ever gonna put you through anything like this again.'" He gave her a diamond engagement ring that night, claiming her as his own. "It was a total surprise—he turns me around, grabs me, kisses me, and says, 'God, do you know how much I love you?' He fishes into his pocket and pulls out a box with this beautiful diamond ring." Yes, I had noticed the large flashing diamond on Tura's finger. Swoon. Elvis's ring. "It's three and a half carats," she smiles. "I said, 'What is that for,' and he said, 'I just asked you to marry me,' and I said, 'You *did*?' At first I said yes. I wasn't expecting it because he knew I had a little run-in with the Colonel."

Then things began to change. Not only was the Colonel out to break up the young couple, his influence over Elvis was becoming stifling. "The Colonel was pulling his strings and Elvis basically let him do it. He often had Elvis strung out, taking stuff to get him to sleep, to wake him up, keep his appetite suppressed. I felt so sorry for him. It was almost like he gave up, especially after his mom died. It was like he signed off." Then Elvis tried to put Tura on that age-old Madonna/whore pedestal. "I told him I couldn't live on that pedestal. I didn't want to be like his mom. I could be his wife and lover, not his mama, but he was trying to combine the two. I didn't mind being worshipped, but I didn't want to be mama."

Tura wore the ring for a while, but Hollywood kept calling the King into the silver spotlight. Elvis told her he didn't want their engagement to be a secret anymore, but he was squiring actresses around. Tura saw the photos in movie magazines. When she tried to return the ring, Elvis wanted her to keep it. "He wouldn't take it; he said, 'That's part of me and you. You'll always belong to me as long as you have that ring.' I said, 'No, I won't. I will not belong to you anymore. From now on I'm gonna go out with other guys and I'm gonna do what I do best.'"

So Tura Satana taught Elvis Presley how to dance, make out, make love, and give head. Then she kissed him good-bye. While Elvis surrendered to the Colonel's manipulation, making less-than-stellar movies such as *Speedway* and *Clambake*, Tura continued to turn heads and raise blood pressure. She drove Francis Albert Sinatra to dizzying distraction and carried on a blazing love affair with Tony Bennett. She also proceeded to blaze distinctly diverse trails. After eighteen years on the burlesque circuit, she landed the sexy role of an unrepentant prostitute in *Irma la Douce*, then made cult history in Ted V. Mikels's films *The Doll Squad* and *The Astro-Zombies*. She's the star of her very own comic book drawn by wizard Mike Hoffman: *Tura Satana: The Ultimate Femme Fatale*. But Tura is best remembered as *Pussycat*'s temptress Varla, whom John Waters calls "one of the best villains in screen history." Ballbreaker Varla definitely kicked opened doors for dolls ready to combine strength with their sexiness. Tura's advice to women? "You can be sexy, you can be hot, you can be feminine—and you can kick ass!"

After his stint in the army, when Elvis brought the teenage Priscilla Beaulieu home to Memphis, he was still thinking about Tura Satana. "He always found my phone number no matter how many times I changed it," she says. "We were friends, but he wanted to get back to the physical aspect of our relationship. I always said no." Slowly but surely, the imported sweet-faced brunette who would become Mrs. Presley started looking more and more like a certain Asian burlesque siren. The hair became blacker, piled high on her head; the eyes thick with black eyeliner slanted dangerously upward. "He told me he wanted a replica of me, and I said, 'She's totally a different person.' He said, 'But I can make her look like you.' I told him it wasn't fair to Priscilla, and he said, 'But I want you, and I can't have you.'"

Ooh, what a night it was, it really was such a night! Slightly tipsy and reeling from all the heady Elvis revelations, I thank the magnanimous Ms. Satana and gather up my stuff. We hug each other and plan to stay in touch. Before I head out into the leafy night, I ask Tura if she ever wished things had turned out differently. "I know Elvis was trying to get off the medications he was on," she says, "but he gained so much weight, he felt he had to go back on the pills. Nobody was taking care of him or feeding him the way they should have. They just let him glut on his favorite foods, deep-fried Southern things that weren't good for him." Tura is suddenly sad and slowly shakes her head. "When he died, yeah, I always felt that if I'd been with him, I would have been able to pull him through. I would have had more influence over him than the Colonel or anybody else." As Tura runs her hands through her long black hair, Elvis's diamond ring shimmers in the candlelight.

Cherry Vanilla

The Happiest Broken Heart

$\mathcal{C}$ herry Vanilla. Just her name evokes the flashy, flagrant, shameless exuberance of her most adventurous decade—the gleefully unapologetic '70s. Look Cherry up on the Internet and thousands of entries emerge, revering this punk high priestess.

> Actress, author, poetess, DJ, and rock star . . . author of
> the libidinous artbook 'Pop Tarts,' her genuinely seduc-
> tive singing voice made mincemeat of the more feted
> female vocalists . . . ranking high among the most influen-
> tial figures on the Anglo-American rock scene. . . .

While I was taking the Sunset Strip by storm in my garters and leopard-print spike heels, I knew I had a sensational counterpart on the East Coast. In those days, the groupie tom-toms were the most reliable form of information as to who was doing what to whom behind closed hotel room doors. I knew Cherry was part of the impudent Andy Warhol posse, that she was a member of David Bowie's tight-knit inner circle and worked for his company, MainMan, as his überpublicist. She traipsed around with lots of stellar rockers and recorded a couple of raunchy rock and roll records of her own, *Bad Girl* and *Venus D'Vinyl*.

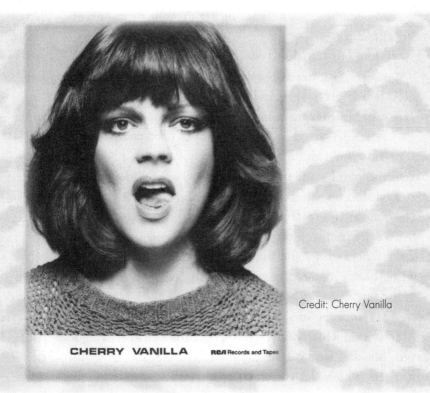

Credit: Cherry Vanilla

CHERRY VANILLA   RCA Records and Tapes

I have crossed paths with Ms. Vanilla at glitzy rock functions through the years and observed her on the arm of the exquisite Rufus Wainwright more than once. We've always been full of mutual admiration, but I never had the chance to get the bona fide lowdown about her hunky-dory history. That changed recently when at I encountered the divine Cherry Vanilla in Fairmount, Indiana—the tiny, exalted town where James Dean was born and buried.

We happened to be visiting mutually dear friends at the same time. Dean historian David Loehr and Lenny Prussack reside on Main Street and help keep the Rebel's flame burning bright in the heartland. Running into Cherry so unexpectedly added a colorful twist to my semiannual visit. One afternoon, I happily dragged her all over farm country, scouring antique malls and thrift stores, while we shared torrid tales. She plans on writing her own memoirs, but after much cajoling, she gave in and agreed to be interviewed about her groupie years. I was tickled hot pink.

Before our scheduled meeting in L.A., I gave her two records a spin. *Bad Girl* and *Venus D'Vinyl* were rereleased as a double-album five years ago, and I got quite a kick out of her nervy lyrics and boisterous tongue-in-cheekiness.

Cherry has lived in the same classic deco two-story building on Hollywood Boulevard for twenty years, and before we start reminiscing, I wander around her classy apartment checking out her eclectic art collection, gaping at photos of her carousing with the famous and infamous.

We settle into a cozy corner on a vintage settee, and when I ask Cherry how she first got into music, I discover that both of us had a memorable early encounter with a certain Italian crooner.

"My mother was a telephone operator at the Hotel 14 in Manhattan, which housed the Copacabana. If I was a good little girl, my dad would take me down the elevators, right into the kitchen, which was the way the stars came into the Copa. I saw Jimmy Durante, Eartha Kitt, and Tony Bennett, and remember mink stoles over backs of chairs, the whiff of perfume in the room, the sparkle of jewelry, the clinking of glasses. And the Copa chorus girls with pastel colored hair! They might have pale blue costumes for Tony Bennett's show, with their hair dyed to match. For Jimmy Durante, they'd have pale orange costumes and orange hair. You can imagine how that stuck in my mind." I certainly can, as every time I've seen Cherry, her hair has been a new shocking hue. In Fairmount, it was bright pink; today it's pale turquoise. "Those are little glimpses I remember," she sighs. "I have a story that's the basis of how I became a fan and a groupie. In fact, my desire to be connected to show business happened right there and then. It was '51 or '52, because I was eight or nine, and Martin and Lewis were still together. I'd seen them on TV and loved their act. In those days, all the same people worked at the hotel year after year. So when the stars came back, they became friends, like a little family. I knew all the bellhops because of my mother, and they decided to play a joke on Dean

Martin. He came in at six o'clock every night to change for the supper show, so one of the bellhops brought me up to his room and sat me on the edge of his bed. I was there all by myself, waiting for Dean Martin! I was already in love with him; he was so handsome. The adrenaline! So I was sitting there fixing my little dress, and in he walked, the most handsome thing I'd ever seen in my life—bigger, darker, shinier, taller, softer, sweeter—everything I had imagined. I remember everything he was wearing: brown wool slacks, brown and white wool tweed jacket, bright white shirt, brown tie, and his black shiny hair. He said, 'Oh, hello! Who are you?' and I said, 'I'm Mary's daughter, Kathleen.' He said, 'Well, nice to meet you.' I don't remember what we talked about, but we *talked*, Dean Martin and me! Then he said, 'I have to go do my show now, so I'll call your mommy and tell her to come get you.'"

I can relate, because when I was thirteen, I put on my frothiest junior high pre-prom dress and was invited to sit in the audience for the taping of Dean Martin's TV show. I was lucky because my exotic uncle Hamil choreographed the successful series, teaching Dino's extremely coiffed, Day-Glo–clad Gold Diggers their provocative steps. I was the perfect age to sigh and swoon over Dean's dreamy devil-may-careness, and gazed at my autographed eight-by-ten 'til his ballpoint signature faded.

Long before she became Cherry Vanilla, Kathleen was the youngest of four Dorritie children, brought up in Woodside, New York. By the time she was a teenager, two of her siblings had already moved out. "There was a huge generation gap. I was a stranger in a strange land. I was from one planet, my parents were from another, and they were never going to understand the planet I was on. That's why when I went to the Copa; I knew I belonged with *those* people, not the telephone operator. My parents and I weren't close and didn't talk about anything. They were good parents, but I felt totally disconnected."

It seems that most music lovers remember the very first record on their turntables. Mine was Elvis's "Don't Be Cruel," backed with "Treat Me Nice." "I was a super Elvis fan too," Cherry agrees, "I had Elvis kerchiefs, Elvis pillowcase, Elvis everything.

Please! 'Love Me Tender'? Sitting on my living room floor the first time I saw him on TV? Oh my God! Unbelievable. But the first record I bought at Sam's Candy Store was Bill Haley's 'Rock Around the Clock.' My sister Margaret, who was eleven years older than me, used to tune in to Alan Freed's show, 'Rhythm and Blues.' Everybody in the family would giggle, 'There's *black people* on the radio!' That's still my favorite music, doo-wop and rhythm and blues. My ears just perked up at that dangerous new sound."

Being raised in a strict Irish-Catholic family hampered Cherry's early explorations. She got a bit of freedom when one of her sisters got an apartment in Queens. "I'd stay with her on weekends so I could go to dances, and that's when I started staying out late. I saw live bands and a lot of the dances were record hops, but I was a little Catholic girl; a virgin until I was eighteen."

Summers were often spent at the family retreat in Lake Carmel, and Cherry was treated to performances by the Chiffons, Shirelles, and the Marvelettes. "I was experiencing all kinds of music. After my high school prom, we went to see Connie Francis at the Copa. And Peggy Lee at Basin Street East. I was absorbing pop, jazz, and soul."

Cherry started working at an advertising agency in 1961, and went to school at night, studying film production and acting. "It was the early '60s when the Peppermint Lounge happened and discos started," Cherry says excitedly. "The first discotheque I went to was Le Club, on East 55th Street. The music started soft during dinner, then got louder and more dance-y as the night went on. It was a revelation, because I was eighteen and ripe for it. After Le Club, there was Le Introde. I worked at ad agencies during the day and was DJ at Aux Puces on weekends. I had a lot of musical influences, but loved rock and roll the best. It was amazing—suddenly, you had the Peppermint Lounge, with Jackie Kennedy and Lee Radziwill shaking and doing the Twist, but you also had 42nd Street hookers. It was the first time you saw this clash of culture, which is what made discos like Aux Puces and Arthur amazingly exciting. People of all income levels, all social strata, and all professions found themselves dancing close together in the same place. That was the biggest miracle of all. I thought, 'Wow, the world is accepting this now. Rock and roll is here to stay.' Then came Flower Power, which we thought was going to be even more spectacular."

Cherry was entering the free and brave new world, but still held tightly to her virginity. "I'd let my high school boyfriend barely get his penis in me, then say, 'No, no!' and have to stop because of the Catholic Church, my parents, and the fear of getting pregnant was *really* big. I had girlfriends whose lives were ruined."

When friends from work invited Cherry to Fire Island for the Fourth of July weekend, her old modes of thinking were quickly hurled out the window. "They had this big white dome house, later nicknamed the Whipped Cream House, for reasons you could only imagine. I got addicted to Fire Island, and I went out there that whole summer. And the next summer I was going on nineteen. I met this older guy out there, and thought to myself, 'I'm going all the way with this one.' I knew it right away. He was a musician, of course—an ex-trumpet player for the army. The next weekend I *thought* he was going to want to have sex with me again, but I got my heart broken. The first time was good—I got an appetite for it. I loved sex, man. I wanted more! Give me more! From then on I became a 'whore.' I wanted drugs and sex. I wanted it all. I met two model guys, and I was fucking them both within the first ten minutes of knowing them. I was a wild child and they were gorgeous male models. And once I tasted psychedelics, I was like, *this* is for me! This Mal Williams, who was once married to Ruth Brown, came over and laid out rows of sugar cubes on a piece of foil. He had bottles and bottles of clear liquid, and took out a dropper, and put so much on 'em, those cubes were just breaking down. The sugar was melting! He said, 'This is a fabulous new thing, like peyote. It's called LSD.' From that day on, I was an acid queen! Because we had the pure stuff, they were incredible trips. The first fifty, I only took on Fire Island. It was very spiritual at the beginning, and I wanted to be in nature. It was a long time before I had sex on acid, though I'd have orgasms. You know how you could just spontaneously orgasm on acid?"

Up until this time, Cherry was still Kathleen Dorritie, but had already begun using witty aliases such as Indian Summer and Party Favor. "During the Vietnam War, I met Richard Skidmore, who worked for left-wing activist Abbie Hoffman. They made tapes that were being smuggled into Radio Hanoi and basically were propaganda from black radicals. I knew I wanted the war to end, but I wasn't politically savvy. They asked me to make a tape as a DJ, play my favorite records and tell sexy stories to entertain the troops. I thought I was doing a fabulous thing by telling them how I fucked this one and that one. I could see a soldier in the field being able to jerk off to it. Years later I wondered, oh my God, what were they *really* using me for? So we were in this makeshift studio, and Richard said, 'You shouldn't use your own name because the government doesn't like these tapes.' I might have seen the name on an ice cream container, but for the life of me I can't remember. So I said, 'OK, how about Cherry Vanilla?' I really didn't intend for it to continue, but eventually I started writing for *Circus* and *Creem*. The first couple of things were published under my name, then they said, 'Why don't you use Cherry Vanilla?'

"Remember 'Hang On, Sloopy?'" Cherry asks. "I met the McCoys at a little club on the East Side. I got to meet the whole band and really felt excited to be around them. Then I met the Guess Who. During the mid-to-late '60s, the scene around Bethesda Fountain in Central Park was amazing. On Sunday, you'd take your acid and go to this huge music jam, all kinds of people playing drums and guitars. I went to the park every chance I got. One day, I heard music coming from the Schaeffer Music Festival. I went to the side door and asked this guy, 'Who's playing?' and he said, 'Oh, that's the Guess Who.' It just happened to be sound check. I was wearing a dress from Mexico that I hemmed so my panties stuck out. I had on platform sandals, and was stoned on *something*. He was kind of flirty and said, 'Come on in!' I went backstage, introduced myself to everybody, and started talking to this guy with curly black hair,

'So, you're in the band?' and he said, 'Yeah.' Then I find out, he's Burton Cummings, the singer. I'm thinking, 'This is the guy with the beautiful voice. Fabulous!' So I'm falling in love already, right? Then he says, 'Do you want to come back for our show? I'll get you in.'" An overjoyed Cherry went home, called all her friends, and gushed about her impending backstage pass. "It's kind of funny, because I had been an advertising executive for years, one of the few female TV producers on Madison Avenue. I always had two or three jobs, no matter how many drugs I took. But there I was, running through Central Park, freaking out that I was gonna fuck some rock star. I had a seat in the first row, and when he sang, he looked at me. *He's looking at me!* 'These eyes . . . are crying . . . crying every night for you . . .' So I went with him to Howard Johnson's on the Upper West Side. I had sex with him and had such a fabulous time. For the next three or four tours, he'd call and I'd get to go see Burton Cummings! I was his New York girl. One night I was with him, and the tour bus was leaving for Asbury Park, and the band was saying, 'Come on the bus with us!' and I said, 'I can't, I have to go to work.'"

Cherry did go to the office the next day, but couldn't concentrate, left early, and hitchhiked to Jersey just in time for the curtain to rise on the Guess Who. But guess what happened? "I was so excited I was going to have another night with Burton. But backstage, he was a little distant. The band kept saying, 'Come with us to Virginia Beach!' So I got on the bus. Not even an overnight bag, mind you, but Burton wanted nothing to do with me. The guys said, 'Oh, you know how Burton is,' because obviously, I was finished. He had cooled on me." But Cherry stuck it out, crashing platonically with band members, wearing the same dress for three days. "They dropped me off in the Bronx, and I had to take the subway in this dirty dress. I felt like everyone was looking at me, I was shameful, and Burton didn't love me anymore. But I wrote a poem called, 'A Groupie Lament.' I didn't think of myself as a groupie, even though I liked musicians, until I saw the film *Groupies*, with Cynthia Plaster Caster. You were in it too. When I saw that, I thought, 'Yeah! It's cool to call yourself a groupie. I'm a groupie! Call me a groupie!' And fuck it, at least I got a poem out of it."

Some musicians had more of an effect than others. "When I met Kris Kristofferson, he was just a little folkie playing coffee houses in the Village. He was *fabulous*, one of the most romantic ones, a very loving guy, and great in bed. This is a funny story: I had seen pictures of him and had heard him sing, and thought, 'I have to have sex with this man.' So I waited on line for the first show at the Gaslight Café. It was a little coffee house with benches that held sixty or seventy people, and I had to sit in the back. When they cleared everybody out, I went to the ladies' room, stayed until the second show, and got a seat right in front of the stage. I was by myself, looking at him the whole time, practically touching him. I wrote a four-line poem and gave it to him as he left the stage. As people were getting up to leave, he peeked his head out of the dressing room and said, 'OK, you got me.' Isn't that cute? 'You *got* me.' So I went backstage and hung out with him."

Kristofferson invited Cherry to the Kettle of Fish bar next door, along with a passel of musician pals. "Patti Smith was there. She'd been doing poetry readings, mostly in the UK. I didn't know if she was romantically involved with Kris, but she seemed mushy with him. Everyone was drinking and carrying on. It was getting late, and I just wanted to go home and have sex with this man." But Kris invited everyone back to his room at the Chelsea Hotel, much to Cherry's annoyance. "I was thinking, 'When am I gonna get to fuck this guy?' It was four o'clock in the morning when everybody left. There was just me, Patti Smith, and Kris, and I was thinking, 'I'm *not* leaving! This is a stand off!' Patti had a morning flight to London to do a poetry reading, and Kristofferson finally said, 'Patti, you've got a plane to catch. Come on, I'm gonna get you a taxi.' And I thought, 'Thank the fucking Lord, I got him!' And we had fabulous sex. The next morning, we had lots *more* sex. Then he wanted me to come sit on the toilet and talk to him while he shaved, which I thought was so cute. He was a loving, beautiful guy. I ran into him again, eight or nine years ago, and he was so sweet. I said,

'I don't know if you remember me . . .' He said, 'How could I forget you? You took me to see *El Topo* on acid and I had pneumonia.' One of the nights we went out, he had what he thought was a cold, so I said, 'Take some acid, that cures everything.' We took acid and it turned out he had pneumonia! I did get a crush on him, but we became friends because he started going out with my friend Nancy."

I comment that it was very magnanimous of Cherry to share her prize. "Oh yeah," she smiles, "we used to give our best ones to each other. And somebody else was coming next week—Leon Russell! So who cared? I first met Leon at the Capitol Theatre on the *Mad Dogs and Englishmen* tour. That was the ultimate run-away-with-the-circus tour for me, when I thought I could get on the bus and never come back to reality. The music was so amazing and the atmosphere so welcoming, so *family*, and a nonstop party. I had an instant rapport with the Okies in the band, most especially Chuckie Blackwell, the adorable golden-boy drummer. He was a little devil and a true sex maniac, able to fuck and fuck and *fuck* for hours nonstop. And playful, maybe a little bisexual, and there were a million laughs mixed with the orgasms. I really loved him, not in a girlfriend way, but as a true sex buddy. Through Chuckie, I eventually got to know Leon—as much as anyone really gets to know Leon. He's a quiet, keep-to-himself kind of guy. Of course, I was madly in love with his music and wanted to be as close to him as possible, which in my head, at the time, meant sleeping with him. Chuckie and Leon were sharing a room, twin beds. I had sex with Chuckie, then Leon called me over, and I had sex with him. I can't say it was the most exciting sex I ever had, certainly not like with Chuckie. Nobody in rock and roll was quite like Chuckie Blackwell when it came to sex. But I got to be close with Leon for a few hours and give him the gift of my loving in return for all the pleasure his music had given me."

Aww, it sounds positively idyllic. "Not exactly," Cherry laughs ruefully. "The next morning in the hotel coffee shop, everyone told me that Leon had crabs in his pubic hair, beard, everywhere! And for a minute I totally freaked out. They were just putting me on and having a laugh, but for a while they really had me going."

While DJing at Aux Puces, Cherry got asked to audition for an off-the-wall play. "I said, 'I'm not an actress.' But they didn't want real actresses. It was called 'Theatre of the Ridiculous,' and they needed people who were crazy and free, so I said, 'Why not?' I wound up in this wild play written by Jayne County, who was actually Wayne County then, *World: Birth of a Nation*. It was all made up of song lyrics. I wore a corset, and we used hot dogs as penises. I'd cut them off and castrate those boys. Andy Warhol came to see us. His play *Pork* was being performed at La Mama in New York with a Broadway actress in the lead role, but he thought she was too trained. *Pork* was going to the Roundhouse Theatre in London, and he wanted a new lead. He asked my director, 'What about that girl who used to go around with the hot dogs?' So I auditioned for Andy at the Factory. I had been around him in the back room at Max's Kansas City, but never had the nerve to sit next to him and start talking."

I'm full of questions about the enigmatic Mr. Warhol. Was he mysterious? Amusing? Quiet? "He was childish with me. He'd whisper in my ear at a party, 'I hear that boy has a big penis. Why don't you go see, and come back and tell me about it.' He was very voyeuristic and adorable, and wanted to hear stories. He would bolster your ego, saying, 'You are so fabulous. If only Hollywood knew who the real stars are, it would be a different world.' Other people had problems with him. I think they became dependent on him for money, but I never did. This was an Equity play and we got a salary and didn't expect Andy to pay our rent. When I auditioned for him I discovered he loved advertising. I had done an ad for Yodora deodorant for black people, which would be so racist now. But we used to say it was made for Negro skin. And he just ate it up! The other subject he loved was Catholicism, so he asked me all about Catholic school."

Cherry diligently rehearsed for the play, but Andy just wanted to hear her sing "Our Lady of Fatima." "I sang terribly, I'm sure, because I was nervous. Probably the worse I sang,

With Mick Ronson.
Credit: Leee Childers

the better Andy loved it. I got the part and walked out of there, thinking, 'Wow, I just auditioned for Andy Warhol. And I'm going to London to play the lead in his play!'"

It was much more difficult in 1970 for a woman to make her mark in the music world. "I wanted to be necessary, I wanted to be needed, so I thought, 'Wow, I'm getting in there. I'm really a part of show business.' Oh, it was the most magical summer! The cast lived together. Rod Stewart came to our apartment, and the band America. A lot of local bands would sleep at our flat. We had a ball. Andy came for a couple of days before we opened. And we had a *fabulous* opening night party."

Cherry was already an underground star in her own right, playing the lead in *Pork*, when she saw David Bowie perform for the first time. "I played Brigid Polk, or 'Pork.' She was supposed to be gross and freaking out on speed. There was a gesture I did all through the play, which was to pop out a tit. Bowie was a Warhol fan and knew we were in town. So at the end of Bowie's

With
Angela Bowie.
Credit: Leee Childers

show, he introduced us in the audience: Leee Childers, Jayne County, and myself—and I popped out a tit. Bowie had long hair and yellow bell-bottoms and played an acoustic guitar. Mick Ronson was on electric guitar and Rick Wakeman played piano. Angie was pregnant, and running the lights. So we all got to be friends and started hanging out." When the play ended, Bowie's new manager, Tony DeFries, kept in contact with Cherry and Leee in New York, eventually asking them to help bring David to America to get a record deal. "In September '72, he brought Bowie to America, and we became the core of MainMan—the management agency. I was the only one with some structured Madison Avenue experience, so I organized the office, did all the contract typing; I was the 'everything girl.' DeFries had this ploy to make David more desirable: he wasn't going to let him talk to the press. 'You can't talk to him. But you can talk to Cherry.' So I was yap-yap-yappin' with the press. I'd had poems published in magazines, and was colorful enough to keep people interested and entertain them a bit. Basically, I started doing David's interviews. I had no idea what I was doing, but it worked beautifully."

Here's a revealing little nugget from Bowie's Web site in 1998:

> *I had decided to give my public life over to an extraordinary woman called Cherry Vanilla, an actress and performer whom I had hired to be my PR. And of course, she just wrote about her own life, like what shows she was seeing, where she ate and all that. If Cherry loved or hated something or someone it was Ziggy/Bowie who loved/hated it. Some of the events she wrote about did happen to me but you can assume that most of anything that is taking place in New York is happening to Ms. Vanilla. The cute thing is that every now and then she'd write how I had just come from seeing this great new performer whom everyone should know about . . . Cherry Vanilla.*

Cherry continues with her intrepid tale: "We were in Boston one night, Angie wasn't there, and I ended up in bed with Bowie. And oh boy, did I want that to happen from the moment I met him! They had this so-called open marriage, but until then I never had the opportunity. Also, I worked for him and Angie was his wife and my friend. So even though I was this wild thing, it did feel a little strange. If I was gonna do it, I was gonna sneak! It was wonderful. Bowie is an amazing lover, because he, too, is romantic. Although with him, one might feel he's acting, but who cares? Bowie is an actor. And I feel that way in life too. Whatever job you get, you put on the uniform, the costume, and act the way you think you'd act if you were in a play. Romance made lovemaking better, but I didn't always go for it. I went home with guys who I knew were into S&M and did some pretty weird things because I wanted to try *everything*. The missionary position between a man and a woman is great, because you can be kissing while you're coming. Who doesn't love it? Bowie was very good, athletic and strong and fun. But being with David was forbidden by Tony DeFries. Members of the staff weren't supposed to do that. We had been in Tony's room earlier, and Bowie made me sit in the same chair with him. DeFries was saying, 'You better have those contracts typed tomorrow.' That made it all the more exciting, because it was forbidden. So were drugs on the tour, but we did drugs anyway. But by the time I was working for Bowie I didn't have much time for sex with anybody else. I tried girls, even Angie Bowie, but girls were not my cup of tea. There were a couple of guy groupies on the road, but by the time I worked for him, '72, '73, '74, my big groupie days were over. They kind of ended with Bowie."

Seems like a pretty good place to stop, if stop you must. "It wasn't enough anymore. Once I got to work with Bowie on a business level and help make him a star, that was much more fulfilling than just having sex and then, good-bye. It wouldn't be satisfying to have sex without that mental connection and respect for what I was doing."

After her lengthy stint with MainMan, Cherry was ready to pursue her own extremely creative side, and started doing a poetry act at clubs around Greenwich Village. "I had written a bunch of songs at Leon Russell and Carl Radle's house in Oklahoma. Then I went to my dear friend Michael Kamen and said, 'I wanna write a rock and roll song.' And I wrote 'Little Red Rooster,' about Bowie. Then I wrote a song called 'The Punk,' about *Punk* magazine in New York, the Ramones, and what was going on in the punk scene. When I went to England, in February '77, it was the first single we recorded. They called us punk rock, but I thought we were lollipop, like a joke. I was being satirical, 'Yeah, I'm a rock star, too!' I made two albums, for RCA UK. The first record was all rock and roll. During the second one, it was romance time with my guitar player, Louie. I thought it was punky to write hymns and love songs, punkier than trying to be punk. Like saying, 'Fuck you! I'll do what I want!' But there were a couple of good tracks. Stuart Copeland, Henry Padovani, and Sting were in my band in England. They worked for me and the Police was my opening act. They didn't have Andy Summers then, and Henry was a real punk guitarist. By then, I was into one boyfriend at a time. I was monogamous, but they weren't, which I found out later. It was always my lead guitar player; I had a string of those."

For the last eight years, Cherry has been working with Vangelis, the world renowned Greek composer/artist, most noted for his stunning *Chariots of Fire* soundtrack. "I met him in the RCA offices when we were both on RCA. He's the same age as I am, sixty-two. He was nothing like anybody I had ever been with before. I always loved skinny, little rock and roll boys. Here was a man my age, an intellectual, and I fell in love with his mind . . . and his kindness. I fell in love in a whole new way. Vangelis kept sending for me, to do little 'talk' things on his records, whatever excuse he could find. Then one time, I wound up having sex with him. We had sex a couple more times, then, it was like, now what? Am I supposed to be your girlfriend? But we both knew we would never be boyfriend and girlfriend, because I was much

With Rufus Wainwright, 2004.
Credit: Cherry Vanilla collection

too independent. So we thought, 'What are we going to do? We love each other, but we know it's not going to work.' He said, 'We will love each other, and be friends forever.' He was right, we are. And here I am, working for him. And look!" Cherry beams, holding out her arm, "He gave me a $15,000 watch for my sixtieth birthday!"

When I ask Cherry if she misses her former life and time spent with all those rowdy rock and rollers, she runs her hands through her tousled turquoise hair and grins, "I still love musicians, and always will. Rufus Wainwright is the love of my life now. Not that I date him, but if I were younger, he'd have been attacked already. He certainly wouldn't be a virgin for girls anymore, believe me!"

A Groupie Lament
   By Cherry Vanilla

Diamonds twinkle beneath my feet
On the Labor Day weekend street
Sunlight shines warm through my hair
You'd think there was no pollution there
Pimples sprout on my sleepless face
Varicose veins show the endless pace
My white dress dirty as I walk it home
But my head is up, so I'll write a poem

I'm feeling beauty in my ghetto land
'Cause I got it on with a rock & roll band
The trip was a long one, the bus was crazed
The guys and I were mostly dazed
We sang a few tunes from old rock & roll
And we hid the dope when we paid the toll
Button ignored me, the silly fool
But the rest of the guys thought I was cool
From Asbury Park to Virginia Beach
I gave head like daybed philosophies teach

I feel good and I should and I even got a tan
On my two-day tour with a rock & roll band

You see I missed the last bus from the Jersey shore
And a taxi driver said that there were no more
So, I went back to Convention Hall
And I got on their bus and I had a ball
The motels were sterile and the food was all plastic
But at their last set on Sunday I got freaked-out spastic
I know they all love me, 'cause they told me so
As for Burton, well, I just don't know

I'm the happiest broken heart, can you understand
'Cause now I'm the friend of a rock & roll band

I'm the happiest broken heart, can you understand
'Cause now I'm the friend of a rock & roll band

Gail Zappa

Love at First Sight

Lenny Bruce, the poster punk for fearless rule-breakers, succumbed to heroin addiction exacerbated by much court-appointed ballbusting in August 1966. I was almost seventeen when I threw on Grandma's velvet finery and headed to Lenny's final resting place to pay my fledgling respects. After joining the colorful fray traipsing 'round the cemetery, I found myself at a tragically cool eulogy held in some hipster's backyard in Woodland Hills. I sat cross-legged on the ground along with many somber-faced groovers, while Lenny's peers paid him furious homage. I listened intently to Phil Spector, who insisted that Lenny had died "from an overdose of police." I tried to focus on the proceedings, but bright colorful splotches from another corner of the yard kept commandeering my attention.

Quietly frolicking on the kiddie swing set was the rock master of unrepentant irony, Frank Zappa, wearing outlandish flowered bell-bottoms, accompanied by a lissome, wide-eyed doll. She was model-pretty, and obviously entranced with him, but plainly holding her own. Although it was a thrill to see the leader of the Mothers of Invention, live, in person, and on a swing, I was curious about the girl perched on his knee.

The wives and girlfriends of my musical heroes were my heroines. I was too young to have appreciated Paul McCartney's

34

freckle-faced actress lovebird, Jane Asher, and unsecretly hoped she would drown in the Thames, but I later revered the Rolling Stones' muses: Mick's cherubic Marianne Faithfull and Keith's wicked Anita Pallenberg, a disheveled dame who had settled on the guitar player after dallying with Mick *and* Brian Jones. Those cheeky dolly birds were in the center of all that mad music, proudly floating beside their satin-clad counterparts, privy to succulent secrets locked behind hotel room doors all over the world. I envied them ferociously.

It was a couple months after Lenny's eulogy that I laid my Twiggified eyes on Frank Zappa once again. My childhood best friend Iva Turner and I were among the hippies and freaks milling around the corner of Sunset and Crescent Heights, protesting the closing of our beloved club, Pandora's Box. Imminent danger wafted through the incensed air, but just before a hundred baton-wielding cops trooped in formation toward us, I spied Frank

Credit: Gail Zappa collection

Zappa in the kaleidoscopic throng. Instinctively, I reached out and touched his rowdy mop of hair, then turned to Iva and marveled, "It's *soft* . . ." My next Zappa sighting happened at the Cheetah Club, and I actually rolled around on the floor with Frank before being formally introduced to the glorious rock icon.

I frequently danced at various Hollywood functions with an assortment of rambunctious girls called the Laurel Canyon Ballet Company. One of the dolls, Christine, worked as "governess" for Frank and his wife, Gail, taking care of their six-month-old daughter, Moon Unit. When she told Frank about her gaggle of newfound cronies, the ever-curious Mr. Zappa invited the five of us over for tea.

Decked out to impress the maestro, we arrived en masse at the infamous log cabin in Laurel Canyon, which was once owned by 1920s Hollywood cowboy Tom Mix. His beloved four-legged costar Tony the Wonder Horse was supposedly buried under the bowling alley in the basement. Upstairs, there was a fireplace the size of a movie star's closet, and Frank sat nearby at his piano, creating works of cryptic splendor.

We giggled and danced and showed off shamelessly for Mr. Zappa, but I kept sneaking peeks at Gail, who was busy making tea and snacks for her goofy guests, while Christine bounced baby Moon on her scrawny hip. Even when pie-eyed Miss Mercy stamped into the kitchen and gobbled up a stick of butter, Gail was gracious about the peculiar intrusion. She's got it all, I thought dreamily: a genius rock star husband, a house full of wild musicians, and her own little bundle of baby-joy cooing along with Daddy's brilliant jingles. How had she done it? With all the femmes on the prowl, how had she captured this coveted rock god?

I have been friends with Gail Zappa for thirty-eight years now and have long known the answer to my ardent teenage question. She quickly became my confidant, guidance counselor, and mentor as I went through my endless groupie travails. Her distinctly droll point of view helped me to deal with my lamentable romantic foibles, and I still go to her for advice of all kinds. She's somehow able to cut through the dross and get right to the heartbeat of the matter. She has raised four superb people, Moon, Dweezil, Ahmet, and Diva, and is now Grandma Gail to Moon's baby daughter Mathilda. She also adored, protected, and tended to one of our most prolific, awe-inspiring musical masterminds, until his untimely death in 1993. I truly believe that Frank Zappa should, and will be, revered in the same way that Beethoven and Mozart are one day. Not only did Mr. Zappa compose astonishing music, he also wrote hysterically astute lyrics!

Betwixt and between our endless pressing engagements, Gail and I somehow find the time to drink several cups of tea in her overstuffed kitchen. Gail has remodeled, but I remember exactly where the intercom was back in my governess days; when the sound of four-year-old Moon's sweet voice would wake me up, asking me to come in and make "breaktess," while Keith Moon waited impatiently in my little guest house, wearing my leopard-print spike heels.

Gail has always laughingly referred to herself as a groupie, although her rock star dalliances ended when she met Mr. Zappa. "Being a groupie is a state of mind," she insists. "There was the negative side of groupies who only wanted to be with groups for the lifestyle. I remember going to a party and there were all these girls designed to find the pop star of their dreams, and hopefully get a castle in England in the bargain. They took groupiedom to a whole other level that you might call 'professional.' Groupies who just got lucky—girls servicing the bands. Then there were the desperate ones servicing the crew or anyone near the band—cousins, road managers, whatever."

I mention that I recently spoke with the infamous Sweet Connie from Little Rock, a proudly unrepentant groupie with no qualms about tending to any and all backstage personnel. I think it's pretty cool that she makes no apologies for her behavior. "And why would she?" Gail wonders. "There are some people who might be outwardly remarkable for something they're known for, but someone else might recognize them as being so special that they take it to a higher level. They have much more humanity than most people would ever recognize—more than the average person could dream of."

After we nosh on piles of spicy Indian food, Gail and I cover many topics while the family dogs snurfle for attention, and cats languidly meander across the tabletop. Even after decades of late-night chatathons with Gail, I discover loads of fascinating new info about her during the next few hours.

Gail's nuclear physicist father, Jack, was a captain in the U.S. Navy, and the Sloatman family traveled hither and all over yon while she grew up. He ran the Office of Naval Research in London, and while living there in the mid-1960s, teenage Gail encountered profound new possibilities when she attended a shindig for an up-and-coming rock group.

"I went to a party for the Rolling Stones and they were all in jeans—a very raw band. I remember thinking, 'Oh, *this* is interesting.' Not knowing anything about their music, I definitely saw something different going on. They were young people who were making up their own lives, and *that's* what got me interested. I didn't know what I wanted to do; I thought I had some idea but figured my options were extremely limited considering I had no money. But here were these people with *nothing*—you could see they weren't making a fashion statement—jeans were what they legitimately found to wear. I thought the Beatles were new and fantastic and different; they didn't sound like anything else I'd ever heard, but it was slick and polished and commercial. The Rolling Stones didn't seem to be like that, and yet they figured they had a shot as well."

Since I have known Gail, she's had an eerily prescient sense of the looming future, which apparently manifested early on. "I had psychic visions on an oddly consistent basis," she admits. "Because my family was on diplomatic passports when I was just barely eighteen, I got my first job in London working for the American Embassy. And I'll tell you this: on March 16, 1964, I was working away and this prophetic poem came to me straight out of nowhere. So I had to type it up, and the reason I know the date is because it was my father's birthday. I came to understand from this piece of poetry that I was somehow protected. All I had to do was wait and this important person was going to come along. I knew this so strongly: he was out there and he would show up. I didn't follow any particular passion because I knew I would meet this person, and my whole life would be unimaginable compared to what it was then."

While she waited for a certain illustrious composer to happen along, Gail decided to experience the burgeoning free-love movement firsthand. "I said, 'Fuck this, everything in the world's all about sex. Everyone I know has had sex and I can't allow this to continue. So I got on a train going to London one day and said, 'I'm gonna sleep with the first guy I meet.' And I did."

Gail was going to the movies with a girlfriend and her date brought a pal along, and it turned out to be his lucky day. After that initial encounter, Gail continued experimenting. "I had flings—I flung myself around quite a bit, actually. But I wasn't influenced by what other people did or what they thought. I kept to myself and my visions. I trusted my internal check and balance, and suspected from an early age that my personal experiences were different from everyone else's." She didn't feel she could discuss her unique gift with her folks, and Gail felt like an outsider. "I felt I was out of the time I was supposed to be in—actually a step *ahead* of it. In fact, when I first heard the Stones' song 'Out of Time,' I thought it must have been written about my dilemma. I was seeing everything before it happened, waiting for it to catch up: silly stuff, like my father will come through the door and say 'X,' then he comes in five hours later and says 'X.' It finally got to the point where in some instances I had a choice in the matter: if it played out the way I had seen it, it was dependant on me responding in a particular way at a particular time. I would fall into trances in school and have visions of things that didn't have anything to do with me; I'd see major world events before they happened."

Gail tells me that this unusual capability eventually waned, but seems to be back on the upswing. "Some things stay with you, events you know are going to happen, and every day, every hour, you know it's getting closer. I have my own way of dealing with that information. I've seen accidents before they happened and thought, 'What's the point of seeing something like this if you can't prevent it?' You come to realize that sometimes

these things are mere preparations: you can't speak about certain things because it's not for you to determine or attempt to
interfere with another person's 'other' experience. I know it may
sound like complete hogwash or *frogwash*, as we used to say,
but it's something that helped me through a lot of difficulties
in my life, especially some of the issues that come up with an
artist. You really can't be the person that exerts an undue influence on the decisions an artist would make, because you'd never
want to interfere with their creative freedom. It's one thing to
be an unwitting accomplice or influence because they choose to
respect who you are, but it's another to say words in a certain
way, which once they're said, you can't undo. You know they
would have an effect, because everything does. So you learn to
keep your mouth shut." I understand that she's talking about
possibly influencing Frank, and I can only imagine the intriguing particulars. Does she consider this uncommon knack to be a
liability, or a bonus feature? "I'd call it a gift. Some people have
the ability to become fabulous musicians, singers, or writers, or
an ability that can be put to some kind of service. This gift has
assisted me in many ways in evaluating a situation rather than to
just react to it; to be a little more thoughtful or considerate about
what my actions would lead to."

While flinging herself around London, did she get real
crushes on anyone? "I had a 'crunch' on Chris Stamp, one of the
managers of the Who. It wasn't anything serious—there was a lot
of sex-for-entertainment going on then."

Gail met her first serious boyfriend, British fashion photographer Terence Donovan, on a modeling shoot. "He was the
third person I slept with, and he *completely* seduced me—it was
fabulous." She continued to see Terence even when she went to
New York at nineteen, where she became friends with the notorious groupie/backup singer Emeretta Marks.

"This is what happens when you don't wanna be the groupie
you thought you should have been if you were really a groupie.
Oh, how many groupies would have been jealous of my situation,
and all I wanted was *out*. I was at a record company party for
Tom Jones with Emeretta at the Carlyle, but it kept getting later

and later, and pretty soon the trains stopped running to Long Island and she disappeared on me. Suddenly it's down to the last few people, and I don't have a ride or any place to stay and I don't know what the fuck I'm gonna do. Apparently Tom thinks I'm a little morsel and says, 'How would you like to spend the night with me?' I thought, 'Well, I wouldn't! How am I gonna get out of *this?*' It was the usual unspoken conversation you have with yourself: you're in a guy's room, they really *do* expect it; they think you're there by design, that it's your intention. I was *so* not interested in him because he represented everything I did not like about the pop world—he was totally commercial, totally serious about taking himself seriously, and I couldn't understand what his thousands of fans saw in him. Anyway, I was stuck in this hotel room thinking, 'What the hell am I gonna do?'"

Gail dashed to the bathroom with the bright idea to stuff towels down the toilet so a plumber would have to be called. "The best news of all was the bathroom telephone. I called my mother and told her I was desperate, stuck in a hotel room, and wanted her to know I was safe, and she said, 'Well, you ought to be ashamed of yourself, and by the way, Lou called and he's look-ing for you.'" Music producer Lou Adler was another of Gail's groovy boyfriends, and after a call from her mom, he saved the night by sending a car to the Carlyle, whisking the mortified young damsel away from certain distress. "He saved my rock and roll ass," she laughs.

And how did Tom feel about her skedaddling? "He was a gen-tleman, and absolutely charming about it, but he was agitated."

She was only in New York for six months, but managed to perk up a young blues man. "In 1965 New York was full of Jew-ish guys playing the blues. Emeretta sang with the Blues Project. One day their leader, Al Kooper, decided that I was his girl-friend. He made this decision without letting me in on it; I had no sexual relationship with Mr. Kooper. I've heard that in his book he says something about sending me screaming into the arms of Frank Zappa, which is not true."

That summer she hitched to Los Angeles with her British friend Anya Butler, and their mission was to get the Who played on the radio. "Actually, I was just along for the ride; it was officially Anya's job, but between the two of us, we broke that record—*My Generation*. We took it to every single radio station from Barstow to San Diego and parlayed it into an opportunity for Anya to do station IDs with her English accent. Everybody in Southern California wanted something to do with real Englishness at that time. We didn't have to participate in any nefarious activities either, it was all innocent fun. Anya met her fave-rave, Brian Wilson—we ended up at a studio where he was making a Beach Boys record. It was my first time in a recording studio and that's when I probably got the bug because I thought, 'Oh, my God, they are *making* that stuff here!'"

Gail and Anya got a Hollywood apartment on the Strip, and Gail started working at the Trip, a very chic club down the street. I remember spending many nights at that club, gazing through the giant picture window at Mike Clarke's back because I was too young to get in to see the Byrds. "Anya was totally fascinated with him, so as you came through the door of our apartment you saw this big honkin' picture of Mike Clarke. I remember the moment we met two of the Byrds. Anya and I were crossing the street and a cop whipped around the corner and gave us tickets—it was so rude! We got busted for jaywalking—can you fucking believe it? These two guys saw what was happening and pulled up on their motorcycles—David Crosby and Chris Hillman. They offered us a ride and we ended up riding around Laurel Canyon with them. Anya later told me, 'I'm gonna marry that guy.'" That guy was Chris Hillman, and Anya soon became his second wife. So much for Mike Clarke, eh?

I can tell Gail enjoys reminiscing when she describes her neighborhood coffee house. "If you go into Book Soup now, there's a closed door at an angle to the main store. That door was always open, and there was a stairway that led up to our apartment. Find that door and imagine there's a table right next to it, then imagine Jim Morrison sitting there every day. The Doors were the house band at the Whisky and I would meet him there for coffee almost daily. Not planned though. I looked at him and he looked at me and he suggested I sit down, and we had this conversation, 'You feel so familiar, look so familiar, I feel like I know you . . .'" How did she resist the obvious charms of the Lizard King? "Let's just say that he had an interesting relationship with every girl that crossed my threshold, but *not* with me. Later it turned out that we had known each other when we were five years old. His father was in the navy too."

When her boss at the Trip, Elmer Valentine, hired Gail to work at his other Strip venue, the Whisky a Go Go, she somehow fended his advances off as well. "I had always heard he was a lecher, but not in a bad way. What *is* a lecher anyway? The Whisky was like a big candy store—who wouldn't want to indulge in the candy? I do know that Mario and Elmer were the best protection and best source of information for any young girl in Hollywood. They were really kind and looked out for you."

Gail thinks she may have met the Lovin' Spoonful at a sound check, or maybe it was an audition. "Rock and roll proper was basically still being invented. There were just a handful of people, industry types. I met the band, and the drummer, Joe Butler, was very polite with me. Besides Frank, he was one of the few guys that asked me in advance for an actual date. We went out a few times, but then a very bad thing happened: this is a typical—hmmm, it might be an *atypical*—story but to me, this signifies the moment when you know you're an actual groupie. One day I locked on to the band's guitar player, Zal Yanovsky, and things just clicked. It was like, 'Oh, yes, we're destined to be together at this very special moment in time and space.' Everybody said, 'You can never be with Zal because he's never interested in anyone; he doesn't misbehave, and even if you end up in his room, nothing will happen.' So I thought, 'We'll just see about *that*.' And we did. Days later, there was a knock at Zal's door and Joe was standing there. He didn't say anything, he simply handed Zal my toothbrush."

Right around this time, Gail also had a date with the cosmos. "Somehow I made a conscious decision to take acid so I could see what everybody was talking about. It wasn't illegal; people were still putting it on sugar cubes and keeping it on trays in the refrigerator. So I dropped acid. When I tried to draw a face, the eyelashes kept moving, then they *wouldn't* move. It was interesting because I came to grips, in a small way, with what I *thought* I thought I knew about thinking." Whoa. I tell Gail to let me take a few deep breaths and a long sip of tea, so I can think about thinking about how to digest that thought process.

"I had to take it one more time to see if that was a legitimate evaluation, and the conclusion I came to was, if you *think* you're going to have a paranoid experience, you can have one. I believe acid did the opposite of what everyone said, which was expanding your consciousness. Instead, it allowed you to narrow your focus in a specific and refined way. If you see one thing clearly, no matter how small it is, everything is contained there. It's a map of the entire universe. It was as deep as you allowed yourself to go. In that way it felt like an expansion of consciousness simply because you were looking at something intently and observing it in a way you never had before. The problem, however, was that you didn't have control over that, and under the influence, your response was limited by time and a fading of intensity. But I did feel I was beginning to get the plot. There were no rules because you were taking huge risks, but you were so young that you didn't think of them as risks. Somebody had been telling you all along that you can't do this and you shouldn't do that or *these* things might happen. Suddenly you realized there never *was* anyone else. It was always what *you* chose to believe about what was presented to you. So I said, 'Fuck *that*, I never *have* to listen to anybody again.'"

In this emancipated state, twenty-one-year-old Gail Sloatman would finally meet her teenage poem's promised reward. A friend took her and Anya to an impromptu meeting in Laurel Canyon where she got her first glimpse of her very near future. "The front door opened, and standing in the door frame was this completely stoned girl. The story was that Jim Morrison was in one bedroom and Van Morrison was in the other, and she was trying to take care of them both. Everybody was supposedly smoking pot or dropping acid at *that* end of the house, and at *this* end of the house it was all business. It was Frank's house and just having a look at him caught my breath and I had a moment with him. I thought, 'This is something completely different; this is the most unusual person I've ever seen.' Anya was terrified and said, 'I've gotta get out of here!' I knew she was completely paranoid, so we had to leave. I mean, Frank just didn't look like a normal human being in any way—certainly he *was*, but he had a very intense and stern countenance. The way I think about meeting Frank that first time was like an inoculation that didn't quite take."

The next time she saw this intense fellow, Gail was running an errand for Elmer. "I had to do all the deposits for the Whisky, and I was in line at the bank when I saw Frank in another line. I left my line and walked right behind him, and probably looked like an idiot because I walked up to him three fucking times and didn't have the nerve to speak to him."

An oddball chick who worked with Gail at the Whisky surprised her one afternoon. "She was one of those girls with long, straight hair, always flipping it around in her hands, huffing and puffing every time she walked by. I never thought she liked me because she always seemed to be evaluating me. One day she started staring at me, so I thought, 'Well, I can play this game,' and stared back. I knew it was going to be about who blinked first—it was that stupid—so rather than blink, she said, 'Okay, I'd like you to come over to my house for dinner,' and that broke the ice with her. When Gail walked into the house on Kirkwood to the smell of sizzling lamb chops, she realized she had been there very recently. The huffy girl was Pamela Zarubica, the voice of Suzy Creamcheese, and her roommate was Frank Zappa. "We hadn't even finished dinner when the phone rang, and it was Frank. He wanted to be picked up at the airport because his promo tour had been cut short. Pamela said, 'He told me not to bring anyone, but *we're* going to the airport.' I remember thinking it was her intention to hook us up. So I went to the airport and it was all history after that."

Since I've never heard the romantic beginnings of my fave rock couple, I listen with rapt appreciation. "I was simply standing there and he walked over and made this gesture—to put his briefcase down between my feet. I refused to back up, so I had to move my legs apart. He put it down right between them so the handle was in line with my ankle-bones. I was standing there with this briefcase between my legs and he was really close to me; we were nose-to-nose, and he said, 'You're cute!' And that was it. My vaccination."

Did they both know that this was *it*? "Well, we went back to the house and he didn't say much, just talked about the tour. At one point, Pamela said, 'I'm going to sleep in your bed so you guys can have mine.' She had a double bed and Frank's was a single. Then she offered me a little black slip to wear. Frank was tired from traveling and we just crawled into bed and snuggled up, but absolutely nothing happened. He was a perfect gentleman."

Was she at all nervous to find herself in the sack with her fait accompli? "Yeah, I was nervous, but you can be nervous and comfortable at the same time. The next morning I woke up, and landing back in my body, realized where I was, and thought, 'Oh God, I think he's awake.' I rolled over and the pillow was like a mountain. All I could see was this one eye, wide open, over the edge of the pillow, looking right at me. I heard my voices saying, 'OK, this is it, and if you do not accept this, you'll never hear from us again.'"

Did Mr. Zappa know *he* had met his cosmic match? "*I* never knew that—I didn't know for years, then I read an interview where he said that when he met me it was love at first sight. It's such a corny thing to say—something you would never expect *him* to say, but he *did* have his way with clichés."

And how did this budding rock and roll liason progress? "I knew Frank was the *one* that morning, but nothing happened. Then he called and asked me out on an actual *date* three days hence. After the Lenny Bruce eulogy, our next date was a gig. I remember I had to stop at the Whisky to run in and get Frank's amplifier. I was trying to drag this giant thing out the front door, and Mario wasn't helping me. He grabbed my shirt and yelled, 'You're *not* wearing a bra!'"

Did the Zappa romance start out divinely? Was their chemistry irrepressible and obvious? Did they know right away that they would be together forever? "I think we both knew we had the makings for a great relationship, but we were babies and didn't know how to do it yet. Frank was twenty-five and I was just twenty-one. But yes, there was a real conscious effort to make it something exceptional. I was recently on a press junket with Dweezil and Ahmet. During the interviews, a couple of times the question came up: 'What was it like, growing up with Frank Zappa?' I had to jump in and say, 'They didn't grow up with Frank Zappa—*I did!*' And it's true!"

While I have the opportunity, I ask Gail to share some all-important tips on how she made her rock and roll marriage work for so long. So listen up, dolls.

"I always believed we were *so* convinced we were communicating that it worked out that we *were*. Looking back, it's actually possible that we had no fucking clue, and just *thought* we were totally in sync because we avoided having conversations about a lot of things. When people ask, 'What did you talk about?' I always say, 'I can tell you we didn't talk about mortgages, *ever.*'" It always seemed to me that Gail and Frank had such an amazing connection. Didn't they ever discuss "serious matters"? Gail raises her eyebrows knowingly, and shakes her head, "*Never.* That would be the most dangerous thing that could possibly happen. We never made 'decisions' together. He was an artist: he did what he had to do and I did whatever I could to make it easier for him. I made a conscious effort to keep everything mundane out of his way and out of his path so he didn't have to deal with that crap. I figured if he was going to put a roof over *my* head and I got the benefit of that, the least I could do was spare him ordinary details. I'm not gonna try to say I knew what he was doing or even *how* to do what he was doing."

Does Gail mean she didn't claim to understand what was going on inside his excessively creative mind? "Yes. That's what *he* did. And that's what I found fascinating to the very end: here's a guy who does *that* stuff, and however he does that, it is way different than my experience."

Having lived with the Zappa family on and off for a few years, I think a lot of the magic I saw between Frank and Gail was that

she *did* spare him from trips to Ralphs market and other triviali-
ties of life. "Oh yes," she agrees. "Bad things could happen at
Ralphs." I tell her that this chapter might be seen as a manual
for would-be groupies. "Whenever I've had to answer questions
in forms that ask, 'What is your profession?' I'd always write
'professional wife.' I never, ever put 'housewife,' or 'wife,' on a
form, because it *is* a fucking job and you can do it well or you can
do it not so well."

I surmise that certain genius artists—Picasso, Shakespeare,
or Mozart perhaps—were most likely not regular guys and
therefore couldn't be expected to function at their highest ability while having to fiddle with mundane day-to-dayness. Gail
chuckles, "It was really more about if he didn't get to do what he
wanted to do, bad things would happen. I just never stood in the
way. I had seen his frustration with the business side of things,
and said to myself, 'Don't think you're going to help him in
business. He's gonna make choices, he'll have to figure it out for
himself, and nothing you say is going to change that.' The other
thing I realized was: don't be part of the problem that stands in
his way—in terms of him getting his work done."

I remind Gail that I have long considered her to be as astutely
brilliant as her spectacular husband was in her very own way. "I
can't drink to *that*," she laughs. "There's curds and there's whey,
you know what I'm saying?"

Something inexplicable between Frank and Gail definitely
worked. There were times I had to put pillows over my head
to get some shut-eye while they went at it. Deep down I hoped
that someday I'd have such a delightfully loud sex life. "Really?"
Gail says, slightly shocked, "I'm so sorry. I had no idea! That's
the thing, sex doesn't get different, it just gets better."

Even with all that love and understanding, Frank was on the
road a lot and had his own fervid groupies. How did Gail deal
with that niggling little detail? "Well *everyone* had groupies. I
mean, you couldn't get around them. There are certain aspects
that were *not* easy and *not* fun, and it's not like you could be
consoled or cry on *his* shoulder over it. But what doesn't kill you
makes you stronger."

Was there ever a time when she thought about leaving Frank? "I never thought about leaving him because of another woman, but I did think about leaving him because sometimes it was way too much. When we were at the log cabin, I *did* leave." *What??* I am stunned. She actually fled their idyllic Laurel Canyon sanctuary? "Yeah, I just said, 'I've had enough,' and walked out one day. I wrote Frank a note in lipstick on the upstairs bathroom mirror so only he could see it, took the baby, and got on a plane. We had become a crash pad! Anybody could live there at any time, there were no locks on any doors, and Moon and I were not a priority. It felt dangerous for me and my munchkin. What you didn't know was that I had no means of transportation; I had to hitchhike to do the laundry. I had to put my thumb out on Laurel Canyon Boulevard to go to the fucking grocery store. There wasn't even a proper floor in the kitchen. Nobody had any time. And then they'd say, 'How come there's no food in the house?' Well, I don't know, why don't you ask Mercy?"

Has Gail noticed any difference in the groupie scene through the years? "There's always going to be groupies for this art form or that art form. Think about how many groupies there were for a guy in a uniform during the war! I happen to be very partial to *real* rock 'n' roll; what they're calling 'rock' now pales. It's not *even* a substitute. Just like original rock will never be that way again, there were people who were interested in musicians in a different way."

I was never ashamed of being a groupie. I bask and revel in the glorious, twangy odes that my songwriter boyfriend, Mike Stinson, writes for me, and I still consider myself a muse.

"I think those of us who were in service to the music—we were vestal virgins," Gail says. "But you have to realize that vestal virgins were not actually virgins, they were just unfettered by other restraints, totally devoted and in service to whoever it was that they were *reserving* themselves for. My observations tell me that the early groupie movement was part of a huge shift in consciousness: part of an awareness that was impossible to ignore. Whether it was a nasty sound on the guitar, or what the lyrics said, the people making that music were telling you that everything you suspected about the world you were entering was true. Rock musicians were saying there *is* an alternative—there is another way to think about things."

I tell Gail that I believe Bob Dylan, my absolute hero, heralded that much-needed shift in consciousness. "Well, I didn't think of Dylan in the sense of hard-core rock and roll, but I did recognize that he was changing what I thought of as an art form. I knew the origin of the songs that people around him in the New York folk scene were singing and writing about. Some were seriously interested in the history behind it and others were performing pop music. Peter, Paul, and Mary were singing traditional folk music, but with Dylan there was a big difference. What he was writing about was totally consistent with the huge shift in consciousness. In that sense he was as much rock and roll as anybody in rock and roll. I remember when I first got to Hollywood, I went to a huge party in the hills. There were big, giant open doors that led out onto a wide balcony. I stepped out to look around, and there was nobody out there. I was alone, standing at this balustrade, and it was a beautiful, *beautiful* night. I was in *California* and I thought, 'This is fan*tas*tic.' As I turned around and headed for the door, this guy came around the corner. It was Bob Dylan and I *knew* it was Bob Dylan. I thought he was so beautiful. I mean, he was just exquisite, as we all were back then. The dilemma was, 'Do I just stop in my tracks and let him pass?' because, you know, it's *Bob Dylan*. But I just kept on walking and we looked at each other in that moment and he said, 'Hello.' I can't even describe this perfect Southern California evening—there you are and there he is. Bob Dylan says hello to you and then you just walk on . . .'"

My Lady D'Arbanville

I've always been drawn to imaginative, uncommonly bright women. As far back as I can recall, I've counted on them to encourage and embolden me to be creatively fearless. From my dear mama to Mary Magdalen to Gail Zappa, the feisty dolls I admire have blessed me with their unique perspective and tilted take on life. So, not surprisingly, all three of my best girlfriends are brimming with inspiration and have been writing their own books. Iva Turner has written an extremely funny and erotic novel entitled *Sex Season*, with salacious sequels to follow. The beauteous Catherine James has recently completed her memoir, and Patti D'Arbanville is hard at work on her outrageous tell-some autobiography.

Years before I met my wild Gemini pals, Patti and Catherine, they had frolicked together on the Greenwich Village streets in their early teens. Catherine left a nightmare behind in Hollywood and traveled three thousand miles following a dream. Patti was a frisky little piece of work, pretty much unsupervised by her bohemian parents, and already familiar with trouble.

I stand in awe of Patti D'Arbanville's cheeky audacity, always hoping to glean a few pointers. Here's an event that reveals her nature perfectly: she had picked me up from my plastic surgeon's office in Westwood, where I had undergone a horrific chemical

Credit: Patti D'Arbanville collection

peel, hoping to erase some of the teen-angst acne scars that had bothered me since high school. I was a drowsy, lolling goof-pot, heavily swaddled, with raw pink spots gleaming between my Vaselined bandages. We were stopped at a red light when a couple of creepy dudes in the car next to us started pointing at me and blatantly snickering, close to *guffawing*, actually, at my obvious medical ordeal. Even in my blotto condition, I was aware of Patti's instant response to their rudeness. Enraged, she burst out of the car, marched over to them, her blonde ponytail flying, and began pounding on their windshield, shouting the consummate obscenities required to put the insensitive schlubs in their place. They quickly rolled up their windows, eyes popping with terror. Patti is definitely somebody you want on your side. She'll always go the extra few thousand miles.

I had heard tales about Patti for a couple of decades before we met. One of the best flower-child albums from the 1970s was Cat Stevens's poetic, genteel *Mona Bone Jakon*, featuring the mournful love song "Lady D'Arbanville." It was all about a lass with lips that felt like winter and a heart that seemed oh so silent to the troubled troubadour. I figured she must have broken Cat's heart to pieces, which of course intrigued me no end.

It was the summer of 1984 when Melanie Griffith called to invite me to a big beachy birthday bash for her then-hubby, Steven Bauer. I was especially curious, because my once-adored boyfriend and Melanie's first husband, Don Johnson, was bringing the girl who had tamed him enough to turn him into the daddy of a baby boy—the beguiling Patti D'Arbanville.

Here's a snippet about our first meeting from my second book, *Take Another Little Piece of My Heart*:

> *There they were, D.J. and My Lady D'Arbanville looking way too good with her yards and yards of wavy blonde hair. Thumpy-hearted, I started through the crowd, and when Donnie spotted me, he grandly stood up and, laughing, opened his arms for me to run into. He told me how gorgeous I looked and introduced me to Patti, who sort of snarled at me like a taunted, ticked-off cat. Oops. After attempting some trivia talk with the two of them—with Patti glaring at me as if I was about to unzip Donnie's pants—I excused myself to find Michael, hoping that a glimpse of my real live husband would make Patti retract her claws. . . . I hung onto Michael, making sure to gaze adoringly, and I could feel Patti finally relax and start to soften. I wasn't a threat after all. . . . A new friend! Meeting a new girl and hitting it off is almost as thrilling as falling in love. In some ways it's even more rewarding because romantic passion and honey-devotion can be back-breaking, feverish work, whereas female kinship is a constant, consistent, uplifting experience you can always count on.*

Two decades later, I still rely on Patti for consistently loyal, exhilarating kinship. We've certainly enjoyed our shared bouts of waywardness, and she has dreamed up the titles for three of my four books, including this one. I believe I have laughed with

Patti D'Arbanville, Melanie Griffith, and me.

Credit: Randee St. Nicholas

abandon harder and longer with Patti than with anybody else on the planet. She is so willing to throw her head back and roar, open her heart to the world and expect miracles in return.

Patti's dear mama drank and her father was a bartender, so she grew up without much parental guidance. At fourteen, she had already driven cross-country with her girlfriends in a five-cylinder Mustang, and she says the first time she heard the phrase "wild child," it was being spoken about her. Patti has been working as an actress since her early twenties. I remember enjoying her fetching portrayal of a naughty nymphet in the dreamy French romp, *Bilitis*, and just last year, she courageously appeared naked in *The Sopranos*, crawling across the room on all fours before getting assassinated by TV's favorite mob. She had a ball working with our old friend Bruce Willis in his latest film, *Perfect Stranger*, but insists that raising her three teenagers is by far her most important gig.

Even though she's penning her own memoir, I persuaded her to share her Cat Stevens saga one afternoon while her offspring were safely ensconced at school.

"I was in London, modeling, and went to Sir William Brown's country house one beautiful, sunny Saturday," Patti begins wistfully. "Stevie Winwood was there, Eric Clapton, Ginger Baker, Jimmy Page. Everywhere you looked, there was an amazing musician. I used to be painfully shy, which should probably come as a huge surprise to you. I eventually overcame it because it was really getting in my way. But to this day, the only person I've ever been tongue-tied around was Jimmy Page. He was the most gorgeous man I've ever seen in my life. He must have thought I didn't like him, but the words just wouldn't come. Jimmy Page was like a painting; therefore, I was unable to say a word."

There was a less daunting fellow at the country house that day. "Across the room I saw this wan, thin, dark guy, smoking a cigarette. We just stared at each other. Then I went over and asked him for a cigarette. He told me he had just gotten out of the hospital with tuberculosis. I said, 'And you're *smoking*?' He told me just as his hit record was peaking, he started coughing up blood. He talked about his parents—his mother was Swedish and his father was Greek. I had no idea who he was."

Patti had been dating singer Barry Ryan, who was in a group with his twin brother, Paul, who just happened to be best pals with Cat Stevens. "I walked in one evening with Barry, and there was the dark guy from the party, playing guitar with Paul—and he smiled. He started coming over more and more, and there was flirting going on every time, but Barry was absolutely clueless. Then one day, a whole group of us went to an amusement park. I'm afraid of heights, and there was this ride with two buckets that went up and down and 'round and 'round at the top. I had never even been on a roller coaster. Nobody would go on with Stephen (his friends never called him Cat), and when he said, 'Who's going on with me?' I said, 'I'll do it.' It felt like I was going to the *chair*. The bucket started swinging and I held on to him—I wouldn't let go. He held me tight and it was the first time since we'd been eyeing each other that we finally got to be alone together. It was extraordinary, and by the time the ride was over, I was totally in love with him and he was in love with me."

The would-be sweethearts didn't know how to break the news to the twins, so Stephen kept coming to the house to play guitar with Paul, and one day, Patti and Stephen found themselves alone. "He said, 'Let's get out of here,' and we went to Hampstead Heath and spent the whole afternoon together. We rolled down hills, kissing in the grass; it was such a beautiful summer day in London, simply gorgeous. We went back to his flat, which overlooked his father's Greek restaurant. His bedroom was painted all red, and the only thing in it was a bed and a piano. His father had a thick Greek accent and his mother had a thick Swedish accent, really bizarre. So Stephen and I were in bed together, trying to figure out uh-oh, *now* what are we going to do? I wasn't going back to Barry's, and Stephen's best friend Paul was Barry's twin brother. So I finally said, 'I guess we're gonna have to tell them.' I called Barry and said, 'I can't see you anymore, I met someone else.' He was heartbroken and wanted to know who it was. I just said, 'You don't know him.'

Patti kept her own flat, but spent most of her time in Stephen's small red bedroom. Of course, I have to ask if he was good in the sack. "He was terrific. He was put together very well. A little thin, but back then I liked them thinner than I do now. I just liked everything about him. He was *very* into it, and we stayed together for quite awhile. Somebody told him he looked like a cat once, and he used it instead of Stephen Demetre Georgiou. It was very clever because that's how he'd know if someone really *knew* him. He'd get phone calls—'Is *Cat* there?' 'Yeah, he is, but *no*, OK?' He was easy to talk to, compassionate, and very passionate. He played music for me all the time. We'd be in bed and all of a sudden he'd have to get up and write lyrics down. I'd be laying there and hear the first couple of notes, like the beginning of 'Maybe You're Right,' or 'Wild World,' the songs he wrote for me. He had a guitar, but he always wrote on the piano. We watched the first moon landing together. It was close to his twenty-first birthday, July 21, 1969, and we were lying in bed watching men walk on the moon."

The passionate songwriter who later embraced the Muslim religion and changed his name to Yusuf Islam was once a naughty boy. "For some reason, a lot of Englishmen have this thing about English schoolgirls," Patti smiles. "I was modeling, and one day I came back from a 'go-see' wearing a miniskirt, well, a mini-*belt*, actually, it was so short. It was about three in the afternoon and I guess Stephen had just driven by a school that let out, and he said, 'Come on, I'm going to take you somewhere and buy you something.' He took me to Marks & Spencer, a department store up on the West End, and we went into the section where they sold school uniforms. We started playacting, and Stephen told the saleslady, 'I have to buy this little girl a school uniform, she's the daughter of one of my friends, can you fit her, please?' The woman was very officious and middle-aged, grandmotherly. Here was this twenty-one-year-old Greek kid with this however-the-hell-old-I-looked young girl. I was really

Credit: Patti D'Arbanville collection

flat-chested and stick-straight, like a boy. I was supposed to be going into seventh or eighth grade, but must have looked about eleven. Every time the woman went to get another piece of the uniform, he'd say, 'I can't wait to pull that skirt up and bend you over the car, maybe even before—in the elevator.' He got me a white blouse and a blue and grey plaid skirt with a little blue sweater, and blue knee socks. Then we got those snub-nosed Mary Jane shoes, a little hat, and a school satchel."

I tell Patti that I'm tickled that he took the playful ploy so far. "Oh yeah, soup to nuts, baby: underwear, little girl's T-shirt, little white panties—all regulation. Then he told me to walk to the next corner. He said, 'I'll get the car and you stand on the corner and wait for me. When you see me drive by, pretend you don't know me; just walk down the street and I'll follow you. Then you decide when to get in.' I wanted to hop in the car immediately, but I made him crazy. I must have walked three blocks, by all those little crooked alleys. Then he motioned me into an alley near Leicester Square, if memory serves. It was about six in the evening, twilight time, and I lifted up my schoolgirl skirt and pulled down my little white panties, and we had at it. We did it on the hood of his car . . ." Patti pauses, reflecting. "Imagine *that*. Sometimes I let him take it all off. And because I couldn't wear the school uniforms to concerts or clubs, I'd wear just the understuff. He liked me to wear the white panties. And so did I."

After a year or so of risqué bliss, Patti became restless. "Yeah, it just kind of petered out, if you will. I remember we had taken acid at my flat and were watching *Juliet of the Spirits*. Stephen was a wonderful artist, and he was drawing my feet. There was something about him being at my feet . . . it was too much adoration, and it freaked me out. I could tell he was really falling in love with me, and I was feeling like I couldn't give him what he wanted. I felt trapped—*and* I was on acid. Feeling trapped on acid is a lot more intense than just feeling trapped. The gate came slamming down with him there at my feet. It felt like I was in the *Invasion of the Body Snatchers*. Suddenly I was in a pod, and he felt me go cold. He said, 'Come on, let's go home,' and I said, 'I *am* home,' and he left."

With his romance in tatters, Stephen was inspired to write the tragi-tune "Lady D'Arbanville." "I cried the first time I heard it, because that's when I knew it was really over. But I saw him on and off for a while, then went back to New York in '72 to see my parents. I remember Stephen sent me a postcard from Paris that said, 'Here I am in Gay Paree,' and in parentheses he wrote, '*Gay* being the operative word.'"

Patti later had another encounter with her sensitive flame in Los Angeles. "I'd been in Europe for three years, so it had to be 1975. I was standing at Dan Tana's restaurant with some friends, and there was this guy next to me—tall, thin, black curly hair, wearing sunglasses, and I had no clue. It was three years later and he was the last person I expected to be standing there looking at me."

Stephen was in the middle of a tour, and on his way to Hawaii. "He said, 'Why don't you just come with me, and it will be like old times?' So we went to Hawaii and met up with people who were into Krishna. We went to the temple and they made us the most amazing food. Stephen talked for hours with these people, and they gave us little wooden beads that he wore for the whole rest of the tour."

I ask Patti if she was surprised when Stephen embraced the Muslim religion, and had to stop playing his beautiful songs. "Oh, yeah, I was flabbergasted, especially because I knew how much he loved music. But when I was with him, he was always searching for something—seeking forever. We were vegetarians together, he was a Buddhist, and wanted me to become one, too. He started out as a Greek Orthodox Catholic, for Christ's sake, *hello*."

Much more recently, Patti ran into Yusuf Islam once again. "I was asked to be on a talk show in Germany. They fabricated an excuse for me to promote something. They were going to surprise Stephen with me on TV, but we got wind of it. I said, 'I can't do that, but I would like to see him,' and he said, 'I can't do that, but I would like to see her.' He came with a whole bunch of men to the studio and I was with my husband, Terry. Stephen, uh, Yusuf said, 'I can't talk to you without your husband in the room.' He was married and had all these kids, and it was not proper. So we sat and had a little chat with Terry. He said some *blah blah blah* about the Koran, then he said, 'Call me *Saf*.' I think he found what he was looking for in the Koran, and knowing him, I think he embraced it on its deepest level. It resonated in his soul somehow and he was transformed yet again."

As the back door opens and chatty teenage voices fill the room, I ask Patti how she got so wrapped up in rock and roll so young. "The music is what moved me, and everyone I found interesting was tied to music somehow. I was just naturally drawn to them. It all stemmed from Beatlemania; we used to go to hotels and scream for the Beatles. Then I heard 'Satisfaction,' and that became my main objective—I wanted to get near Mick Jagger. I wanted that satisfaction." I laugh out loud, "Yeah, we *all* did!" And eventually we all *got* our satisfaction, but that's a story for another time.

Patti stands to welcome her brood. Emmelyn and Alexandra are both two years older than she was when she started going out, and Liam is twelve. "They're all pretty sheltered in a way that I never was. I know where they are all the time and they actually report to me. Imagine that!" She smiles knowingly, "If you can dream it, you can be it, and if you can be it . . . well, then you know how to be two steps ahead of your very clever kids."

The Elusive Miss James

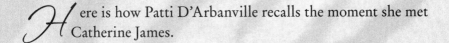

Here is how Patti D'Arbanville recalls the moment she met Catherine James.

It was one of those sexy-hot days that we seemed to have all the time in the summer of '64 in NYC. I was kittening down MacDougal Street in my mini, certain I looked like the goddess of the world: shiny blonde hair that reached my shoulders just right, perfect, tight fanny, long, long *legs (for my height, 5'3", quite remarkable), champagne-glass titties ready and at attention. My mother had always told me that I was the most beautiful girl in the world. Naturally I believed her and never had any reason not to think she was telling the absolute truth. On my way to Washington Square, I ran into Lizzie Derringer who was talking to a tall, lanky blonde girl with her back to me, and when Liz saw me she said my name. I still see this in slow motion: the girl spun around, her long, long (just* better) *honey blonde hair swirling around her. She had storm-tossed, sea-green eyes, an aquiline nose, and a smile that could break your heart and fill you with joy all at the same time. She, too, was skinny, perfect, and her breasts were really there, quite a handful too. I*

Credit: Catherine James

*was devastated. She was the most beautiful creature I
had ever laid eyes on, she had a great story, knew amazing people, and worst of all, I learned that day that my
mama did lie.*

Yes, Catherine James was the most alluring of the classic rock
and roll temptresses. She appeared on the Hollywood scene after
I had taken the Strip by storm, and to borrow a line from Dylan,
I immediately wanted this tall, elegant eyeful to go back to from
where she came. Jimmy Page had been romancing her for quite
some time when he first began to pursue me. We briefly wrangled for the exquisite rock prince, but Jimmy shattered her heart
in favor of mine that time around.

The nineteen-year-old elusive Miss James turned up unin-
vited at my twenty-first birthday party during my long-distance
British phone call from the wicked Mr. Page. I was tripped out

on acid, and she stood there glaring at me, draped around her glamorous prop for the evening, Pink Floyd's delicious David Gilmour. For a few months Catherine and I circled around each other in the clubs, hissing like spiteful cats, and I got my wish when she suddenly vanished from the scene.

Surprise, surprise! A year later, when I moved to London to stay with my new boyfriend, Marty, owner of the supertrendy Granny Takes a Trip, guess who came to tea? Marty's partner and roommate, Gene, also had a new live-in lady-love, Miss Catherine James. Not only were we forced to be civil to each other, there was just one bedroom, where all four of us had to sleep in two big beds jammed together. Catherine's ringleted baby boy, Damian, slumbered along with us in his little cot in the corner.

It didn't take us long to realize how alike we were, despite how differently we were brought up. Catherine had a wildy eccentric absentee father and the mother from Hades, and I was an only child, swathed in adoring attention. While I was safely sequestered within my cozy Reseda tract home, living my teen-dream, Catherine was running away from a West Coast orphanage, in search of her then mentor, Bob Dylan. From the age of fourteen, she found herself in situations that boggle the heart.

We avoided the topic of Jimmy Page, but soon bonded over boy talk, big, fat hash joints, and our crazy love of music.

John Mayall wrote a song about Catherine called "The Elusive Miss James." And the lyrics Jackson Browne penned describe his muse well: "you're a warm and lovely mystery/abandon your sad history/and meet me in the fire . . ."

Catherine has just completed her memoirs (with much encouragement from me), but happily, I have convinced her to share a few tales, which are merely a teasing peek into her sizzling rock romances.

Catherine has rarely lacked male attention. She always seems to have several suitors, as she calls them, vying for her charms, yet she has always been a very old-fashioned girl. When life overwhelms her, she needs quiet time alone, which irks her gentlemen callers no end. I often joke that she gets "the vapors," just as swoony damsels did in days gone by, taking to their beds while handmaidens cooled them with fancy lace fans. I think this is partly why she is so intriguing to the opposite sex. She speaks her mind, but she is also enchantingly vulnerable.

After a scrumptious dinner at a darkened Italian bistro near her place in Malibu, Catherine and I sprawl out on her chaise longue while her hyper teacup Yorkie puppy, Jack, gnaws on everything within his reach. All through our reminiscing, Catherine's lilting laughter bounces around the candlelit room.

It was patently obvious that Catherine was a stunner, with her long Barbie-doll legs, flawless body, and golden mane of hair, but she never believed it. "I didn't *feel* pretty. I knew I commanded a certain amount of attention, but I wasn't sure why. My mother constantly insisted that I was the ugly duckling. As a young woman I felt like an imposter. Even as a Wilhelmina model and with the attention I got from every boy that caught my fancy, I still felt like the great imposter."

Catherine's sweet nature belies a childhood full of terror at the hands of her devious folk-singing mother, Dian. She did unspeakable things to her lovely little daughter, such as dropping her off in strange neighborhoods and telling her to find her way back home. By the time she was eleven, Catherine was blossoming into a beauty, which enraged her jealous mother even further. When she broke her arm, Dian refused to call a doctor, insisting her injured daughter finish ironing a huge pile of clothes. It was probably a life-saver that Dian sent Catherine to an orphanage, where she spent much of her childhood before heading east, looking for a savior.

Since her parents' relationship was brief and calamitous, and her father was rarely around, I ask Catherine if his absence created an attraction to bigger-than-life, seemingly unreachable men. "At that time, my mother was married to Travis from Bud and Travis. She always had famous people around her—Leon Russell, Hoyt Axton, Tommy Boyce, and Bobby Hart—I didn't go looking for heroes, they were in my own backyard. I lived with my parents in the bohemian folk world and these were the people in my universe. Peter Yarrow of Peter, Paul, and Mary was after me when I was fourteen. There were no rules back then, no one was watching, but he certainly wasn't blabbing around town that he was interested in a fourteen year-old."

Dian was a hopeful folk singer, who recorded an album, *Dian and the Greenbriar Boys* for Elektra, and her producer, Jim Dickson (who later managed the Byrds), was smitten with young Catherine. "He got my attention under the guise of being a protective father figure, which I desperately needed. I was still too young to understand the love vibe, so I just ignored it. When I was released from Los Padrenes, a state institution, I was sent to a homier orphanage in west L.A. I used to call Jim a few times a week from the pay phone on the grounds. One day I called and heard a strange voice. 'Who's this?' I asked. 'It's Bob.' 'Bob who?' I said. 'Bob Dylan—have you ever heard of me?' I said, 'No, I only have a minute to talk. Can I speak to Jim?' Jim was also a photographer and had taken several black and white photographs of me; and these artsy pictures had been blown up and scattered around the walls. I was only thirteen, but the photos made me look more like sixteen or seventeen. So Bob says, 'Well, don't you wanna talk to me?' and I said, 'No, and if you don't let me talk to Jim, I have to hang up.' I was only allowed two minutes on the pay phone, so I hung up on Bob Dylan."

Jim had permission to take Catherine out of the orphanage on weekends, and one night they went to Santa Monica College to see the upstart folk singer. "After the show we went backstage and Jim introduced us. Bob shook my hand and said, 'There's a party after the show. Do you wanna come with me?' I had just turned thirteen. He didn't ask how old I was, but I was cunning for my age because I'd spent so much time around adults. Before the party we stopped at the store. I was already smoking cigarettes and told Bob I'd like some Marlboros, please, and he bought me a carton. I was like, 'Oh, my God, a whole carton!' I'd never had a whole carton of cigarettes in my life."

Even though Catherine carefully hid her secret stash behind a windowsill, the warden in charge soon discovered and confiscated her coveted contraband. "I yelled, 'You can't take them! They were a present from Bob Dylan!'"

When the future bard was in town, he began to pick Catherine up on weekend afternoons. "One time Bob showed up wearing the coolest soft suede jacket I'd ever seen. He said, 'Let's go get you one!' I was almost in tears because I never had anything new of my own. We went to Fred Segal, which back then was just a tiny hole-in-the-wall store on Santa Monica Boulevard. We searched through all the jackets, but no matter how tall I stood, they were all clearly too big for me. Another time we went to the Santa Monica pier, to a funky little café on the beach. He'd only released the self-titled album, the one before the stunning *Freewheelin'*. He was carrying two bags, stuffed tight with songs he'd been writing. The Beatles had just come out with 'She Loves You' and 'I Wanna Hold Your Hand,' and we put a couple dimes in the jukebox and talked about the Beatles. He loved their chords and music changes. Then we talked about me, what I was gonna do, and why I was living in the institution. He gave me some pretty insightful information. He said my almighty mother would be all alone one day, and that I should feel sorry for her. He said she would have no love in her life and would have to live in the hell she created. I thought to myself, 'You don't know my mom; she'll never be alone. She's beautiful, powerful, and really scary.' I thought he didn't understand because he'd never met her, but he turned out to be right. It took a while, but my mother is, indeed, completely alone now."

The last time Catherine saw Dylan in L.A., he gave her one more shot of wisdom that has resonated throughout her life. "He said, 'It's only life—it's *your* life.' For a thirteen-year-old, it was slightly cryptic, but I understood the essence. I was *free*."

Her beloved grandmother, Mimi, had long been trying to get custody of Catherine, and when that failed, the disobedient girl was told she would be sent to Los Padrinas, a tight-security orphanage that she describes as a "lockdown kiddie prison with barbed-wire fences." This was her cue to fly the coop.

"I went upstairs, packed a Mexican straw bag, and walked out the back door. I'd made up my mind. I was going to New York to be a singer in Greenwich Village, and maybe see Bob again. First I went to my secret hangout, the Troubadour, where

I sometimes sang with David Crosby and the Dillards. There was a certain amount of leniency for me because my stepfather, Travis, played there. The police and a social worker were already on my tail because they knew my MO from the orphanage. It was now or never, so I took a seat next to a stranger who was watching Ramblin' Jack's final encore. The cops were showing my picture to everybody, so I said to this guy, 'Pretend you know me.' He put his arm around me and I slid down in the seat. I said, 'I've gotta get out of here. The police are chasing me.' During the ovation, we got up, he put his coat around my shoulders like we were a couple, and we slipped out the back."

That night, Michael Stewart from the folk group We Five was her saving grace. He took her to meet his brother, the Kingston Trio's John Stewart, and she briefly nannied for his children. But when she heard there was an all-points bulletin out on her, she hitched a ride to Berkeley. More adventures ensued, including a trip to Massachusetts, which put her closer to her Greenwich Village goal. "I had twenty dollars in my pocket and was dropped off on the corner of Bleecker and MacDougal. I wanted to be a folk singer and see Bob Dylan again. Of course, by then, Bob had become a world-renowned entity. I didn't know a soul and there I was on Bleecker Street. I said to myself, 'I *think* this is the place,' and I had nothing but me."

Catherine says people might not believe what happened next. "Actually, I never tell anybody this because it sounds too unbelievable. The sun was setting and I was a little scared because I didn't have anywhere to go, didn't know anybody, and didn't have enough money for a hotel. I was talking to some kids sitting on a stoop, and I said, 'I'm from California. I don't really know anybody here but I'm looking for Bob Dylan.' They gave me the raised eyebrow, like 'Yeah, sure.' There was slow moving traffic, and just then a car stopped in front of me, and there was Bob! I said, 'There he is!'" I'm amazed and ask Catherine why she didn't mention this cosmic little anecdote in her own book. "Because it sounds like I made it up. But I swear on the Bible—there he was, on the corner of Bleecker and MacDougal. I ran up to the car and he rolled down the window and I said,

'Bob, I made it to New York!' He told me he was leaving town to go away on tour. Then the traffic moved and I said, 'OK, goodbye!' and off he went into the flow of traffic."

The sweet sound of music drew Catherine to Washington Square Park and her fear soon evaporated. "It was like a love-in, everybody was playing guitars and they all looked like Dylan, wearing little caps and playing harmonicas. I met this guy, Bill Miller, he was in a band called the American Dream, and as beautiful as a boy could be. He lived on 8th Avenue in a six-floor walk-up, and when I told him I didn't have a place to stay, he said, 'Why don't you come stay at our place?' So I moved in with him and his whole motley band."

She quickly made friends in New York, and one of them, the infamous groupie Emeretta Marks, took her the RKO Theater where Smokey Robinson and the Miracles were doing a sound check. "It wasn't to meet the musicians," Catherine insists. "We just wanted to see a great show. Cream and the Who were playing, but I didn't know anything about them. I just wanted to see Mitch Ryder and the Detroit Wheels and Smokey Robinson. He was the big act."

Another new pal, Liz Derringer, unwittingly introduced Catherine to her future. "Liz was on the scene with this English band in their posh hotel. She said, 'I've been seeing this English guy Denny in the Moody Blues, and he's really cute. They're having a party and you should come.' I got there and when Denny walked in, it was instant 'Aahhh . . .' between us and we rudely forgot about Liz."

The Moody Blues were in New York for two weeks, performing Murray the K's concert series, so Denny and Catherine had plenty of time to fall in lust. Not quite fifteen, she told him she was eighteen and he didn't question her. "We did it 'til dawn, and I was in *love*. I used to get up early and put on my false eyelashes and eyeliner: the full fabulous Mary Quant look, hoping he wouldn't realize how young I was. Then I'd get back in bed, totally made up like I'd slept all night. I figured if he saw me without makeup, he'd know I was a child."

After the Moody Blues played the British Invasion shows, Denny took his newly beloved on a vacation to Puerto Rico. But despite her clever makeup job, when the rest of the band got a load of Catherine, they insisted Denny send his obvious jailbait straight back to New York.

Mushy love letters flew back and forth across the pond. "I couldn't tell Denny how old I was so I kept putting him off. He wanted me to come to England, but I was still a runaway and didn't have permission to leave the country." The heat had died down in L.A., so Catherine went back and found a place to stay with Johnny Rivers. In exchange for room and board, she became his hippie housekeeper.

"Denny and I stayed in touch, and when I turned sixteen, he sent for me. I didn't have a round-trip ticket when I got to London, so the customs officials told me I would have to go back: 'You're sixteen, you don't have a ticket home or any verifiable residence here.' I was about to have a heart attack because they were going to call the authorities. I'd be found out, and worse, they'd call my mother. Denny was waiting outside customs and he finally came in and said, 'What's the trouble, luv?' When they told him I'd be on the next plane to California, Denny said, 'I'll vouch for her. She'll be staying with me and my friends and I'll get her a ticket back home.' Suddenly one customs guy perked up and said, 'Hey, aren't you Denny Laine? I saw you on *Top of the Pops*, and I love that song 'Go Now.'"

Sixteen-year-old Catherine moved to a foreign land knowing next to nothing about her latest Prince Charming. "I knew he was gorgeous, he was English, and in London. It was all very exotic for a teenager from California. I was crazy about him, or maybe it was the newness of our sexual chemistry."

For a brief time, all was peachy in Catherine's swinging pop paradise. "We went to recording sessions and over to George Harrison's house. We went to happening clubs and hung out with Paul McCartney and danced with Ringo and Maureen. I was hanging with the Beatles! We were taking acid with Brian Jones and smokin' hash with George and Pattie Harrison."

Unfortunately, things soon took a turn for the worse. Catherine was so accustomed to dealing with abuse that she attempted to take Denny's mood swings in stride. "It was unpleasant but not shocking when the *real* Denny stood up. He was a possessive maniac: insecure and jealous. He started knock-down brawls and turned into a raging bull. Just like my mom—he was unreasonable and started irrational fights. Sadly, I was familiar with bad behavior. I kept thinking I could win him over and he would stop. But if I even *looked* at somebody, he didn't believe I loved him. He would chase double-deckers down High Street if somebody whistled at me, and if I *smiled* at someone it started an instant war. I had to walk with my head down just to keep the peace. I felt like a prisoner."

Denny was overjoyed when Catherine found out she was pregnant, but the impending love child didn't temper his violent streak. "It was a day-to-day thing. I loved him, or at least I *thought* I did. I left him several times while I was pregnant, but kept going back." She went all the way to New York, got an apartment, and started modeling, but Denny promised he'd change and convinced Catherine to have the baby in England. "He tricked me. The argument we were having the day I left for New York picked up exactly where it left off. When I was in labor he got annoyed because it went on for so long. He said, 'Either we're going to the hospital or we're going to sleep, which is it?'" Damian was born exactly on his due date, but the proud papa didn't alter his mean-spirited, jealous ways.

Yet another platonic savior came to the rescue while Catherine contemplated her fate. "My friend Jimmy Webb, the songwriter, was in town producing 'MacArthur Park' for Richard Harris. He's always liked me, and when he saw how unhappy I was, he said, 'You're coming back to California with me.' For a while I lived in Jimmy's big house next door to Ozzie and Harriet in Hollywood."

Believing she was finished with Denny for good, Catherine eventually got her own Hollywood apartment, sharing it with her friend Linda Lawrence, who had a toddler son by Rolling Stone Brian Jones. The two single rock moms shared babysitting chores and Catherine got a job as hostess at Thee Experience, the crazy club-of-the-moment.

The presence of little Damian didn't seem to stop Catherine's determined admirers. "The boys were even *more* interested because we were a ready-made family. They saw this girl on her own with a baby and wanted to swoop me and my cherub son into their arms."

One late night at the club, someone arrived just in time for Chuck Berry's encore. "The show was almost over so I told this beautiful boy he could go in for free. He said 'What time do you get off?' I still had half an hour to go, but I said 'Right now.' There was an instant attraction between us."

Catherine and the appealing young songwriter, Jackson Browne, quickly became an item. "He was a sweetheart. He'd take me to work at Thee Experience and pick me up so I'd be safe. This was before his first record, but he was writing such beautiful songs. I would listen to him sing and play 'Doctor My Eyes' and 'Jamaica, Say You Will' on the piano. He wanted to write for other people, and we would visit his musician friends and he'd play for them. I remember he was trying to get Rita Coolidge to record his songs. I said, 'Jackson, you should sing your own songs, don't give them away.'"

Catherine says that she and Jackson fell fast in love. "He wrote me a beautiful song called 'Under the Falling Sky.' It goes, 'I've got lightning in my pocket and thunder in my boots/Have no fear/I've got something here/I want to show you/Our angels wait to take us higher and higher.' Jackson was a sweet and romantic lover, the one I should have stayed with."

She hadn't heard from Denny for over a year when a mutual friend gave him her number. "I was over him, but he started calling me secretly, begging me to come back. He was in a new band, Air Force, with Ginger Baker. He told me about his sprawling house in the country and the Jaguar he'd buy me for my birthday. He finally convinced me when he said he really wanted to have his son with him. So I left Jackson. He was very upset, but such a gentleman. He even took me to the airport."

English country living didn't turn out to be as comfy-cozy as Denny promised. "There was no heat, so I had to stoke coals and bring in the firewood. The bathtubs in England are bigger than usual, and it took fifteen trips carrying buckets of heated water up and down the stairs to get the bath half full. We were getting along quite well, but I was freezing out there so I convinced Denny to get us a little place in London."

One of the backup singers left Air Force and a replacement was needed immediately. Catherine auditioned for Ginger Baker and suddenly she was a singer in a rock and roll band. "We traveled around doing concerts with Cream, Jimi Hendrix, the Animals, and Donovan. It was all wonderful, except Denny and I were starting to battle again, and we couldn't seem to fix it. I walked around with my head down, not making eye contact with anybody because of his bloody jealousy."

Air Force was booked on the *QE2* to sail away on an American tour when Ginger Baker abruptly changed his mind. "The night before we were supposed to leave, Ginger Baker decided he was going to go to Nigeria to play drums with the Nigerians, and the tour was canceled. That same day, a friend of Jackson's, Ned Doheny, arrived in London and called to say hello. I was talking to him and Denny asked, 'Who is that?' When I told him it was a friend from California, he hauled off and slugged me in the face."

Catherine escaped out the bathroom window, scaled the wall, and hailed a cab. She was bleeding so badly the kindly cabbie gave her a free ride to the hospital, where she got five stitches over her left eye. Since her bags were conveniently packed, she grabbed Damian and left Denny for the last time. An innocent flirtation she'd been having with Gene Krell from Granny Takes a Trip instantly changed course, and that night she moved into his house on Carlyle Square. A month later, I arrived from California, and for a couple of months, we were one big, well-dressed, wacky family.

The romance with Gene didn't last long because Denny, still obsessed with Catherine, began following her around London, shouting threats and obscenities. I remember vividly the day we were strolling along the King's Road and he tried to snatch Damian out of her arms. "Denny was with his father in the Bentley, and we were running down the street with them on our tail," Catherine recalls. "I was going to take Damian back to America and wanted one last night at the Speakeasy before I left. They sat me across from Eric Clapton, and when he saw the black stitches in my pale white skin, he said, 'What happened to you?' I told him about Denny and that I was moving back to America. And he said, 'Come to Hertswoood Edge and stay with me instead.' He had my trunks picked up from Kensington and taken to his estate in Surrey, and I spent the summer as his chef and trusted friend."

There was no hanky-panky between Catherine and the guitar god because he was gaga over another music muse. She was not only Clapton's cook; Catherine also became his confidant. "Eric was in love with Pattie Boyd Harrison, but it was still a big secret. I got to listen to him write 'Layla,' and I was the only person who knew it was for Pattie. Not even the band members knew."

She's told me about the delicious meals she created for Derek and the Dominoes, who were all living at the house. How did she learn to cook so well at the tender age of nineteen? "I had a cookbook from Alice's Restaurant," she laughs. "Everybody enjoyed my cooking, and I loved it in the country—all that amazing music! Damian toddled around the manor, coloring on Eric's walls. The dogs frolicked, and I was the lady in residence. Denny kept trying to woo me back, and I started letting him take Damian for a day or two." It was during one of Damian's visits with his father that Catherine had a dreamy, steamy encounter.

"Eric was throwing a big party for the drummer, Jim Gordon. It was his birthday, and everybody was coming, including George Harrison and Pattie. I was glad when Mick Jagger arrived. He'd been to visit Eric before, and even though we'd never really interacted, we knew about each other. He knew there was a girl at Eric's that he liked. That night somebody spiked the punch with mescaline, and before we knew it, we were all lost in ecstasy. It was getting late so I thought I'd better call

Damian at Denny's to say good night. I went into the study and could still hear the music. I heard George Harrison say, 'Here's my new song,' and he started playing 'My Sweet Lord' for Eric, then everyone joined in. It was unbelievable. That gorgeous song could be heard all over the entire village at full volume. As I was talking to Denny on the phone, somebody walked into the study. I heard the door close, and he walked right up close to me. The mescaline was coming on, and I looked over and saw houndstooth trousers. The black and white fabric was undulating with psychedelia, and when I looked up, Mick was standing there. He knew exactly where I was; he had found me in that little room. The vibe was so intense. I told Denny I had to hang up and he said, 'Why?' I said, 'I just have to get off the phone,' and he said, 'No, I don't want you to hang up.' I said, 'I *have* to go now . . . good-bye!' Music was filling the whole house, and when I hung up the phone, Mick just picked me up, pressed me against the wall, and started kissing me passionately."

While the band played on and the Eric/Pattie/George/Layla drama played itself out in the other room, Catherine was literally swept off her feet.

"Mick was unbelievably gorgeous, and I was instantly smitten. He kissed me hard as we slid down the wall, then we were on the floor, passionately making out. We went outside and walked around Eric's garden and found a little path that led to a trellis with a seat just big enough for the two of us, and we kissed for ages. We must have been gone a long time because when we got back to the house, a lot of people had left or gone to sleep. We went up to my room and made out until the sun came up.

"Mick called later that day and asked Eric and I to go see Stevie Wonder's concert with him. I dressed in my finest silk velvet and wore my silver platform boots covered in crescent moons and stars." After that night, they had several sweet late-night phone chats. "I started taking the train into London to see Mick. After a few dates I was finally going to spend the night at his house. It was his twenty-fifth birthday, and he had a huge party. Believe it or not, we were both nervous, and chatted in bed for half an hour before we even *did* anything. I thought 'Oh my God, this is finally going to happen.' And of course, we had incredible sex."

Catherine gets up and mixes us another round of lime martinis. "I've been so lucky to experience this amazing life," she says with a giggle. "I know what the possibilities are." She takes a slow sip of her cocktail. "After about our fifth date, Mick asked me to move in."

Catherine transferred all her earthly possessions, including her adored toddler, from one rock god's estate to another. "Damian was about two years old and Mick loved him. He was so sweet with him. He'd show him magic tricks and say, 'Where did you find Damian anyway? You must have found him under a mulberry bush!'"

I imagine life must have been particularly sweet living with the most coveted rock star on the planet. "We walked around Chelsea, and he'd tell me about the architecture, the carriage houses, who once lived in this house or when that home was built. He taught me all about the Pre-Raphaelites. We'd go to fancy little restaurants for dinner that weren't on the map, places that nobody knew about. We'd stay home and listen to music, get high, and drink champagne. He'd put on a James Brown record and do his Mick Jagger dance for me. We listened to Stephen Stills, Gram Parsons, Clifton Chenier, and all those fabulous blues artists he loved."

But how long could this kind of ultimate rock and roll bliss last? "Two months after I moved in, the Stones were going on a European tour, starting in Brussels. While Mick was away, I decided to use my ticket to California that I'd had since I saw Eric at the Speakeasy. Before we left, Mick asked me to go to Paris for a little vacation, and we stayed at Johnny Halliday's house—he's the French Elvis—and we had a perfect time. Really, it was so lovely. Johnny had this beautiful house in the French countryside and we'd go out in the forest and search for rare truffles. At nighttime, we'd go to fabulous country inns and eat carpaccio. After our holiday, we were only at Cheyne Walk for one night, and when he kissed me good-bye to leave for the Stones' tour, I didn't even wake up all the way. I just stayed in bed and fell back asleep."

During what she thought was a brief stay in Los Angeles, Catherine started seeing disconcerting photos of Mick in the newspapers alongside a dusky, dark-haired dame who looked very much like the Stone himself. "At first, he called me a lot, then the calls came less, then they stopped altogether. I tried calling him to see if the tabloids were right, and *she* answered, '*Halloo.*' I just put the phone down. I didn't take it that hard because we never really broke up. We didn't argue or anything. There was no discussion; it was just *over.*" Bianca's presence certainly curtailed Mick's extracurricular activities, because the same thing happened to me when I called him right around that time. Bianca answered the phone and growled, "Don't you ever call here again."

If you don't count Catherine's occasional tête-à-têtes with Jimmy Page, she hasn't dated a musician since 1971. By then, she had experienced enough rock and roll to last several lifetimes. She decided to disappear to the country, taking Damian to live in a cottage in Connecticut where they spent the next seven years. "I've seen Jimmy, I've seen Denny, I've seen Jackson, but I haven't lived that rock and roll lifestyle since I was nineteen. I had smoked a ton of hash and did my share of LSD. I probably would have dropped dead if I'd kept it up. I moved to the middle of nowhere so I wouldn't get sidetracked. I gave things up for Damian because I wanted him to have a good life. I was asked to go to Paris to model but couldn't afford a nanny. I became a model with Wilhelmina in Manhattan out of necessity. I took the train into town and my son came with me." Amazingly, Catherine is now a grandma to Damian's son, sixteen-year-old John. "I speak to Damian every day. He's thirty-eight and still likes to talk about his unique childhood."

Jimmy Page took a couple of limo trips to Catherine's Brookfield hideaway, and in 1975, when I was doing the soap opera *Search for Tomorrow* in New York, I paid her a visit, bringing along a fellow from my acting class who later became her hus-

Credit: Catherine James
collection

band. "Yes, thank you for ruining my life," she says wryly. "I
spent six years with Joe, then five more with Steven, my very
interesting British husband." Today she happily juggles her
quartet of suitors with ingenuity and finesse. Catherine just isn't
herself unless she has a couple of besotted swains dangling on
the line.

Her last encounter with Zeppelin's guitar wizard was ten years
ago. Over dinner, Jimmy pulled all the old romantic lines out of
his crushed-velvet pocket, and Catherine was close to caving in.
"Thank goodness I caught myself in time. He looked different,
but his eyes were exactly the same. When I gazed into his eyes,
it was Mr. Page, all right. I thought 'Maybe,' then, 'Nnnnoooo.'
He was still too dangerous. The hand grenade is totally viable."

Music continues to be paramount in Catherine's life. Whenever Al Green comes to town, she's front and center, swaying
and swooning. Among the family photos on her library table

there's a recent shot of her beaming at Smokey Robinson the night they met at a charity event. "I've been exposed to every kind of music there is since I was a baby girl. My great-great-grandmother was a classical violinist, my great-grandfather was a concert pianist; and my grandfather played with all the big bands and wrote boogie-woogie. I miss the sound of a guitar or piano in my house. I miss the music vibe all around. After all, I was right in the middle of the revolution that changed the world."

Cynthia Plaster Caster

Kicks

From the moment my creative mentor, Frank Zappa, titillated me with the tale of Cynthia Plaster Caster back in 1968, I have been fascinated by her brazen art. Riotously enamored with rock stars myself, I was also impressed by the ingenious way she set about meeting her personal faves. Frank believed Cynthia was an innovative groundbreaker and had decided that the shy, chubby, dark-haired girl from Chicago should join his wacky ranks, even though her particular art form couldn't be captured on vinyl. Thankfully, our squealy first meeting *was* captured when Frank introduced us on the phone and recorded our giggly call for a track on *Permanent Damage*, the album with my all-girl group, the GTO's.

Cynthia has been praised as "The Rodin of Rock," an apt description for such an undeniable artiste. I have watched people blush and stammer, fume and pontificate, laugh uproariously and bow down to her audacity, her *spunk* (so to speak) when discussing the merits of Cynthia's artwork. Some of them might not consider what she does (making plaster replicas of rock stars' penises) to be an art form, but those folks are supremely uptight, shortsighted, and don't have a very good sense of humor.

Just to set the record straight, I looked up the word *artist* in Webster's:

One who professes and practices an imaginative art.

That's for sure! And the meaning of *art* truly helps describe what Cynthia does so well:

skill acquired by experience, study, or observation (the art *of making friends); an occupation requiring knowledge or skill (the* art *of organ building); the conscious use of skill and creative imagination.*

God bless Merriam-Webster, I couldn't have put it any better myself! Cynthia and I have been friends since the day Frank threw two kinky kindred spirits together. We found we were besotted with the same spindly, frizzy-haired British rock star,

In the 1970s.   Credit: Cynthia Plaster Caster collection

Noel Redding, and bonded immediately. I've long known about her stifling upbringing and thorny, troublesome relationship with her mother, a portentous, pious presence she still calls "the Warden." I have been privy to many of her infamous antics and treasure trove of plaster casts. I've had the unparalleled pleasure of sleeping among the many shapes and sizes during my frequent visits to her pad in the Windy City. Something about their proud, silent presence makes me feel right at home.

I'm always chuffed when our fun-intensive schedules allow for a little visit, so when Cynthia called to tell me one of her favorite new bands, the Redwalls, asked her to appear in their upcoming video here in L.A., I jumped for joy. Of course, I invited her to stay with me, and in between our lively dinner party and shopping sprees, Cynthia and I manage to curl up on the couch and trip the light fantastic.

Just like me, young Cynthia was struck hard by the limey lightning bolt called the Beatles. Up until then, she had been a devotee of show tunes and live theater, and when she saw a picture of the four mop tops in their matching outfits, she thought they were a new comedy troupe. "Then I heard 'I Wanna Hold Your Hand' and was blown away—because they were good-looking *and* made proportionately great music." Virginal and completely ignorant about the facts of life, Cynthia still realized there were far more fascinating prospects to consider. "Fuck the high school swills. *This* is what *I* wanna date!"

Swimming, gymnastics, and ignorant high school lads were all but forgotten as the Brits triumphantly invaded U.S. soil. "As each new British Invasion band arrived, I got more interested, but so did more and more *other* girls: competition, and this growing number was becoming a big problem for me." In 1965 the disorderly Rolling Stones came to town to record *12 X 5* at Chess Records. "I realized they stayed at a hotel, so *that* had to be mecca. I also figured out that when I called I should ask for the least popular band member, and that's how I found the Stones at the Water Tower Hotel. I asked for Bill Wyman."

The first day Cynthia showed up with her best friend, Pest, there were three girls waiting at the hotel; the next day there were six. Cynthia giddily gave Brian Jones a box of cough drops and got Mick and Keith's autographs, but knew there had to be a far superior way to meet the bands.

Up until Cynthia briefly met Gene Clark of the Byrds, she thought all she wanted was to make out with her musical heroes. "We talked to Gene and he said, 'Oh, you're virgins, huh? Why?' 'Well, why *shouldn't* we be virgins, huh?' 'Because sex feels *good!*' 'What, Gene? You're kidding!' Pest didn't believe it either, and we wondered, '*How* does it feel good?' I mean, nobody in high school talked about it."

Cynthia's mother had thrown her father out of the house years earlier due to heavy boozing, and had no use for the opposite sex. Not only was the Warden a hard, chilly taskmistress, she neglected to tell her daughter a single thing about s-e-x except that she considered it to be a very evil deed. "I'd been wanking off since I was five, but didn't know that was considered *sex*. I didn't know *what* the fuck it was! I never talked about it to anybody and nobody asked me about it until I was thirteen and my high school music teacher saw me wanking off behind my desk and yelled, 'What are you *doing?*' as I moaned loudly. It so embarrassed me that I didn't do it again for a long time."

The first British group the girls managed to spend valuable time with was the Hollies. "They were the first band I actually hung out with, one-on-one. But not the cute ones; they were Bobby Elliott, the drummer, and the teddy-bear bass player, Eric Haydock. We somehow got into their hotel room and *laughed* with them—we *loved* British humor. And because they were not the main rock stars in the band, we felt more like their equals."

Their semi-comfy experience must have triggered "I want more of *this!*"

"Yeah, it subconsciously told me I could hold a conversation with them. I was more comfortable if they made me laugh and I could make them laugh. This was a *real* important discovery because I figured that was the only way I could get laid, which I found out was something that was supposed to feel *good*; part of the sexual process that my mother said was a very *bad* thing for me." When Cynthia read in the paper that the Beatles took their girlfriends along on a vacation to the Virgin Islands, she naturally assumed they'd be sharing hotel rooms.

"I figured that fun/sexual reproduction was going on in the *Virgin* Islands, and thought, 'Okay, if that's what *they* want, that's what *I* want.' The same time this realization came about, we learned about Cockney rhyming slang. Most importantly, we learned the dirty words. The slang for 'dick' was Hampton Wick and 'wank' was Barclay's Bank, which was the key to opening the door *behind* the hotel room doors—our first *really* successful means of getting close to rock stars and indulging in conversation."

Clever, clever, clever. As the competition got as stiff as you-know-what and girls piled up in the lobbies, Cynthia and Pest were on the fast track to possible pop paradise. They began leaving naughty letters for the bands. "We incorporated Cockney rhyming slang into these goofy notes, like, 'Hello, Gerry and the Pacemakers. We are the Barclay's Bankers of Chicago. We have convenient nighttime hours. Would you like to make a deposit?'"

Cynthia slipped the Pacemakers a note, including her phone number, through the window of the tour bus. "I gave it to the drummer. They all looked me over and I thought nothing of it until he called me at *home*. The Warden's in the next room of our little bitty apartment, *looking* at me. I was *so* impressed because back then, long distance was very expensive, probably put through by an operator. He called all the way from Ohio and found out very soon that I didn't know what the fuck I was talking about in the note, and politely hung up." Cynthia handed over a few more bold missives and got more calls and scathing looks from the Warden, but fate was about to dial her number.

In April 1966, the Dick Clark Caravan of Stars was in Chicago and this particular tour starred Paul Revere and the Raiders. "Their song 'Kicks' was number one on the charts, which was *really* hot! Because as you know, part of the appeal of being a groupie is to impress your friends with the fame and success of the band—especially when we were young. It was a real treat, besides the fact the guys were good-looking and talented.

"I was an art major, and was on my way out of art class to meet Pest and find the hotel. We didn't know how we were gonna meet them, but presumed we'd try the 'passing the note' trick. I stopped dead in my tracks when my art teacher gave us the homework assignment: 'Make a plaster cast,' he said, and the object had to be solid. '*Solid!* Wait a moment,' I thought. 'Don't *Hampton Wicks* get *solid*? Okay, let's make it really absurd.' I took extra plaster, put it in a brown paper bag, and wrote PLAS-TER so it was official looking. I couldn't wait to tell Pest, and her reaction was the same as mine—we *screamed* our heads off! We took the kit to the hotel and found Paul Revere and the Raid-ers' rooms."

Cynthia had never even seen a penis, and didn't have a clue how to handle one when she and Pest knocked on the first hotel room door. The Raiders were good sports, telling the girls they'd come up with a great idea, sending them on to the next room until they finally got to the singer, Mark Lindsay.

Mark had company, but was intrigued enough to invite the cunning plaster girls to come back at midnight. They both called home to fib about spending the night at each other's houses, and were back at Mark's door when the clock struck twelve. "He was really fascinated, especially by the fact that we were virgins. He thought we were funny, and it was so romantic being on his fire escape with him, like a scene out of *West Side Story*." Cynthia had to invent another tall tale for the Warden because Mark was tantalized enough to invite her back the next day. "I wasn't sure what would happen but I had a funny feeling I was gonna be *relieved* of something, and I was right. He took care of the job in forty-five minutes, then had to be on the tour bus. Even though it was really speedy, he was flattering and a real good kisser and had a gorgeous naked body. Oh, my *God* . . . it *did* feel good." Cynthia actually fans herself, recalling her very first time.

"Virginity was a *major* appeal. Virgins were becoming an endangered species. It was so *groundbreaking* for me. I mean, I thought I was in love, but you know what was *most* on my mind, even though I had never spoken the word 'fuck'? That plain old *me* had fucked Mark Lindsay. That's all I knew—that's all I was thinking about. And that the road to getting laid was paved in plaster."

For homework, Cynthia turned in a plaster vegetable, but her sights were soaring much higher. "After that weekend, Pest and I became the Plaster Casters of Chicago. It was so silly, but silly was all we ever wanted to be! I put a generic-looking logo on the side of a small case, and thought, 'We should really learn how to do this, put all the materials in the suitcase, and make ourselves look like salesmen, traveling from hotel to hotel.' The bands thought it was hilarious, and the word got around really fast—way before we ever figured out how to actually *make* a cast!"

As Pest and Cynthia practiced British rhyming slang and discussed plaster casting at a local pizzeria, an eavesdropping chef listened in and asked if they had ever heard of alginate, a substance used by dentists to make impressions of teeth. His description made it seem plausible, so Cynthia bought a can, hoping she'd soon have use for the fluffy pink powder.

As "The Last Train to Clarksville" scurried up the pop charts, teenybop fans believed the Monkees were as squeaky clean as their cutesy tunes, but groupies knew better. The mod TV foursome came through Chicago, and as Cynthia and Pest waited outside the hotel, a couple of roadies invited them upstairs. "We were out there with a large number of girls and were *singled out* because of that fucking suitcase."

The Plaster Casters of Chicago soon found themselves in front of a very willing Monkee. "I tried to open the can, which in those days opened up like Planter's Peanuts, and it's dangerous because you can really cut yourself. Which I *did*; my pinkie finger wouldn't stop bleeding." As Peter Tork stood ready, able, and naked, Cynthia had to make apologies. "That got me off the hook, gratefully, because I found out later you have to be more scientific with alginates. The water can't be too hot or too cold. The best way to mix is with your hands, kind of slowly, not get too many air bubbles, and keep monitoring the water temperature."

The next brave young bloke willing to proffer his member for the cause was Gary Brooker, Procol Harum's lead singer. But sadly, the daring attempt failed. "Yeah, all he got was a mountain of pink barf on his dick," Cynthia concedes. I marvel at how these fellows offered up their private parts for an untried, untested, brand new concept! "It was a *major* part of the sexual revolution!" she enthuses brightly. "They had a social obligation to put their dicks into something new and different."

Cynthia and Pest were in serious rock star pursuit. "By then we had calling cards: 'The Plaster Casters of Chicago: Lifelike Models of Hampton Wicks.'" The girls tried various substances, such as wax, sand, and oatmeal. "That wasn't gonna go over too big; and *nothing* was gonna go over big with sand and water."

As she pondered these deep artistic issues, problems were brewing at home. "All this time the Warden had been reading my diaries—each and every one of them. So she found out I was no longer a virgin and grounded me for a month."

Instead of dashing around town with her suitcase, Cynthia moped around the house, eating to assuage her pent-up resentment. She gained forty pounds in thirty days. But a month later and a tad chubbier, she was right back at it. Pest "retired" and Cynthia met her next "plater" (rhyming slang for "*Plate* of Meat=eat"), Dianne, hiding out on a hotel fire escape. "She was willing to join ranks with me because I paid the for the pricey dental mold—it was $4 a can—and learned how to mix it. *I* remained the mold and plaster-mixer, and Dianne became the designated plater. She discovered she had a certain skill: she was *very* good at giving blow jobs. She had a gentle touch that the bands liked."

As much as she was thriving in college, Cynthia had to quit and get a job. "It was scary. I didn't know what the Warden might do to me when I fell asleep. She was sneaky, trying to control me behind my back, like throwing out Beatles memorabilia—she threw my Beatle dolls away!" How dare she! The nerve! The injustice! And because of the Warden's punishment, Cynthia had put on forty pounds at exactly the wrong time.

"We had our heyday for about two or three years, and throughout it all I was fat. It was really hard to lose that weight once I escaped from the Warden. I had one more little scene with Mark Lindsay, but I had gained weight and I think he was no longer attracted to my body. In fact, the next time he came to town he was with another girl and I was crushed."

Brokenhearted yet undaunted, Cynthia stayed the course, and soon turned her attention to another rock star: a certain scrawny British bass player. The Jimi Hendrix Experience was coming to Chicago and Cynthia wanted to be ready. "I was thinking, '*OK*, this is a band I've really gotta learn to use alginates for.' So I practiced on my college friend, Joel, who said, 'Oh, somebody's gonna give me a *blow job*? I'm *in*!'"

The Experience was playing two concerts at the Civic Opera House and after the first show, Cynthia, Dianne, and Marilyn, another avid rock fiend, followed the Hendrix limo to the Hilton Hotel. "When we held up the suitcase with our logo on the side, they started waving and following us. We couldn't believe it—they were *the* hottest band at that time. Noel came along with a new way of looking groovy in Britain: big Afro-curly hair and psychedelic clothes, this impish little guy; there was nothing more English than the elfin look. When we got to the hotel, they're looking at *us*, we're looking at *them*—in the flesh! And Jimi says, 'Ohhhh yes, I've heard about you from somebody in the Cosmos—come on up to my hotel room.' The first big thrill was riding in the elevator with the band for a change instead of charging up the fire escape. There were six of us: Jimi, Noel, Mitch, me, Dianne, and Marilyn, in this little bitty elevator. And we didn't say a word."

The Plaster Casters had been boning up for this very occasion, and although the band seemed calm and ready for action, Cynthia freely admits to freaking out inside. "Jimi was so flamboyant and gorgeously dressed, wearing an orange and yellow panne velvet top and a gaucho hat. And what a body! He had the body for casting—one of the most beautiful bodies I ever saw in my life. Oh, his thighs were really muscular but graceful at the same time, almost like a dancer's legs—shapely but skinny. He had a round butt—my God, he was so *perfect*. Anyway, we set up shop in the hotel room, and Dianne started giving Jimi a blow job while Noel and Mitch just sat there, quietly watching."

All these years later, I am still downright impressed that Hendrix took this newfangled experience in stride, as if having his penis plunged into plaster for posterity was an everyday occurrence. "Yeah, he was perfectly comfortable," Cynthia asserts. "Dianne gives him a blow job and he has this really big, honkin'—it's *true* what they say about black men. So he dipped his dick in the alginates—we used Vaseline or Kama Sutra oil, but I hadn't lubed him much—and his pubes got stuck in the mold. Jimi was in the mold for a *long* time, longer than we planned, but he was very mellow, cooperative, adaptable, and patient. He was fucking the mold while he waited."

While all this phallic magic went on, Cynthia was cognizant of Mitch Mitchell and her fave-rave, Noel Redding, taking it all in. "They were real nice; not lofty at all. None of them were. They were quiet and curious about us. Marilyn was a virgin, and never having seen a dick before, she hid behind a piece of paper. I liked to get stoned when I measured alginates, but I'd lose count between twenty-five and thirty-five, so I let Marilyn write down how many scoops I measured."

After the nouvelle deed was done, Hendrix and the band played another show, then invited the plaster trio to party with them. "It was not only monumental because we were with *them,* it was the first time I knew of an English band going to a party in Chicago. Graham Nash was there and I didn't even know he was in town! It was totally groovy, unreal. My horoscope that day said, 'You rarely get everything you want in life but today you *will,*' and it was *true.*"

In 1967 I danced in one of the first music videos, a short film to promote "Foxy Lady." When Mr. Hendrix made it known that he fancied teen-green me, I was too agog and virginal to succumb to his palpable prowess. Cynthia had the same reaction when the guitar god gave her the come-hither eye. "Noel was more approachable and besides, he had that pixie/fairy look:

hunched over and *so* pale with bad posture." We both heave sighs recalling the dazzling splendor of malnourished English musicians. "I had posters of him in my bedroom before they came to town, so I was ready for him. He didn't come on really *strong*—we got to the hotel and somehow I wound up in his bed. He weighed a lot less than *I* did. I was twice his weight. We had great, straightforward sex. I was so happy it was good with him." Cynthia and I agree that Noel was right at home under the sheets, and taught us both that sex could be a bundle of fun and feel very good indeed.

Cynthia was terribly shy, a fact that most people find difficult to believe due to the audacious nature of her art. "Back in those days I had a hard time bonding with the guys I worshipped because I was in disbelief that they'd want anything to do with me. I had trouble with the great in-between: the ability to relax and feel that I was up to their level or that they were down on my level—that took a while."

Despite that, the next time the Experience came to Chicago, Noel found himself with Cynthia again—in the sack and in the alginates. "Noel's was the first cast to come out twisted. That happens when they have a curved dick and when they start to lose their erection; instead of going straight down it twists around and the pressure of the alginates pushes it down further. But the only way that can happen is if they have enough *length* to begin with, folks, so don't laugh. It happens with a normally, a slightly curved, long dick."

Let's take a peek at Cynthia's casting journal:

NOEL REDDING
March 30, 1968
Conrad Hilton Hotel (Chicago), Room 1136
Dianne—Plater
Cynthia—Mold and Plaster Mixer

I would like to note that Marilyn was present to resume her duties as general assistant. However, at the time, being very stoned, she was unable to offer any service,

*save a couple random scratches on a newspaper with
a marking pen. Being under the same circumstances,
I (Cynthia) could do little better, and faced with the
additional chore of counting scoops (meanwhile trying
to ignore Marilyn's insensible mumblings: "Sixty-two,
sixty-three, sixty-seven, sixty-nine . . ." she was only
trying to help). There was a short delay in getting the
alginates measured (I lost count 3 times) and heaven
knows how warm or cold the water was. It was SUP-
POSED to be a 28:28 ratio (water to alginate powder),
but what with my scrambled measuring and the huge
overflow from the vase when I began mixing, I doubt
if it was even alginates. Still, it molded SUPERBLY.
Dianne applied some baby oil to Noel's hair, and he only
got stuck for five minutes. I had been counting aloud
the time before we thrust Noel in the mold, and when
I announced the crucial moment, he became panicky
and started to get soft. Thus, instead of diving might-
ily straight in (to the vase), we had to shove and pound
it in, and it twisted like a worm. This is just what the
cast looks like—a worm peeking out of the ground. We
managed to get the balls (or ball, I'm not sure) and, I'd
say, it's well, humorous. And very life-like, although
that is NOT the best Noel's rig can do. Noel said that
my counting aloud didn't help matters, and when it
came time to put his rig in, he grew frightened his rig
might not stay hard at precisely the right moment, and
all would be ruined (Niagara Falls divers and motorcyle
jumpers will know what he means) . . . and so his rig got
butterflies. He didn't KNOW HOW his rig felt inside
the mold, and gasped, "This is INDEED an EXPE-
RIENCE!!" Yes indeed, Mr. Redding. He expressed
a desire to make a second attempt in the future. YES
INDEED, MR. REDDING!!! Noel is one of the Jimi
Hendrix Experience and is my favorite person in the
world . . . Bass Player . . . English . . .*

A few months later, the Experience returned, and Cynthia wanted to cast Mitch, but wound up in the sack with him instead. "I slept with Mitch, and Noel was with somebody else." Ah, yes, in those heady days there sure was a lot of sharing and sharing alike going on.

It seemed as if the fine art of plaster casting would take off, so the girls set about honing their craft. "As we tried it with more people, we learned things. Before Dianne started plating, she would ask them, 'Do you happen to know how long you can maintain a hard-on once I start getting you hard?' and 'Once Cynthia starts mixing, get ready to stick your dick in the mold roughly *two* minutes later.'"

Cynthia and Dianne found more willing subjects, among them Eddie Brigati, singer for the Young Rascals, and Wayne Kramer and Dennis Thompson of the MC5. "Wayne and Dennis wanted to be done simultaneously—it was a brotherly thing. I only had one mixing container, so all I had for Wayne was the actual alginate container. That didn't work so well, and it set prematurely before he was able to penetrate it all the way, so it looks like all Wayne has is a thimble, but he's got a *long* shaft. He was a very good sport about it. I always tell people that Wayne is one person who has not fully been captured."

On another hopeful casting excursion, Eric Clapton was the catalyst for a thunderous, life-altering event. He suggested Cynthia ply her craft on his band's opening act. "That was pretty unbelievable! We found Cream's hotel and went up to Eric Clapton's room. Dianne and I just chatted with him—he was nice as pie. We asked if he was interested in being casted and he said, 'I might be, but I have a friend who may even be more interested—Frank Zappa.' Deep down I'm thinking, 'Ooh, isn't that guy a big drug addict?' But Eric took us to meet him and he wasn't scary, not scary and loud the way I thought he'd be. He was intelligent, respectful, and very curious, and he seemed interested in my idea about having a rock-cock museum."

A couple months later, the Mothers of Invention were headlining the Kinetic Playground, and the owner, who had previously ignored Cynthia's shenanigans, breathlessly told her that Frank Zappa was looking for her. "I said, 'You're *kidding*. Does that mean we get in free?'" Frank had been pondering her handiwork and was full of grandiose ideas. "'I want to help you further your dream of collecting more casts for the museum of rock-cocks you told me about,' he said. 'I want to bring you out to Los Angeles and pay you a stipend to create more *cock*.' For a girl like me, that was unheard of. I mean, I was a keypuncher! I had just escaped from the Warden and didn't have much hope for a future—I wasn't raised to think about what I wanted to do in life because my mother *told* me what I'd be doing: taking care of *her*."

The GTO's were in the throes of recording our album, and before she made the move to the West Coast, Cynthia was featured on side B, track 7, called "Miss Pamela's First Conversation with the Plaster Casters of Chicago."

Our high-pitched voices joyously trilled and burbled over each other when we realized we had the same drooly crush on Noel Redding. Because of this and other breathy discoveries, we knew we were rock sisters forever and couldn't wait to kiss and squeeze each other. I hurriedly made plans to spend a wintry week with my newfound friend in Chicago.

It was love at first gaze. I soon realized that Cynthia was surprisingly shy and tender hearted, and the pounds she had added to her slender frame exacerbated her already low self-image. I told her how beautiful she was. We divulged our deepest secrets, played loads of records, and the days flew by, even though I had all the wrong clothes for the subzero, snowy weather. I remember my lips and toes were numb as I staggered through the slush in vintage chiffon and spike heels to see Fleetwood Mac on New Year's Eve. We dribbled over Peter Green and marveled joyously at Mick Fleetwood's testicles that seemed to be hanging out of his trousers while he bashed the drums. Later we were told he wore a pair of red wooden balls on his belt for good luck, but we didn't believe it for a minute. We lounged around for hours, gushing over Noel Redding and various other rail-thin rockers.

On the wall next to the canopied bed, Cynthia had tacked up a poster of the dangerous new British quartet, Led Zeppelin. "Just my type!" I crooned, but Cynthia warned that they already had a severely roguish reputation. She should have paid attention to her own stellar advice, because shortly after I left, she cast their scandalous road manager, Richard Cole, and had an encounter that left her sadly dazed and confused. "I'm saving that big, juicy story for my own book. There was a routine involving Robert Plant, John Bonham, and Richard Cole. Robert was the bait, and Bonham and Cole were the violent ones. Jimmy was always off with a girl, and John Paul was horrified by it." Let's just say that Zeppelin lived up (or down) to their bad reputation.

"I felt like shit. It made me wary—it didn't make me want to stop being a groupie or Plaster Caster, it just made me realize I couldn't go into any band's hotel room without researching them first. To this day, I tell young girls to find out whatever they can about a band before going into their hotel room."

Eric Burdon and the Animals were faves, but when it came time to work, Cynthia became flummoxed due to another giant crush. "I tried to cast Eric, but it was a mold failure—and he wouldn't let me do it again. I was distracted by the guitarist, John Weider. He was helping me mix the mold and that made me fuck it up. I was turned on by him, but of course I was too fat."

Right around this difficult time, Dianne fell in love with a drag queen and retired her plating crown. Used and abused by Zeppelin and minus her beloved partner, Cynthia's artistic vision never wavered. "First I did it to meet the bands, secondly it satisfied my collector's impulse—I used to collect stamps before that. It was Frank Zappa who told me it was an *art form*. I said, 'You are telling me it's an art form, so it must be an art form.'"

Frank's earnest heart was in the right place, but when he imported her to town, Cynthia and La-La Land didn't exactly merge. "I hated L.A. The first week I did not like the people I met, they didn't seem to like me. Put it this way: I didn't laugh for ten days, until I met Alice Cooper—he had Midwestern humor like mine."

As she tried to adjust to the frantic Hollywood pace, Cynthia thankfully found a new plater called Harlow. This capricious original already had a scintillating past as a member of the gender-bending Cockettes, and together she and Cynthia immortalized a few rock boys. "I casted somebody from a band called the Churls; I casted the drummer Keith Webb from the Terry Reid Band; Eddie Brigati, the singer in the Young Rascals; and Aynsley Dunbar from the Mothers. And Zal Yanovsky from the Lovin' Spoonful. That one turned out good and it was a good experience."

Because of her teenage addiction to musical theatre, Cynthia pursued playwright/actor/singer Anthony Newley and enlisted my pal Iva Turner as plater. "Cynthia was one of the few people I knew who loved Anthony Newley as much as I did," Iva tells me. "In fact, we shared the fantasy that he might want to be casted some day, and made a pact that I would be his

Cynthia with Jimi.
Credit: Jim Newberry

plater. So, when she called and excitedly gasped, 'Guess who's coming over!' I guessed it on the first try and rushed to her apartment. Mr. Newley arrived a few minutes later. He was adorable, sexy, and enthusiastic about being inducted into the Plaster Caster Hall of Fame. After a bit of preliminary chitchat around the dining room table, Cynthia went into the kitchen and began scooping alginates, while I coaxed our honoree into the bedroom. As I lovingly labored to bring Mr. Newley's cock to its full potential, I could hear Cynthia counting down the seconds, 'Ten, nine, eight . . .' and when she got to *one*, the door seemed to blast open, Mr. Newley jumped to his feet, Ms. Plaster Caster held the container to his crotch, and together they shoved his hard cock into the mixture. 'It's cold!' he declared. (Don't worry. I warmed him up later.) Cynthia was the consummate professional. Gently removing his pubic hairs from the mold, she congratulated him on a job well done. She could tell immediately that the cast was going to be a good one, and if you look at Mr. Newley's cast, you'll see that she was absolutely right. It's a beautiful example of her signature amalgamation of sex and art."

While Cynthia mixed plaster, and the GTO's continued romping around Hollywood, Mr. Zappa attempted another brave undertaking. He wanted to capture the groupie spirit by publishing Cynthia's diaries, along with mine. He even asked Noel Redding, who kept copious road notes, if he'd like to round out the proceedings. Cynthia and I spent long days reading our diaries aloud while Frank's proper secretary, the *veddy* British Pauline, typed up the frisky endearments for future generations. Sadly, even the possibility of her own fame couldn't keep Cynthia in Tinsel Town.

Her Hollywood apartment was robbed, and Frank's shyster manager, Herb Cohen, offered to put her all-important casts into his vault for "safekeeping." "I was passive and easily intimidated, I didn't want to argue: Frank trusted him and *I* trusted him, so I agreed." As if being burglarized wasn't bad enough, she got hit by a car and was badly hurt crossing the street on the Sunset Strip. At that point, even Mr. Zappa's enthusiasm wasn't enough to hold her here. Cynthia wanted to go home. "Times were changing: for one thing, when in Chicago, bands wanted to be casted, but in L.A., they only wanted to date beautiful models. And the sexual revolution was changing in 1971; people were starting to get married instead of sleeping with strangers. It was no longer trendy to be in my collection, I guess, so I didn't capture people of the magnitude of Jimi Hendrix. Suddenly, everything was going wrong; it was a really bogus time for me."

Back in Chicago, Cynthia settled into a normal typesetting job and didn't whip up any alginates for ten long years. "I didn't care for the '70s music. The rock was getting too hard for me, and I worked a straight job. Plaster casting does not lend itself to the time I had to go to bed. Usually the golden hour for a dick to go in my mold was 3:00 A.M., and I had to get up for work three hours later." In the early '80s, Cynthia came out of semi-retirement. "Punk rock started up and that's when the music got really exciting for me again."

Due to the gathering obsession and keen yearning for the days of Hendrix, the Doors, and Zeppelin, the more mythological the '60s heyday became, and the more Cynthia found she was garnering a new kind of respect. And she was once again svelte and miniskirted. "It was different, yeah. I was no longer fat, I got more respect, people wanted to be on the same mantel with Jimi Hendrix. It started building over the space of fifteen or twenty years—and to this day, the pace is still mounting."

In 1986, my first book, *I'm with the Band*, became a bestseller, and Cynthia and I were happily reunited on the first salacious groupie exposé on MTV. "Even before I moved to L.A., the media jumped on the Plaster Casters, and I didn't expect that. Slowly even *more* media became interested and started to call me an icon. I try not to think about it too much or it makes me crazy." Cynthia smiles. "But it does come in handy when things are down. The fan mail keeps me goin'—it really helps."

The icon continued pursuing musicians that moved her, and in the '80s and early '90s she generated a plethora of artistic achievements, among them Jon Langford of the Mekons, Chris Connelly of the Revolting Cocks, the Dead Kennedy's Jello Biafra, and Richard Lloyd, the guitarist for Television.

Encouraged by the burgeoning fascination with her "sweet babies," Cynthia politely asked Herb Cohen to return her casts. His response left her stupefied. "In the late '80s it became apparent that I should get them back because interest was building. I said, 'I'd like 'em back, please,' and Herb said, 'No, I *own* them.' I thought, 'I can't afford to get them back. Holy fucking shit: *now* what?' At various points of my life I felt like a loser. I could never win; people took advantage of my passive nature. And this Herb Cohen trial was a turning point in my life. I didn't think it was humanly possible, but I actually found lawyers to represent me for nothing because they *loved* the idea of the case. My attorney thought what had happened to me was horrible."

It took five years for the Case of the Stolen Plaster Casts to come to trial at a Los Angeles County courthouse, and Cynthia made the front page of the Calendar section of the *L.A. Times.* "Exhibits A through Z were the *casts.* I know the paparazzi were there to shoot them. I had to testify about dicks on the stand for two days, and *you*, my doll, were my only witness." Yes, I was a character witness for a true character, and even in the face of attempted character assassination, I was confident that the precious truth would prevail. A puny, fresh-faced bumpkin attorney brandished one of my bygone "love letters" to Cynthia as proof that we had been lesbian lovers, insisting that my testimony would therefore be tainted. With C-minus dramatics, he scornfully recited my flower-child prose.

"February 10, 1969: My true love, my dear piñata face, how I love you and long to see you. Please come here to work. I loved your letter, my sweet. Write sooner than soon as I will have my heart tied to the mailbox. If each long mile between us were just a single kiss, I'd buy a mileage ticket, and not a mile I'd miss . . ." The judge wasn't going for it. At the end of the four-day spectacle in which the bronzed penises in question stood proudly in the hallowed halls of American justice, Cynthia was awarded her casts, and Herb had to fork over $10,000 for the pleasure of returning them to their rightful owner.

Cynthia became an equal opportunity plaster caster a few years back when she started casting rocker girl's mammary glands. "I was liking as many girl bands as boy bands, and girls were not just great singers, but instrumentalists and songwriters, so it was long overdue. The first girl I casted was my friend Suzy Beal from L7, and it worked like a charm. I've casted both sisters in the Demolition Doll Rods, the only band I have a complete set of: Danny's dick, and Christine Doll Rod and Margaret Doll Rod's tits. I've got Laetitia from Stereolab, Sally of the Mekons, Karen of the Yeah Yeah Yeahs." Cynthia and I have been talking about casting each other's titties sometime in the future, a thrilling possibility.

Cynthia's untamed life in art was captured in 2003 when the documentary DVD *Plaster Caster: The Rock and Roll Adventures of Super-Groupie Cynthia Plaster Caster* was released by Fragment Films. I was interviewed and so was our long-ago fave-rave Noel Redding, who passed away soon after filming. "Before the shoot, he called me long-distance," she says, still impressed by all those miles between Cork County, Ireland, and Chicago, Illinois. "God, I'm proud and honored and really sad, too, that his last appearance on film was in my cockumentary."

Considering that most folks believe Cynthia to be a left-field eccentric, I ask if she thinks of what she does as outsider art. "I've been trying to figure out whether I'm an outsider or not. A lot of people believe a true outsider is insane, unlike *me*. I know what I do is absurd and funny, and most outsiders don't realize their work is absurd. In fact, the reason I *do* it is to be as absurd as possible." Cynthia's work has actually become accepted by much of the mainstream, but how does she feel about actually being *revered* by her fans? "It sure is bizarre, but I'm *lovin'* it. I just want to have a good time. I've really been burnin' to write my book—and I would love to find the time to draw. I've been doing still lifes of very *still* dicks and tits. Some people do gardening, some people do still lifes."

In 2002, Cynthia founded the Cynthia P. Caster Foundation, a legally sanctioned not-for-profit institution whose mission is to give cash to cutting-edge musicians and artists in need of financial assistance. The foundation raises money through donations and the selling of Cynthia's magnificent limited-edition art objects, which include her art school sketches of the Beatles, the Byrds, Noel Redding, and Jeff Beck's crotch (you'll have to read *her* book for that story).

Up for grabs at her Web site for a mere $1,500 is a numbered replica of the Hendrix cast, which Cynthia describes thusly:

> *The Godfather of Whopper Choppers in my collection!*
> *Because this was one of my first shots at plaster casting, the*
> *end result came out kind of gnarly. I prematurely cracked*
> *the mold open, only to find a still-moist, broken cast*
> *inside. So yes, Jimi did in fact, break the mold! But thanks*
> *to Elmer's Glue, I managed to reconnect the head to the*
> *shaft to the testicles. Very statuesque and antique-looking;*
> *like Grecian art. The Canadian underground paper* Geor-
> gia Straight *called it the "Penis de Milo." There's no deny-*
> *ing that Jimi towers over most of my collection. His long,*
> *thick shaft combined with his disproportionately small*
> *head brings a shudder to the spinal cord!*

She has had art showings at superchic art galleries in New York and San Francisco and also does hilarious spoken-word show-and-tells at open-minded universities and rock clubs. We did a rave-filled night together not long ago at L.A.'s Viper Room and happily brought the house up.

It's way past bedtime, and as we stand in front of my bathroom mirror, rubbing endless creams into our somehow dewy faces, Cynthia and I discuss the impact the Warden has made on her life. I find it astounding that she still speaks to her aged mother almost *every* day. No matter where Cynthia happens to be on the planet, the Warden thinks she's safely tucked into her apartment in Chicago. "I'd call what she did to me *terrorism,*" she says ardently. "I *feared* her more than anything when I was a little girl. I studied psychology in college about how really strong hereditary and emotional disorders were—I was afraid I was gonna turn into her."

Through pioneering artistry and scorching soul-searching, Cynthia has finally come to the conclusion that she is *not* an extension of her mother; and for almost forty years she has pulled the proverbial wool over her mama's sneaky eyes. Amazingly, the ninety-year-old harridan still has no idea that her infamous daughter is the notorious Cynthia Plaster Caster of Chicago.

For over three years, Cynthia has made ends meet without having to work an insufferably confining nine-to-five job. Her only line of work these days is being Cynthia Plaster Caster. "I feel more me. I feel like I fit into my skin more compactly. I say whatever I want to say and it makes me say even *more*. I have never felt more *me* than I do right now."

Dee Dee Keel

Hey Little Girl,
You Wanna Come on the Bus?

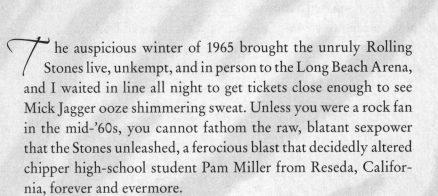

The auspicious winter of 1965 brought the unruly Rolling Stones live, unkempt, and in person to the Long Beach Arena, and I waited in line all night to get tickets close enough to see Mick Jagger ooze shimmering sweat. Unless you were a rock fan in the mid-'60s, you cannot fathom the raw, blatant sexpower that the Stones unleashed, a ferocious blast that decidedly altered chipper high-school student Pam Miller from Reseda, California, forever and evermore.

Safely sequestered in my seat that November night, I watched agog as several fans seemed to lose all semblance of normalcy. Aroused in spanking new ways, fire-eyed girls hastily unbuttoned their pert cotton blouses, hurling unsullied white Maidenforms onto the stage where five British ruffians played music that sneered.

Halfway through the short, strutting set, one brave fan had somehow gotten backstage and was rabidly descending the long gold drapes behind the band, scuttling closer to Charlie Watts like a demented spider in a matching pastel sweater set. Landing on stage, the star of her own teen dream, she managed to glom onto Keith Richards's leg before being hauled off by a crew-cut guard. As manic as I was about the Stones, I did not remove my slightly padded bra, nor dare attempt such a high-risk feat, but I

101

envied those who made sure they were precisely in the spinning center of the action.

Years later, in my early groupie prime, I prided myself on being an indispensable Whisky a Go Go girl. I was invited into the all-important club most evenings and didn't have to pay because my unbridled dancing got people out of their seats and onto the floor. And yes, there were many nights I was escorted through the door on the arm of a rock god. Even though I considered myself a vital part of the Hollywood music scene, I secretly revered the sassy girls who *worked* at the venerable rock club. The ticket takers, waitresses, the girls who ran the office for owners Mario and Elmer—they all seemed to harbor hushed secrets behind their long bangs and heavily made-up eyes. These girls never missed a show or a beat. They were first to know who was coming to town, they were always allowed backstage, they had automatic cachet and respect—and often had first dibs on the most coveted local and visiting rock stars.

One of these intimidating dolls was Dee Dee Lewis, a slim strawberry blonde who won the highly prized job of Whisky

With ex-husband Ron Keel.   Credit: Dee Dee Keel

office manager after her lovely predecessor, Gail Sloatman, met Frank Zappa and became what we all wanted to be. I vividly remember Dee Dee's thick mod-girl lashes, tomboy stance, and in-crowd allure.

Lucky for me, it's a small rock world we live in, and when she heard I was working on a book about groupie histories, Dee Dee contacted me through my Web site. This is her response to my e-mail asking whom she had "groupied" with: "Here goes: Jeff Beck, Cozy Powell, Chick Churchill, David Cassidy, the entire Hollies band, Ian Paice, Keef Hartley, Johnny Almond, Tony Stevens (traveled with Foghat, Humble Pie), Peter Grant (yes, I went BIG!), Lee from Chicago, many, *many* roadies (I didn't mind if I got to hang with the bands), Iggy & the Stooges (married the light man; lived with Iggy), Van Halen, Mötley Crüe, Ratt, married Ron Keel, and toured the world with many famous bands . . ." I called her instantly, and after a few minutes on the phone, I knew she had to have her own chapter.

Dee Dee Keel (nee Lewis) arrived at my door carrying loads of scrapbooks and photo albums. A mother of six, the still-striking strawberry blonde looks far younger than her fifty-some years, and she is bubbling over, seemingly pent-up with tawdry tales she can't wait to disclose. She makes no apologies for her devil-may-care dalliances with the boys who played Satan's music. Her ribald memories are essential to her, and she joyfully wears them like a coat of many conquests.

To jump into the thick of it, I suggest we begin at the middle. "I think my favorite adventure was with Jeff Beck. He was what I aspired to, followed through with, and ultimately attained. The odd thing about the Whisky was that the girls who worked there had little camps. They'd see an album cover and say, 'He's mine,' and I wondered, 'How do you know who's gonna like *who*?' At first, I couldn't figure out how I'd get *this* one because everybody wanted him. Since I had just started working there, and was low on the totem pole, I coolly said, 'I'll take Cozy Powell.' At that time Cozy and Jeff Beck were very close. My devious side knew if I did something spectacular, it would get back to Jeff." So how did she go about meeting Beck's notorious drummer? "I simply left a message for Cozy at the hotel, then found out who he knew in London and the names of a couple obscure places he frequented, so when he returned my call I was ready, 'Hey, it's Dee Dee from the so-and-so club!' I named the people I supposedly met him with, and he said, 'Wow, what are you doing in L.A.?'"

I am duly impressed, and Dee Dee still seems happily amazed that the ruse worked so well. When the strangers met up at the Whisky that night, Cozy said, "You know, my memory's a bit rusty—come give me a sock in the jaw so I'll remember who you are." Dee Dee giggles, recalling that she hadn't told her Whisky coworkers about her mischievous stunt. "I loved myself! I bought this purple velvet cape and wore skintight jeans and boots. You should have seen the looks on everyone's faces when Cozy walked in. And I thought, 'OK, it's show time. What am I gonna do?'" She had nothing to worry about; Cozy acted like Dee Dee was a long lost lover. "I could tell all the girls were wondering, 'How did she do *that*?' I was thinking, 'I'm in deep trouble.' So I recruited one of the waitresses, Charlotte, to hang out with us, and we had a great time. At the end of the night he said, 'Are you gonna take me home with you?' and I said, 'Sure am—with *her*,' and he said, 'Right on!' I figured I had to show him what I got if I expected him to tell Jeff something phenomenal happened—and the three of us played all night long."

Yes, the naughty ploy worked, but Dee Dee didn't go all the way with Cozy Powell, and she made it clear that she had a crush on Jeff Beck. "At that point, I would only do oral things— cuddling and playing. I wasn't gonna do it." Smiling, she adds, "I shed that feeling later and started doing everything to everybody! But I thought if I had sex with Cozy, I wasn't gonna get Jeff. I had an ace in the hole: I knew Jeff was into cars, and I had a killer '69 purple Cougar stick, and I let Cozy drive it back to the hotel. I went to the Whisky early the next night and got a booth. When Jeff came in, he kept trying to get my attention, but I ignored him. Finally he tapped me on the shoulder and said, 'Are you the one?' and I said, 'Why, whatever do you mean?' 'Are you the one Cozy told me about?' When I said, 'Yeah,' he said, 'All right, when are we leaving?' At this point, Charlotte let me know she really wanted him and moved in as the Alpha canine—Jeff was gonna be *hers*. She thought I had gotten him for her, and I was OK with that. I was a real follower then; I didn't have my own identity until I was well into my thirties."

Dee Dee sometimes shared an apartment with Charlotte, and at the end of the night, they left the Whisky, heading for their tapestry-covered couch. But was Dee Dee really OK sharing her Top Rock Dog with her cunning canine roommate? As soon as the door closed behind them, jaunty Jeff clambered onto the bed, inviting both girls to join him. "We each go to him, and when I smell him and feel him, I think, 'Oh my God, this is a real rock star, this is a real man, *this* is what I've been waiting for.' When he was kissing me, *she* started to go after his fly, and he leaned to me and said, 'Is there someplace we can be alone?' Charlotte stormed off to her room. We went into my room, but suddenly I felt like shit. He said, 'Come on, you can't be upset about her,' and I said, 'But I have to live with her tomorrow.' I said, 'I know, let's all take a bath together!' So I ran this big bath, lit all the candles, and got us in the tub." Did she wind up sharing her prize after all? "No, because he didn't want Charlotte, and he was gonna have it *his* way. I had him in her room, on her bed, with her watching. I was a bit nervous, but after a while I thought, 'I don't really care. I just wanna be with Jeff.' He really enjoyed it and when he leaned over me, the cross around his neck dangled just above my face. I can still see it. Then he wanted me on top, and it was the best experience I'd ever had in my life. The next day the two of us went cruising. I let him drive my car all around Hollywood, and he gave me tickets to the show, then he had to leave town. That was my first big groupie hurrah. I was hooked."

Dee Dee speaks openly about her X-rated early life, and her lack of remorse is quite charming. She laughs freely and her sky blue eyes shine when recalling raunchy three-ways or when telling me tales about her six adored children. Her youngest daughter, Kelly, appears to be following in her mama's platformed footsteps, and Dee Dee promises to bring her over the next time we get together to gab.

How did her obsession begin? What made young Dee Dee Lewis desperate to be in the spinning center of the action? "At thirteen, my fantasy was to get to the Rolling Stones. I loved their music. I wanted to know all about them. I wanted to *be* them. I wanted to be a cool dude like that." When she went to Wallach's Music City to buy her Stones concert ticket, she met a savvy older girl in leather who gave her a new perspective. "From that minute on, I was gonna be this tough little leather chick."

At the Stones' 1965 Long Beach show, Dee Dee and her girlfriend were way ahead of me, literally crawling through a bathroom window to get backstage. I'm astounded when she reveals that it was her friend who clambered down the golden curtain and attached herself to Keith's scrawny leg that November night. "They didn't throw us out, just tossed us by the side of the stage. I realized I could get that close. I was standing right there when they came out to the car. 'These guys are real, these guys are cool, my parents don't like 'em . . . I'm *there*.' It was very powerful."

She was fifteen when the Stones played the L.A. Sports Arena and the father of a friend managed the venue. "Does it get any better than that?" Dee Dee grins. "So I buy myself gold stockings and I'm ready to go. We're backstage after the show, and here comes the band. Keith Richards walks up and says, 'Hey, little girl, you wanna come on the bus?' My girlfriend grabs my arm, 'Oh, we shouldn't do *that*.' I look in Keith's eyes and know at that moment exactly what could happen if I get on the bus. But her father arrived and whisked us away. I thought to myself, 'I really want to be on their bus—and I really want to know what that *look* meant.'"

She soon found out what *that* sort of look actually meant when she got pregnant at seventeen after a brief fling with a dashing family friend. But that didn't stop her from exploring the Sunset Strip and pursuing coveted rockers. "I just went about my business, pregnant or not, and started following the Young Rascals. That's when I made a wonderful discovery: I would pick the least popular guy in the band—in this case it was Gene Cornish. I found out where they were staying—which wasn't hard—and would just call the hotel and leave a message. Curiosity always killed the rock star," she assures me. Gene Cornish was a tad bummed that his mystery caller was seventeen and pregnant, but Dee Dee started hanging out with the band whenever they hit town. She became dazzled by singer Eddie Brigati's L.A. girl-friend Amy and soon named her newborn daughter after the blonde model.

"I had a lot of adventures with the Rascals. They just accepted the fact that I was gonna be there. I didn't know they had different girls in every town, but when I began to realize that Amy was Eddie's L.A. girl, I thought, 'I wanna stay in nice places like *they* do. I wanna ride in limousines and go on airplanes. I want to live this life.' Later on, I would say to certain musicians, 'I'll be your L.A. girl,' because I just wanted to be *something*—some kind of monumental thing to them."

While her daughter was safely ensconced with her exasperated parents, Dee Dee became assistant to Whisky owner Elmer Valentine. "My parents weren't thrilled because I started renting a house with Charlotte. For a long while I'd have to work my job at the Whisky, which ended at 7:00 P.M., then I'd go take care of my baby, then back out partying all night. I did that for years."

Despite her quickie with baby Amy's father, Dee Dee was surprisingly insecure at this early stage; most of her sexual experiences consisted of oral favors. But after a wild night with one of Led Zeppelin's roadies, gossip got around, and she caught the eye of their gargantuan manager, Peter Grant. "One day I was sunbathing at the Hyatt House pool. I noticed Peter had his eye on me. That night he took me back to the hotel from the Whisky in the limo."

I knew Peter well. When I was with Jimmy Page, the big man took divine care of me, and I felt I knew a side of him that few others were privy to. I'm happy to know that Dee Dee saw his sweet side as well. "Down deep Peter was one of the sexiest, nicest men I had ever spoken to. I was drunk, yes, and the idea of this enormous man . . . I thought, 'Hey, I wonder what *that's* like! Nobody else seems to want to know and I'm not getting any Robert Plants.' I had on these five-and-a-half-inch patent leather heels with heart cutouts, this little top, and a tiny velvet skirt. He was so sweet to me. We were drinking, more drinking, and pretty soon we were making out. I said, 'Wanna see my sunburn?' and he said, 'Oh, *do* I!' and off came the clothes. I put myself down on the bed and said, 'Come here to me,' and he said, 'Darlin', I'll crush you.' So *he* got down on the bed first."

Peter's horny kindness encouraged her to branch out even further. "He called me sweet names; he adored that I was a little blonde thing who touched him and liked him. It was good—it helped me to get a little bolder as to what I might be able to do."

Dee Dee's stories come hard and fast now. She spent twelve years, day and night, at the hippest club in the trendiest city, and gaily took advantage of her priceless vantage point. Even though she has a thick scrapbook crammed with memories, her escapades are all jumbled up, and I hear about that keyboard player, this drummer, that bass player . . . and through it all, she carried on a tempestuous, clandestine relationship with her powerful boss, Elmer Valentine. He treated her like a princess, and perks were plentiful. "I almost got caught once when I was down on the floor under his roll top desk, and one of the girls came in. I looked up at him and he looked down at me and suddenly I was brilliant: I grabbed whatever I could find on the floor, peeked out, and said, 'Found it!'"

People think *I* was brazen in revealing my rock star intimacies, but Dee Dee's unabashed saga makes my tales sound kindergarten tame. "I *do* have a wild story about the Hollies," she says with a wink. "I was with all of 'em!"

The British foursome was heavily coveted among the Whisky chicks, and every girl had claimed a Hollie for herself. The stakes were even higher because the band was going to be in town for a few weeks recording a new album, which made them potential boyfriend material.

"They all came into the Whisky and I stood behind the lead singer, Terry Sylvester. He kept turning around, and every time he did I made an awful face. Finally he said, 'Are you trying to take the piss out of me?' I'd never heard that phrase before and started laughing, and he said, 'Get over here. Talk to me.'"

It must have been quite a night, because once again, Dee Dee remembers exactly what she was wearing, "I had on a little rainbow sweater with 'Hello' knitted into it and he thought that was really cute." At the end of the night, Terry asked Dee Dee for a ride to the hotel, and she sashayed out of the club with her prize while the other girls shot dagger eyes. "As we were driving, he explained that the boys in the band were well aware of what the Whisky girls wanted, but they were all married or in relationships. I made it clear that I didn't want to destroy any relationships, I just wanted to have a good time." Terry took her up to the room where the other three Hollies were watching TV. "He said, 'Look what I brought home.' And I did my famous 'Let's take a bath, boys!'"

Dee Dee had come up with this routine when she realized that British rockers' bathing habits weren't quite up to her standards. "I had so many encounters that I developed the Bathtub Game. There is nothing worse than going *down there* when . . . yuck! So, I ran a bath with the Hollies, took off my clothes, got in the tub, and said, 'Come on in with me.' Of course they all couldn't fit; some were sitting on the edge, and they were so cute, that's when I decided to have sex with whoever wanted to do it—and it was glorious."

They all basked in Dee Dee's largesse except for cutie-pie Tony Hicks, who stayed in front of the TV. "He was a little 'tsk-tsk' about the whole thing while the rest of us had a good time. Afterward, he frowned and said, 'Well, what are you gonna do with *me*?' I got down on the floor in front of him and they all gathered 'round to watch." After hearing about Cynthia Plaster Caster's unique way with a dick, Dee Dee had been trying to come up with her own sexy gimmick. She asked Terry to go to the fridge and get some ice cubes. "I was gonna put them in my mouth and give head with 'em. I wanted to be called the Ice Princess, but it never took off . . ." Yikes, no wonder. Lucky for Tony, there weren't any available ice cubes, so Terry came back with a carton of yogurt. "I poured out the yogurt and gave him head. He came all over and I licked the yogurt off him. From that minute on, he adored me. We had the best time; the whole

band made a date with me every night that week, and we created little games. One of 'em was 'We'll pull up in front of the
Whisky and you'll be wearing just a trench coat, stockings, and
heels, and pretend you're hitchhiking and don't know us.' They
would take turns having me flash 'em. I'd pretend I was Marilyn
Monroe and they'd be total strangers. The girls were so angry,"
Dee Dee says proudly. "They never could figure out what I'd
done and how I had 'em all!"

She was having a blast, but couldn't seem to keep the promise
she made to herself and her Hollies beau. Dee Dee began falling
for Terry and things soon got sticky. "He started coming into the
Whisky often to see me, and I knew it was out of line. He told me
he wasn't in love with his wife but promised he'd be there for her
and they'd have a child. I respected that, I really did, although I
would love to have stolen him away." Dee Dee sighs, "The last
time I saw him, we couldn't even touch each other because it
would have been *love*making, not just fun. I cried and begged
and whimpered; then I had to pull myself together." Sounds like
the age-old groupie's lament to me.

There were plenty more guitar-playing fish in Dee Dee's
aquarium. There was Leigh Stephens, lead guitarist in Blue
Cheer, and Tony Stevens, the handsome bass player for Foghat.
"And I had an encounter with Emerson, Lake, and Palmer. It
was actually Carl who picked me out as I walked by their booth.
That was another thing: strut by the booth enough times and
you might catch their attention. Mario used to assist in telling
the guys which of us were the 'clean' girls. And Elmer would
always say, '*This* is the girl you want.'"

All the while, her relationship with Elmer never abated. "He
was with me the first time I ever gave a girl head. Suzette was one
of the cute little things who used to hang around in the office.
I liked boys, not girls—I really didn't know what to do with
that sort of anatomy, but I did the best I could. Suzette crashed
her car the day after I'd been with her, and tragically died. This
is the kind of humor Elmer has—he said, 'Dee, you give *killer*
head.'"

In the midst of a semiserious fling with Johnny Almond of the Mark Almond Band, Dee Dee cavorted with a few other rockers. "I began to see, on a very serious level, Ian Paice, Deep Purple's drummer. He wanted to marry me and take me to England. At the same time I was seeing LeRoy Jenkins of Quicksilver Messenger Service, but he had a teeny-weeny peenie. And there was also a lighting man, Erich Haddix. I really wanted to marry Keith Robertson, the roadie for Fleetwood Mac, but one night he went out with someone else. It broke my heart because he really loved my daughter Amy." In retaliation, Dee Dee picked up Keith's best friend at the Whisky and took him home. "Keith was so peeved, he ended up crawling through my bedroom window, screaming at me. I thought, 'OK, I'm a tramp.' So I just went Eeny, Meenie, Miney, Mo. I did process of elimination and married Erich Haddix. But I remember standing in the church with my flowers, realizing 'I can't say *I do*,' and crossing my fingers."

She may not have been sure she married the right guy, but Dee Dee certainly gave it the royal try. The mismatched couple had three sons together, Marlon, Jeff, and Erich Jr., before breaking up in 1980. "I did have a stable time when I was doing the Betty Crocker/Suzy Homemaker thing, but I guess temptations were pulling me because the entire time I still worked at the Whisky. We were developing the Roxy and the Rainbow and were quite busy booking all these great bands. There I was, under the table, sucking Elmer's cock, then going home—'Hi, did you pick up the dry cleaning? Let's make dinner!'"

To make the setup even more unusual, Erich's erstwhile boss, Iggy Pop, was a frequent houseguest. "He had nowhere to live so he ended up living with us for years. I spent my honeymoon night at an Iggy and the Stooges concert. I had on this beautiful long black gown with rhinestones and brand-new wedding-night panties with roses on them, and Iggy walks into the room. He was comfortable with me because we'd been hanging out for so long. He points at me and says, 'You. Take off the panties.' My husband says, 'You'd better just do it,' so I pull 'em off and give 'em to Iggy, he puts them on, and says, 'Now I'm ready to go onstage.' He went on that night wearing my panties and a pair of boots." Dee Dee is suddenly struck by vivid recollection, "Outside of David Cassidy, Iggy has the most enormous cock I've ever seen in my life. It's *huge*! I don't even know how anybody can deal with that thing. And he's such a bad boy. He'd see my little daughter and say, 'Come here, little girl. There's a mouse in my pocket.' We'd have to slap him and say, 'Come on, she's three years old, stop!' Yeah, Iggy was really naughty. He was pretty bad off when Bowie was in the picture—when they were having their little *thing*. They were lovers, very much in love. My ex-husband has some drawings that Bowie did of Iggy having oral sex with him, and he's got a tear in his eye. It was when they were breaking up."

Dee Dee and I agree that there were a lot of same-sex relationships back in the day. It was a way people expressed themselves, but it didn't necessarily mean they were gay. "There was more freedom," Dee Dee says assuredly. "I walked into a bedroom at a party one night, and Rod Stewart was with a real cute guy, giving him oral. I wasn't shocked, just embarrassed and felt bad that I'd intruded. I just closed the door. I *did* see some pretty outrageous things at the Hyatt House. I was with Jeff Beck on our way upstairs and he wanted to stop at this certain room. When he opened the door some roadies had a girl on the bed, putting champagne bottles inside her. If I hadn't gotten close, I would have thought they were in the middle of a poker game—you know, men yelling and taunting; that sort of thing. When I got closer, I thought, 'Oh, dear, I don't want to find *me* there next.' I saw the same scenario later in Iggy's camp—some girl messing with sticks of butter. And I thought, 'What will these girls do to be accepted?'"

Toward the end of her marriage to Erich, during a rocky marital spat, one of Dee Dee's girlhood wishes decidedly came true. As we peruse her numerous backstage passes, stickers, and photos, one shot stops me hot. "Isn't that David Cassidy?" I ask. "Yes, I finally got that fantasy fulfilled. I had a crush on him from day one, but he eluded me." That is, until she heard the teen idol was having marital strife himself. At a baby shower, a good friend of Dee Dee's sneakily got David's home phone number by asking his wife, Kay Lenz, out to lunch. "I feel extremely guilty about this. We waited until Kay was out of town and me and my girlfriend called him. He was home by himself. We made sure he knew he was gonna meet somebody who *really* wanted him. It was that easy." The excited girls arrived to find their pop hero in his new mansion, amid chaotically stacked packing boxes, sitting alone in the dark. "He wanted to give us a tour of the house, and when we got to the bedroom, we stayed there . . . of course." When I ask if a three-way ensued, Dee Dee shakes her head. "My friend was more of a watcher. Hey, it was my treat!"

It's no secret that David Cassidy is mighty well-endowed. He spells it out in his autobiography, *C'Mon Get Happy: Fear and Loathing on the Partridge Family Bus*, in no uncertain terms. "He's so big that when I was trying to give him head, I couldn't even do a quarter of it," Dee Dee says, wide-eyed, "and I have a huge mouth! We saw him a couple more times when Kay was out of town. He began to call me at the Whisky, but it was a dark time in his life when he was tragically depressed. I was married too, and I found out I was pregnant. David would kiss and hold my belly—he wanted a child so badly. I always wonder what would have happened with us had I not been married."

Dee Dee developed her own superpowers when she started booking bands at the Whiskey. "Whoever got in Dee Dee's pants got the best booking!" She hired the New York Dolls, and Elmer gave her a raise. Next it was Iggy Pop. After booking Van Halen, she went on to help them get a record deal. "I started having escapades with guys in the heavy metal bands. I groupied with all the members of Ratt except *one*. In fact, he and I were at a club one night and he got drunk and said, 'When's it my turn?' I was like, 'You are *so* wrong. It's never gonna be your turn. I'm not a horse and we're not taking rides! I booked Mötely Crüe. We were all best buddies, and I partied with all of 'em except Nikki, who I *did* play with a bit. I can still walk in somewhere, see Vince and Nikki, and it's all hugs and kisses." When she booked Ratt, singer Stephen Pearcy temporarily drove her to distraction. "Warren DeMartini was the hottest, but Stephen was my favorite. He was the sexiest thing I'd ever laid eyes on. He was an odd one, though. He's the only guy I ever met with a tremendous mole on his dick. And he was darned proud of that dick. He used to call me on the road and say, 'You gonna fuck me yet? You're fucking everybody, but not fucking me.' We did lots of stuff, but, uh-uh, I couldn't get past the mole. I kept running back to him, though. I've been told that his song 'Back for More' is about me because I'd dump him, then go back. It was always, 'So, you're back for more?'"

As a result of her back and forth exploits with Stephen Pearcy, Dee Dee met the man she'd spend the next eighteen years with. She thought Stephen was using her to get to one of her pretty friends, and though she was crazy about him, she was starting to feel jerked around by the rocker with the fearsome mole. "One day he came upstairs and there was a picture of the Stealer Band on the wall, which Ron Keel was in. When Stephen asked me to meet him that night at the Whiskey, I said, 'No, I have a date— with *this* guy,' and pointed to Ron. I didn't really and had to call their manager to say, 'I need to meet with your singer—fast!'" Talk about rock and roll clout. "That night, Stephen takes one look at me with the singer from Stealer, and says, 'Well, *steal her* away.' Then he says to me, 'If I walk out that door, I'm not coming back.'

"It was all game playing in the heavy metal days," she admits. "Total debauchery, partying, do it with anybody in the bathroom stall. I had finally had enough and was standing in the Whisky with Ron, and I said, 'Go away, that's it!' I turned to leave and he yelled down the hall, 'But I love you!' I said, 'What?' He said it again, and from that minute on, we were together."

Dee Dee married Ron Keel, who later formed the hard rock band Keel, and they had two kids, Kelly and Ryan. In spite of going out on the road and all over the world with bands like Mötley Crüe, KISS, and Bon Jovi, Dee Dee considers her years with Ron to be "pretty normal, even though we were a rock and roll family. Having kids never hindered me from doing what I wanted to do. We toured with all our friends and I helped out

With Ron Keel.
Credit: Dee Dee Keel

other bands." Life was cram-packed, and Dee Dee felt it was finally time to call it quits at her feverish stomping grounds, the Whisky a Go Go. "I really loved Ron and was afraid to leave my rock guy home alone. I figured if I was gonna grab him, I'd better grab him now. It was '83, and the Whisky was on a downswing. Elmer said, 'You know, I'm getting old and it's not happening anymore. We're gonna have to start renting out the club. But I want to keep you on . . .' So I continued to see Elmer. It seemed to never end." I ask if her boyfriends and husbands ever knew about the ongoing tryst with her longtime boss. "Hell, no!" she says. "That was my secret life."

As promised, when she next comes to visit, Dee Dee brings along her daughter Kelly, a sleek, canny twenty-one-year-old bass player that her mother calls "my groupie wild child." Kelly also arrives bearing photo albums teeming with snaps of her posing with various modern rockers—tattooed, made-up fellows from bands such as Sinnistar, the Toilet Boys, and Static-X. Dee Dee is obviously proud that her backstage wiles have been passed along to her music-loving daughter. "The very first time I got backstage, I had to admit Mom was right about everything," Kelly says. "I was fifteen and wanted to go this concert festival because I was obsessed with Kitty. They were angry girls just like I was and they played guitar and rocked through their hearts. We were driving around the Palladium and my mom's like, 'Well, just look for a Ryder truck. You can get in, and you won't have to pay.' We went to the back and the entire band was standing by the truck." Dee Dee chimes in, "They said, 'You wanna go backstage with us?' and I said to Kelly, 'I'll be back to pick you up at one.' After that it was great because she'd come home and say, 'I went to a show and I totally pulled a *Mom!*'"

I ask Kelly when it dawned on her that Mommy had such a vividly colored past. "Well, she would say stuff like, 'When I turned twenty-one, I was hanging out with Led Zeppelin, and Axl Rose rubbed my leg . . .' and I said, 'Yeah, but you wound up with Ron Keel!'"

Kelly obviously has tangled emotions about her absent rocker dad, because after this blatant put-down, she reverses course. "Now, anytime I go to a concert I know just what to do. I saw Radiohead at the Hollywood Bowl and went to the back where they were having a huge party. All I said to the door guy was, 'Do you know who I am? I'm Ron Keel's daughter,' and they let me in. I love my dad. I get along with him, but not on a daughter-father level. He doesn't know how to be a parent, so I just hang out with him like he's another teenager." I comment that most rock stars never seem to grow all the way up. "It's true. He is really sixteen," Kelly sighs. "That's just the way it is."

As more of Dee Dee's tales tumble forth, it's obvious by Kelly's mixed reaction that some of the explicit details are more than she needs to know. When the topic turns to Zeppelin, she is perplexed about her mother's fling with the hefty Peter Grant. "How do you do it with somebody who weighs three hundred pounds?" she wonders. "They don't get on top of you," Dee Dee informs her curious daughter. "Have you ever seen those commercials where the girl is riding an electric bull doing *this*?" She demonstrates with one hand high in the air, bouncing around on the couch like she's competing at a raunchy rodeo. "*That's* what it's like."

When the subject of Elmer and the late Suzette comes up, Kelly raises her eyebrows in semi-mock shock, "Mom! I didn't know you swung both ways." But Dee Dee barely notices. "I dream about Elmer to this day," she confesses. "He wasn't very happy when I fell in love with Ron. He was jealous and angry because I was getting distracted and coming in a little late and wanting to leave a little early."

I know that Dee Dee has been on her own for several years, raising Kelly and younger son Ryan basically by herself. What happened to the romance with her beloved hard rock husband? "It got quite tough. The Jack Daniel's and the cigarettes came first. My family's big in real estate and I had a lot of property.

With Taime Downe of Faster Pussycat.
Credit: Dee Dee Keel

Here's the kicker: I sold it off, piece by piece, band by band, record by record. It came to the big finale in Arizona—Ron wanted to do country-western. He was turning forty—the end of the world was coming! And that *was* the end; there was nothing more to sell. It's interesting because last week he came to town to see Ryan in a play, and he brought flowers for me. I looked in those eyes thinking, 'You chose the wrong road. I would have stayed.'" So what finally made her call it quits? "His multi-daily cheating: the booze, the drugs. The *real* last straw was when I opened the car door to drive the kids to school and out rolled the straw and bindle of coke. I went upstairs and said, 'Why would you do this?' And he looked me right in the face and said, 'Why *wouldn't* I?'"

"He was hiding money from us," Kelly adds sadly. "And I saw him snort stuff in front of me all the time."

"Yeah, that was the end," Dee Dee continues. "And the truth is, it's really hard for me now because I know he wants to get back together, but I've already rebuilt my life. Quite frankly, I discovered I can still get guys—*young* guys!"

How does Kelly feel about the resurfacing of her mother's rambunctious ways?

"I understand now, and more power to her—she can be with whoever she wants—but when I was sixteen, I was so pissed off when she flirted with the bands I hung out with. I was like, 'Stop being a whore in front of me! I hate it!'"

"But I wasn't," Dee Dee insists coquettishly. "*They* were flirting with me!"

The comfort level between these two dolls makes it clear that Kelly seems at peace with her offbeat rock and roll upbringing. "What bothered me then doesn't bother me now. I know that my mom and dad aren't like everybody else's mom and dad, but she's a good mom. I'm proud of her because I grew up more and I realize she's had a hard life, and she should do whatever she wants. She doesn't have to listen to anybody."

"Yeah, I suppose I have had a hard life," Dee Dee concedes, "but I don't regret any of it. Had I been a groupie with talent,

The Keel family.
Credit: Dee Dee Keel

perhaps I would have been able to record an album like Kelly's done, but my talents weren't in the musical sense."

"I'm sure you had talents, but they just weren't indulged the way you encouraged mine. Like, you bought me a guitar and gave me all the CDs I wanted and told me to do whatever I wanted to do creatively."

"I had to do what I had to do to hang out because I loved the music so much," says Dee Dee. "I was at the Tubes' show recently, and Fee Waybill, who I'd loved for so many years, tried to get me to come backstage. I know I could have had him that night, but I've matured enough that I thought, 'Nah, it's better in my memory, better you want me next time around,' and I was able to walk away. The old me would have gone for it, but I started to realize that the chase was sometimes more fun."

Now that Dee Dee is making her way backstage again, I wonder if she's planning on embracing the music scene the way she once did. "Used to be I wouldn't sleep very much because I was afraid I was gonna miss out on something. It was like that one night I didn't go to the Whisky, that one guy was gonna be there—so I *had* to go. I'm not like that anymore, but sometimes I still feel like I'm gonna miss out on something. I love a good time, I love a good rock show, and I love a good musician."

Miss Mercy's Blues

Shock Treatment

*I*t was the mind-blowing, heady summer of 1968, and I was
happily floating around in my own private Laurel Canyon
bliss-out with my wacky Hollywood girlfriends. Frank Zappa
was fiddling about on the piano while his lovely wife Gail
fetched tea for a kaleidoscopic assortment of humanity. Miss
Christine, dressed in her outlandish Dr. Seuss garb, balanced
baby Moon Unit on her scrawny hip, as Misses Lucy, Cynderella, Sandra, and Sparky pranced around the room showing off
their infinitely small mini-mama getups. Alice Cooper was on
hand, making goo-goo eyes at Christine, a few of the Mothers of
Invention decorated the premises, along with Captain Beefheart
and a couple Magic Band members, who were avidly listening to
Frank's stellar composition.

Ahead of his time, as usual, Mr. Zappa had already decided
that the teeming cadre of flagrant, dancing groupie girls should
become a rock group and cut a record of our very own. He
had already christened us the GTO's—Girls Together Outrageously—and the six of us were in the process of writing tunes
for our stimulating upcoming stint in the studio.

Yes, we were in the midst of a rosy, harmonious joyfest when
Mercy Fontenot plowed through the Zappa's open double doors

like a carnival in progress. Her panache momentarily blotted out the sun, and a woozy cloud of patchouli oil wafted through the layers and layers of scarves, belts, skirts, vests, necklaces, and jangling bracelets that reached all the way to her elbows. She haughtily surveyed the scene in the log cabin, and with a sweep of her kohl-smudged, raccoon-painted Theda Bara eyelids, boldly entered the fray. I knew there had to be a pair of eyes in there somewhere—what were they seeing? Behind the zaftig gypsy girl loomed the caped Carl Franzoni, aka Captain Fuck, who loudly introduced her to all and sundry. "Hey, everybody, this is MERCY. She's from San Francisco."

Miss Christine, a true speedfreak of manners and grace, was the first to introduce herself to the audacious newcomer. And despite my trepidation, I, too, stuck out my hand to make her acquaintance. As Mercy from San Francisco slowly scanned my girly, pink chiffon presence, I noticed that both her earlobes had been split down the middle, still managing to accommodate loads of spangly coin earrings that drooped down to her shoulders. Her mouth was a brazen crimson slash, and her fierce eyes poked me like a pointy red fingernail to the solar plexus. Then Mercy briefly touched my hand, and merged into the commotion.

A few moments later, Frank made a stunning announcement. He declared that Mercy Fontenot would become the seventh GTO, proclaiming that she added "an imperative bizarre element" to the proceedings. Our hero had spoken. Mercy looked around at our thunderstruck faces and said, "Don't worry. I'm not a dancer. I'm not a singer. I'm a gypsy. I come from a long line of Fontenots out of New Orleans." Then she yanked a small shimmering bag from within her copious bosom and shook it at us. "And this is John the Conqueror root."

It took a little time, and some turbulent convincing from Mr. Zappa, but it wasn't long before the nomad neophyte became Miss Mercy, a proud member of the GTO's. If one of my many psychic soothsayers had taken me aside that day and told me that Mercy would become one of my closest, dearest, forever girlfriends, I would have checked her forehead for a fever.

Wild woman of the GTO's.

Credit: Baron Wolman

Mercy Fontenot, aka Judith Peters, grew up all around the greater U.S. of A., carted hither and yon in finned American cars by her bigger-than-life gambling daddy. She remembers always seeing a racetrack from her bedroom window. "My dad was a car salesman, mother was a nurse, and they both gambled. We picked up and moved over and over because he was always in loads of trouble—they were gonna put cement shoes on him." Since she lived all around the country, Judy was treated to a wide variety of music. "I would hear all this stuff on the radio. Even as a little kid. Rhythm and blues, country and western, all the roots music. It shook me up. My mother listened to Jerry Lee Lewis, my dad played Sinatra." Little Judy lived in Seattle, Dallas, Oklahoma City, St. Petersburg, and Sarasota, but the family kept returning to San Mateo, California—situated near the handy-dandy Bay Meadows racetrack.

Judy's pop, Donald W. Peters, a flamboyant, swarthy dreamer with a penchant for crooners and cocktails, often disappeared, once returning home with an angular *Vogue* model. "I was about twelve when my dad brought the model home," Mercy recalls, raspy words spewing out of her mouth like chewed-up Red Hots. "Her name was Janis and she was a very famous *Vogue* cover girl. My dad started taking speed with her because she was desperate to stay thin. Dad and the model took me for a ride in the car, while Mom waited in the house." This troubling incident, and too many more like it, shredded the already troubled marriage, so Susan Fontenot Peters finally snatched Judy and hightailed it to another part of town. For a while, her bickering parents tried to make the shaky marriage work. "I didn't see my parents fight. But they did argue a lot about the pope. Dad was Protestant and Mom was Catholic. I've always had a crush on my dad, but I didn't know him very well. He was a gambling cowboy groupie drug-taking guy."

Since Judy's mom was a nurse, Judy had no problem getting fistfuls of diet pills, but still couldn't seem to lose weight. She didn't have many friends in junior high, so music became her saving grace. "I was a pudgy girl and I think fatness made me feel like an outsider, but I did win a twist contest in eighth grade

Credit: Mercy Fontenot

with One-Eyed Jack O' Rourke!" Mercy suddenly recalls. "But mostly I had to live outside my realm. The uppers helped intensify the radio waves that called me, so I started chasing bands. It just fell into place, you know? I came alive in '65. The first group I met was the Beau Brummels. I saw them on Ed Sullivan and thought they were cute. Then it was the Stones. We followed their car to the hotel and Mick was pacing, you could see his shadow. We listened to him scream about Keith, who had just gotten arrested. The door was open and Brian was sitting there with his suitcase, and Charlie Watts—or maybe Bill Wyman, they seemed the same to me—had been locked out of his room, and Brian was showing us his psychedelic shirts. I was attracted to the powerful fame frequency early."

What made little Judy Peters from San Mateo think she could meet the Rolling Stones? "Well, first of all, at fifteen I changed my name to Mercy, so Judy Peters wasn't about to do anything! And how can you answer why? I wanted to know the people who made the music," she says simply. "For some odd reason, music was the most important thing to me. You have to meditate on what you want. That's the main thing."

Luckily, San Mateo is very close to the show-stopping heart of San Francisco, where a vivid music scene was burgeoning. "From where I was living near North Beach, I started getting into the blues. The beatniks were blasting Lightnin' Hopkins and Muddy Waters in the local record shops." She was barely in her teens and getting into big trouble at school, but Mercy's musical taste was coming together beautifully.

"It all happened so fast. Everything seems to merge together in a big mountain of Mounds Bars! A girl gave me LSD when I was fifteen, so everything's all one big spin. She said 'Do you have lemons in your mouth?' 'cause she wanted to make sure the acid was working, making my mouth pucker. I could see her wicked smile in the car mirror and she cackled at the effect it had on me. Then she took me home and left me there. My parents were in the next room, fighting or fucking, then the walls started to breathe. All the gypsy bracelets turned into snakes and crawled up my chubby arms. I looked out the window and there was a huge circus going on in the carport with Ferris wheels, clowns, fireworks, and a fun house raging. I didn't know how to tell my parents what was happening, because I'd never heard of this stuff. I knew I'd lost my mind, but *they* didn't have to know. I was totally terrified by this external trip, but the unknown had captured me, and my internal vision would never regain consciousness. My mind was no longer a virgin and would lust for lunacy for many moons. I went right into the radio, sliding into the airwaves every time a song played. I crawled inside the radio, and never came out again."

It was when she heard Don Covay's sultry "Have Mercy Baby" that our brave new worldly doll unloaded the dullsville "Judy" and never looked back. She discovered that the beatniks had fled touristy North Beach and taken over a coffeehouse across from "Panhandle Park" called the Blue Unicorn, where electricity brewed with the coffee. "My first screwing experience was with a beatnik, an older man, up in an attic with rows of mattresses. He ripped open my virginity and took it, and Bob

Dylan plugged in an electric guitar, moaning contagious words of wisdom, and took the world's virginity too. And here came the hippies! I think I also fucked one of the members of the Sopwith Camel."

Mercy soon ran into the multiethnic Bernardo, a breathtaking androgynous creature who inspired her to throw away the bellbottom jeans and become more multihued. She was gaga over the ringleted Romeo, but he had a penchant for the boys. Still, they recognized a similar madness and became quite an alarming team.

Just like most parents of teenagers in that disorderly era, Mercy's hardworking mom didn't have a clue how to handle her suddenly unrecognizable daughter. "I didn't have a home life. My mother was at work all the time and my dad had already tried to commit suicide three times. The poor man had no idea what amphetamines were doing to him. He destroyed his liver and pancreas and couldn't drink. I never wanted to go home, and when I did they told me I couldn't go to Haight-Ashbury anymore. So I said, 'Just take me to the juvenile authorities. I'd rather be locked up.' So they did."

Mercy was in and out of juvie, and the worst part for her was when they confiscated her diet pills. She remembers arguing with fellow bad-girl inmates about what station to listen to. "We fought over the radio. The blacks had the radio on Sunday, which *I* didn't mind at all because I loved black music by that point." Strangely, despite her being incarcerated, some of Mercy's new friends spotted her out on the scene. "People would say they saw me at Fillmore when I was locked up because I was transcendentally meditating myself to places I wanted to be. I'm serious."

One deep night something happened that briefly catapulted Mercy out of her teenage jail cell. "Juvenile hall was way up on a high hill and I woke up when this light started flashing in the playground—this thing spun down, a saucer, just like you see in the movies, a big silver disc—it hovered above and in color vibrations it said, 'Walls cannot hold your soul,' then Star-Trekked down to the ground. I never forgot that. Walls cannot hold your soul." Soon after this extraordinary incident, a kindly probation officer from Youth Authority took pity on Mercy, giving her an afternoon to gather some belongings to bring back. Silly man. Instead, she flew the coop with Bernardo, splitting immediately for L.A.

Mercy hadn't been in Hollyweird long before she found herself ensnared in Miss Christine's vault bedroom at the Zappa cabin with six GTO's. We madly scribbled nutty prose for the upcoming album, while our newest member crossed her arms and glowered. From somewhere under her zany layered ensemble, an embellished diary appeared, upon which was scrawled "Scarlet & Merry Gold." Astoundingly, she began to jot down some words of her own, then presented her offering, a startling little ditty entitled "Shock Treatment." A few days later she handed us our album title as well—*Permanent Damage*. A condition she was obviously quite familiar with.

Gradually Mercy began to grow on us, like a garish barnacle with a screw loose, and the discovery of the obsessive groupie heart lurking under all those belts, vests, and scarves clinched the deal.

We were lounging on Christine's ancient multipatterned quilt after a songwriting session, and we opened a box of crayons to write our rock star sex wish lists on the wall above her bed. Mick Jagger was my number one, and since Brian Jones was Mercy's pick to lick, we bonded in empathetic Rolling Stones awareness. It turned out "Scarlet" was her secret name for the brazenly bisexual Bernardo, and "Merry Gold" was a reminder of Mr. Jones's cheeky wit and gleaming golden locks. Despite her eerie aura, I soon discovered Mercy was a chick after my own heart. We got sisterly close, but it was years before she revealed Judy Peters, the flip side of the fearsome Mercy Fontenot.

Brian was the only white guy on Mercy's list. The rest were fine black soul brothers. I forget her entire list, but I do recall several old blues guys like Howlin' Wolf, Bo Diddley, and Muddy Waters. Also Bobby Womack and Wilson Pickett, along with a Temptation or two. I remember she adored David Ruffin, and that ingenious ol' sleazeball Chuck Berry. We all believed that our horny wishes would come true. I managed to merge with my entire hit list with the exception of Bob Dylan—but hey, I'm not dead yet, right?

Oddly enough, Mercy discovered she had a penchant for country music. This unlikely notion came through our pal Gram Parsons, cofounder of the very first country-rock band, the Flying Burrito Brothers. Gram called this newfound genre "cosmic American music," and together Mercy and I glammed up in nutty gypsy feather lace chiffon cowpoke outfits to check out the Burritos in all sorts of seedy country-and-western dives. We somehow managed to dance our colorful asses off to original Burrito tunes and country ditties such as "Six Days on the Road" and the tragic George Jones opus "She Thinks I Still Care." The rest of the GTO's snickered about our devotion to Merle Haggard and Waylon Jennings, but Mercy and I were proudly broadening our musical horizons. She certainly enhanced my appreciation of the blues and the steamy sexiness of R & B.

Even though I was consuming plenty of illegal substances myself, I worried about Mercy's constant state of intoxication. She had already taken hundreds of acid trips, and was way too familiar with a cornucopia of pharmaceutical delights, thanks to her dad and his skinny model gal pal. She was always up, over, under, sideways, or down, to paraphrase the Yardbirds, but her special relationship with angel dust really freaked me out. She huffed that sickly sweet, minty joint and her mind conjured up all sorts of twisted out-of-the-question scenarios. When she started dabbling with heroin and needles, she was really breaking the rules. I was perpetually worried that our mentor, the oh-so-drug-free Mr. Zappa, would find out about her nasty illegal habits and bust up our groupie group. In fact, several of the GTO's were breaking that critical rule and becoming hard drug devotees. Even after a blotto Brian Jones drowned in his Winnie the Pooh swimming pool in the British countryside, Mercy kept on popping, dropping, and shooting up with alarming frequency.

She was heart shattered about Brian "Merry Gold" Jones succumbing to his hellacious habits, the first rock star to hit the high road at age twenty-seven. And she was devastated when

Otis Redding and most of his band, the BarKays, died in a plane crash soon after she saw them perform at the Monterey Pop Festival. She carried around a photo torn out of *Jet* magazine—a chilling shot of the soul god, covered in icicles, frozen to his seat after being pulled from the cold, merciless sea.

Sure enough, my frantic fears were realized when Mercy and Christine were caught crimson-handed with the bad goods. Christine's folks took her back to San Pedro, but Mercy spent a couple dismal months behind bars at Sybil Brand. Meanwhile, Frank disbanded and disowned the GTO's, even threatening to shelve our treasured *Permanent Damage*.

When Mercy got out of the clink, her newfound friend Chuck Wein was there to gather her up. Also known as the Wizard, Chuck was a cosmic director-protégé of Andy Warhol embarking on his own feature film, *Rainbow Bridge*, to be shot in Hawaii. He gave Mercy the choice part of playing herself, and she was soon perched on the edge of a volcano with costar Jimi Hendrix. "Jimi broke down and did the movie when they gave him angel dust," she recalls. "I danced on stage with him. I was really high on pot and dust. It changed all the dimensions. I loved that horrifying drug." In one of Mercy's zonky visions, she saw the gloomy future. "Over this bridge comes Jimi and his manager, Michael Jeffries, and I'm looking at them and it's very Star-Trekkie. Suddenly they turn into little glimmering things and fall to the ground, like holograms. I saw them both disappear into thin air, and then they really did." True, Michael Jeffries soon died in a plane crash, and Jimi OD'd in London. "The first time I ever saw Jimi at the Monterey Pop Festival, I thought he was Mick Jagger in black face," Mercy suddenly remembers. "I was high on the STP they put in the punch, and he was at the top of the stairs with Brian Jones. I thought they were Brian and Mick."

While the GTO's waited around, hoping our personal opus would be released, Mercy decided to hitchhike to Memphis so she could be in close proximity to the remaining BarKays. She had just taken up with an extremely talented youngster, seventeen-year-old guitar whiz Shuggie Otis, son of legend Johnny Otis, and they were in the process of driving each other crazy. A few weeks earlier she had dreamed she would soon meet her future husband and described the boy pretty accurately. She moved in with the family and enjoyed being around blues masters like Big Joe Turner and Charles Brown, who recorded for Johnny's label, Blues Spectrum, but she was spun out on speed and too wrapped up in the troubled teenager. "I just wanted to get away from Shuggie because he was all I could think about. He dominated my whole life, and it wasn't *going* anywhere—and besides, I always had a crush on the BarKays."

After a perilous cross-country hitchhike, Mercy and her friend Marquise found their way to mecca—the parking lot of Stax Records. But the vibrant white chicks weren't alone for long. "Yeah, I wanted to sleep with the BarKays," Mercy admits. "They were freaky looking, talented blacks." Instead of the BarKays, however, the girls were approached by legendary musician Teenie Hodges, who wondered if they'd like to check out another studio across town. "These were session guys—the Hodges boys from Hi Records. They took us out to the ghetto, to this little poverty-stricken Royal Studios, and cut some tracks really fast. They were amazing, and I said, 'Oh my God, *listen* to these guys.'" After the tunes were recorded, Mercy and Marquise went along for the ride to meet the singer. "They took me over to a tract house to pick up this guy from Detroit. When he opened the door, he said, 'My name is Al Green,' and I said, 'Fine.'"

The singer's slick suit and trenchcoat seemed pretty square to Mercy, so when he asked if she'd like to share a little intimacy, she declined. "He didn't seem like my type. At that time he had a hit record, a cover of the Temptations' 'I Can't Get Next To You,' and we ran around to the record stores looking for it." Then they all went back to the studio so Al could lay down his vocal tracks. "And then I said, 'Oh my God! What is *this*?'"

After the mind-boggling session, the group headed for Hernando's Hideaway, a club partly owned by Elvis himself, on the outskirts of town. Everybody was smoking pot, and Mercy was kicking herself under her stratum of skirts for turning Al Green down. "Of course, if I had heard him sing I would have said yes right away."

Martin Luther King Jr. had been killed a year before and civil unrest was raging, but Mercy was such a progressive misfit she didn't understand why she and Marquise had to duck down as they drove through certain parts of town. "I was an out-to-lunch hippie. I didn't know why I had to get out of the car in certain areas, and why whites and blacks were meeting at Hernando's Hideaway. The house band was Ronnie Milsap. A lot of black musicians were playing with Elvis at the time and they talked about how great he was. You had Steve Cropper, the BarKays, and Booker T. meeting on the outskirts of town."

Mercy says being with Teenie Hodges in Memphis was like hanging out with God. "The BarKays started paying attention to us and we even got Ike Turner in that mix. We were the only white people in the place." I ask Mercy if she felt exotic. "What do you mean *exotic*? We were *white*! Ike Turner took us to the hotel where these crazy lesbians were eating each other out, and he asked me to stay, and I told him Marquise was my girlfriend." Poor cheatin' Ike, Mercy had her heart set on Al Green. "I tried to call Al from a phone booth and a girl answered, so I let it go."

Back in L.A. Mercy got more hung up on Shuggie, but since he was running around with other girls, she decided to write Al Green a little note and included her phone number. "I walked in the door one night after a date with Shuggie and my room-mate tells me Al Green called. In front of Shuggie! It was a few months after I met him, and Al was getting really huge, filling auditoriums." Turns out Al Green had called Mercy from Disneyland, where he was performing. The next time he called, Mercy was home. "I picked up the phone and he said, 'Come on over here.'"

Al was tantalized by Mercy's letter, asking if she had written it by herself. "I told him I didn't have anybody write it for me and he was amazed. I was on speed and the whole thing was very dramatic." Mercy was much thinner and wore a long, white, clingy Moroccan robe to seduce America's foremost soul singer. "I was kinda cute then and he said, 'Oh my God, you've lost a lot of weight.' He smoked pot you know," she adds conspiratorially. "Here was the greatest sex star on the planet and there I was, getting high with him." Mercy remembers that Al had an elaborate tape deck system, and as they made love he played his own songs over and over, the entire time. "It was all set up," she recalls. "I remember thinking he was ego ridden. All through the sex, he listened to himself, one tape after another."

Mercy didn't know whether to be offended or grateful the next morning when Al opened a suitcase full of money. "The finishing touch was when he gave me five dollars. His entire suitcase was full of cash, because he got paid the night before at the Forum. He opened it up and gave me *five dollars*. Thanks, Al, yeah . . ." When Mercy opened the hotel room door to leave, she says two of Al's female employees had their ears pressed so tight to the door, they literally fell at her feet. "I read later they were blackmailing him," she says. "I didn't see him again because soon after that, I moved in with Shuggie."

When she hears Al's music, does Mercy think about that long ago night? "Always. It trips me out. I go back to being there with him. He was an extremely funny guy. I don't know why I didn't pursue that one."

As the GTO's came to an end, Mercy's lovefest with the teenage guitar genius and her dangerous liason with speed consumed her life. Shuggie was high on coke and often on the road with his dad. He was also dallying with the daughter of a blues great as well as one of the Otisettes. Because Mercy was jealous and wanted to make Shuggie green-eyed too, she had an encounter of the strangest kind at the Happiest Place on Earth the night Johnny Otis opened for edgy legend Chuck Berry. "I had my uppers and downers and Valiums and everything, and I took a handful of meds and got *really* loaded. Shuggie was with this girl, Terry, and they just disappeared together."

Mercy had always been intrigued by Mr. Berry, so when he rolled down the road at Disneyland, she was ready for him. "This Cadillac comes creeping along and Chuck gets out and I say, 'Oh, man, I've been waiting for you all my life,' and he says, 'Well, come on!' So we go into his trailer and I have two things going in my brain at the same time: I really want to go home with Chuck because I want to see what his life's all about, and the second thing is I'm gonna try to make Shuggie jealous. I had this dueling banjo in my head, and like I said, I was so loaded that I cannot remember what took place in that trailer. I think I went to bed with Chuck because his wife showed up, mad. And he had this fascination with people going number two, so he had me go to the bathroom in this bucket—I do remember *that*—and he took a photo of me and said, 'I have a collection of everybody that I have sex with.' There's a knock at the door and someone says, 'You're on, Chuck.' So I get up and I walk out of the trailer with him, and he lets me carry his guitar. I'm thinking, 'Oh, man, this is it. This is *really* it; I am gonna make Shuggie so jealous!' But I look around and there's nobody backstage to witness this."

In spite of the pie-eyed chaos and constant tribulation, months later, when Mercy got pregnant, the only recourse was for her and nineteen-year-old Shuggie to tie the knot. "I'm sorry, but I don't really remember my pregnancy. Here I am, getting fat again, after I got skinny—but I thought I was happy at that point."

During her pregnancy, Mercy's father finally managed to kill himself—sitting at a table in her mother's apartment, dressed up in a suit and tie. Always a fan of celebrities (he kept a snapshot of himself posing with Ann-Margret in his wallet), he addressed his suicide note to a couple of stars of current TV commercials: "I've had a good life here, don't be sad. I want to say goodbye to Rodney Allen Rippey and Morris the Cat."

Mercy did stop taking speed while she was pregnant, and I remember visiting her in the hospital. Originally she was going to call her baby boy "Jinx," but thought better of it and finally settled on "Lucky." But even the precious bundle couldn't change the misery around him. Once Mercy came home to find that Lucky's daddy had hacked off all his divine blond ringlets. "Shuggie had a violent, violent, violent, violent, violent temper. They were giving him antidepressants—he was chemically imbalanced. One time he tried to choke me and his dad came

With Lucky.
Credit: Shuggie Otis

in and hit him. He said, 'I've never hit you before in your life, but you cannot choke your wife.'" The raucous marriage lasted three years.

Mercy took Lucky and moved in with her mother in Santa Monica where she continued self-medicating with a vengeance. "It's in my blood, from my father," she sighs. Arriving back in town, Mercy discovered a raw new sound shattering the big-haired complacency. "Anywhere something starts rumbling, I'm there," she insists. "From the hippies on, every decade, I've been there. I started getting into the punk scene. You could feel the energy of something erupting."

Mercy became an integral part of the punk world, went to beautician's school on Hollywood Boulevard, and soon had her bejeweled fingers in ducktails and beehives all over town. "I don't know how I got into hairstyling. I could just take somebody and alter their looks and I loved that." Her specialty was "extreme rockabilly," and she created radical looks for the Rockats and Rockabilly Rebels, and even got her hands in Darby Crash's bristly locks. She got romantically involved with Brendan Mullen, the astute entrepreneur who opened the infamous Masque nightclub in Hollywood. "He invented punk," she spits. "OK?"

It was about this time, when Mercy was skinny, spiky, and punked out that she ran into a certain well-muscled up-and-comer on a neighborhood street near the beach. "This guy picked me up by the belt loops and asked me to come visit him. I only recognized him because he was all over the TV—his first movie had just come out." Mercy turned up at the stranger's home and smoked pot with him and his bodybuilder buddies. "He was telling me all the things he was going to do, how famous he was going to be. He probably even told me he was going to be governor and was already plotting that." After some small talk, Arnold Schwarzenegger grabbed Mercy by the arms. "He pinned me up against the wall and said, 'I'd like to know what it's like to go to bed with you.' And I said, 'You'll never know.' He was scary to me, even though he's much smaller in person than you think he is."

When her mother got breast cancer and passed away, Mercy's life became even more rough and tumble, and Lucky went to live with her former in-laws, Johnny and Phyllis Otis.

Through her old GTO partner Miss Lucy, Mercy slammed into Love's wild man Arthur Lee, who was trying to help Lucy get into an AIDS clinic. He was in between jail stints and Mercy soon found herself in grubby porno hotels with another of her favorite musicians. "Well, he watched porno. I didn't," she says firmly. "But I've always idolized him. He's such a genius in the studio." They had a brief, crazy affair until they met up with the cops late one night. "Art and I stopped seeing each other when we got pulled over by the police. They almost took him away, until I said, 'Do you know who this guy is?' I started singing 'My Little Red Book,' and they cut him loose. He took me to Jack in the Box and said, 'You know, we've gotta split up,' so we did."

I had been concerned about Mercy's death-defying habits for a long time, but even at her lowest point, she still retained her acerbic good humor, firebrand quotability, and gaudy élan. Somehow her total and utter *Mercyness* stayed intact.

When she hooked up with a fellow she met on the crack circuit, I knew I was in for more hand-wringing. Leonard was dark eyed and good looking, a former air force vet with a monthly paycheck, which was part of the reason Mercy moved in with him and eventually married him. "We were a lot alike, but I had no idea he was so violent or I would have never dealt with him. One day he just started beating the crap outta me, but by that time I was too far gone. Once you start doing crack, you just dive into it." They smoked Leonard's entire check every month, and pretty soon the rent became an afterthought and they were living on the street, sleeping under the Hollywood freeway. I often found Mercy pushing a shopping cart, prodding through dumpsters for leftovers or something to sell. "Was crack your every waking thought?" I ask. "*Waking*?" she snickers. "There was never any *sleep*." It went on for years.

"Yes, it went on and on, and when he bashed my face in I was gonna leave but I *couldn't* because I was stuck to him financially and I thought he'd *change*."

It took awhile, but amazingly, Leonard *did* change. He put crack down and picked up a decent job at a Goodwill store downtown. But Mercy stubbornly kept smoking until the Easter Sunday she couldn't find her pipe. "I had put it out by the garbage cans and couldn't find the damn thing. So I said, 'That's it.' Never to pick up again." After a beat Mercy adds, "Well, you gotta hit *bottom* sometime." She started going to AA meetings and reconnected with her gifted, charming, and tolerant son, Lucky.

I've made certain to stay in touch with my outrageous pal, whatever shape she might be in, and our friendship took an unforeseen shift in 1998 when my sweet mother, Margaret, moved in with me. I took the newly clean and sober Mercy to the hospital to visit with her, and it was evident in their comfortable chitchat that, despite appearances, down deep Mercy and Mama were kindred spirits. Although Mercy worked part-time at Goodwill with Leonard, she came to my house and entertained

With Lucky.
Credit: Pamela Des Barres

my mother three days a week, which blessedly gave me time to run errands and write.

Three years later when Mama passed away from a lifetime of puffing Pall Malls and Virginia Slims, Mercy made an eloquent, wry speech at her funeral. She surprised us all by putting a toy gorilla that sang the "Macarena" in Mom's casket to keep her company—because it had cracked them up so many times.

Mercy is now an auction clerk at www.shopgoodwill.com in Los Angeles, listing an array of unique hand-picked items that are snatched up daily by happy bidders. She is eight years sober (yay!), but sadly, Leonard went back to his dismal old habits and they haven't seen each other in over two years. She lived with me for awhile after she found him smoking crack with a hooker, and recently got her own pad in a grandiose, antique building downtown, not too far from Skid Row.

Luckily (it's good she didn't call him Jinx!), her son Lucky was blessed with the bluesy Otis bloodline. He played bass with his revered grandfather in *The Johnny Otis Show* for several years and is an esteemed musician in his own right. Her lanky, hazel-eyed boy is now hosting his grandfather's radio show, showcasing the same music that his mother was devoted to back in juvenile hall.

That Mercy is here to tell this tale is a downright miracle, since her hazardous life has consistently been in jeopardy. The night Janis Joplin OD'd, Mercy was with their dealer. "He was on his way to see Janis and he said, 'I want you to try this heroin,' but didn't tell me why—so I did it while he sat by with a shot of coke. I said, 'I'm going down too fast,' so he gave me the coke to bring me up, watching everything I did. Later that night, I heard on the radio that Janis had *died*."

So much of her time was spent high and looking to get high, does Mercy wonder what might have happened if she had made different choices? "Oh, yeah, all the time," she admits freely. "Opportunities just knocked at my door and I sat down and got stupid . . . got *stupid*. But I married Shuggie, who I *dreamed* I was gonna marry, who I really wanted to marry: that was my main goal in life. And I'm sure it was to produce Lucky. Yeah, sometimes I go back and think, 'Why didn't I pursue Al Green instead of Shuggie Otis?' Maybe things would have changed, maybe I would have ended up with Al. But if I had taken any other road, there would be no Lucky, and as much as I've screwed up with him, he's the real reason I'm still on the planet."

After all the ups and lowdowns she has experienced, Ms. Mercy Fontenot is still the most memorable, uncompromising, point-blank woman in any room. Her very presence is a vivid reminder that walls cannot hold your soul. "If I could sing," she tells me finally, "the title of my song would be, 'The Blues Ain't Nothin' but a Color, Baby.'"

Michele Overman

Love in Her Eyes and Flowers in Her Hair

I was twirling all over the dance floor at the Palomino club as the Flying Burrito Brothers played their cosmic American music to a handful of devoted diehards. Lost in the final notes of the strum and twang, I was pleasantly brought back to the smoke-filled honky-tonk by a blonde sweet-teen who had noticed the sparkly cross around my neck. "I know you're wearing that cross because you love Jesus," she purred. The chiffon-clad sylph soon joined Miss Mercy and me on the floor, and as the evening progressed, she and I fell in love the way only hippie-chick flower children could back in the intoxicating spring of 1969.

I immediately wanted to touch her, and she returned the favor, stroking me with babysoft intensity, her huge aqua eyes brimming with delight. After a couple more tunes, we rushed to the ladies room to find out more about each other, and it was quickly revealed that she was there to see the Burritos' front man, Gram Parsons. They had recently spent a romance-filled four days in New York, and Michele was taking a chance tonight, hoping for a reunion. Alas, it wasn't to be, as Gram had just gotten back together with his ladylove Nancy, but Michele put on a brave, beautiful face and took it in stride. My adored Chris Hillman wasn't giving me the time of night either, so Michele and I kissed each other's rock and roll wounds and found wistful solace in our instant camaraderie. The impish newcomer from Manhattan and I quickly discovered we were soul sisters, simpatico spiritual seekers, and, eventually, roommates.

In spite of our full-plate lifestyles, Michele and I have remained close friends, and I hop a jet to Portland to hang with her for a few days. When she throws open the door of the apartment she shares with her (much younger) boyfriend Evan, I marvel once again at how childlike she is. Michele has retained all the qualities I was mad for the day we met—open-hearted innocence, wide-eyed expectancy, and an innate sweetness that lights her up like a candle in the moonlight.

After a couple of days catching up, Michele takes me to a vividly green park where we spread out on a blanket and reminisce. She has amazing recall. "I remember very well the first time we saw Zeppelin together," she laughs. "We hitchhiked out to the Long Beach Arena, which was our typical mode of transportation in those days. You knew Jimmy was interested in you because everybody kept sending you messages telling you so. Robert and I were together already and he told me, 'Jimmy really wants Miss Pamela,' and to pass the message along. Ah, yes, I remember it well."

Before young Michele danced with me at the Palomino, she had already dallied with Zeppelin's twenty-year-old singer during their debut American tour. "When I first met Robert, they were staying at this second-tier hotel, the Gorham, and every groupie in New York was after him. He was *un*believably gorgeous."

On both coasts, word was out that the four lads in Led Zeppelin were way too risky. "I saw them at the Scene and everybody said, 'This guy Robert really likes you,' but I was intimidated by him because I knew every groupie, including the really hard-core chicks like Devon Wilson, was after him, and I didn't want to get involved. The night of their concert we were at Ratner's, a Jewish dairy restaurant next door, and Robert saw me and came over. 'Oh, there you are. Would you like to come up and see my etchings?' He literally said that to me. He was just a boy, a

February 1969.
Credit: Michele Overman
collection

man-boy, and I was slightly intrigued, but then they *played*, and after that . . ." Yes indeed. When you saw Led Zeppelin play, it was all over but the orgasm.

"I was standing in the back of the theater, and I could not believe my eyes. He was wearing a green velvet suit and he threw the microphone up in the air and introduced himself—'My name is Robert Plant.' I thought, 'If this guy likes me the way everybody says he does, he's gonna get me because he's totally IT!'"

Long before she attracted the Golden God, Michele had already led quite an unorthodox life, raised by her bohemian maverick mother in a tiny Greenwich Village walk-up, surrounded by hipness. "My mother, Gina, was definitely one of a kind, way ahead of her time, and took a lot of flack for her beliefs. In those days, it took a lot of guts to be different. She was absolutely gorgeous. I think she was just born weird. But as nutty as she was, her kids came before everything, so I always felt loved and cherished."

She was adored but free as an uncaged canary, haunting coffee bars and rock clubs while her mother worked nights as a waitress. "When I was very young I wanted to live like Ozzie and Harriet," Michele admits. "I wanted stairs with carpeting and a pool in the backyard, a dad in the house and a kitchen where we'd all have breakfast around the dining table in the morning."

Michele and her older sister, Franny, never saw their missing-in-action father, however, and Gina served up dishes that Beaver Cleaver couldn't even imagine. "My mother was a spiritual seeker. She got into Zen Buddhism and was one of the first people in New York on the macrobiotic diet. When I was eleven, she became a vegetarian, and I grew up on brown rice."

Living with an eccentric mother sometimes took its toll on the girls. "When you're a kid and your mother is weird, walking around barefoot, even in the Village, people made fun of her and it was embarrassing. But she was true to herself and brought us up the best way she knew how."

At least Michele didn't have to sneak out to smoke her first joint. "It was kind of cool, I smoked pot with my mom one time and she said, 'You know, this is very nice, but I'm like this all the time *anyway*.' It was true."

Even though I know Michele grew up with music all around her, I ask why she started falling for musicians. "My very first love, my first crush in kindergarten, was Elvis Presley." I should have known since I also discovered Elvis at a very young, love-me-tender age and never got over it. "I had fantasies that he would come pick me up from class and wheel me away on a cot. I actually got as far as lying down on this portable bed with Elvis. Pretty precocious, huh?"

As a young teen, Michele was free to roam the world's trendiest streets. "My mom knew a lot of jazz musicians and artsy people, so it wasn't a foreign milieu to me. In those days there were folk singers in the park every weekend, and I was always around people playing music, so it was normal. The first job

February 1969.
Credit: Michele
Overman collection

I had after school was at the Night Owl Café, where a lot of groups got started: the Lovin' Spoonful, Dylan, the Mamas and Papas, the Doors."

Even a freewheeling hippie chick had to make a buck, and Michele's second job had her modeling in the window at Betsey Johnson's original Greenwich Village boutique, Paraphernalia. "It was so much fun. All the gay guys would come up to me and say, 'We just want to tell you how *fab-u-lous* you are; we love watching you dance in the window!' I have this incredible photograph, a double exposure of me on my little platform—and an old couple, a man and a woman, looking in the window, smiling at me."

It made perfect sense that Michele's first love would be a musician. Ralph Scala was eighteen and Michele only fourteen when they began their passion fest. "When you're first in love, the whole world revolves around this person—all your happiness hinges on them." Ralph's band, the Blues McGoos, had a hit song, "Ain't Seen Nothing Yet," and he took Michele on the road with her mother's blessing.

The band moved into the au courant residential Hotel Albert, home to a plethora of struggling rockers, and Michele moved in with them. "I was literally getting fucked during lunch break, then I'd trot back to high school. And sexually, I had no idea how lucky I was. I didn't know yet that all guys weren't so considerate of their partner's feelings. He was an incredible lover, and I remember my first orgasm. I wasn't trying to have one, when all of a sudden, spontaneously, it felt like my insides were rushing out my body, and I thought, 'So *that's* what everybody's talking about!' I was fifteen years old."

Despite the divine orgasms, Michele was getting antsy, thinking about other rock guys while gamboling in the sack with Ralph. The young couple broke up, and she soon came across another sexy fledgling musician, Steven Tallarico. "In '68 there was a club in the Village called Stone the Crows, where this wild guy sang with his band, Chain Reaction. He was oh-so-cute with his exaggerated Beatles mop top." Steven Tallarico later altered his Italian moniker somewhat, formed Aerosmith, and became Steven Tyler. And he still makes the little girls swoon. But back in 1968, the beloved only child still lived with his folks in Yonkers.

Steven's upbringing mirrored Michele's, and the two renegades were soon crazy about each other. "His dad was a jazz musician and his parents were away a lot, so Steven had the house, just north of New York City, and it became an essential hangout. We did so many drugs—not anything really serious, we took a lot of acid, smoked tons of pot. The one and only time I did chloroform was with Steven. You put it on a cloth, inhale, and get really fucked up."

Seventeen-year-old Michele and nineteen-year-old Steven had a chaotic fling that lasted almost a year. "Steven was a maniac, he was just nuts," she marvels. "He had *so* much personality—just one of those people with no brakes, no filter, just total id. He used to freak me out, doing things like squashing a banana through his teeth. He had this huge mouth and the goop would come squirting out everywhere!"

Modelling at
Paraphernalia.
Credit: Michele
Overman collection

I think Steven Tyler is one of the hottest men ever, so I ask about their amorous adventures. "He was the *best* lover. I mean, he was the *absolute* best," she assures me. "He lived in the attic on the top floor of the house. He had speakers on either side of his pillows, and when you laid in bed, you were immersed in this wall of sound. He used to make this sexy blowing noise in my ear," she says, demonstrating with a gentle whooshing sound. "Yeah, I gotta give him all the credit for being a wonderful lover. He was very uninhibited, physically and sexually free, and in touch with his body." Does she remember any of the music coming out of those pillowside speakers? "He used to play an album by the Hollies all the time, and now, whenever I hear that song 'Hey, Carrie Ann,' I think of making love with Steven Tyler."

Chain Reaction played the coolest clubs in New York, and Michele enjoyed watching Steven take over a room. "One night they played Salvation, a circular club with a dance floor in the middle. Steven was the front man, but he played all the instruments: the keyboard, the lead guitar, the bass, and he got behind the drums. You knew he was gonna be famous because he was such a madman. You *had* to be that kind of brave, brilliant, and over the top to make it."

The Yonkers house became a crash pad, and Michele had to step over piles of stoners to get ready for school. "He picked me up from high school one day, and I even remember what I was wearing: this pretty, fitted dress made out of an Indian bedspread. He handed me a pill and I asked, 'What *is* it?' and he said, 'Oh, it's just a mild upper,' so I took it. I brought it up years later and he swears it didn't happen this way, but I remember it well. The acid was very strong, and we got wrecked at the Circus club in the East Village that actually had a circus going on with trapeze artists and clowns."

The ribald ride became a bit overwhelming for Michele, and she spent less and less time romping in the sexy attic. "As much as I loved being with Steven and was attracted to him physically—and the sex was phenomenal—I realized I just wasn't in love with him. And the drugs didn't help any. In the end, it didn't jibe with my romantic vision of how it was supposed to be. I wasn't even eighteen and just too young to be tied down."

It was just a few weeks later that Michele dolled up in her suede Pocahontas mini to see the Flying Burrito Brothers at the Scene. "Oh my God, I loved their music. I played *The Gilded Palace of Sin* 'til my ears fell off. It was always the music that got me, and if the guy was gorgeous like Gram was, it certainly didn't hurt! He had just gone through a horrible break up with his fiancée and his heart was battered. He told me I helped him heal, that I was good for him. He was really genuine. Ooh, he had this incredible skin," she gushes, "and those hands—oh my God, the most unbelievable hands I've ever seen."

Which brings us back to that sultry night at the Palomino. After the Burritos gig, Michele came home with me and stayed.

It wasn't too long before we had our thumbs out, hitching a ride to the Long Beach Arena to see the bad boys of rock, Led Zeppelin.

"When I met Robert, his album was 'number eighty with a bullet.' He wasn't famous yet, but you could see the writing on the wall. I can literally say I met him before the world knew who he was. He was so excited. For a country boy from the Midlands, being on the charts was a very big deal." Michele's time with Robert in New York was all too brief. "He said, 'Damn it, why didn't you take me with you when we first got here? We could have had a couple of weeks together!'" The day before he flew back to his little family in England, Robert got Michele high and they focused on a calendar full of fairies and elves. Michele says they "totally clicked."

"Somebody had spilled a cup of coffee on the calendar and ruined it. He was really upset because his aesthetic was, like, the depths of Mordor, Gollum, gnomes, and all that, so we spent the last day looking *all* over New York, trying to find another calendar. I was thinking, 'I really want a boyfriend, but this guy doesn't live in America.' Then I saw a picture of his baby daughter, and thought, just like Scarlett O'Hara, 'I'll think about that another day.'"

When Zep came back to the United States on their second tour, a pal called to tell her she had bumped into "that guy Robert Plant" at the Scene. "He told her that I was the only person in America he wanted to see. Of course, I was flattered." Robert brought his wife to L.A., but her brief presence was only a temporary setback. "Sure enough, as soon as she left, I contacted him and he told me to come over and we started going out. Whenever he was in L.A., he would call me and I was, like, his L.A. chick. The news really got around; everybody knew about us. Sure, I was aware he was married, but was somehow able to compartmentalize that. I just didn't think of the consequences and started to fall in love with him."

I had a similar experience when I tried to avoid Jimmy Page's long-distance advances. And when he had his road manager, Richard Cole, pass me a note requesting my presence at the

Hyatt House, I simply tucked it away. But he somehow wrangled my phone number and gallantly invited me to their Long Beach show, and my flimsy resolve deserted me.

"You bought this little gingerbread man dressed up like an astronaut to give to Jimmy as a greeting gift, remember? We hitchhiked down to Long Beach, and Richard Cole put us right on the side of the stage." We were the only girls onstage that night, and Michele and I still savor the remarkable feeling of being welcomed into that irresistible inner sanctum. It was the headiest, swooniest rock and roll experience possible. Jimmy was just about to entertain the surging masses, and when he saw me there, his angelic face lit up. Those were the heaviest heavenly moments in the world. Michele agrees, laughing, "Yeah, and you know what's funny, now that we're talking about all this stuff? You're starting to look just like you did back then! It's true, your face just morphed into this eager twenty-year-old."

Our gushing recollections:

Michele: I remember we got so excited at one point you reached back and grabbed my pussy.

Pamela: I don't remember that!

Michele: After the show, Robert introduced you to Jimmy, and you two were inseparable. He flew you all over the place—Robert never took me anywhere because he was married and had to be discreet.

Pamela: How did it feel to be romantically involved with Robert?

Michele: Ahhh, I remember he had these gorgeous golden curls at the back of his neck, this perfect row of ringlets, and he had hair on the small of his back. He was so leonine. He *is* a Leo, a gorgeous *lion*, a honeypot of a man. There was incredible power and heat that came off his body.

Pamela: He sure had reams of self-confidence.

Michele: Very much a Leo—outgoing, warm, and passionate. Even though he told me years later that he was nervous in those days, he never gave that impression to anybody.

Pamela: Remember those shirts I made for Jimmy?

Michele: Yes, each one was so unique, and I decided to make something for Robert: a hand-embroidered vest of purple felt. I put his initials on each side surrounded by rhinestones, and sewed each sequin one by one, then embroidered Alice in Wonderland holding a bottle with "DRINK ME" on one side, which was my little alter ego. On the other side was a lion, of course. On the back I embroidered the Cheshire cat in a lemon tree—because "The Lemon Song" had just come out. I gave it to you to give Robert because you were going on the road with the band.

Pamela: We went to New York that time.

Michele: I put you on the plane and you went off with Jimmy. I was so thrilled. You brought me a letter from Robert that said, "Dear Alice, My face is too creased from the smile to say much. I'm writing from my place amongst the branches." He went on to say how much he loved the vest, and signed it "Cheshire Cat." He wore that vest at every single concert for that entire tour. I think he wore it until it fell off his back.

Pamela: It was such a blast when we all hung out together.

Michele: Yeah! Remember that time you teased Jimmy? You and I went to Disneyland on mescaline and the lecherous Three Little Pigs chased us. It was like all the characters came alive and we frolicked with them, tripping out of our brains. And when we got home you and I spontaneously started making out . . .

Pamela: Was that the first time?

Michele: No, we had kissed before. I wanted to keep going, but you said, "I can't do it," and I said, "Don't stop now!" But you weren't ready, so we didn't go any further.

Pamela: That's the closest I ever came to actual girl-girl sex.

Michele: So you told Jimmy that we had made out, and of course he totally wanted a replay so he could watch, and I thought, "You little vixen, that's why you told him—you *knew* he was gonna get all hot and bothered!"

Whenever the mighty Zeppelin slammed into town, Michele was installed in Robert's room but sometimes felt like a shameful secret. "He didn't want our relationship to become too public because he was married. He was being interviewed once and they were taking pictures. As usual, I was *there*, but had to be off to the side. He took my hand and put it on his head so at least some part of me would be in the picture."

There were a lot of married Brits on the road, but the family back home didn't seem to put a dent in their love lives. Robert proudly displayed Michele at the clubs, and one steamy night, he told her he was in love with her. "He only had eyes for me, and it was such a feather in my cap because everybody wanted this guy. Their nose tips were twitching—all the groupies were having a feeding frenzy—but it was ME he wanted."

She could never actually feel secure because the man she adored always went home to his wife and baby, so Michele made sure Robert knew there were other men in her life. "I remember him telling you to take care of me and keep me away from the 'Flying Hot Dog Brothers,' because I told him I was in love with Gram Parsons. It was only half a lie, and Robert *was* married." Did she ever feel guilty about the duplicitous romance? "I was too young to fully realize the actual impact. I was *so* naive. When he was with me, he was mine."

Robert thought he should meet Michele's mother, so when Zep played New York, he called Gina, and he and Jimmy took her to dinner. The two rockers and the madwoman from Greenwich Village got along famously, discussing blues and jazz and beat poets. This encounter gave Michele hope that Robert was getting serious about her.

Waiting and pining between tours didn't suit her, so Michele decided to make the daring move across the pond. I was already living in London with my fashionable Granny Takes a Trip clothier boyfriend Marty when she arrived. My adorable girl soon realized that her knight was already entangled in yet another illicit affair. "The whole time I was seeing Robert, he was involved with his wife's sister. How could he have been in love with her and in love with me and . . . ?" I remind her that Robert was just a kid back in those glory days. "Yeah, a kid in an ice-cream shop," she agrees, "and with all those *flavors*. Why not have double-chocolate dip and French vanilla?"

When Michele arrived in England, Robert suggested she stay with Zep's infamous road manager, Richard Cole, at his house in the country. But not wanting to be sequestered, Michele opted to move in with a wild friend in the heart of London. "I loved Jeanette dearly, but she took a lot of pills and hung out at the Speakeasy. Robert wasn't happy I was staying with her, but I was too young to be tied down to a married man. It was unbearably difficult—he wanted to keep me out in the country, but I didn't want that kind of relationship. He was very upset, and said, 'That's it, we've lost her. She'll be down at the Speak every night taking Mandrax.' I think that was when he decided to stop seeing me, because he wanted to keep me pure in his mind." Still, when she complained about being lonely, Robert attempted to make his California girl happy.

For a few days, she danced on hallowed ground when he invited her into Led Zeppelin's truly private party. "He took me to Headley Grange where they were recording the fourth album. It was this big, drafty old barn, totally secluded, where they could make all the noise they wanted. I stayed with him for a few days, listening to all their new songs."

Some of Robert's gorgeous lyrics were written about his wife's younger sister. How in the world did he juggle it all? When Michele had to leave for an appointment in London, Robert waxed romantic. "When I left, he said: 'Little girl, I have a feeling you and I are gonna be together for a long time. Don't you ever feel that way?' I said, 'No, because I don't want to be disappointed.' I don't know why I said that, but I remember it vividly. In retrospect, maybe I should have stayed and not gone off to that stupid hair appointment. Who knows what might have happened?"

When she complained about being a taboo secret, Robert bristled. "He said, 'That's not gonna get you any closer to the altar,' and it was like, fuck you! How dare he be so cruel to me?" The memory still irks Michele. "I was totally devastated. Meanwhile he was writing 'What Is and What Never Shall Be' for his wife's sister."

Michele saw her erstwhile rock prince only once more in London. "He took me to visit some people selling jewelry from Morocco and said, 'I should buy you something.' I knew it was a parting gift. Then taking me home in the cab, he said, 'Hold me. I just want to remember what it was like.' I recall seeing sweet, sorrowful Michele standing at a bus stop on the King's Road in a dismal gray downpour, sobbing her heart out. "I was very, very heartbroken, as you know." Yes, it definitely was a heartbreaker.

Michele eventually headed for Europe where she spent a few years seeing the sights and driving men wild, then wound up back in New York. Her incomparable mother, Gina, who had become "Govinda" due to a spiritual relationship with guru Meher Baba, passed away and Michele was the one to find her, sprawled on the floor of her tiny Greenwich Village walk-up. Michele spiraled downward and even her closest friends didn't know how to find her. But she never lost her faith. Down deep she was still that sanguine flower child I met at the Palomino. "I think God—my higher power—helped a lot, and realizing I didn't want to be a fucking casualty. I still had self-respect and wanted to do *something* with my life—painting or writing a book. I knew didn't want to die without having contributed anything to the world."

At this tenuous point, Michele met Chris, a restaurateur who took her to Portland, where she still lives. Their relationship lasted several years. Now she's with Evan in the cheery apartment with their beloved pug, Ollie. "My whole life changed when I came here," Michele says as we stroll the shady streets. "I started getting in touch with people I hadn't seen in years—I saw Robert, and Steven, and you—so many people have come back into my life."

Six years ago Aerosmith played Portland and Michele thought it was high time she saw her lusty teen dream again. "I'd seen him in the '80s. I knew his first wife, Cyrinda. We had a mutual friend who said Steven told her I was the best sexual experience of his life, and *that's* on the record."

With Steven Tyler,
October 1997.
Credit: Michele Overman

Michele was busily painting a mural, listening to the radio, and heard that Aerosmith was playing the Coliseum that very night. "I got the backstage number, left a message, and Steven called me back and said, 'Get down here right away!' The concert was great. I hadn't seen him in years and I couldn't believe how energetic he was. I mean, the guy had just turned fifty and he was doing backflips—it was amazing."

While a pack of teenage dolls gave Michele the evil eye, she was escorted backstage just like the good old days. "Steven was really happy to see me, and kept telling me how beautiful I looked. He said, 'I can't get *over* you,' and held my face in his hands. He looked so good and was so sexy, hugging me—his skin was like velvet. We caught up on old times and it was really wonderful."

A few years ago, Masters Page and Plant graced Portland and Michele got up to some old-fashioned mischief. "I marched up to will call and said there were tickets waiting for me, because if Robert knew I was there, he would want to see me. She took my name and came back five minutes later with two tickets and two all-access passes! The band did a great set and Robert said somebody special was in the audience and it was bringing back incredible memories from long ago." Michele looks dreamy eyed. "To be spoken about from the stage was really a trip after so many years. I never thought I'd get that kind of high again, but it happened."

Before Michele left that night, Robert made sure she wouldn't forget their time together. "He said he couldn't understand why we had stopped seeing each other, the years we wasted, the fun we could have had. It was amazing how he remembered every-thing—how we met, that my mother was a Meher Baba lover, the Alice-in-Wonderland vest. He actually remembered the line he used to pick me up: 'Come up to see my etchings.'"

The two passionflowers reignited their specialness again last autumn when Robert hit Portland with his groovy new band, Strange Sensation. "When I saw him backstage, we were totally focused on each other. He was holding me and said, 'So this is what we felt like together.' I laughed and told him, 'I've gotten a little shorter since then,' and he said, 'I have too!' He told me he was talking with his assistant, and she asked if he'd ever been in love with no boundaries to his passion. He said, 'Yes, one time—and that was with you. I should have come back, I *would* have come back, but I had my daughter, Carmen.' I told him I was *so* in love with him back then. He told me he sang 'Going to California' to me that night, that I was the epitome of that era for him, and repre-sented the whole '60s hippie love thing. Then he said we never stop loving somebody, we just paint it a different color. I told him that if I didn't have a mirror or a memory I'd think I was fifteen, because I didn't feel any different. Losing a love relationship when you're that young forms a neural pathway in your brain that never goes away. That old love stays with you and will always be there." Michele smiles, "Especially if your old love happens to be Robert Plant."

As we get closer to Michele's pad I ask how she came to be such a music lover and eternal rock muse. "It couldn't have been a cultural influence, or peer pressure, because there *was* no peer

With Robert Plant,
Portland, Oregon,
September 27, 2005.
Credit: David Sarapina

pressure then; we were making it all up as we went along. We
paved the way for a lot of freedom women take for granted and
don't appreciate. We were the first generation of women openly
expressing our love for music; and the music, obviously, was
extremely sexual. But more than that, it was magical, and the
magic was actually larger than the groups that played it."

I remind her that some people saw groupies as oppressed
and exploited. "But we were doing *exactly* what we wanted to
be doing! We were in love with the music—these guys were the
answer to our prayers. They *wanted* us there, and they treated us
like goddesses."

> "Made up my mind, make a new start
> Goin' to California with an achin' in my heart
> Someone told me there's a girl out there
> with love in her eyes and flowers in her hair . . ."

Cassandra Peterson

The Virgin Groupie

I knew my friend Cassandra Peterson for a decade before discovering we had such profoundly kindred rock and roll hearts. Not too many Elvira fans have a clue that the rib-tickling multimedia Mistress of the Dark was once an unabashed groupie maiden.

I met Cassandra at a swinging '80s soiree for Ringo Starr. Manic-eyed Phil Spector roamed the palatial grounds along with Roseanne Barr, my old label mate Alice Cooper, übergroupie Britt Ekland, and the pouty-lipped dead ringer for her daddy Lisa Marie Presley. I recall that Cassandra was equally intrigued with the King's ravishing offspring and commented on her facial expressions and familiar half-lidded gaze as we gobbled down skewers of jumbo shrimp.

Pinning the hardworking mistress down has been quite a challenge, since we're both such busy little beavers. She fits our interview in between a personal appearance at a comic book convention and an Elvira calendar shoot. I've seen the vivacious redhead in action several times, wriggling around in her sultry Elvira drag, captivating crowds with her combo of crass sass and clever quips. Above all, Cassandra is a quintessential comedienne, and I'm jazzed at the prospect of capturing her droll, knowing nuances on paper. As we enjoy a meat-free, dairy-free lunch at the scrumptious nouvelle Real Food Daily on La Cienega, we hearken back and wax nostalgic.

Like so many of my devoted groupie comrades, Elvis was numero uno, but Cassandra's second boi-oi-oing moment came when she heard the Beatles. "My parents were huge fans of Elvis, so I grew up loving him. The first present I remember getting was '(You Ain't Nothin' but a) Hound Dog,' and at three years old, I made up the kookiest dance for it you've ever seen. Then the Beatles came along and *boom*, I was a Beatle freak. I first saw them at eleven or twelve and went out of my mind. I switched all my girlfriends at school because they didn't like the Beatles, and held Beatle birthday parties with all my new Beatle pals. First I liked Ringo, then switched to George, then Paul. By the time I was thirteen, I loved John and stuck with him. He was my only rock idol I didn't meet. And my favorite. I've met all the other Beatles. I guess it wasn't meant to be," she sighs. "Besides, I'm not Asian. And it's too late now."

Credit: Cassandra Peterson

There was nothing stopping the perky high schooler and her like-minded girlfriends from meeting any musician that came through Colorado Springs. "Back then you could just go backstage and knock on the door. Me and Kathy and Eileen would knock, and they'd literally say, 'Come on in!' We were pretty much into making out with every boy we met. I'd be flirting, pretty soon we'd be kissing. They'd ask me back to the hotel and I'd say, 'Oh, no I can't. I have to get home.' I made out with the Young Rascals' drummer, Dino Danelli, and Buffalo Springfield's drummer—I always had a thing for drummers."

The keyboard player for Mitch Ryder and the Detroit Wheels must have had the grooviest gift of gab because he was the first rocker to talk Cassandra into his motel room. "I got in bed and took off all my clothes except my bra and panties and made out with him, but wouldn't let him touch me. He called me for months, wanting to marry me because I was the only groupie who wouldn't actually have sex with him. Being Italian, he thought the only way to screw a nice Italian girl was to marry her, but I wasn't Italian!"

One of Cassandra's early cohorts was her sister Melody. "Here's the difference between my younger sister and me: she was screwing everybody and I wasn't. I remember her standing on my shoulders to get into Buffalo Springfield's room, and she ended up screwing Stephen Stills and I made out with the drummer, Dewey Martin. I liked Stephen but my sister immediately went off with him and I was pissed! My parents had drilled into me that if I ever had sex they would kill themselves, so I was worried they would think I was a slut. If I came home late my mother called me a whore and I said, 'I'm a *virgin*!' But I might as well have been boppin' everybody, because I had the *baddest* reputation. Kids at school called me a big slut because I was hanging out with bands, I was a go-go dancer, and I had big boobs. If you had big boobs back then, you were automatically a big tramp in school."

I understand the process of protecting the precious pussy, because I had done the same thing by perfecting the fine art of giving head. But somehow Cassandra managed to keep even her mouth virginal while spending many hours in the sack with rock

Yummy young
Cassandra.
Credit: Cassandra Peterson

greats. "Yeah, but I'd get myself in *situations*. At sixteen I had a terrible experience with Eric Burdon when he was touring with War. I drove him back to the Holiday Inn, we were making out, and he said, 'Come upstairs to my room.' So like a doofus, I did. We played around in bed and when it started getting serious, I said, 'No, I don't do *that*, I'm a virgin. Leave me alone.' He said, 'You're kidding!' So he took my car keys, dropped them down his pants into his underwear, and said, 'OK, if you want your keys, come and get 'em.' I chased him around the bed but he wouldn't give them back, so I ran out the door and he said, 'Where are you going?' I said, 'I'm going to call the police because you stole my car keys!' So he threw them and hit me really hard in the back with that sharp set of keys." Alas, there's nothing like a rocker scorned.

Close calls such as this did nothing to stop Cassandra from more tantalizing meet and greets. When the Yardbirds arrived in Colorado, she convinced her auntie to drive her and sidekick Kathy to their hotel. "Our mothers wouldn't let us go, so my aunt loaned us these dorky skirts and sweaters, dropped us off, and said she'd pick us up in a couple of hours. We went to the bathroom and rolled the skirts up five thousand times and got all boobalicious.

"We went to the first floor, second floor, third floor, systematically listening at doors, until we heard somebody dorking around on a guitar. We knocked and Jim McCarty opened the door in Keith Relf's room, and said, 'Oh, come in!' Keith was drawing designs with Magic Markers and he gave me one. It was beyond thrilling.

"We were two hysterical little girls, practically fainting, gushing about how excited we were, acting like dweebs, and they loved it. I actually washed Jim McCarty's hair, then Jimmy Page came in and said, 'Why don't you come to my room with *me?*' He was the one I liked best in the band, so I was dying. But being with Jimmy Page almost became date rape, and that phrase wasn't even invented yet. When I wouldn't do what he wanted, he got pissed off and ripped off my clothes. He didn't hurt me, he was just very insistent, and wouldn't stop when I said *stop!* I ran out of his room with my skirt pulled up to my waist, my sweater torn, screaming, 'I'm gonna call the police!' The elevator opened and it was full of people looking at me with my hair a mess, my skirt hiked up, my bra showing. After two hours we went to meet my aunt, and she said, 'Oh, did you girls have a good time?'"

This particular dangerous encounter also stands out for another unforgettable reason. "Jimmy's was the first *penis* I ever saw. It was the longest, skinniest thing ever—like a snake or a worm. But that night didn't stop me. I continued to get myself into these situations."

The Svengali guitarist may have shredded her auntie's mohair, but Cassandra still yearned for rock romance. "I cried and pined. I was in love with him forever; it didn't matter that he treated me like an asshole. When Zeppelin came out, I was so in love, I told everybody I had made out with *Jimmy Page*. I thought I was in love with everyone. I had the same teasing thing with Doug Ingle from Iron Butterfly. I also liked Eric Brann, the guitarist with the little bowl haircut. I did this with band after band after band. I was madly in love after I saw them play, then I'd have to get backstage and meet them. We'd make out and I'd maybe let 'em feel me up. I had huge bazoobies and they loved that. So I kept getting kicked out of hotel rooms, but I felt like I had made a conquest, and oh, wasn't it *great!*"

Cassandra left many of her favorite musicians thwarted and throbbing after promising make-out sessions. "I think about it all the time: why did I do this? It was so attractive; they're performing, people are looking at them. I think I wanted to *be* them, and it was my little way of sharing a piece of them, their fame. So what if one of 'em threw me out of his room. I had just made out with him! Big deal. I got what I wanted—sorry *you* didn't. God! I was obsessed."

Cassandra agrees it's a shame that the word "groupie" has slowly become synonymous with "harlot." "'Groupie' wasn't a bad word. It was almost prestigious. *I* thought it was prestigious anyway. I would tell everybody *I* was *with the band*! It was a good thing, like, 'I'm on the road crew. I'm almost *part* of the band.' There was never any shame. We were their little home away from home. I took Steve Miller and his whole band to the zoo in Colorado Springs. I took Queen antique shopping all day. I hung out with Frank Zappa and the Mothers. No sex, just talking and joking—they were so wacky. I would say, 'I'm a big groupie!' They thought it was so cool."

For me it was about adoring the music, and I know Cassandra feels the same way. "The music was so magical," she enthuses. "It wasn't so much about screwing them. And it wasn't just about the fame. I had to like the music they played. I met the Guess Who once and I thought they sucked so bad. I had breakfast with them but I did *not* want to make out with any of them! The lead singer came on to me, but he said something that made me get up and leave the Holiday Inn coffee shop: 'We're going to be bigger than the Beatles.' I was like, 'Ha *hah!* Let's get out of here, these guys are too conceited!'"

While Cassandra frolicked at the Denver Pop Festival, police threw canisters of tear gas into the audience. While she tells this story, Cassandra imitates everyone's voices, including her own teen-queen falsetto. "One canister hit me in the head, I had a huge lump and the liquid stuff burned my skin. The paramedics rushed me behind the stadium to wash it off with boric acid. As I was leaving, a big black bodyguard with a giant Afro says, 'Hey, you wanna meet Jimi Hendrix?' 'Yes, I *do*!' 'Well, come over here to his trailer.' So I run on over and there he is, wearing his little costume. He says, 'What happened to you?' And I say, 'The pigs were throwing tear gas, man.' Jimi goes on a ranting rampage about America and how he wants to get away and never come back. 'Fuck those bastards! Are you OK? Let me see where they burned you.' He was so sweet." Jimi rinsed a cloth in cold water and gently placed it on Cassandra's back, then asked if she'd like to share a joint. "So we start smoking pot and just talk and *talk*. Then we kiss and make out, rolling around, smoking,

Come-hither eyes.
Credit: Cassandra Peterson

having the greatest time. He never even tried to get serious. They call him to go on and he says, 'Here's my number at the hotel. Call me tonight and we can get together.' I thought, 'Uh-oh, I know what'll happen if I go to the hotel . . .' Back at my seat, I told my girlfriend, 'Oh my God, Liz, you'll never believe . . .' and she said, 'Shut up! Jimi Hendrix is about to come on!' and I yelled, 'Listen! *This* is his phone number!'"

As we order maple tofu dessert, a swarm of attractive young dudes enter the restaurant and take over the table next to us. Black leather jackets, spiky hair, earrings, boots, eye makeup. "Obvious rock band," I comment. "No doubt about it," she agrees, and we both crack up. Why are we still attracted to rockers? "I don't know," she says. "I wonder sometimes if it's because we want to be famous ourselves." "But you *are* famous," I remind her. "Well, I am now. Musicians are exciting and romantic and adventurous and cool. They're everything you want to be, so you're in love with what *you* want to be, and you hope a little rubs off. I wanted to be creative like they were, but didn't know how it would transpire. I loved music, but didn't play an instrument. I tried guitar for five minutes and thought, 'Ow! This is *way* too hard! My fingers are killing me!'"

More than a little bit of creativity rubbed off on Cassandra. At fourteen, she saw Elvis and Ann-Margret in *Viva Las Vegas* and, from that stimulating moment on, was determined to become a Vegas showgirl. "I thought about it all the time. When I told people, 'I'm gonna be a showgirl in Las Vegas,' they laughed. I might as well have said I was going to be a Martian. Even my mother said, 'You can't be a showgirl, they have to be talented and beautiful.'"

She had already moved out of the house, but when her folks planned a trip to Sin City, Cassandra begged to go along. "We went to a big show at the Dunes, and because you had to be twenty-one to get in, I put on three hundred pairs of eyelashes and a million falls in my hair and tried to act sophisticated." As they waited for the showgirls to shimmy on stage, the host appeared at the Petersons' table and asked Cassandra if *she* was a showgirl. "I said, 'Uh . . . *no.*' My parents were letting me have a glass of champagne and I thought I was gonna be sent straight to jail. He said, 'Stay right there,' and went to get a woman named Fluff who turned out to be the dance captain. She asked, 'Are you in any shows here in Vegas?' When I said no, she said, 'Would you *like* to be?'" Cassandra's folks were moved to the best table in the house while she was escorted backstage. Fluff had her do a few steps, then told her she'd be perfect for the upcoming the summer show, aptly titled *Viva Les Girls*.

Her far-fetched fantasy was in the process of coming true, but Cassandra was not quite eighteen and her parents put up a fight. "They said, 'No way in hell,' and dragged me out of there by my falls. I had only two or three months left of high school, and for the rest of my senior year I threatened to run away, kill myself, and finally they said, 'OK, for God's sake, just get out of here!' The day I graduated, I threw my stuff into my Firebird and drove to Las Vegas. I started rehearsals and became a showgirl."

Part two of Cassandra's determined dream-come-true involved the king of rock and roll himself. "Elvis came to see *Viva Les Girls* and my roommate was dating his road manager, Joe Esposito. He invited her over after the show. I said, 'Please, *please* take me with you!' and since I was *the* biggest Elvis freak, she took me. Up in his suite, Elvis and I sat at the piano and sang harmony together." Cassandra has never told me her divine Elvis story in detail, and I'm palpitating. "That's almost as good as fucking him!" I shriek. "It *was* pretty hard to believe," she agrees. "I was seventeen, and I think he had respect for young girls. He was very gallant, and respected women, even though I'm sure he screwed a million and one of 'em. We went off in a corner; just me and him, one-on-one, no one else. He talked about his parents. He asked if I'd ever smoked pot or done drugs, and when I told him I had, he said, 'Don't ever do it again!' He was *so* anti-drug. He told me he had just met Nixon, and brought out this gigantic gold belt buckle he had given him. He was so excited! He said, 'The president of the United States gave me this!' He must have been thirty-five, but seemed so naive and young."

Because of his "respect" for her, Elvis didn't escort Cassandra to his kingly boudoir. "Since Elvis knew I was a virgin, he was too damned respectful," Cassandra mourns. "I could have kicked myself a hundred times for not . . . can you *imagine*? Unfortunately I met Elvis before I came across the cad who de-virginized me. But we kissed a lot," she smiles. "I was so busy thinking 'Oh my God, I'm kissing Elvis, kissing Elvis, *kissing* Elvis . . .' that I don't even remember how good it was. From about two until eight the next morning, we never stopped talking. He told me about spirituality, numerology, religion, and I just listened. He had this whole bizarre theory and wrote down a bunch of things for me, which I still have. It was all about how numbers correlate to letters, how they spell different things like 'Christ' and 'Heaven.' And he gave me the most important advice of my entire life. After we sang together, he said, 'You have a good voice. Have you ever taken singing lessons?' I said no, and he said, 'You ought to get out of Vegas. If you stay here you'll wind up like one of these old showgirls. You won't have anything when you get older, and that'll be the end of you.'" Elvis suggested that Cassandra start singing lessons right away and form her own band. "If anybody else had told me that, I would have thought they were full of shit. But he was *Elvis*."

The very next day she found a vocal coach, and it just so happened a few weeks later the showgirls in *Viva Les Girls* were asked to audition to sing a number, and Cassandra got the part. "Not only did my money go way up, but I became a featured player. From there I moved on to Europe and became a singer in Italy. Elvis absolutely changed my life. I thought I'd peaked, reached my dream, hit the heights. I really *did* think I would stay in Vegas and be a showgirl for the rest of my life."

One hot night after Cassandra trilled her new so-called lesbian number "A Good Man Is Hard to Find" alongside the rest of the sequined Les Girls, a renowned Vegas titan wearing tight shiny trousers came calling. "Our show was voted Best Show in Vegas. It was very cool and hip for the time; a tits and feathers show. Tom Jones arrived and invited the showgirls to meet him and party afterwards. I looked like such a baby with my big round face, but he was flirting with me and bringing me drinks backstage. The rest of the girls were in their thirties, one was forty, so I was fresh meat. Tom seemed gentlemanly and nice, so when he was jumpin' on me a few hours later, I thought, 'Well, if I'm ever gonna do this, it might as well be with Tom Jones.'"

'Fess up, I demand. How *was* Mr. "What's New Pussycat?" Cassandra shakes her head and groans, "It was *not* a good experience. It was painful and horrible. Afterward, I couldn't stop bleeding and he said, 'You'll be OK, don't worry about it. Here's some money for a cab.' When I got home and told my roommate, she said, 'You'd better go to the hospital.' I ended up in the emergency room getting a couple of stitches. Talk about fun! I don't know if I was so tiny or he was so big. Of course I was madly in love with him afterward, and thought he *must* be madly in love with me. I thought sure we were gonna run away together and get married! I went backstage to see him the next night, but he was with his two background singers, the Blossoms, and was all *over* them. I was devastated. I remember sitting backstage in my dressing room for the next week playing that song of his, 'I who have nothing, I who have no one . . .'"

Cassandra relates the sad story of how on Good Friday, when she was not quite three years old, she clambered up a chair to the kitchen stove to peer at a pot of boiling Easter eggs, and tipped the scalding hot water all over her. She underwent several painful surgeries, but still ended up with unsightly scars that caused her heartbreaking embarrassment during her teen years. Not only did her first real lover turn out to be a heel, he had the sensitivity of a cockroach. "I saw Tom in Vegas years later, and I'll never forget what he said to me. I got backstage at his show and said, 'Hi Tom, do you remember me?' And he said, 'Yeah, you're the one with the scars.' That killed me. I was really sensitive about my scars. Almost 35 percent of my body is skin grafting, mostly on my back and shoulders. My whole life has been about dealing with the freaking scars, and it was like saying to somebody with an amputated leg, 'Yeah, you're the one with the peg leg!' Really subtle, eh? I've always thought that was brutal, and it certainly ruined my love affair with Tom Jones."

Following advice from the King, Cassandra continued singing and fronted a band called Mama's Boys with seven gay men.
They were traveling the frenetic disco circuit, performing in
Provincetown, Massachusetts, when she was hit with tragic
news. "I can remember the exact second I heard that Elvis had
died. It was very heavy for me, just horrible. I put a Joan Baez
song in the show, 'Never Dreamed You'd Leave in Summer,' and
dedicated it to Elvis every night. I couldn't get through the song
because I'd start sobbing. Of course I had wanted to see him
again, but you could have probably reached the pope easier than
Elvis."

Always the music lover, when she moved to Los Angeles,
Cassandra easily fell back into the rock scene. "Musicians are
children in disguise—they just don't grow up. Their lives are so
insane; they're big kids and so much more fun to be around than
normal guys with a job." Cassandra quickly landed her own
job in the music biz as an A&R scout for *Don Kirshner's Rock
Concert* TV show. "I was a production assistant and checked out
all the new groups in town. It was during New Wave, and for
years I spent every single night at the Roxy, the Rainbow, or the
Whisky. I saw every freaking band that existed."

Cassandra didn't know it, but her carefree groupie days
were about to come to a halt. "I was checking out this new act,
Johnny Cougar (later John Cougar Mellencamp), trying to get
backstage—of course—to jump on him. What else is new? He
was really cute then, *small,* but cute. Mark Pierson was guarding
the door; he was the guy *not* letting people backstage. But the
band invited me to a party and I wound up with Mark instead
of John Cougar, and we were together twenty-four years. My
ten-year-old daughter Sadie says, 'Thank God you didn't marry
John Cougar, Mom, or I might have been a dwarf!'"

During her stint as an A&R babe, Cassandra continued to
pursue a career in show biz. "I segued from dancing to singing to acting and was doing stupid parts on *Fantasy Island* and
Happy Days." While she was on her honeymoon, she heard
about a director looking for someone to introduce local TV
horror movies. "He wanted somebody funny but sexy; kind

of like the '50s character Vampira. When I got back, they still hadn't found anyone, but playing a late-night local horror movie host sounded kind of dorky to me. And it only paid, like, three hundred bucks a week, but I thought it would be some money coming in while I looked for other acting work. I auditioned as myself and got the part, and had to come up with a *look*. My best friend from Mama's Boys drew a picture of me with a Ronettes hairdo—it was called the 'knowledge bump.' He got my makeup from a Japanese Kabuki book, and drew the black dress as sexy and tight as possible. I put that all together and started doing the show."

The timing was wickedly auspicious. Cassandra had been honing her comedic timing as a member of the fledgling comedy troupe the Groundlings, performing madcap improvisational skits with the likes of *Saturday Night Live*'s Phil Hartman and Paul "Pee Wee Herman" Reubens. "I was working on a character, this really stupid valley girl actress. She was basically the Elvira character without the drag. Even though I thought 'This does *not* work together,' the spoofy juxtaposition that didn't work created this bizarre *creature*. And I'm still doing it. I'm still humpin' that bra for all it's worth."

Every October it's impossible to get in touch with Cassandra, so entrenched is she in her saucy alter ego. The only way to see her is to attend one of her annual Halloween extravaganzas, and for several years I took my son Nick to Knott's Berry Farm (Knott's *Scary* Farm in October). We were dazzled by her high kicks and high jinks, peppered with sly double entendres and titillating tunes. Cassandra's career highlights would take up several pages; this doll is a self-made whiz. Along with her two hysterical movies, *Elvira: Mistress of the Dark* and *Elvira's Haunted Hills*, she's done countless TV appearances and has written a series of humor/mystery/horror novels. She launched her own perfume, "Evil," as well as lines of greeting cards, candy, comic books, bobble head dolls, action figures, and slot machines. Then there are the bestselling video and computer games and Rhino Records music compilations. She has her own Elvira pinball machine, Revell "Macabre Mobile" model car,

Credit: Cassandra Peterson

and, of course, the endless array of award-winning Halloween costumes and witchy paraphernalia. For many years she's been a strong animal rights activist and in 1990 won PETA's Humanitarian Award. Cassandra makes umpteen personal appearances every year, but still manages to include rock and roll on her busy dizzy schedule. "As Elvira I opened for Mötley Crüe a couple of times, and told a few jokes, and I opened for Rob Zombie and Alice Cooper. I also introduced U2 on their Zoo tour from Knott's Scary Farm." Being around all those rockers, was she ever tempted to explore her former wanton ways? "I was married twenty-four years, but still flirted unmercifully with bands," she admits. "It's sad because I had a lot of opportunities. I could have had flings as Elvira. I could have had *anybody*, but I was out of the playing field. It's so ironic," she laughs, "because now I'm too old." Right. I'm sure the leather-clad devil gazing at her over his glass of squeezed greens would beg to differ.

"I had a blast recently with REO Speedwagon at a Harley Davidson gathering in the desert," Cassandra says as we down the last drops of our café lattes with soy milk. "I picked out the clothes they wore, we danced on stage and laughed together; it was hysterical. Most of 'em were married and divorced and married and divorced. They're still on the road three hundred days a year! Two women came backstage and immediately took off their blouses, '*Look*, here's our tits!' The band was messing around with their guitars, and said, 'Yeah, that's interesting.' They couldn't have cared less."

She may have romped with one too many rockers, but Cassandra doesn't have any regrets. "Come on, it was exciting. Sex is the best exercise; it's good for your brain and your blood! The weird thing about having a lot of partners is that it's still OK for a guy to say he's had a million partners. But it's *not* OK for women. When I was starting to come out, so did the birth control pill. Those little round dial packs changed everything. For most people my age, that solved the whole problem. I didn't even think about disease. I felt very free; women were supposed to have as much sex as guys did and enjoy it too. But I wouldn't advocate that lifestyle now."

It still annoys her that groupies were harshly judged for doing the same thing everybody else was doing. "So *we* were bad for screwing a bunch of guys in bands? My girlfriends were also screwing everybody, but the guys weren't famous. It doesn't make it better, but it certainly doesn't make it *worse*."

As we get up to leave, "All You Need Is Love" pours out of the speakers, and Cassandra's Beatlemania springs to life. "God, the Beatles were brilliant beyond magical," she sighs. "They changed the whole world with their spiritualism, introducing the Eastern religion to the West." When I tell her I finally met my fave Beatle, Paul McCartney, last year, she raves about his latest live show in L.A. "Oh, Jesus. Unbelievable. The entire audience was singing and swaying. Talk about being in the *now,* it was like being somewhere *else*. I had tears pouring down my face. Seeing and hearing that kind of greatness is like meditating. You are so focused on getting energy from the music; you

Credit: Cassandra Peterson

are here now and there's not enough room for any other energy to exist. It's like mountain climbing or any of those dangerous sports people play. You have to be focused a hundred percent."

"There's a line by the poet Neruda," Cassandra says as we open the double glass doors to the West Hollywood heat. "'We have only to convey to others who we are.' That's what creativity is. That's what these artists are saying to us: 'This is *me*, this is who I am; I'm unique.' And you can relate; you get a connection going because you realize, 'Yeah, *I'm* like that too.'"

Lori Lightning

Absolute Beginners

By the time the brand-new batch of budding groupies appeared on the Hollywood scene, I had almost had my fill of rock royalty. I was twenty-three years old, and although I still had my fave-raves, I'd found other fantasies to pursue. Thanks to Keith Moon's smashing largesse, I had been able to join the Screen Actors Guild and had appeared in a couple of brilliant B features: the groundbreaking *Massage Parlor* and the unforgettable masterpiece *Carhops*. I was seriously studying acting and thought I was ripe and ready for my close-up. I would always love the men who made rock and roll but desperately wanted to stir up my own creative potential.

Whenever I went to the Whisky, I steered clear of the skinny prepubescents littering the Sunset Strip in their itty-bitty mini-shorts and towering platforms. I considered them more of a nuisance than a threat—even though one of them dared to call me "an old bag" in front of Elton John one rude night. They teetered around in a pack, just like I had with the GTO's, but these brazen junior high schoolers were competitive and just plain backstabbingly *mean*, especially their acne-scarred platinum boss-baby Sable Starr. There was Queenie, Corel, Lynn, and Sable's closest confidant, a dusky, gangly child with layers of thick black curls who called herself Lori Lightning.

Despite my grand thespian plans, whenever Led Zeppelin barreled into town, I found myself back at the Continental Riot House, nestled in the slim white arms of the Dark Lord, Jimmy Page. We had broken up two years earlier when he met a red-head named Charlotte on his birthday, and supposedly fell in forever love. I was crushed almost beyond recognition, but had since recovered enough to join him in the sack for long nights of irresistible revelry while his London ladylove pined back home. (C'mon, what did she expect?)

On a particularly memorable evening, Jimmy had called from the previous city on the Zep tour, asking me to meet him at the Whisky for a round of merriment, which I assumed would last for the rest of the night. Unbeknownst to me, Jimmy had also looked up little Lori Lightning after seeing her precious pouty mug in the short-lived teen bible, *Star* magazine. For most of the night, I occupied the middle red booth in my usual hallowed spot between Jimmy and Robert Plant, and when Jimmy called for the limo I gathered myself and innocently followed him out the front door. The sleek black car was idling at the corner, and as Bonzo, Robert, John Paul, and roadie Richard Cole climbed in, Lori suddenly appeared and Jimmy grabbed her, tossed her into the limo, slid in next to her, and they were gone in a flash. Stunned, I stood there with my face on fire and a fluorescent spotlight pointing directly at my mortified heart.

I consider that night to be the lowest point in my métier as a groupie. Jimmy's churlish behavior put a black spot on an otherwise joyous seven-year rock romp. I wanted to blame Lori, but she was only thirteen years old. I had barely put away my Barbie dolls at her age, and here she was, cavorting with a whip-wielding heavy metal icon pushing thirty.

How had Lori Mattix found her way to the Sunset Strip at such a tender age? Where was her mother when she left the house wearing five-inch heels, skimpy Lurex tube tops, and nonexistent short shorts on her way to certain bacchanalia?

Lori, Sable, and their lip-glossy mob reigned over the scene for another few years, especially when the "Mayor of the Sunset Strip," Rodney Bingenheimer, opened his integral glitter-palaces,

Credit: Lori Mattix Collection

the E Club and Rodney's English Disco. You could see them draped all over musicians of the moment, haughtily perched on velvet-clad laps within the coveted, roped-off center of the room. I heard that Jimmy eventually trampled Lori's girlish heart as well, but that didn't stop her from careening from one rock god to the next, next, next.

We often came across each other at rock events, and Lori and I have gradually made peace. We've frequently been interviewed for the same TV shows and documentaries, and all these years later, we find our tempestuous rock and rollicking history mutually amusing. Robert Plant has come to town and once again we are a few seats apart in the fifth row. During Robert's latest stellar version of "Black Dog," Lori and I look over at each other. But when he looks skyward and calls out "Miss Pamela" from the stage, tossing his curls, I get a jolt of age-old groupie pride.

Even though we're misty eyed with nostalgia and still can't seem to get the Led out, we laugh at the absurdity of it all.

No longer the lissome waif, Lori is a bosomy, boisterous force of nature. She has a palpable zest for life, and you always know when she's in the room. At Robert's aftershow bash, I watch with amusement as she happily bosses her current boyfriend around while he obviously enjoys catering to her every whim.

I've always been curious about the real story behind her illegal relationship with Mr. Page, and since we're in the wayward throes of Zeppelin nostalgia, it's a perfect time to hark back to her promiscuous past. On a rare day off from her high-powered managerial job at the chic Theodore boutique, Lori joins me for a few cups of English breakfast tea and empathy.

"I knew nothing about you, that you and Jimmy had been an item; I had no idea that you were gonna be with him at the Whisky that night," Lori says emphatically. She has told me this before, of course, and I assure her I harbor no groupie grudges. "Sable had already told me that she'd kill me if I went near him! She wanted him and I thought *they* were gonna be together. When I saw you with Jimmy, it freaked me out and he said, 'I told you I'm gonna be with you,' and that's the night he kidnapped me." When I ask how Jimmy knew about her in the first place, Lori's answer is a shocker. "Sable was fucking Michael Des Barres, so we were always hanging out with Silverhead. He took photos of Sable and me on the Hyatt House balcony, wearing little red boas. When he went back to London, he showed the pictures to Jimmy and said, 'You gotta meet this girl. She's thirteen, she's *this* big, and she's got hair just like you.' Then *Star* magazine came out and he saw how young I was. Jimmy *loved* young girls—babies—and that's how it happened." I've always known that Michael had a fling with Sable, but I never knew that before we even met, my future husband unwittingly set me up for such an ignominious fall.

So, how *did* such a baby girl find herself half-naked in front of the Whisky a Go Go? "I got there by accident," Lori insists. "Lynn and I went to school together, and she was friends with Sable. They were working with *Star* magazine. That's how I got dragged in—Peterson Publishing discovered me." Lori wasn't even aware of the risky lure of rock and roll when she became a pinup doll for lascivious musicians. "I didn't know anything. I was still a virgin, I knew *nothing* when they started putting makeup on me and dressing me up for magazine covers. The whole glitter rock scene was decadence; that's when we really captured our style and got bold. Platforms got bigger and skirts got shorter, hair got wilder."

It was 1973, and since many Brit bands had been on the road for years, hotels and venues started looking too much alike. Even though they had a chick (or three) in every city, rockers were getting bored and seemed to require ever-increasing and varied stimulation. Keith Moon was driving town cars into swimming pools, while Mitch Mitchell spent all evening gluing his hotel room furniture to the ceiling. *Star* magazine, featuring the likes of Lori and Sable, arrived on the scene just in time to stave off the predictable tedium of touring. The underage glam-babies were a spanking new treat for jaded eyes.

How did Lori's mother cope with the sudden change in her young daughter? "It was very difficult because she was a single mother. I had three sisters; she was raising us alone. She was a waitress and working every night, so we would sneak out and back again before she got home. Sometimes she wouldn't know, but she finally got wind of it and went down to the Strip and asked Mario, the owner of the Whisky, 'Where's my daughter?' He reassured her, 'Val, don't worry, we're looking after her. She's fine.'"

There was only so much the fatherly figure at the Whisky could do, however, and Lori soon found that her innocence was a highly prized asset. "Rock stars started pursuing me. One night at the E Club, Mick Ronson arrived with David Bowie, and that was my first encounter with him. He said, 'I want to be with you. I'm *going* to be with you,' but I was terrified and ran into Rodney's arms yelling, 'No, I can't go with you!' It was ridiculous!" It was six months before Bowie came back to town and the songs Rodney played at the E Club sent Lori reeling. "I found my music: Slade, the Sweet, Silverhead, T. Rex—and Bowie. On the next trip he played the Long Beach Arena, and

With Jimmy Page.
Credit: Lori Mattix collection

his bodyguard, Stuie, came up to me. 'David wants you to come have dinner with us tomorrow night.' Sable was with me and was freaking out because *she* wanted to fuck Bowie. She was a year older, and I was still a virgin and *terrified*, so I said, 'You have to come with me. I can't go alone!' The next night I waited in front of my house with my mother, and a limo came and got me, then picked up Sable and took us to the Beverly Hilton where Bowie was staying. After dinner, we ended up at the Rainbow, and that was the night David got attacked—some guy called him a faggot and jumped him. There was this big fight, so we ran back to the car and that song was playing, 'Even though we ain't got money, I'm so in love with you, honey . . .' Sable was wearing her Hollywood underwear, singing, 'Even though we ain't got honey, I'm so in love with your money.' It was classic."

Back at the Hilton, the youngsters joined Stuie and David in their snazzy adjoining suites. "There was a big living room with fluffy white shag carpet, and Stuie rolled this humongous hash joint—one of those huge spliffs. I had smoked pot before, but it wasn't like this. I got *so* fucked up. David went into the bedroom and said, 'I'm going to take a bath.' All of a sudden, the door opens and Bowie is standing there with that gorgeous white skin and carrot-red hair, no eyebrows, wearing a kimono. It was in his early Ziggy Stardust era, and that was the first time I thought, Oh, I *want* him! Sable was like, 'I'll kill you if you go with him because *I* want him and you can't have him.' He came out and said, 'Lori, could come over here?' and I said, 'Alone?' I was *so* paranoid—*stoned* and paranoid, and he said, 'Yes, please, just you.' I go in and he's about to close the door, and I'm looking at Sable and she's in tears. I was so nervous. I had boyfriends in junior high; all the smooching, but I'd never had intercourse. So he escorts me into the bathroom and takes off his kimono, gets into the bathtub, and sits there staring at me with those different-colored eyes. You have to understand—he's so gorgeous, his skin is so white and flawless. So he says, 'Can you wash my back?' and that was just the beginning. He knew it was my first time, and he was so gentle with me. We started to fuck in every position possible. Then I told him I felt *so* bad about Sable, and he said, 'Well, do you think we should go and get her?' I said yes, and we walked into the living room and she was fogging up the windows, writing, 'I want to fuck David!' So he called her into the bedroom and we all spent the night together. David Bowie was the one who devirginized me."

Lori says that for the next few months she went through a "little guilt period," and attempted to walk a semistraight line by spending more time at home and at school. But during this interim, Michael Des Barres showed Jimmy Page her photos, and the rock and roll tom-toms were loudly pounding out the message that Zeppelin's guitar god wanted to meet Lori Lightning. Much to Sable's chagrin, Lori once again beat her to the pop star punch. Lori turned up at the Whisky that fateful night and was whisked back to the Hyatt House with the rock and roll master of romance. "I met him that night; he had called from Texas and told me he *had* to meet me and I hung up on him. I think he was obsessed with me because he loved that I looked kinda like him: eighty pounds, hair down to here, skinny as can be." Yeah, and I remind her that it might have helped that Jimmy also knew she was an *infant*. "Yeah, well, I didn't know that then!" Lori laughs loudly. "The obvious factor! That night turned out to be so beautiful though, because I fell in love with him," she sighs. "He was the first man I ever loved, in the sense that he was on this huge pedestal. I loved the way he moved. He was so gentle in bed, and that *face*. He was like this whimsical celluloid creature—I don't know how to explain it. In my whole life I've never met anybody like him."

Their torrid affair went on for more than two years. Except for those rare occasions when he was with Charlotte in London, Lori actually believed that her knight in shining satin was being true to her. "I was so naive. I had no concept of it being any other way. I was a *baby*! He was this god to me—it was like being in love with Elvis Presley. I mean, I'd go to the Forum and there were thirty thousand people, all there for him, and he was with *me*. He was twenty-nine when I was thirteen," Lori adds. "And you know how old his wife is now? Twenty-nine!"

How did it feel to be caught up in that particular web? "It was like being with the pope. You don't get concerts like that anymore, massive stadium concerts with a hundred thousand people. And you don't see that kind of magic anymore, that great rock era—three nights at the Forum, thirty thousand people with candles shining . . ."

To prove that she was the one he loved, Jimmy encouraged Lori to listen in on phone conversations he had with Charlotte. "He told me it was over with Charlotte and that it had been for years. He'd call her and let me listen so I wouldn't worry. He'd go, 'Charlotte, can you go get a number upstairs for me?' and instead of picking up the phone by the bed, she'd go all the way upstairs and take twenty-five minutes, and come all the way down and go, 'I can't find the number,' and he'd say, 'Why the fuck didn't you pick up the phone up there? Are you stupid?'"

In between Zeppelin jaunts, Lori continued her in-demand teen model career. "I made a few hundred dollars on a job and that would buy my little outfits—I needed money for platforms after all! I didn't even know what money was when I was dating Jimmy. Once he sent me out to buy a dress and gave me $300. I said, 'I can't spend that much money!' Once I wanted this beautiful scarab necklace and he got it for me. He liked me in long, flowy skirts. He wanted me to look like a gypsy all the time; an *innocent* gypsy." With so much time together, what did they talk about? "Love," Lori gushes. "I didn't have much else to talk about at that age! We fucked all the time, you know? I'm kidding; we talked about everything! He was so romantic and wonderful. I never thought of him as crazy—he was so possessive and protective over me. He wouldn't let me drink, and one time I was smoking cigarettes and he went crazy. He made me smoke a whole pack of Salems until I was gagging. I never smoked again. He was like a dad sometimes." For a few moments we marvel over the many sides of James Patrick Page. "And then, one day I found a picture of this transsexual she-male and I'm like, 'What's this?' and he said, 'I wonder how that got there. I don't know where that came from.'"

Lori says Jimmy called her every day when he got back to England, and in 1975 when Zeppelin played Madison Square Garden, he flew her to New York to stay with him at the Drake Hotel. "That was when their gig money got stolen and the FBI was investigating. Everybody was paranoid about me being around because I was underage. Zeppelin's manager was flipping out. He said, 'You've gotta send her home. She can't be at the hotel with the FBI sniffing around.' We had been up all night in the studio. Jimmy was hanging out with Joe Walsh because his daughter was killed in a car accident. They were writing a song for her, and Jimmy was so affected by Joe's sadness that he couldn't sleep. He'd been awake for two days, and that's when I went home."

Lori had invited an attractive new acquaintance, model Bebe Buell, to hang out with her and the band in New York. "She was my friend, so she brought her pet monkey and got an adjoining suite with Jimmy and me. This is where the whole thing gets all screwed up—Bebe was *my* guest." Oops. Lori went back to L.A.

for a few days until the FBI cleared out, then hightailed it back to Pagey paradise. She had her own key to the suite, and when she strutted in, expecting to fall into his slim, waiting arms, she was horrified to discover Jimmy in bed with her pal Bebe. At least the monkey was nowhere to be seen.

"I was never supposed to walk in and see that!" Lori fumes. "When I saw him in bed with her, I couldn't deal with it. It destroyed me. I don't know about him, but for me it would never be the same because I trusted him. I thought we had this perfect love and my man on the pedestal had turned into a pig. How dare he be with my girlfriend! It was so disgusting to me."

Brokenhearted Lori never darkened Jimmy's bed again. "My innocence was shattered and that's what he loved about me. Once my innocence was gone, what was left to love?" When I ask why she thinks Jimmy left her for Bebe, Lori becomes incensed. "I don't think he *left* me for her! I don't think he ever planned on leaving me. I think he was gonna fool around with Bebe on the side. Yeah, he could have been cheating the whole time, and was gonna keep his little innocent thing put away. I think it tore him apart too, because I was so young, and he knew my heart was pure. It took me years to trust a man again—*years*! Especially because of the cold and callous way Jimmy did things—he told me he was loyal the whole time and I believed him!"

After experiencing adult heartache at such a tender age, she was determined not to fall for another musician anytime soon. "I had to grow up all of a sudden. I went from this golden heart full of love to a crushed bubble. I shut myself down emotionally, physically, everything."

As her heart healed, Lori found she was still crazy about rock and roll and was soon cavorting rampantly with her favorite willing rockers. "Music was in my soul. I was with everybody from David Bowie to Mick Jagger to Jeff Beck to Ronnie Wood to Mickey Finn of T. Rex. I saw Mickey on and off for years; there's another bad-boy lunatic. I went after bad boys because Jimmy had been so sweet and gentle with me, and I had to get him out of my system. Once I had a three-way with Mickey Finn and Angela Bowie. I remember he was slapping her ass so hard, then picked her up and threw her into the air conditioner. I was hiding in the closet because I was so scared. I had Angie's kimono on and was trying on her shoes. They came in and got me and said, 'Okay, come out now!' I was wearing her shoes with pom-poms on them, and she gave them to me. I also saw David Bowie on and off for years. I was in that whole circle—you could either fuck a roadie or you could fuck a rock star. I mean, sitting in a room with Ronnie Wood, why would you want to fuck the roadie? How do you turn that down? Ahh, Emerson, Lake & Palmer. I was with Keith Emerson, of course. He was fun because he used to take me riding on his motorcycle. Then later on I had a little thing with Carl Palmer, too! He was so good looking; he was a fucking *god*. I definitely had flings, but it was all playful, I didn't have another boyfriend for a long time because I couldn't get emotionally involved."

How had she caught Mick Jagger's roving eye? "He was an accident," Lori smiles. "I used to go the Record Plant every Monday night for Jimmy Keltner's fan club sessions, with incredible

With Iggy Pop.   Credit: Lori Mattix collection

musicians like Jesse Ed Davis, Tom Scott, Stevie Wonder, Bobby
Keys. One night three Beatles were recording there, and Stevie
Wonder and Mick Jagger, all at once! Mick was having ego problems with John Lennon: they both wanted to sing and they were
both Leos or something." I remind Lori that John Lennon was a
Libra. "Well, *Mick* was having an ego problem, so he was pouting in this back room that had beds and shackles. I was there too,
escaping from the studio for a while and my friend said, 'There's
somebody you need to meet.' She took me to the room where
Mick was pouting." And how was her frolic with Mr. Jagger? "It
was very interesting. I think he was high; he had a little trouble
getting a hard-on and coming, but it was fun. We rolled around
and kissed and fondled each other and had a blast. After that, I
didn't see him for years until I went to New York to stay with
Freddie, the drug dealer. Mick was there and we had another
little fling. The third time I saw him was at Keith Moon's birthday party at the Beverly Wilshire. Mick came up to the bedroom and that's when we had the best wild sex—he fucked me
on the bathroom floor while Keith Moon and everybody were
in another room celebrating Keith's birthday! While we were
on the marble floor in the bathroom, Bianca was downstairs. It
was after she'd had surgery or something; she was recovering at
the Beverly Wilshire. People have always told me I resemble her,
which I found very flattering. But I was never in love or serious
until I met Jimmy Bain, who played in Rainbow; he was probably the most serious boyfriend I had after that awful Jimmy
Page nightmare."

The spangly, glam-slam glitter scene was suddenly history,
and Lori settled in with Mr. Bain and got a job working for Deep
Purple's Ritchie Blackmore as his assistant. "The English Disco
was what kept everybody together and I think it all fell apart
when Rodney's closed—everybody went in different directions.
Times changed, *Star* magazine closed, Peterson Publishing
folded, punk started coming in. That was when Sable moved to
New York with Johnny Thunders and the New York Dolls. I
bailed 'cause I was more into the rock scene. I never got into
punk, like Stiv Bators. I thought it was all dirty and ugly—I was

never into that heroin chic. It was also tragic for me because during that period Jimmy got into heroin, which killed me."

When Sable got back from New York, Lori went to visit her at an apartment in Huntington Beach. "The last time I saw her, she'd had a baby, and I think she was doing a little bit of heroin. She told me she'd gotten pregnant by some skateboarder or lumberjack guy and had named her son Denay. This is the honest-to-God truth: her sister, Corel, played tennis, and this was classic Sable. She said, 'Yeah, I named the baby after Corel's tennis racquet.'" This absurd story reminds me of the time I ran into Sable after I had my son Nick, and she suggested that I have another baby "just in case something happens to this one." I hear Sable now has two kids and deals blackjack at a casino in Reno.

Through her modeling connections, Lori started working in the fashion industry and slowly got caught in an upscale Beverly Hills nightmare. "Everybody was doing disco drugs and getting high in the '80s. I was going to the Daisy, Pip's, and the Candy Store. O. J. Simpson was hanging out every night; it was disco hell. Cocaine creates insanity after all." In her early twenties, Lori says she finally became "responsible" after several friends died. "I ran in to John Bonham at the Rainbow one night and it was the turning point for me. In that teddy-bear voice of his, he said, 'Lori, I've been coming here for fifteen years. I don't want to come back in fifteen years and find you still here.' Something rang very true in Bonzo's statement, and I looked around and saw all the same girls—they'd been on the Strip forever. I remember leaving that night and I went out and got a job and got my life together."

Lori has had several long-term relationships, one of which produced her son Sean, who is now nineteen. "He's a great kid. He surfs every day and wants to be a pro surfer. I raised him and he didn't need his dad around. When I found out I was pregnant, my AA sponsor said, 'You have to turn your will and your life over to the care of God, and this is God's will for you.' I had to finally grow up, and that's what changed my life."

Thankfully, Lori also has a good relationship with her mother. "She knew I was seeing Jimmy because he asked her permission. I think because she had three other daughters getting into so much trouble, my trouble seemed lightweight to her. My sisters were dating low riders and getting arrested for grand theft auto, while I was dating a rock star. I mean, what could be so bad?"

We've been gabbing for hours and Lori has to get to Pilates class. As she takes her last sip of tea, and gathers up the gypsy skirts she still wears, I ask how she feels about the sadly tarnished G word. "I feel like it's been degraded somewhere along the way, and it was never meant to be negative. Groupies in the old days were girlfriends of the band. They were classy and sophisticated, but now you hear the word *groupie* and you think of hookers and strippers. In the grand rock days, the groupies were Pattie Harrison, Marianne Faithfull, Linda McCartney, Anita Pallenberg. They didn't give blow jobs to get backstage—and neither did we!"

As turbulent as it was, Lori wouldn't have missed a moment of her impassioned past. "I had such a monumental time. I don't regret one second of it. It was such a different time—there was no AIDS—and you were free to experiment. I always asked, 'Why me? Why did this incredible person choose me?' It was all so random, and I felt so blessed to be there. I'm on stage, watching Led Zeppelin play in front of thirty thousand people—why me? Or I'm sitting in the studio with three of the Beatles thinking, 'Wow, this is pretty incredible—why me?'"

Sweet Connie

There's Only One Way to Rock

Fifteen years ago, while promoting my second book, *Take Another Little Piece of My Heart*, I subjected myself to the slings and arrows of Jenny Jones's envious TV audience, adroitly ducking the verbal blows like the pro I had become. One disgruntled middle-ager in Bermuda shorts refused to believe that her sockless hero, Don Johnson, had cavorted with the likes of *me*. She insisted that the photos of us in my book had been doctored, "touched up," she smugly proclaimed.

I may not have had too many fans in Jenny's peanut gallery, but I certainly had one on stage. Beside me that harrowing afternoon was another defiant groupie, the renowned Sweet, Sweet Connie from Little Rock, Arkansas. When she told me on camera, in front of technicolor America, that I was her hero and she had followed in my footsteps, I was mortified. After all, Connie Hamzy proudly admitted to having sex with no less than thirty music men in *one* lustful night. What could that kind of behavior have to do with me? I was a one-at-a-time rock star gal, looking for long-term love and romance.

After recently spending twenty-four hours with Sweet Connie, I'm mortified about being mortified that day. This straight-talking Southerner makes no apologies for her still wildly wanton lifestyle, and I greatly respect her for it. Her beautiful smile is genuine as she reverently offers herself up on a self-designed, sequin-splattered platter to musicians and their compatriots: roadies, soundmen, lighting guys, guitar techs, managers, and promoters. Y'all come! These travelin' men keep Connie's seemingly out-of-control world spinning sweetly on its phallic axis.

Her list of conquests *is* quite astonishing. Members of the Who, the Stones, Fleetwood Mac, ZZ Top, KISS. She made naughty videos with clean-cut Rick Springfield, and got it on with a willing girl in the tour bus while Huey Lewis and the News (and their entire crew) cheered. From all of the Allman Brothers and Van Halen, two of Led Zeppelin, and a threesome with two Eagles to heated cunnilingus with Johnny Carson's bandleader Doc Severinson (!) and a salacious encounter with then governor Bill Clinton, Connie's horny history is unequalled in the annals of groupiedom. She was eternally immortalized in 1973 when Grand Funk Railroad celebrated her expertise in the classic song "We're an American Band": "Out on the road for forty days/Last night in Little Rock put me in a haze/Sweet, Sweet Connie doin' her act/She had the whole show and that's a natural fact." These four lines enhanced Connie's burgeoning reputation and made sure Little Rock was on tour itineraries. Notice that she "had the whole *show*" and not just the band. Most groupies believed it was beneath them to extend favors to the crew, but from the very beginning Connie spread the love to everyone involved in the creation of the rock and roll spectacle.

Back in swinging 1974, an intrepid journalist from *Cosmopolitan* magazine ventured into a broken-down part of Little Rock known as "Dogtown" to have a discussion with nineteen-year-old Connie at her parents' humble one-story house. As her weary mom, Joetta, hovered uncomfortably nearby, Connie happily admitted to already "taking care of two to three hundred people in the industry." This interview took place thirty-one years ago, and she still hasn't come up for air. The writer describes the shabbiness of Connie's teenage room, the rag dolls on the bed, the hamster rattling around in its cage. It all started when she was fifteen, Connie said, when she was invited backstage at a Steppenwolf concert. She made

Me and Connie.
Credit: Connie Hamzy
collection

eyes with the band and paid strict attention to the lyrics of the
song, "Hey, Lawdy Mama," all about "cock-teasing girls" who
didn't "put out."

"I kept thinking, gee, they're probably on a plane somewhere
thinking, 'That Connie, she's just a C.T.' And I decided that I
would put out to the next group that came to town."

I couldn't imagine writing this book without including the
most notorious groupie of them all, and I've been looking forward to some hometown hang time with Connie. But I've had
to change my Little Rock travel schedule a couple of times, and
it's made Connie nervous. Her distinctive rasp has eaten up quite
a chunk of my voice mail by the time I finalize the flight and
wing my way south. Her house is a mess, she says, warning me
about her four twitchy felines and less-than-stellar housekeep-
ing skills. She isn't quite convinced I'm coming anyway, insisting, "I'll believe you when I see you, *Paaam*ela." Up in the sky,

I open a recent *Spin* magazine to peruse a story entitled "Oldest Living Confederate Groupie Tells All."

The second paragraph reveals an encounter Connie had with a certain American icon: "So I'm out on the tour bus, smokin' dope and blowing roadies . . . and who comes into the back lounge? *Neil fucking Diamond.* Neil looks me up and down and nods his approval, then he gets high with us, and disappears backstage. A few minutes later, his manager says he wants to see me in his dressing room. So I knock on the door, and there's Neil waiting for me in a blue robe. And I didn't just suck him, there was fucking, too." I decide to stop here and get the whole story from the practiced mouth of the muse.

The humid summer air in Little Rock is as sticky as cotton candy as I climb out of my rental car in Connie's driveway. She is nervously waiting for me on the tiny screened-in front porch, scarily gaunt, wearing skinny, tight shorts and a Van Halen T-shirt. "You *made* it! Come on in," she shouts, before warning me again about the state of her house, which I discover isn't all that bad except for the pungent aroma of kitty cat. A bit tattered and funky around the edges, Connie's quaint little cottage is almost paid for, a fact she proudly announces, showing me her most recent mortgage bill as proof. She seems honestly thrilled that I've come to visit, and I'm struck by the dichotomy of her world-weary guilelessness. The walls overflow with photos of Connie on laps of rock stars, along with autographed pictures, backstage passes, posters, laminates, and concert tickets. She grabs the remote, hoping to surprise me with a video of our long-ago MTV groupie interviews, and when I decline she's disappointed. "I'd rather go to your local haunts," I tell her, and after musing that she might miss an important call from "*Edward* Van Halen," we head to Bennigan's, not too far from her pad on Green Meadow Drive.

We climb onto the barstools and, bubbling over, she pulls my first book out of her bag, introducing me to the owner, the bartender, and a couple of patrons as a "famous writer" in town just to interview *her.* Connie's enthusiasm is infectious. Even when locals look at her disdainfully, she's happy to get the attention, and cackles, "We were on *Jenny Jones* together!" Here, she orders her first white wine of the day and doesn't stop imbibing until well after midnight.

As she sips her chardonnay, I ask how she became music obsessed. "I was an only child, and I think that's one reason I became a groupie. I always wished for an older brother and becoming a groupie, I got a lot of 'em! Even before I hit puberty—in the fifth and sixth grades—I went to see the *Dick Clark Caravan of Stars*. Sam the Sham and the Pharaohs, Paul Revere and the Raiders, and the Yardbirds played. I always saw these good-looking gals backstage and thought, 'I don't want to be out here with all these people. When I get older I'm gonna do *that*, I'm gonna be back *there*.'" In the ninth grade, Connie was invited backstage at the fateful Steppenwolf gig, where her controversial future was secured. Her friend hooked up with singer John Kay, and Connie wound up with drummer Jerry Edmonton. "I was a virgin then, but he *did* get me out of my shirt. I said, 'I'm on my period, and I can't do anything anyway because I'm a virgin,' and he said, 'Have you ever heard of oral sex?' I said, 'What does that mean? *Talking* about it?'" She later found out that her rock conquest wasn't referring to public speaking and quickly set about learning the delicate art of giving head.

Following Steppenwolf's anti-cock-teasing lyrics to the letter, Connie was determined to "put out" for the next band to come through town. The drummer for Detroit's Frijid Pink happily removed the obstacle of Connie's virginity and was also the lucky recipient of her newfound oral knowledge. The soon-to-be Sweet Connie was on her merry way.

She's world infamous for her blow jobs, so I ask how and why that practice began. "Because you can't get pregnant doing it! And I was desperate for a backstage pass to Three Dog Night. I went to one of the roadies and said, 'I don't care what it takes. I'll blow everybody on your crew to get me back there.' And I did." Did she get to the band? "Yeah, the drummer and Chuck Negron. I blew him during the drum solo in the backstage restroom, sitting on the toilet while he stood in front of me." Was giving head an enjoyable experience? "Yeah, definitely. For one thing, it doesn't take very long and it isn't really messy." Did she swallow? Dumb question. "Hell *yeah!*" When I mention that a lot of girls don't swallow, Connie shrieks, "Then a lot of girls are sitting out there in the fucking *crowd*, aren't they? I don't know what I enjoyed more: the blow jobs or standing on stage waving at all those people from North Little Rock Old Main High School."

After knocking back her glass of wine, Connie wants to take me to the Canyon Grill, a favorite haunt. Obviously warmly familiar with her, the bartender pours wine while Connie introduces herself and flirts with a pair of young cops. Then we pick up where we left off. "After Three Dog Night it began to get around, because I had to blow and fuck promoters to get to roadies and past the security of the building. I started on the ground level and worked my way up."

Spotting backstage stickers on guitar and amp cases gave her a brilliant idea. "I went to a printer in Little Rock and got five hudnred paper stickers made that said 'Connie in Little Rock — 501.753.1005' and you know what happened? The very first batch got ripped off and some asshole plastered 'em around town and people called my parents asking, 'What's this?'" How *did* her folks deal with her blossoming popularity? "They did not have a clue for a long time—until the *song* came out, and then they began to get wind of it." What did they think all the guys were calling about? "Selling cookies for the Girl Scouts, I guess—and I sold candy for the Future Teachers of America."

Connie says she got along fine with her mom until she hit puberty. "Then she turned into a bitch. I think she was just afraid and insecure, even though my father was a good man. My mother had an agenda—she was a cunt and is to this day. She thought if she gave me enough rope, I'd hang myself. When they found out I'd lost my virginity and was fucking around, all hell broke loose. And that came about because I got the clap. I tell you what: when I lost my virginity, they couldn't have been any more hurt than if I had lost a limb."

Her home life was hellish, but even though she spent many nights at concerts, in tour buses, and in hotel rooms, Connie somehow kept her priorities straight. "It was never a question that I'd graduate high school and go to college because I knew the bands and crews wouldn't respect me if I was just some drop-out loser."

Her parents couldn't keep her at home, and conquests came fast and furious. She had a grand ol' time with Grand Funk Railroad, she "got it on" with all the members of Chicago while everyone watched the proceedings. The same happened with the Allman Brothers. A trip out of town with her mom backfired when Connie discovered they were staying in the same hotel. "The Allmans were there for a couple of days. I did the road-ies. I did everybody. They all got a kick out of it—knowing my mother was right upstairs. It was a real picnic when we got back to Little Rock and she told my dad. 'You mean all she did when you all got there was chase them bands? I sent you all over there to get her *away* from them! I can't do anything with her! We might as well put her in a juvenile home or send her to the nut-house!' They threatened that repeatedly."

Concert promoters took advantage of Connie's oral largesse and began inviting her to gigs in nearby cities. "They flew me to Oklahoma City to see KISS and to St. Louis to see the Who, which was where I wound up with Keith Moon the first time. I got flown to Shreveport to see Alice Cooper. I started fucking him way early in the ball game because I would drive to Memphis to meet him."

Gene Simmons, the monster bassist for KISS, is a longtime friend of mine, and I'm curious about his bedside manner. "He was pretty good. He's well-endowed, but you know what? The time I got it on with him, I had bad anorexia and he spent a lot of time chewing me out for being underweight. I was never with Ace Frehley. He got drunk and threw a roomful of furniture out of the hotel room next to me. I fucked Peter Criss, I fucked Paul, and he was wonderful! He told me that I've got a clit like a little dick. But when I hooked up with Peter, it was usually Peter from then on."

While her parents were on vacation in Vegas, Connie took the family car to a concert in Memphis and spent more time with Three Dog Night and their opening act, Black Oak Arkansas.

With Paul Stanley
of KISS, February
1988.
Credit: Connie Hamzy
collection

One upstanding quality Connie got from her folks was honesty, and when they got back to town they confronted her. "They said, 'When we called from Vegas, you sounded like you had something you wanted to tell us,' and I said, 'Well, you always told me to tell you the truth and while you all were gone, I drove to Memphis to see Three Dog Night.' Man, I really got an ass whipping that night. My father had a horrible temper, but then he was apologetic."

Connie and I have more in common than we realized: Waylon Jennings, Jimmy Page, and Keith Moon. She met the brilliant, manic drummer for the Who when a promoter took her backstage in St. Louis. "I was in the dressing room after the show—security wasn't the way it is nowadays—and Keith and Roger were not getting along. For some reason, Roger decided to upend a whole table full of food, then he started crying. Keith and I started fooling around, and before I knew it he had my jeans off and was fucking me with a banana to ease the mood and break the tension. Keith was that kind of guy. After you see somebody get fucked with a piece of fruit, you forget what happened five minutes earlier! Then he said, 'Come back with me to the hotel,' and I spent the night with him at the Chase Park Plaza. The whole time I was with Keith I thought, '*This* is that guy I used to see on *Where the Action Is!* He had the most beautiful facial features when he played the drums. When we weren't making love, he had a little 45-rpm record player and played a stack of records and sang along to 'em. He'd go down to the bar for booze and bring it back up to the suite and we'd sit there and drink and sing and fuck. We sang 'This Diamond Ring' and 'Love Potion Number Nine' at the top of our lungs. He invited me to go to with him to Detroit and I said, 'I can't go. I live with my parents and I ain't got any clothes.'"

Connie and I also have my early mentor, Frank Zappa, in common, but in a decidedly different way. He was always captivated by out-of-the-ordinary individuals, so their encounter doesn't surprise me. "Gosh, I was only with Frank one time and he was such a dear—and he was *so* apologetic. When I first met him during the sound check, I was fooling around with the crew because they had taken care of me all day and given me a pass. I was walking with his roadie into a little tuning room, and Frank got on the microphone and said, 'Okay, Connie, I guess that makes number ten.' He turned out to be a great lover, and that night when we were in his hotel room, he said, 'I wanna apologize to you for saying that.'"

When she was almost nineteen, two things happened that finally got Connie booted out of her childhood home. "Not much had happened with Grand Funk other than me blowing Don Brewer and Mel Schacher, and if memory serves, I took care of the keyboard player a time or two. In June of '73, I was sitting on a towel at the beach with my transistor radio on. Most of my girlfriends were out on rafts in the lake when the disc jockey said, 'Ladies and gentlemen, we just got the new song by Grand Funk Railroad, and you all are not gonna *believe* this—you know that dark-haired girl you always see backstage at concerts? Listen to the first few lyrics of this song,' and I started jumping up and down, screaming for my friends to come listen!"

Not long after "We're an American Band" blasted the airwaves, Connie's startling tell-all article shook up the community. "I got out of the house because of the interview in *Cosmopolitan*. When *that* hit the stands my mother said, 'OK, enough's enough. You're talking in this national publication about sucking dick and swallowing. You're outta here!'"

We say our good-byes to the rookie cops at Canyon Grill and on our way out, I spy a colorful store across the street offering vintage frocks. Whenever I travel I have to check out the native collectibles, and as I inspect a black velvet tunic, the salesgirl recognizes Connie and she gets a hoot out of it. She is a well-known local character of indeterminate infamy around town. For several years she was a substitute teacher, and complains she was canned due to her off-color notoriety. Nobody will give her a decent job, she claims, but Connie refuses to live anywhere but right here because Little Rock is where she is so well-known. And of course, she's listed in the phone book just in case rock stars want to look her up.

On the way back to Green Meadow Drive, Connie surprises me by suggesting we drop by the Little Rock Zoo. It seems she has to tend a small vegetable garden she has growing on zoo grounds. "I was a wonderful teacher," she says as we peer into cages at the small animal sanctuary. "They stopped me from doin' it because of who I am, and I got press to prove it. The kids loved me but they don't want me teaching school 'cause I'm so controversial. I am who I am and that ain't goin' away." I get another shock when she tells me about her part-time job. "Well, *Pam*ela, I rent wagons and baby strollers here." In fact, her little veggie patch is situated behind rows of gleaming rental buggies. She ambles over to a leafy plant and, beaming, reveals a fat, red tomato.

Back home, Connie shows me her favorite picture of bright-eyed grade-schoolers and tells me how "precious" they had been to her. "But I have dedicated my life to being a groupie!" she shrieks, as wine gurgles from the spigot attached to a Gallo box in the fridge. "Thanks to you! You started me. It's your fault!" I remind her that she was stalking Dick Clark's fresh-faced caravan before I wrote a single word of *I'm with the Band*. "I know one damned thing: *that's* when I realized that them broads backstage looked a lot more comfortable than I did out there in a pile of people."

Sweet Connie got out from under what was left of her parents' control just in time to meet up with Led Zeppelin. "I got my own apartment in the cool part of town called the Quarter, and was doin' fine when the Concerts West promoter flew me to Dallas to see Led Zeppelin. That was such a special evening. It's been chronicled in all the Zeppelin books because the tour was based in New Orleans and they were hanging with a lot of drag queens. Everybody flew the coop that night—Jimmy, Robert, and John Paul Jones went back to New Orleans; Bonham was gonna stay in Dallas because from the balcony of the hotel he saw a Corvette in the parking lot that he liked. Bonham was take no prisoners—'if I want it, I want it!' Well, he went down there and sat on the hood of the car until the owner came out. He said, 'Man, I'm John Bonham, the drummer of Led Zeppelin, and I wanna buy your 'Vette.' The guy said, 'I like y'all a lot, but don't ask me to sell my car.' So John decided to stay in Dallas until this guy sold him his car.

"That was the first time I ever had caviar—with Led Zeppelin when I was nineteen. I'll never forget that big tuna-salad fish mold covered with black caviar. And you know, I don't even *like* caviar! Sex with Bonham was real good and he just kept saying, 'I'm not leaving Dallas until I get that 'Vette. I'm gonna have 'em put it on the back of a truck. I'm gonna take it to California and drive it around.' And he got what he wanted." Did she ever spend time with Bonham again? "No, I didn't, but I *did* see Keith Moon after that and told him I'd been with Bonham and he said, 'We're gonna do something together eventually.'" Sadly, that meeting of remarkable minds never manifested.

Connie splashes more wine into her glass, then leads me into a dusty room crammed with photo albums and starts yanking out pictures of her with Rick Springfield, Ginger Baker, Ronnie Lane, Dr. John, et al. But when I ask about the picture on the living room wall of her sitting cozily with Eddie Van Halen, she's briefly at a loss for words. "It's hard to explain my relationship with Van Halen. It goes back to 1979." Questions about the virtuoso guitar player are verboten, but when I ask if I might allude to her relationship with Edward, Connie smiles slyly, "You can *allude* to it." And what about David Lee Roth? Was she ever with the last great front man? "Oh, yes, David and I were very intimate in an oral sense. We were together with another girl in the production office. We were fooling around, getting ready to blow him, and the promoter came in to watch. Then they called in David's bodyguard to watch . . . everybody had a good laugh and then he had to go onstage. By the next time they came around, David was history." I assume she then went on to Sammy Hagar. "Yeah, Sam was a lot of fun, but I believe he's mad at me. I don't think he wants me talking about it, but that's too bad. He never said *don't*."

She's been telling me all day about Doe's, the laid-back neighborhood hot spot and well-known Clinton hangout where the owner is treating us to dinner. "Who knows," she sneers. "Clinton's in town; he might even be there." Connie promises she'll divulge the details of her encounter with our former charismatic president of the United States over a colossal plate of garlicky shrimp.

After taking a gander at the shots of the handsome prez with local celebs that line the restaurant walls, I toast Connie with a glass of wine, and soon we are gaily gabbing with a table full of traveling salesmen sitting next to us. She, of course, tells them all about what brought me to town, and it turns out that one of them had read my books. We both sign autographs and pose for snapshots, feeling like the divas of the diner. Crustaceans are served and while we dig in, Connie launches into her anti-Clinton tirade. I soon discover that she doesn't share my admiration for William Jefferson Clinton.

"I sometimes went to the bar at the Riverfront Hilton for happy hour and the manager said, 'If you're a regular here, you're more than welcome to use the pool!' Rush had stayed there a few days earlier and we all partied at the pool. Anyway, I was the only person out there that day. No bands, everybody was gone. I was in my bathing suit, writing in my diary, minding my own business until two guys came up to me. One of 'em used to live near me, and he said, 'Connie? I thought that was you. It's Mike Gaines. I used to be your neighbor. I'm working for the governor's office now.' Then he said, 'The governor wants to say hello to you.' I said, 'Well, Mike, I met him before, at an Olivia Newton-John concert.' He said, 'He wants to say hello to you *again*,' and I said, 'I don't have any clothes on.' He said, 'That's exactly why he wants to talk to you.'" Connie threw a towel around her shoulders and followed Mike inside. "Clinton's standing there saying, 'I just want you to know you made my day, laying out there in that little purple bikini. Do you have a room here?' I said, 'No, Governor, I don't.' He said, 'You *sure* you don't have a room?' I said, 'No, Governor, I just snuck in to use the pool, sorry.' He said, 'Well, where can we go? Looks like we can't go in there,' he opened another door and said, 'We can't go in there,' then he opened the doors to the laundry room and we go in there and proceed to start groping and fondling. I stroked his cock—he's very well endowed—and right when we were about to get to it, he moaned and somebody popped her head up from behind the washing machine. He said, 'I guess we'd better get out of here.' We stepped back into the hall and he said, 'You gonna be here later?' and I said, 'I'm gonna be here all afternoon, Governor.' He said, 'I'll call you or come back. I gotta be up at the Capitol to direct the legislature.' I swear to God, I never addressed that cocksucker any way other than 'Governor.' Afterward, I go in the bar and tell the manager about it and he says, 'Yeah, I know, the governor is a whore *dog*.'"

I wonder why Connie is so vitriolic about the Clinton skirmish. Apparently Big Bill later denied that it ever happened, and honesty is paramount to Connie. Her mom warned her to keep mum, but the tale of the groupie and the governor soon got around and the *Arkansas Democrat-Gazette* ran the sordid tale on the front page. When denials came from the governor's office, the right-wing *American Spectator* asked Connie to take a lie detector test. "They were *so* out to get his sorry fucking ass, they said, 'We'll pay if you'll do it,' and I said, 'Hey, I've got the balls to take it.' They said there was a 50/50 chance I might not pass and I had to live with that. I smoked dope, I drank wine the night before, and told the polygrapher exactly how much I drank, how much I smoked. I said, 'Look, I was nervous, but I guarantee you, I'm telling you the truth.' They gave me the test three times and I passed it all three times."

Connie may have aced the lie detector test, but the odds were with Clinton, and the scathing press and negative fallout wore her to a frazzle. She still fumes with anger. "I started talking about what he was way before Paula Jones. The Clinton deal almost put me on the streets. He is a bigger groupie than either of us *ever* was; he may not be sucking any dick, but it ain't all about the dick sucking, it's about the handshaking and glad-handing. I might be a slut and a whore, but I ain't no liar."

I wonder if Connie ever attempted to settle down, and she tells me that only once did she give domesticity a try. "I got engaged spring of '83—he was a bond daddy, one of those guys who sells stocks and bonds—and he always had blow. We got along great until a gig came to town, then we didn't get along worth a fuck. I told him from the get-go that I'm gonna keep goin'. But he was enamored about who I am, you know, 'Oh, *I'm* dating Sweet, Sweet Connie, she's got celebrity status.' Plus I got him to the gigs because he was selling blow. But I'd tell him, 'Don't be hoverin' over me because I'm gonna be *gone*, I'm gonna be way out of your line of vision—in the bus, in the dressing room, I'm not gonna be wantin' to hang around with you.' When there weren't gigs, we were havin' a great time; havin' great sex—he had a huge cock—and my parents were happy. Their little girl was finally gonna give up all that bullshit and get married. My mother and I looked for a dress, and I knew better than to get a white one, so we got a little sundress because I wanted something I could wear to gigs. I've still got it. He and I sort of tried to hang on to the threads, but one thing led to another and we broke up."

Fortunately, Connie has always been listed in the phone book, and shortly after her engagement unraveled, she got a surprise call from a certain raconteur. "He said, 'Connie, this is Jimmy Page,' and I said, 'I don't believe you.'" Jimmy put Phil Carlo on the phone, a record exec she knew from her days with John Bonham. "He said, 'Connie, it's Phil—that was Jimmy. We want you to come to Dallas. He's doing the ARMS tour and we'll prepay your ticket.' I was substituting that day and went to the airport when school let out." Connie spent the next three days trading rooms with Jimmy and Phil. "I *did* make Jimmy mad because it was during my anorexia period and Phil called me aside and said, 'Jimmy does *not* want you throwing up in his suite anymore.' The anorexia manifested when I got engaged. I was torn between what's right and '*I wanna keep doing what I wanna do!*' I thought, 'I'll just kill myself.' It didn't work out, but it made people take notice." Did she still have ribald relations with Jimmy even though he didn't want her hurling in his suite? "Yeah, as much as possible, but I mainly gave him head. He was doin' a lot of nose candy." Connie pauses to light up a bowl. She offers me a hit of pot, but I have to decline because I'm on the job. "The majority of the time I was with Jimmy he spent bitching about Robert. And I know what they were bitching about: they were blaming each other for Bonham's death. But Phil was *fabulous*."

When her dad died in October 1984 with bad blood still brewing, Connie drowned her grief with another pop star. "Rick Springfield came to town and I guess I really needed to let my hair down. It was the first gig I'd been to since my dad died and Rick and his crew treated me real good, gave me passes and let me hang out in the dressing room. I got it on with his massage therapist, and they made a movie to watch on the airplane. He was Dr. Noah Drake on *General Hospital*. It was just something to get my mind off the fact that we had buried my dad, and two days after the funeral, my mother stopped speaking to me."

Since that day over twenty years ago, Connie and her long-suffering mother have been estranged. Has she ever had the desire to patch things up? "Well, yeah, but she's got an unlisted phone number and if I show up she'll probably have me arrested."

With Rick
Springfield,
September 1985.
Credit: Connie Hamzy
collection

Connie bought her house in Little Rock when she sold her diaries about her unrepentant life. I applaud this brash, unabashed woman, and I'm glad she'll always have a place to hang her laminated passes. As I gather up the photos and articles she's given me, I ask the same cliché question that everybody asks me: does she regret anything she's done? "Not really—nothing that's related to the music business anyway. Actually," she grins, taking another drag, "I'm very happy, *very* content." I tell her I love how she proudly admits that she's a bit off her rocker. "Notoriety will drive anybody nuts," she says simply.

Connie Hamzy may have reached the ripe middle age of fifty, but she has no intention of behaving like an adult anytime soon. "As long as I can do this, yeah, I'll do it, but hell! Now I gotta pace myself a little differently. But I'm gonna make up for lost time *this* weekend. Like, OK: I know the lay of the land on Dylan and Willie comin'—they're doin' Memphis the night before they play Little Rock, they'll be leaving Memphis and gettin' here about three A.M. Tommy, the guitar tech, said he wants to come over here because he doesn't have to start working on both guitars until about two in the afternoon, and I live close to where the gig's gonna be. When his bus pulls in I'm gonna jump up, run over there and pick him up, bring him over here. On Friday I'll run over to the zoo, get my check, water the garden a little, then run to the bank, cash my check, come home, sleep as much as possible until Tommy calls and says, 'The buses are here, come get me!' Then after we fuck around I'll take him back to the gig and spend the rest of the day and the evening with him and . . . what I'd *really* like to do is go with him on the road because on the Fourth of July, Willie Nelson has his picnic in Fort Worth . . ."

Sweet Connie can't wait to get on the road again, and that's a natural fact.

Gayle O'Connor

Crazy, Crazy Nights

*I*t's a soggy, gray afternoon in Seattle, and I'm sitting in one of a zillion rustic coffee houses, waiting for a compelling woman I met on the Internet to arrive and divulge her wanton tales. From her e-mails, Gayle O'Connor seems to be a seasoned, unrepentant, music-crazed biker chick, and I can't wait to take a trip back to her 1970s groupie years. I've just ordered my second chai tea when I hear the unmistakable thunderous vroom-vroom of a gargantuan motorcycle. I peer out the window to watch Gayle climb from the snazzy Harley-Davidson, pull off her helmet to reveal short, spiky platinum hair, and stride purposefully into the caffeine establishment. I had told her about my ludicrously red hair, and she recognizes me as soon as I reach the bottom of the stairs to greet her. Gayle is clothed top to bottom in black leather. Her eyes sparkle, crinkling at the corners, and her teeth are impossibly white. She gives me a hearty, firm handshake, and her smile pulls me right in.

She orders a large black coffee and we take our drinks to a quiet table upstairs. Gayle speaks in quick, clipped sentences and laughs raucously and easily. From my first question, she is off and sprinting.

"My first rock and roll memory? I was nine years old, sitting in the bedroom with my sister, listening to the Rolling

Stones—early stuff, like 'Paint It Black.' In '68, '69, we lived in Laos. My dad was in the Vietnam War. He was with the CIA, Air America stuff, going into the jungle, training the troops. He was a raging alcoholic, and there was a lot of drinking overseas. They only had one radio station in Laos, one hour on Sundays. The bathroom was the only place we could get reception, so we'd sit in there and listen to American music. The first album I had to have was the soundtrack to *Easy Rider*. And the Beatles' *White Album* had just come out. My very first concert was the Monkees. Peter Tork was my first rock and roll crush. Micky Dolenz came to my high school for our homecoming game, but that was years later, and no big deal at that point. I was probably out smoking pot.

"I was the rebel in my family, but my mom thought I was really good. I'm in the middle. My two sisters and brother always grouped together, and I was way over on the other side.

Gayle at forty
years old.
Credit: Gayle O'Connor

They would always tell my mom, 'Gayle is the worst. You don't know what she's up to.' Starting in my teens, they separated themselves from me. My younger sister thought my older sister walked on water. And my brother was full of teen angst because my mom and dad split up. My dad left and didn't contact us: no Christmas cards, no presents, no nothing. After that, we were basically raised by two women with no man around. You can read between the lines if you want to.

"I remember I had a poem on my bedroom mirror, even before I started the groupie scene, that said, 'Music is my first love/ it will be my last/ Music of the future/ music of the past/ To live without my music/ would be impossible to do/ In this world of troubles/ my music pulls me through.' I would shut the bedroom door and blast Pink Floyd's *Dark Side of the Moon*. I started taking drugs in seventh grade, starting with LSD. I was altered at thirteen! I did a lot of LSD and a lot of pot all through school. I was drinking then too, and the very first time I drank, I blacked out. I used my allowance to buy it. And I stole money from my mom. I stole a lot. I was a big thief.

"My first concert was here in Seattle—Alice Cooper. It was '73, and I was a junior in high school. I went with my friend Michelle, and I had this blue halter dress, but my mom wouldn't let me wear it, so I changed on the way. I had a big star painted over one of my eyes, with glitter. Some guy from Alice's entourage gave us passes, and we ended up backstage. They were going to Vancouver and said, 'You girls should come to Canada.' So Michelle and I packed a bag and got a ride to the border. But we weren't allowed to cross because we didn't have concert tickets. We said, 'Oh, no, no. We're with the band.' But the border patrol said, 'Sure, *right*,' and sent us away. So we went through the woods in our huge wedgie platform shoes—mine were green snake skin—and kept heading north, heading north. We hid anytime a car went by, and stayed in the woods. Swear to God! And I was only seventeen. Eventually, we hitchhiked and got a ride to the Bay Shore Inn where the band was staying. It was the middle of the night and we ran into a couple of roadies in the lobby. Bottom line: my friend ended up in one bed, and I ended up in the other. I wasn't a virgin, but I'd only slept with maybe two guys. I guess I was ready to embrace the rock and roll experience because I didn't say no. We got passes for Alice Cooper, partied like crazy, and came home.

"That was the beginning, and once I started, it was *on*. I needed to do it more because it made me feel like I was somebody. It was very heady. The guys were famous and I was with them, getting in and out of limos. I suppose they were just flings, although I wanted more. I wanted be their girlfriend, but I didn't go about it in quite the right way. My next big groupie experience was with Bad Company. I was with Phil Carlo from Atlantic. He was a beautiful man. I went to San Francisco with them, and then to Arizona for a couple weeks with Phil. He was taking a sabbatical and called and said, 'Do you wanna join me?' We rode horses and stayed at the Camelback Inn, where we sat in the swimming pool and drank. What a life. Oh, and Mick Fleetwood was one of my first big ones. I look at pictures of him now and I'm mortified. He was one of my first big ones. He was at least twenty years older than me. That was before I got picky, but he was very nice, so I don't want to say anything assholey.

"My first job out of high school was selling clothes at Jeans West, a slick clothing store. I robbed them blind. When I left that job, I was nineteen and started topless dancing. I was making a ton of money stripping, enough to keep myself in drugs and booze. During that time, Kansas came to town and I was with their manager, Jeff Glixman. He was beautiful, with a big nose, and long, curly hair. It was the first time I tried MDA, which is the ecstasy of today. It didn't matter if I was with a roadie or a manager, I just wanted to be a part of that scene and be set apart from normal people. I wanted to be special and I was. It was such a fantasy life. I'd get so sad when they left and promised to call. Sometimes they would and a lot of times they wouldn't. But sometimes my goal was exactly what I got, and then I got outta there. *Next!* It was power.

"I had a wild night with Stephen Stills in L.A. He was nasty, yeah, we had a nasty time. He was pretty raw. But he was also very rude afterward. He was great when it was to his advantage, but then he became hurtful. He was one of *those*. I did spend the night, but the next day, he was done. I had a crazy night with Davy Johnstone from Elton John's band. Apparently he was dating Kiki Dee for a while. I remember being in bed with him, sitting on top of him while he was on the phone with Miss Dee. I remember thinking, 'I am so *it* right now!' There were a lot of guys I felt good about. I partied with Peter Frampton's group one night. There was Barry Brandt from Angel, and David Flett, the guitar player from Manfred Mann—I had a great time with him. But before they even came to town, Roger Earl, the drummer for Foghat, was the only one I *had* to have. I said, 'That will be mine, somehow. I don't know how, but *that* will be mine.' There was something about him. That's when I learned about going down to the local radio station when bands were being interviewed.

"I ended up with Pat Travers when he came to Seattle and he asked me to go to Portland with him on the bus. On the way back, I was really tired, so I crawled into one of the beds to sleep. I woke up and felt hands on me; touching my hair, rubbing up behind me. I reached back to grab his hair. Pat had long blond hair, but this person had short hair. I sat up and said, 'What the fuck?' It was one of the roadies. Pat had told him, 'Go ahead.' I was devastated and so hurt. That was mean. Pat Travers was an asshole, and you feel free to put that in print.

"I went backstage and met Chicago. Walter Parazaider, one of the sax players in Chicago, was a huge one for me. I have pictures of him in boxers with this little stuffed Pooh bear. He was very married. A *lot* of them were very married. Ringo Starr came to a party for Chicago. And for me, the Beatles are on another plane. I dated George Harrison's road manager or PR guy, can't remember which. I was in the car with him and he said, 'I gotta stop at George's house.' It was up there in the hills. He told me the story about the street signs getting stolen—Blue Jay Way. We walked in and I was standing in George Harrison's house—in front of one of the Beatles! He was very nice and polite. I didn't know if I could say, 'Oh my God!' I didn't, because I was being

At Pride in 2005.
Credit: Gayle O'Connor

cool. Oh, and one of the best was Alto Reed. He played in the J. Geils Band and with Bob Seger in the Silver Bullet Band. He was *awesome*. He was so real. No man had ever told me that my body parts were beautiful. I'll never forget it. I was mortified because I was so young. He sat down there between my legs, touching me, looking at me, then looking into my eyes, saying, 'Just look at it. It's beautiful.' He's the one who taught me to be vocal, how to talk during sex. I just got goose bumps thinking about that. Then in '76, KISS came to town.

"First I slept with Paul Stanley, and then I slept with Gene Simmons. Gene was fantastic! He is so smart and polite. He's just real. We had a great time. I hung out with him at the Sunset Marquis, and they left town three weeks later. I was living with this girl, Debbie. The phone rang and it was Gene. I said, 'Hey, what's up?' I was gesturing to Debbie, going, 'It's *Gene*, oh my God!' He said, 'We're taking a break before we do the next album. I was wondering if you'd like to come to New York for a couple of weeks?'

"Did I take him up on it? Yes, of course. Did he pick me up at the airport? No, of course not. He was staying on Riverside Drive. I got there and I was dyin'! We shopped, went to restaurants, did normal things. It was during the time KISS wore makeup, so we could just walk down the street. Now mind you, he was wearing six-inch platforms and skull rings on all his fingers. He had skintight jeans and was so tall anyway. Nobody recognized him, but he still looked like a freak. The night I really remember was at a well-known restaurant. We went to the door and there was a private party for Hall & Oates going on. So the doorman said, 'I'm sorry, there's a private party.' And Gene, very eloquently said, 'Oh, well, thank you anyway.' We started to walk away, then the doorman said, 'Hey, wait a minute, aren't you Gene Simmons? Oh, you can come in!' I was twenty years old, and in this room was Rod Stewart, the Rolling Stones, Hall & Oates, Bad Company. I was standing against a cigarette machine with my heart racing, thinking, 'I can't believe I'm here!' And I was with Gene so it was a huge night.

"Gene's mom came to visit and she was very Jewish. His real name is Chaim, and she'd always call him that. She wanted to feed us and kept asking, 'Are you hungry? You want to eat something? Let's feed him, he's too skinny!' One day we went downstairs and the table was just filled with food. She was a sweetheart. Gene had a hobby of cutting and pasting every single article ever written about KISS—German magazines, Chinese, Japanese—an unbelievable collection of everything written about him. One day I was sitting downstairs with his mom, looking at these KISS scrapbooks, and we finally went through the ones we had. So I said, 'Let me go upstairs and get some more.' So Gene gives me more scrapbooks for us to look at. I unzip one, and it's *filled* with naked women and beaver shots. I about died, but his mom says to me, 'Oh, my son, I know he's kind of a naughty boy, but he's a good boy.' Poor mom. I took my pictures out of his scrapbook. Yeah, I took mine right out of his little book.

"Gene knew I had already been with Paul Stanley, but he didn't care. And when I wound up with Gene, did Paul care? No, he didn't. Those were the days. Gene took me to the studio one afternoon, and it was the first time I hung out with Peter Criss, and we just clicked. Gene was very square. When I even had a glass of wine at dinner, he would say, 'Are you OK to talk? To walk? You've had some wine.' So after the session that night, Peter and his wife, Lydia, came to dinner with us. Well, the chemistry between Peter and I was just raw. We went back to Gene's house after dinner. When I went to get something to drink, Peter came after me, and in the kitchen, it just happened. We were on each other like flies on shit. With Gene and Lydia right upstairs! I was going to be leaving in three days, and I thought, 'What am I doing? I'm here in New York with Gene and I'm making out with Peter. Oh my God, what are we going to do?' So we go back upstairs, and I'm trying to be cool. About five o'clock in the morning, I was in bed with Gene and the phone rang. He answered the phone, handed it to me, saying, 'It's for you.' It was Peter saying, 'Can you get away? I'll meet you downstairs.' Gene turned over and went back to sleep, so I slid out of bed, went downstairs, and jumped in Peter's sports car, and we roared off. We went to his manager's apartment for three days. It was a very white New York apartment. We fucked our brains out, ordered in, and did so much blow. Oh, Peter was off the hook. And hung like a horse. Peter was huge! Oh, it was *on!* I called Gene and he said, 'I think it's probably time you come get your stuff, huh?' He was cool. I went and got my stuff, and to this day when I see Gene, he's totally cool.

"But I still have sadness because I fell madly in love with Peter. He was probably my first real love. I thought he was going to leave Lydia and come to me. He got in a whole bunch of trouble because he delayed the recording of the album. I have no idea where his wife thought he was. The next time KISS came to L.A., I spent the entire week with Peter at the hotel. They were photographed for the Christmas cover of *Circus* magazine with fake snow all over them, holding red candles. I still have that red candle. Peter brought it back for me. He had this drug box that we kept our blow in, with three plastic containers. I still have that little jewel case too. A month after KISS left town, I found out I was pregnant. He was the only one I had been with, so it was his. I was devastated. I called him and he said, 'Since we can't have it together, then . . .' Whatever guys say to make you get an abortion. So I got the abortion the day before Thanksgiving in 1977. And I cried and cried.

"Usually, I partied with roadies, managers, just having a good time. My friends would ask, 'Why are you hanging out with him? He's just a roadie.' I wasn't starstruck in a way that would make me sleep with somebody I thought was an asshole. If David Lee Roth had been nice, I'd have slept with him in a heartbeat! But he was an asshole. I was at a party for the Who, and I was a stripper at the time. Another woman there was also a stripper. Roger Daltrey turned to her and said, 'Why don't you fucking dance for us?' and I looked at him and said, 'Why don't you fucking sing for us? She's not working right now!' He was cocky and belligerent, like David Lee Roth. They thought they were God's gift. Roger Daltrey? An asshole *and* short! But that night, we were all partying and it was pretty crazy. Keith Moon sat next to me on the bed, locked my eyes, and proceeded to act out the Randy Newman song '(Beware of the) Naked Man'—'Old lady standing on the corner/middle of the cold, cold night . . .' He was so crazy. He put his room key in my hand, closed his fingers over it, and said, 'Be there in an hour.' I said, 'I don't think so,' and handed it right back to him. I started talking with Pete Townshend, and I could tell he was coming on to me. I chose Pete that night, and he was friggin' *wild*. I was wearing boots that I bought at Nordstrom—red cowboy boots. He picked me up and took me in the shower. He turned the water on, and we did it against the shower wall. I had my fucking red boots on and they got ruined, and I'll never forget it, 'cause Nordstrom took 'em back! Yeah, Pete was really nasty. We had great sex. It was off the hook, all over the room, and it was just raw. And he was cool the next day. He was nice. I remember leaving there feeling really good. You know, I wasn't there to fuck the stars. If it happened, it happened. When I ended up sleeping with people of Pete Townshend's caliber, I thought, 'Wow, I guess I just slept with Pete Townshend!'

"One night that really stands out was when Foreigner came to town. I was with Rick, I don't remember his last name or what he played, but he was the only Rick in Foreigner. When they came to Seattle, a lot of bands wanted to see Jimi Hendrix's grave. So we'd jump in the limo and I'd take 'em out there. That night, Foreigner wanted a really nice dinner. So we went to Iver's Seafood House and I was the only woman at the table. It was the whole band and the management. They put me at the head of the table and I chose the wine. I was treated like a queen that night.

"In the late '80s, I was dating a married man, Tom. A band I partied with was in town that night and I had a pass to the show. My phone rang on my way out the door, and Tom said, 'If you want me, I'm walking out on my wife. Come get me now.' I made a choice to not go to the show. I picked up Tom instead, and that was the start of my life with him. I actually took him to a couple concerts with me. I took him to meet Patrick Moraz from the Moody Blues. By the way, Patrick and I are back in touch. I sent an e-mail to his Web site and got a note back—I could just hear his sweet British accent—'Oh, how are you my love? I think about you often.' So Tom and I got married in '89, and he was just happy that he married a woman who fucked Jimmy Buffett, because Jimmy Buffett is his icon. It was at a party after a concert, and Jimmy had a broken leg at the time. I was in the kitchen making drinks and he was hobbling around. He made some comment about what a great bartender I was, and maybe I'd like to be his *private* bartender. We ended up leaving the party and having our own! Let's put it this way, he was on the bottom.

"I got into bodybuilding because I missed the lights. I started lifting and exercising, and the trainer at the gym said, 'Wow, you have great potential to be a bodybuilder.' He was right, because I've got the symmetry. So I started lifting, and decided to compete before I was forty. I took second in my first show! I did that for six years during my marriage. We moved around a lot because of Tom's jobs. My son, Seamus, was born in Sacramento and he's lived in San Diego, Florida, Texas, and now Seattle. Tom and I were together for twelve years. What happened was we started having three-ways. We were in San Diego, and Seamus was about eight. I said to Tom, 'I think I'm gay.' He said, 'No, you're not.' I was crying, and said, 'Yeah, I think I am.' He said, 'I think you have the propensity to like women too. I'm willing to let you explore that side of who you are.' So I proceeded to meet a woman and fall in love. Tammy was a big bodybuilder with a gorgeous body. I'd gotten sober in '87 and hadn't had a drink in eleven years. Well, Tammy introduced me to GHB, and that was the beginning of my demise. It took me down really far. It's a drug that affects the same dopamine receptors as alcohol and makes you feel high and giddy, like you're the life of the party. It only lasts an hour or so, then you need another little dose or scoop. Tammy told me it would enhance my bodybuilding, but I had stopped going to AA and forgot I was a dopehead. If you sip a little bit too much—one minute, you're there, the next minute, you're out. Just *out*. I have a scar on my chin to prove it. But it wasn't until I bought my first drink that I thought, 'Wow. I'm drinking. I haven't had a drink in sixteen years.' In April 2001, I checked myself into a women's treatment center here in Seattle. I was their first GHB case, and my withdrawals were very scary, acidlike. I was lying in bed with the ceiling moving, fighting it. Then I thought, 'You know what, Gayle? If this is what it is, just go with it.' While in treatment I met a girl named Melody and started having an affair. When I got out, I left my husband in a horrible way. He was still madly in love, hoping we could resurrect us because of the treatment. Instead, I went off with this woman and my son.

"The only job I could find, at the age of forty-four, was making $12 an hour. Talk about humbling. Mel and I split up, then I met my girlfriend Deb. And over time, with Tom working his program, and me working mine, we've come to a better place. Now I'm a marketing director for a legal software company. Who'da thunk it? But I'm still edgy. I worked in the library of a law firm for fifteen years, and no one would have guessed. I'm a chameleon. I can play the part, put on the suit, but I can totally go the other way. But they respect my work, so I get away with it. I bought my house a year ago. I'm an avid Harley rider. I have an '05 Softtail Deluxe. I love my bike. I'm glad I didn't ride before, because I probably would've wrecked it. That's why God didn't bring it into my life until now. So I ride with friends, and life is good. And guess what? I'm five years sober today, April 11. I'll betcha there are some men who read this that'll say, 'Thank God she quit drinking!' I'm going to the meeting tonight where I checked myself in to rehab, to get my five-year coin. I've got good friends; I'm healthy, which is a miracle. I love what I do. Deb and I have broken up more than once, but what else is new? Welcome to the world of lesbian relationships. She thinks it's horrific that I'm doing this interview, but I see that time in my life as full of great experiences, and so much fun! I have absolutely no regrets, but Deb thinks you should put experiences like I had under the rug. She takes more of my mom's attitude, and I say, 'Get over yourself! It was a blast!' Her problem, not mine. Being in recovery, I certainly have codependency problems, and that's all about letting go of your partner's issues. C'mon, that was twenty-five years ago, a whole different era.

"Many times I've sat in reflection, and because of all my using and drinking, I blew what could have been a dream life with one of these guys. I could have turned a few of those relationships into something more. I was probably pretty rough to be around sometimes. There's a Moody Blues video, and it begins with a woman ironing in her kitchen. She had obviously been a groupie, and she starts thinking back about her wild life, wondering, 'How did I get *here*?' And there were many years when I felt 'Wow, my life is so boring, look what it's come to. Now, in sobriety, I treasure the memories, but when I buy a ticket and go to a concert, I don't want to be in the friggin' audience in my seat! I want to be up front, up close, I want to feel a part of it. About ten years ago I went to an Aerosmith concert by myself. I was watching the show and this roadie handed me a pass and said, 'Come back after the show.' 'Oh my God,' I thought, 'I'm almost forty years old and I've still got it!'"

Margaret Moser
and the Texas Blondes

Slow Dazzle

A few years ago I was invited to speak as part of the first-ever groupie panel at Austin's annual South by Southwest Music Conference by the queen bee of Austin's mind-blowing music scene, Margaret Moser. It was one of the best-attended panels that year, and we had an unbridled blast enlightening the industry hipsters about the tricks and trials of groupie-dom. Margaret and I hit it off like we'd been hanging out for decades.

When she invited me to another groupie panel at the ROCKRGRL Music Conference in Seattle, we crazy-glued our bond and also got to swap sensuous tidbits with Penny Trumbull, formerly Pennie Lane, founder of Portland's Flying Garter Girls.

A few years younger than me, Margaret used the GTO's as role models when she pulled together a group of love-minded, music-blinded dolls to create the Texas Blondes. They became notorious in no time, and although their reign lasted barely three years, the comely clique made an enduring impression.

I've been enjoying Austin since that first groupie panel, and this honest-to-god music city has become one of my homes away from home. I've made lots of friends, including Margaret's flamboyant younger brother, Stephen, who writes the uninhibited style column for the *Austin Chronicle*.

Woody Harrelson, Margaret Moser, and Willie Nelson.

Credit: Margaret Moser

Margaret has been married a couple of times, and is now happily in love with Burnin' Mike Vernon, guitarist in one of Austin's most revered bands, 3 Balls of Fire. It's SXSW time again, and in between our absurdly chaotic schedules (checking out hot bands), I somehow finagle a chatty hour alone with her over plates of spicy Mexican food. She is a senior staff writer at the *Chronicle*, and for over twenty years has produced the prestigious Austin Music Awards. Just last night she inducted the cult band the 13th Floor Elevators into the Austin Hall of Fame.

"I come from a literary background that encouraged reading of all kinds," Margaret tells me, dipping chips into fresh salsa. "I'm the one who read the cereal box at the breakfast table. I read *anything*, but also read between the lines. Not just people being written about, but the ones doing the writing. I remember being in eighth grade, looking at Janis Joplin's 45, 'Down On Me.' The song on the flip side was called 'Bye-Bye Baby' by Powell St. John. I had no idea who that was, but the name stuck in my mind. I read music labels the way other girls didn't. 'What does *producer* mean? Who are these people on the liner notes?' So to induct Powell St. John as part of the Elevators—and remember looking at that Joplin label—it was full circle for me."

How did Margaret go from reading about the music world to being in the thick of it? "You didn't have a lot of options in San Antonio; even kids who liked the Monkees didn't care who was writing the songs. Could N. Diamond who wrote 'I'm a Believer' be the same Neil Diamond my mother listens to? Are C. King and G. Goffin the same people writing those girl-group records? I was connecting the information, but it wasn't going anywhere because I didn't have kindred spirits. But when I picked up the *Rolling Stone* groupie issue, I thought, 'Yeah, hey! *This* is what I wanna do!' I didn't have the sense that groupies were sluts—they looked like glamorous, fun-loving young women to me. I felt like an outcast, so it was a way to distinguish myself and be some-body on my own. I'd go back to school after a show, and think, 'Ha ha, you jackasses paid five bucks for a concert last night, and *I* was backstage.' My first experience emulating the GTO's was in '71. I made baby-doll outfits with my girlfriends, with hands sewn over the breasts. I was putting together my first written collection called 'The Groupie Papers,' and I reviewed records, but didn't know how to get them published. I didn't have the guy mentality like Cameron Crowe. So groupiedom was my way in, my entrée. I went in on my knees and kept my eyes wide open."

I always enjoy finding out how it all began. "The first time I weaseled my way backstage was for Joe Cocker's Mad Dogs and Englishmen. I just nosed around, and the bug bit me. The first musician I slept with was Norman Mayell, who was drum-ming for Blue Cheer. The next thing I remember was a concert with Badfinger, Leon Russell, and Quicksilver. We were hang-ing over the backstage waving at the guys, letting them look up our dresses. I ended up sleeping with John Galley who played keyboards with Leon Russell—I've always had it bad for key-board and bass players. Then I was with Robert Cardwell from Mother Earth. He was my first experience with cocaine and a big dick, and that notched the whole thing up. I'd get there around three P.M. for Jethro Tull or John Mayall's sound check and weasel my way backstage and wind up with *some*body!"

At sixteen, Margaret fell in love with Gary Kellaher, an eighteen-year-old like-minded music lover, and after moving around, they wound up in Austin in 1973. "Willie Nelson just had his first picnic; ZZ Top had the Barn Dance, and this was a dope-smokin' hippie haven. We were *home*! And there were all these young, upcoming musicians, including a set of brothers: Jimmie Vaughan and his younger brother, Stevie Ray. I started gearing more toward the blues, hanging out with all the blues musicians."

By spring 1976, Margaret was freewheelin' again and looking for her own creative outlet. "I picked up the local underground newspaper and they were looking for somebody to clean the office, and I thought, 'That's for me!' I started tidying up and answering phones at the *Austin Sun*, and the first thing I did was nose around the music department. There was a new column called Backstage. We were at a staff meeting and the editor asked, 'What's gonna be in Backstage this week?' Nobody said anything, so I said, 'I know Randy California from Spirit. I can get an interview with him.'"

Although she had only met Spirit's singer once, Margaret was tight with the owners of the Armadillo club. "It was the cultural center of Austin's hip community, and I could *sail* backstage anytime I wanted to. People like Waylon Jennings and Gram Parsons played there. Spirit did a show, and I got the job to interview Randy California. I hadn't a clue as to what I was doing. I took some notes with me and he was *so* hot—I remember how sexy he was—and he said, 'Do you wanna do the interview back at the hotel?' I said 'Sure!' We ended up in the bathtub, and later I sat on the toilet in my underwear, interviewing him for the *Sun*. The sex was pretty quick—I'm sure there was cocaine involved—but I *do* remember him sinking down in that huge bathtub, his beautiful, curly hair all wet over his shoulders. I did my little interview, which I didn't fact-check, and messed up the name of his label. But I turned it in and they printed it. That was my way in, and I made myself fairly indispensable at the

Margaret Moser, Candye Kane, and me way after bewitching hour.
Credit: Pamela Des Barres

paper. I was just starting my writing career and Rolling Thunder came to town. What a zoo! I took a cab to the Driscoll and the party was in full swing. I was dressed to the nines, walking up the marble staircase, and *down* the stairs comes Bob Dylan. He was so handsome, and he was *Bob Dylan*. He smiled at me, took my hand, and said, 'Nice to meet you. Hope I see you later.' I was just as high as could be—I don't think I've ever been higher; there was cocaine flying around like crazy. Everybody was in and out of the bathroom, so I walked in there and ran into Mick Ronson. He grabbed me, pulled my dress up, and was fucking me within thirty seconds. I hardly knew who Mick Ronson was, except that he was really handsome: I wasn't into Bowie, but I liked this guy's accent and he sure was cute. So I wrapped my legs around him and we went at it."

I know Margaret still frequents Austin's divine Driscoll Hotel. Does she ever walk by the restroom and recall that decadent night? "I was there in November with John Cale, laughing my ass off about it. I was in that bathroom with Mick Ronson for twenty minutes, having sex and snorting coke. Afterward, I went into one of the bedrooms and saw Roger McGuinn. He was wearing a big belt buckle covered with rhinestones—it had to have been the size of your tape recorder—and I was dazzled by it. I was wearing one of those '70s dresses, made of *Nyestra*—shiny, clingy polyester that snagged on *anything*. I was staring at Roger because I thought he was so handsome. He was sitting on the bed and I was standing up, and he grabbed me and started kissing my breasts. I said, 'You've been a hero of mine since seventh grade,' and he said, 'How old were you in seventh grade?' I said, 'Oh, eleven or twelve,' and he said, 'Did you have to wear a school uniform?' I thought, 'Maybe he'd like me to wear anklets and black patent leather shoes too.' I was completely entranced, and next thing I knew *we* were in the bathroom and—yes, I know, sloppy seconds and all that. From the waist down, my Nyestra dress was shredded. It was never wearable again, but I kept it anyway."

I try to imagine bespectacled folkie Roger McGuinn going at it atop the bathroom sink. "He was something else! I was loving it because he was all over me—and I *knew* who he was, unlike Mick Ronson. I walked around knock-kneed for the rest of the party."

Margaret says that was when she "embraced groupiedom." But she also had a fledgling writing career and made an important decision that night. "I wondered how I was going to compromise the pussy and the brain, both of which were going full tilt, so I decided not to sleep with local musicians anymore—that was where I drew the line." Margaret laughs, "I just continued to sleep with national and touring musicians."

Taking the advice of a music-savvy friend, Margaret decided to check out an Armadillo show by a former member of the Velvet Underground. "The moment I hit backstage, I was thrown into the dark, feeling my way around, and ran smack into this guy wearing a hard hat and camouflage. He looked down at me and I looked up at him. I gasped and could hardly breathe. I didn't know who he was, but he led this group of people onstage and I just went 'Uh, uh, uh . . .' It was April 17, 1979. I fell in love with John Cale on the spot."

John's set mesmerized Margaret, and pulling a poster off the wall, she asked him to sign it for her. "He smiled, and asked my name. When I told him, he gave me an odd look and wrote 'Best Wishes, Margaret.' I reached for the poster and he pulled it back so I had to lean forward. He said, 'What are you doing tonight?' and I said, 'Anything you want.'"

John invited Margaret back to his hotel, but a dear friend came to her with his heart shattered. She felt she had to console him, so her rendezvous with John Cale had to wait. "John was playing an outdoor show two nights later in San Antonio. I showed up that afternoon wearing a strapless sundress and high-heeled slides, and walked backstage, looking around for him. I heard 'Pssst—hey! Pssst!' I looked up and he was leaning out the backstage window, so I dashed up the stairs. There were four lines of cocaine on the counter and we got *right* to it. My dress was in a circular heap thirty seconds later. Someone banged on the door, 'John, you're onstage!' We had to finish quickly and he yanked his pants up. That night we stayed at the St. Anthony and I remember massaging him in the bathtub, ordering room service—I was falling in love." Margaret starts fanning herself. "My God, Pamela, my heart is racing so hard right now."

Years ago, John Cale was married to one of the GTO's, Miss Cynderella, and I found out recently that the youngest member of our group had died mysteriously. It's hard to believe that there are only three Girls Together Outrageously left: Sparky, Mercy, and me. "We had our first Texas Blonde death four years ago, so I understand. It was heartbreaking," Margaret says sadly. "She was one of my best friends, and such a free spirit."

It was shortly after her first shimmering experience with John Cale that Margaret gathered her own kindred clan. "I'd never forgotten the stories I read about the GTO's. At that time I was between newspapers and had just split up with my photographer husband. It all began the night John played the Armadillo. That show completely ripped the top of my skull off, and I wanted to do nothing but immerse myself in music. I was absolutely besotted. There was a burgeoning new wave scene, with bands like the Romantics and Psychedelic Furs coming through town. I kept running into the same group of girls, and we started hanging around together. Then in '81, John was at the Armadillo again, and I found out he was playing the Whisky in L.A. for three nights. I gathered up the girls and we rented a car and drove to Hollywood. We got a room at the Tropicana where John was staying. I got to be good friends with his band, and they'd come to our room after the show, because we were the party girls with all the drugs and alcohol. Their backup singer, deerfrance, had this cute little girl voice, and one night she said, 'You're all blonde and you're from Texas. You're the Texas Blondes.' And I said, '*Yes!*' We showed up at the Whisky the next night, drunk with being the Texas Blondes. Suddenly we had an identity. And I knew exactly what we could do with it, because of the GTO's and the Plaster Casters, who were our role models, too. We were in the Whisky bathroom that night, with our glittery eye shadow, applying brilliant red lipstick, and this dark-haired girl walked in and said, 'Who are you?' We looked at each other, and grinned back at her, 'We're the Texas Blondes!' Saying it out loud affirmed it. We went to L.A. just a group of girls, and came back the Texas Blondes. Through the years we had Mexican girls and black girls, because it wasn't a color thing, it was a state of mind. And we got really famous for it. Guys loved having us on their arm. We were great eye candy, and lots of fun."

A few months later, Margaret was hurled back down to earth when John brought Reza, the girl he would marry, to Austin with him. "I was trying to be brave," she says, "but my heart was bleeding all over the place."

It was a festive whirlwind while it lasted, but by 1982, the Texas Blondes started winding down. "I was never the pretty one in the Blondes, I was the smart one and the leader. I knew who the pretty ones were—and they walked three feet in front of me and we all got in. But my heart just wasn't in it anymore." There *was* one last hurrah, however. "One night, a local promoter called and said, 'Iggy Pop is in town, and we're bored.

Why don't you rustle up some of your girlfriends and meet us at the hotel?' I called three of the girls and pulled on my old Velvet Underground T-shirt. We arrived at the hotel, and Iggy was standing there shirtless while all my girls flitted around him. I was sitting with the promoter, and all of a sudden Iggy stood up, yawned, looked at me and said, 'I'm going back to my room. Do you wanna come with me?' I said, *'Me?'* and he said, 'Yeah.' I said goodbye to the promoter and shrugged at the girls and walked down the hall with Iggy. He pulled out the key to his room and I said, 'Why did you pick me? My roots have grown out, I haven't shaved my legs, and I'm twenty-five pounds overweight.' He said, 'I like you, you're smart.' I said, 'And I've got big tits,' and he said, 'That too!' We talked and talked, did coke, drank, and talked. Iggy was one of the most fun musicians I've ever been with because we went on tangents, chattering on about books and films. I think both of us were surprised to find this similarity in each other. And it added to the sex."

Margaret had just gotten married for the second time when she saw John Cale again. "It was February of '85, five years since I'd seen him. I remember it well because it was two months to the day after I'd gotten married. Rollo was a tattoo artist and hated John Cale with a passion. John was now married and had a baby. When he asked me to come back to his hotel room, I thought, 'Oh my God, what am I gonna do?' This was the moment I'd dreamed about for years. We kissed a little bit and I said, 'I just got married and you've got a wife. I can't do this.' But I did stay out late with John that night, and when I got home there was hell to pay. When I got in the shower, Rollo thought I was washing away my guilt, and I said, 'No, I didn't, I didn't, I *didn't.*' Now I wish I had."

For the next few years, it was awkward when John came to town. "After that, he never tried again. I think I wounded his ego. But I'd see him whenever he came through, and I guess he realized that I was gonna be here every time he came to Austin. He'd arrive at the airport looking for somebody to pick him up, and there I'd be. In 1988, I picked him up and took him to the Driscoll. The doorman took us to the room, opened the door, and John walked in. Then the doorman held the door for me and said, 'Here you go, Mrs. Cale.' Just for a second, I had the luxury of being Mrs. John Cale." Margaret sighs. "When I read John's biography, I found out his mother's name was Margaret. Now I know why he gave me that look the first time I told him my name."

Margaret was with Rollo for fourteen years, with the last few years of married chaos spent in Hawaii. "I was so devoted that I put my feelings for John on the back burner and tried to not acknowledge them. Everything I did was defined by Rollo, and when he got strung out on heroin, I felt alone and betrayed. I felt like a fish out of water surrounded by all that ocean and was anxious to come back to Austin. It was '93, and I hadn't been home very long when I read Ann Powers's review of your second book in the *New York Times*, and once again you inspired me from afar. Her article made groupies sound like the Florence Nightingales of rock and roll, trading gracious bedside manners for blow jobs. I sensed that all along, but had never been able to put it in words. Here was another woman saying it for me. And using my role model. I took it to SXSW and said, 'There's a panel in this.'" Since then, Margaret has been avidly involved in the annual convention, hosting panels and directing the snazzy annual *Austin Chronicle* music awards.

I was a presenter again in 2006, and while dashing off stage, Margaret introduced me to Dayna, one of the Texas Blondes. "Dayna's worked with me the longest," Margaret informs me. "And in every case, it was what we learned being groupies that's given us the ability to work with bands so well. We know all the tricks."

I ask Dayna for some memorable Texas Blonde tales. "I was with Iggy Pop for a while," she says, efficiently holding her clipboard. "He liked me from the jump. Sweetheart that he was, he'd say, 'Aw, you're my little shithead, come here, darlin'.' I was very young when he took me on tour, and finally his manager said, 'You cannot be dragging a fourteen-year-old girl across state lines. You're going to prison.' I said, 'Well, I've got to go back to school anyway.' Shortly after that, Iggy decided he needed me with him to write. He came and stayed with me and my mom and dad while I went to school. That lasted a week or so, until my mom made him do dishes. Then he got a hotel and I stayed there with him. I look back and think, 'What a pedophile!' I must have been a novelty to him. Sexually, I probably didn't please him like a grown woman could. He's got a massive cock—like the size of your right arm—and I couldn't take it all the way because I was so young." Dayna hands an award to the next rowdy presenter and quickly returns. "There was one person I stayed in touch with for years—Jerry Harrison from the Talking Heads. He was always there for me and I loved him dearly. Every time he came to town, we got together, and when I moved to New York, I stayed with him. He's one of the most stand-up guys I know. But I was never treated poorly by *any* of them. They gave me emotional strokes I never got in high school, which contributed to the self-esteem I developed later. People say, 'Oh, poor thing, you were young and taken advantage of.' Yes and no. Logically, I can see it that way, but don't think I didn't get something out of it! Everybody knew how powerful Margaret was, and being under her wing, nobody fucked with me. I went where she went, and before you knew it, there were several of us. The publicists would have bands in town and say, 'Can you get those *blondes*?' Suddenly we emerged and I thought, 'I'm in this cool group that can go just about anywhere. I meet all the great guys, and I can tell those people who thought I was a loser in junior high to kiss my ass!'"

The next afternoon, I was hosting the annual Rajiword party, introducing cool acts like the Faces' Ian McLagan and sexy Steve Poltz, when I met Alice, an altogether different type of Texas Blonde. I snagged her between sets and she told me about the night U2 came to dinner. "It was 1982, and Margaret let me come with her to sound check when she interviewed U2. Since I'm the born-again Christian in the Blondes, I kept dropping hints that I was spiritually on the same page as they were. I had a long talk with Bono and asked if they'd like to come to church the next day, and three of them came with me. We went to lunch afterward, and I invited them to dinner at my mom's house in

Houston the next night. They liked the idea of a home-cooked meal. This was only their second time in America. They were excited about everything they were into, and wanted to share it. So they came over for dinner. We were all really young at the time, just nineteen or twenty. They were young and fresh, very honest and likeable, with a sweet naivete. Even then, they very much cared about people and justice and mercy. Mom cooked some casserole, and it was a lovely dinner. We talked a bit about their church group back home. They belonged to a little church that met in a house. My mother loves Ireland, and they enjoyed talking about that as well. Had they not already been married, or with girlfriends, I'm sure I would've tossed my hat into the ring. I did get to give the drummer, Larry Mullen Jr., a back rub. He had a really painful shoulder, so I gave him an intense back massage. And it worked. I saved the show with my magic massage."

Marriage must suit Margaret Moser, because she is engaged again, this time to guitarist Mike Vernon. "One of my favorite all-time posters was for 3 Balls of Fire. It was a picture of Mike playing guitar, wearing this big ol' cowboy hat. He's lit from below in a very striking way, with flames on either side of the guitar. It's really badass. Whenever they put out a CD, it got uniformly great reviews from me. I wrote a funny, prescient one just four years ago: 'Mike Vernon plays with a lover's touch that leaves you breathless.' Who else am I going to fall in love with? I'm tired of artistic pussies. I've dated doctors and lawyers and married a tattoo artist and a photographer. I've been with artistic types and nonartistic types, and I ended up falling in love with a politically conservative guitarist. A friend of mine in her sixties said to me, 'Conservative men make good husbands.' I'd never thought about that. But Mike's conservatism is very much a part of his commitment and willingness to stick with things. And I'm perfectly willing to let him have views that I don't agree with. I'm not a flaming liberal anyway." Her new beau accepts Margaret's heady past, and her long-term fascination with John Cale. "The very last time John was here, we had, hands down, the most uninhibited, friendly relationship we've ever had with each other. It couldn't have been better, and Mike was fine with it. Mike and I do think alike in a lot of ways. Last week we made one of our joint concepts come true. We invited thirteen of the best guitarists around town to get on stage and play Link Wray's 'Rumble.' Mike came up with the idea of the Guitar Rumble, and we originally played around with the idea of fifty guitars. We were driving down the street, and I said, 'Fifty guitars will never work.' I was thinking hard, and finally came out with, '*Thirteen* Guitar Rumble,' and he almost drove off the side of the road. He said, 'Oh, that's brilliant! We'd only been going out ten days, and he was already saying, 'I'm going to marry you.' I said, 'Okay, bud, you're on.'"

Pleasant Gehman

Flesh for Fantasy

My goddaughter, Polly Parsons, recently had her splashy nighttime wedding shower at a venerated Moroccan restaurant on Sunset Boulevard, where patrons gleefully dig into mounds of spicy chow with their bare hands. Polly's hungry guests were halfway through the tabbouleh and shawerma when mysterious, sensual music wafted through the mirrored curtains, and Princess Farhana undulated to the center of the room. I've always known this vibrant scenester as Miss Pleasant Gehman, infamous punk/singer/writer/hipper-than-hip journalist, and here she was in yet another incarnation, wriggling and shimmying to beat the band, decked out in sheer, sequined, coin-laden odalisque garb. Her curvy midriff bare, Pleasant began her dervish whirls, clanging her finger cymbals, seducing us one by one. Our jaws dropped as she performed outrageous belly rolls and provocative bumps, her exultant dark eyes sparkling like desert moondust.

Thanks to the musical savvy of various teenage babysitters, at the age of four and a half, precocious Pleasant Gehman was already obsessed with the Beatles. Pleasant and her baby brother performed "I Want to Hold Your Hand" for their parents while strumming badminton rackets and wearing fuzzy lamb hats as Beatle wigs. She remembers meticulously studying the black and white photo on the cover of *Meet the Beatles.* "One of the first things I said to my mom was 'Where are their penises?' You can tell I was doomed from birth!"

After I enjoyed another evening of her dazzling hip sway-ing, the vivacious, va-va-voom Pleasant takes me into a velvet-curtained hideaway and regales me with tales of her tender years. "I had a thing with the Beatles and the Rolling Stones. I grew up with them, watching them on Ed Sullivan. I was obsessed with Ringo because of the way he dressed. I thought George was the cutest, but anytime I had the chance, I'd get these rings out of gumball machines, and my brother and I would put them all on. My father yelled at him, 'You look like a fag!' which we misinterpreted as 'tag.' Obviously if Ringo was a 'tag,' it had to be a great thing. So we put on every fucking piece of jewelry we could find, and in the middle of this big dinner party we came downstairs and said, 'Look everybody! We're tags!'"

Pleasant's mom taught theater at Wesleyan College and her dad was a jazz critic for *Down Beat* magazine. And although there was always music playing at their house in Middletown, Connecticut, a lot of Pleasant's basic training came from a glam-obsessed babysitter, who just happened to be a "tag." "Gary Morris, who runs one of the most noted film Web sites, Bright Lights, and lectures all over the world, introduced me to 'Liar, Liar' by the Castaways. I'd paint his toenails blue while we lis-tened to all this crazy '60s pop. My mother's sheets became Gre-cian gowns and we acted out Supremes songs. When I was eleven he gave me my first copy of Andy Warhol's *Interview*: 'Here's Candy Darling, she's fabulous, and this is Mamie Van Doren, she's amazing, look at Mick Jagger, look at Rudolph Nureyev.' I quickly started catching on to this insane outré aesthetic, and right about that same time I discovered *Creem* magazine. By age twelve I was getting stoned, but it *was* the '60s and early '70s. My mother screamed at Gary about statutory rape, and we both laughed because he was such an obvious 'tag'!"

At the new local mall, Pleasant bought a T. Rex album because she had been "flabbergasted" after seeing glitter-god Marc Bolan on TV; then she spied David Bowie's *Aladdin Sane*. "That was the first time I shoplifted anything other than bubble gum, and I stole it just 'cause of the way the cover looked—then the next week I shoplifted Iggy's *Raw Power*, and those are still two of my favorite records on earth."

Well, if you're gonna steal, steal something worth stealing, right? When she ripped off a pair of white hot pants and wore them around the house, her mom was horrified. "Instead of asking where I got them, she said, 'You look like Lolita.' I said, 'Who's Lolita?' She told me to read the book so I went up to our guestroom and started reading. I apparently didn't hear when she called us to dinner, because I was in there, dumbstruck. I didn't think of *Lolita* in a pedophile way, instead, 'Wow! A grown-up could be that excited over someone my age? Woo-hoo!' I started pondering this power I had, and in that same week I saw *Cabaret* with all those clothes and the crazy three-way. Forget it, I was never the same. I discovered Bowie and Lou Reed and it was an upward spiral into heaven. I knew what my path was. I wanted to be a completely glamorous creature—a '30s movie star mixed with a courtesan. Then I honed it to 'I wanna go to L.A., get high, and fuck rock stars!' I spent most of my adolescence and twenties not thinking I was attractive, but when I look back at pictures I think, 'Oh my God, I could have ruled the world!'"

Soon Pleasant and her friends were busy shoplifting outfits to wear at rock concerts, hiding the fishnets, Lurex tube tops, and platforms under tie-dyed jeans and puffy Snorkel Arctic parkas. Their first secret adventure was to see Alice Cooper. "We stole everything we wore, including green nail polish, and put all our normal clothes in the locker at the Greyhound station. We put on makeup, sparkles, and beauty marks, then walked five blocks to the New Haven Coliseum in hot pants and tube tops, uproariously drunk and stoned. The guards wouldn't let us backstage. Then I remembered reading in *Rock Scene* that Alice Cooper always stayed at Holiday Inns. I knew his manager's name and called the first Holiday Inn. 'Hi, can I have Shep Gordon's room, please?' They just put me through, and I heard a raging party going on, so we hitchhiked over there. They let us party with them, but since we looked like fucking fetuses, nothing happened—even though we wanted it to."

What made Pleasant believe she could just sashay into Alice Cooper's hotel room in the first place? "I just didn't feel separate from them. I listened to the records over and over and always felt we would become friends if we met. I did feel like a fan but I also thought they would love me. I just thought we'd get along like gangbusters."

Due to a wild array of circumstances, including red-handed sex and drugs, Pleasant was sent off to boarding school in Massachusetts. "I got a full scholarship. My mom thought it was going to be good for me, but little did she know I was fucking out of control, having sex with everybody and taking drugs, which was opening new realms for me. Then she told me we were moving, but didn't tell me where, and I cried for four hours because I finally had a bunch of friends that didn't think I was crazy."

She wasn't bummed for long because her mom had gotten a job at 20th Century Fox in the City of Angels—mecca for any

Princess Farhana.
Credit: Don Spiro

rock fiend. "I thought it was going to be Somewhere Horrifying, Iowa, and when she told me, 'We're moving to Los Angeles,' I dropped the phone. I finished that term and got to Hollywood in the middle of my junior year. I had my first date with Rodney."

That would, of course, be Rodney Bingenheimer, L.A.'s finest late-night DJ, Mayor of the Sunset Strip, who was always on the lookout for new girls in town. "He showed up at my door in his Cadillac and a pink Granny Takes a Trip suit, à la Rod Stewart. I was a foot and a half taller in my giant silver platforms. He was like an octopus." I tell Pleasant that dear Rodney also tried to feel me up the night I met him long ago, but you can't blame a fellow for trying. Rodney introduced Pleasant around town, and she was instantly welcomed into the budding prepunk scene.

After sharing a welcome-to-Hollywood joint with "hot old man" Tony Curtis at a Tubes concert, she met a couple of soon-to-be punk heroes. "A few rows in front of me, I saw George and Paul, who later turned into Pat Smear and Darby Crash. Georgie was dressed like Alice Cooper, and Paul was all in white with an Aladdin Sane lightning bolt and red hair. I threw them a note with my phone number: 'Aladdin Sane, you cosmic orgasm, call me.'" The next day, Pleasant spent the afternoon slumming around vivid Hollywood Boulevard with her new pals. "Two or three days later they asked, 'Do you like Iggy?' They knew where he lived and asked if I wanted to go. 'Oh my God, *yeah*! Are you kidding? Am I *breathing*?' So we took the bus over to Flores Street. I'm so naive, I thought we were going to a Jed and Granny Clampett *Beverly Hillbillies*-type *mansion*, but it was a 1920s apartment. I'm thinking he must be in the penthouse, but no, he's in this hellish tiny, dark basement hovel up to your knees in clothes and fast food containers, beer bottles and open guitars with glasses full of cigarette butts on them, just horror."

Hellish hovel, yes, but Pleasant was about to meet her very first rock god in the glistening flesh. "Iggy comes out of the bathroom in tiny cutoff shorts with the fly open, and that was *it*. I was in dumbfounded amazement 'cause he looked so beautiful. His hair was all platinum and he was tan and healthy looking.

He was completely incoherent, but had the most beautiful body, and that platinum hair, and it was Iggy POP!"

Despite Pleasant's rather sophisticated upbringing, she had never even been in a man's apartment, let alone nestled amid the squalor of one of her heroes. "This is what was going through my mind: I had this $99 Sears plastic stereo and I would play *Raw Power* incessantly, and I'm sitting there thinking, 'I can't believe I'm meeting the person who made that record.' I was just being quiet and he said, 'Hey, nice to meet you,' acting like a lounge singer or someone's dad, shaking my hand with *two* hands. In hindsight, I think he may have been in the throes of meth-mania. I thought he was gonna be real mean and tough, but he was all nice with a big, pretty smile. 'Come on in! Here, sit down,' clearing shit off the bed, cups from Taco Bell flying. So we're sitting down and there's kind of a lull in the conversation. I was trying to take this all in and he asked if anyone had a cigarette, so I gave him one and we

With Iggy Pop.
Credit: Jenny Lens

smoked. I was all nervous and he said, 'Anybody got any drugs?' I had a joint in my purse, so I said, 'I do.' I'm sitting there thinking, 'OK, I'm gonna try to keep this roach forever.' I couldn't believe I was giving *Iggy Pop* drugs."

Pleasant now lived on the outskirts of Beverly Hills and went periodically to Beverly Hills High. "I would wear my bathing suit under my clothes. I'd cut the first period or two, arriving in time for nutrition, long enough to get salads thrown at me and get called a faggot 'like David Bowie.' I'd drop in on my art class because I liked to draw pictures of dominatrixes, then I'd walk across the street with my girlfriend to the Beverly Hilton. We'd go through the back door, take off our clothes in the ladies' room, grab towels from the maid cart, go out to the pool, and wait for people from Bad Company or whoever to buy us drinks—because they always would, you know."

From the moment she arrived in L.A., Pleasant knew she wanted to write about rock and roll, and when she finished high school in 1977, she did just that. "I loved all the writers at *Creem*. Lester Bangs was amazing, but most of the stuff I saw in local publications was so dry and stupid. I thought, 'I can write about music better than these people can.'" She submitted samples and wound up working for several local rags, which helped get her right where she wanted to be—backstage. "I was at all those early underground punk shows and crazy parties at people's houses, so I decided to start my own magazine, having no idea how to do it." She called the fanzine *Lobotomy*. "I copied the Frederick's of Hollywood bag and added, 'Where Glamour Is a Way of Life.' The first issue had the Mumps on the cover. Lance Loud was the first person I ever interviewed and he knew it, and said, 'You're doing great!'"

Pleasant ran into Iggy Pop a few times and he was charming, but she'd been too nervous to attempt meaningful chatter. It had been over a year since she last encountered him. Between Devo's sets, her editor at *Slash* excitedly told Pleasant that Iggy Pop was in the audience. "'You know him, right? Go ask him for an interview!' I said, 'Well, I know him, but I don't *really* know him.' I had toppled over a balcony the night before and I felt ugly, fat, young, and stupid, with bruises on one side of my face, and this big bandage with stitches. I looked like a pudgy baby prizefighter, you know? I had on a Spiderman T-shirt with safety pins all over it and striped stockings with Converse high tops. I was embarrassed but went up to him. 'Hi, would you like to do an interview for *Slash?* Do you remember me?' and he said, 'Of *course*, why wouldn't I remember you! Why don't you just say hi like you're a human being?' We started talking and he said, 'What are you doing after this?' He was with Toni Basil, David Bowie's choreographer, totally fucking Black Dahlia beautiful, with a giant orchid in her hair, and two tall, gorgeous, long-haired Farrah-y blondes wearing nice dresses. I felt like an idiot, so he says, 'What are you doing afterward? Wanna go to the Whisky?'" She was thrilled, but had come with Pat Random of Dangerhouse Records, and didn't want to be rude. Then Iggy asked her to meet him at Barney's Beanery, and she told him she would have to bring her date. "This guy was all excited because it was *Iggy*, and when we were getting his car from the parking lot, we saw Iggy driving this huge '60s white convertible, a giant fucking tank, with Toni Basil and the two girls. It was just the *picture* of glamour."

Pleasant wanted to stop for cigarettes, and as she was going into the liquor store, she was surprised to see Iggy coming out. "He said, 'Let's ditch everybody and go see the Dictators at the Whisky, come on!' Iggy and Pleasant abandoned their dates and soon she was smack dab in that dreamy, incandescent picture of glamour, zooming through the night in the big white convertible. The Whisky was packed, so Iggy invited her to his pad in Malibu. "We were driving through that greenery part of Beverly Hills, and he had his arm around me. He was being super-nice and I was really stoked, but a little weirded out that we had ditched people."

It got bone chilly cruising through Pacific Palisades, so Iggy gallantly pulled over to manually yank up the top, fiddling with the numerous old-fashioned snaps. "I was sitting there wondering 'What do I do now?' Then he looks at me and says, 'I feel like Richie Cunningham in *Happy Days*.'"

Iggy was exuberant and upbeat about his upcoming trip to Berlin to record *The Idiot* with David Bowie. In fact, Bowie had rented the house in Malibu, which was quite different from the seedy apartment on Flores—more in keeping with Pleasant's idea of how the venerated shock-rocker should live.

"He opened some red wine and we walked out to this rock jetty and sat down and talked about communism, the Romanoffs, Russian deconstructive arts, Berlin, cabaret, and Sally Bowles—because he was going to Germany. We talked about loneliness. I mean, we were discussing really deep shit, but I don't have the full-on gist of the conversation because we were pretty drunk."

Back at the pad, Iggy played Pleasant demos of his new music. "Then he said, 'Let's go to sleep,' and we went to bed and had sex, like, seven times. It was insane! I hadn't experienced *any*-thing like that yet. I also had nothing to compare it to—at least not on that level. I had been having sex, but I'd go with someone, try a door on someone's nice car—if it was open, we'd climb in the back seat and have sex. Anyway, Iggy was totally fucking awesome, he has a great body, which everybody knows, and a really huge dick."

The next day, Iggy asked Pleasant if she'd like to move in for a while. Since she still lived at home, she told him she would commute back and forth. "The first time I stayed three or four days, and this guy, David, was also living there, acting like a houseboy. I'd sit on the couch, looking at a book and when I reached for a cigarette, there'd be David with a light. One day Iggy was completely high out of his mind and David mumbled, 'Oh, he's just painting.' But I didn't know what that *meant*. Iggy was in this insane period: he had the whole house plastered with butcher paper and he covered himself in gallons of house paint, acrylic paint, spray paint—all this shit—pouring it over himself, running to the walls and jumping against them. He was making full-on body prints."

The whole thing must have been overwhelming for a teenage girl from Middleton. "It was crazy," she agrees. "All my friends were very impressed, but I was a bit scared. I didn't know how I was supposed to act, it was so much to absorb. I hadn't been in these kinds of situations before. If I had just been ten years older . . ."

Along with the lunacy, a bit of tenderness found its way in. "We *were* very romantically involved, and sometimes I took care of him. He asked me to get the paint off him in the shower, so I scrubbed him with a scrub brush meant for the floor. It was on in layers, peeling off in plasticky-like curls, but some wouldn't come off. It was under his nails and in his nostrils—he had dreadlocks of paint. One night we went to the Whisky and he was covered in paint. I was underage, but of course we drank loads of cocktails."

She was the baby of the duo, but Pleasant felt strangely protective of Iggy and was often concerned that he got so wasted. "I had a huge crush on him and we were having great sex, but it was beyond my realm of understanding—the amount of drugs he was doing, running into walls and stuff. In a lot of ways I acted like his mom, but he was protective of me too. It was sort of domestic bliss in a twisted way."

At the end of summer, Iggy left Malibu to record with Bowie and explore the depths of Berlin. He told Pleasant he would stay in touch, but she didn't expect him to keep his promise. When he didn't call, she didn't crumble. "It lasted on and off for the summer and it was really interesting and *cool*. But I didn't have any thoughts about the future—I almost couldn't believe any of it had happened anyway. There was absolutely no context to put the whole experience in. I felt sort of lucky. I wouldn't say it was a blessing, but I felt like it had been a *privilege*."

Iggy moved on and so did Pleasant. Her fanzine was shaking things up and she went on an extended trip to New York. "New York was run over with all these beautiful English boys, punks and teds," Pleasant recalls. "Also Sid Vicious was in town, right before the Nancy Spungen murder. We used to see him all the time. We'd look at each other, batting our eyes, saying, 'Oh, he looks like a vampire, he's so tall and pretty.'"

When she returned to L.A., Pleasant succumbed to the extreme rockabilly charms of Levi Dexter and the Rockats. "The Rockats were all cute. They looked like horror movies in a great way. They had all these fashion models draped around them, and Marianne Faithfull sniffing around. They were the It Boys and converted the punk scene into rockabilly." There was a photo session set up with the Rockats and the girls who hung out at the Masque, but Pleasant wanted to stand out in the punked-out, green-haired leather crowd. "I thought, 'I have to look like fucking Sophia Loren or Gina Lollobrigida.' I did my nails, movie-star makeup. Instead of putting grease on my hair and spiking it, I let it be all soft. I wore this bias-cut zigzag '50s blouse, high heels, and the tightest pencil skirt I could find. I walked in there, wearing my bullet bra, and the photographer says, 'Why don't *you* stand right between those two?' meaning Levi and Smut. It worked like a charm."

I remember when the scorching punkabilly Rockats bebopped into town with their Brit Teddy-Boy sneers and radical rocka-billy pomps, helped along by Miss Mercy's scary scissors. All the girls groveled over Levi, but Pleasant's blatant charms won him over and they became a hot item. When Levi was on tour, Pleas-ant continued down the same rocky road, wild about a stunning British up-and-comer, Billy Idol, the lead singer for Generation X. She wrote glowing reviews in *Lobotomy*, then promptly sent them to his record label in London, along with spray-painted Gen-X T-shirts and a bluntly candid love letter.

Luckily, her old friend Rodney Bingenheimer was fast becoming the hipster DJ at KROQ and invited her to come to the studio the night Billy was calling in from England. "So I'm hyperventilating, and Rodney says, 'OK, someone wants to talk to you.' I say 'Hello, this is Pleasant,' and Billy goes, 'Oh, I got your package last week.' We were on the phone for an hour and a half."

A few weeks later, Billy came to town and didn't have a bit of trouble tracking Pleasant down. Another would-be groupie followed them around the market, trying to horn in while they were buying vodka, so Pleasant did what any self-respecting cat-eyed doll would do: she let the air out of her tires. She took Billy up to Runyon Canyon for a glittering view of Los Angeles. "I thought it would be a really bitchin' place to bring him because it had a crazy pirate, jungle vibe, loads of L.A. history, and you could see the whole city. We had already smoked pot, and one hit of pot to me is like three tabs of acid. We were looking at the view and it was just like, 'Fuck, it's beautiful.'"

So what was it like to gaze at Billy Idol in the moonlight? "He was one of the most beautiful human beings ever. His skin was like cream. No shit, I mean, he looked like someone carved him perfectly out of pearls. His hair was white and he looked like a baby chick in a good boy way. Fucking beautiful eyes, and he was really funny. He had a great wit, a funny laugh and a sharp sense of humor. Maybe he wasn't the most cerebral person on earth, but he was quick, well read, he caught onto things and was sarcastic but not mean tempered. He had a nice skewed view on things. He could have been a big asshole but he wasn't."

As the lights twinkled below, Pleasant and Billy drank spirits, passionately made out, and thought they were alone. Then Pleasant heard rustling noises. "I was nervous in this total sixth-grade way but trying to be unflappable. From the corner of my eye, I saw this amorphous shape and screamed at the top of my lungs! I jumped on Billy, my legs wheeling around like a Road-runner cartoon! The shape flew up, and a bum clambered out of a sleeping bag, and said, 'Got a cigarette?' Any form of cool fled in that moment, and the ice was broken."

The next day Pleasant took Billy to a big bash and the insistent groupie from the market was back and wouldn't lay off. "She was being totally uncool, and I was no stranger to brawls and bar fights. Joan Jett was there and said, 'I got your back,' because it looked like there was going to be a big chick fight. I don't think I was planning to set her hair on fire, and I wouldn't dream of doing it now, but it seemed like a good idea at the time. So I lit up a good chunk of her hair with a lighter." Pleasant measures about three inches with her fingers, smiling sheepishly. "Like about that much."

To raise money to print *Lobotomy*, my dear friend Michele Myer, who booked the Whisky, suggested Pleasant hold benefit concerts. On one of these nights, Billy was the guest of honor.

"It was just our friends helping out, but the bills were *crazy*—the Go-Gos, the Weirdos, the Germs. Joan Jett lived right across the street, so whenever we went to the Whisky, especially for *Lobotomy* nights, we'd prime the pump at her house. Gil Turner's Liquor delivered booze, even though no one was even close to twenty-one, because we'd answer the door in black underwear with handcuff belts and high heels. We'd start the order with a gallon of vodka and get blitzed. On this night Billy came over to Joan's, and we fucking outdid ourselves. We had this girl, Nancy, tied to the bed with socks and sheets and clotheslines. There were three or four different kinds of whips. We were all on Quaaludes, and the Sex Pistols were *blast*ing. The front door was open and the coffee table was *covered* in beer bottles. The show must have been really late: we heard this yelling, and Michele Myer came from the Whisky and burst into Joan's apartment. She saw all the beer bottles, the trail of clothes, and Nancy spread-eagle bare on the bed. Billy was holding a gallon of vodka and a cat o' nine tails in mid-swing. She yells, 'You—the show producer—get to the fucking Whisky. *You*—the stage manager—get to the fucking Whisky. And *you*—the fucking guest of *honor* . . .' she screams at Billy, shaking her finger. And he says, 'Sorry, madam.'"

Pleasant spent some sincere quality time with Billy. Then his acclaimed gal pal Peri Lister came to town. "I was totally crushed out, but she was so beautiful. I pretty much wanted to sleep with both of them, but didn't know how you went about doing that. I had slept with my girlfriends and a guy, but never a guy I had a crush on and a girl I didn't know who was his girlfriend. He said he had to spend time with her and that was fine. I mean, I had no claim on him. I'm not like a guy, where the conquest is all, but that was a great, crazy conquest."

All the while Pleasant romped with Billy Idol, Levi Dexter was conveniently on tour. "Oh, he was in England fucking someone else, or actually he might have been in New York at that point with Belinda from the Go-Gos. I told her to fuck him so he wouldn't fuck some stupid girl. I mean, we totally switched, and I took care of her boyfriend, Bill Bateman from the Blasters.

This was the way you kept people *true* in the '80s, right? Have them fuck your best friend. I think Jane also fucked Levi, but in the late '70s/early '80s, 'cause of Quaaludes and coke. It was like free love in leather. We shared boyfriends and crushes, it was no biggie. It was just a crazy pass-around. I either had sex with or made out with most of the girls I knew, like Belinda and Jane. I actually had a little affair with Jane that started one night when we locked ourselves in a bedroom at somebody's parents' house. While Levi and the Rockats jammed with the Rockabilly Rebels, Jane and I had a long make-out lesbo session, and it went on for a while after that."

High jinks aside, when the long arm of the law threatened to deport Levi, extreme measures were called for. "We decided to get married because he had been coming in and out of the country so much and they weren't gonna let him back in. I was almost twenty and I couldn't imagine not seeing him anymore. We had a huge ceremony at Cathay de Grande, the punk club, when I was booking it. The wedding was at a Unitarian Church. Bill Bateman of the Blasters was one of the best men, Belinda was the maid of honor, and all the bridesmaids were in leather. Our wedding was mistakenly scheduled at the same time as a low-rider wedding that had powder blue tuxedos and matching carnations. We tossed a coin and our wedding came up first. I thought, '*Cool*, we get the blue flowers!'—Levi had blue hair at that point. My wedding dress was a Salvation Army white prom dress, my hair was white, and I had a big white veil. The wedding was just insane and the reception was even crazier—a total who's who of the punk scene." Someone special was on hand to lend a yowl to the festivities. "Billy Idol was there, *screaming* 'White Wedding.' And he's the one who caught the garter!"

The Dexters moved into a cockroach- and pop-star-infested apartment house that Pleasant called "Disgraceland." Unfortunately, the powder blue wedding turned out to be the best part of the turbulent two-year punkified marriage.

"As soon as we got married he started with the domestic violence. He'd wake me up punching me. He stayed home smoking pot all day while I took a forty-five-minute bus to Century

City with a huge hangover to work as a secretary in clothes I borrowed from my *mother*. Finally I said, 'You have to get up.' He gave me a black eye and shoved me against a concrete wall, trying to rub off a tattoo I had just gotten. I said, 'Get out of my fucking house!' but he wouldn't." To make sure Levi vacated the premises, Pleasant ran off with a gorgeous skateboard champion and had a ragingly naughty fling in San Francisco. "When I got back, Levi said, 'Were you *fucking* him?' I said, 'Yeah, of course—that was the whole point! We're over. You have to get out.' And he finally realized it."

In the mid-'80s, Pleasant made one of her far-flung dreams come true by fronting the Screamin' Sirens, then the Ringling Sisters. "I decided I wanted to sing, because ever since high school I wrote poems and songs. I could make the noise of every guitar solo, but never learned how to play anything. But everyone said I was so flamboyant and outgoing, I thought, 'OK, I'll sing.' I totally sucked at first. I have the kind of voice that's popular now—a girly Phil Spector voice. But in those days you had to be a punk screamer or sing like Aretha Franklin. I wanted the band to be all girls because it was working out really well for my friends, the Runaways and the Go-Go's. I thought, 'I'm gonna have an all-girl gang band and I want us to be a cross between Old West saloon girls and bikers. And we're gonna play country music!'" The band toured a lot, and besides delighting fans with her trilling, Pleasant threw her entire body into the mix. "Through the whole set I was dancing and shaking, nonstop for forty-five minutes."

Pleasant had long been fascinated with anything to do with the Middle East. So when a woman at Club Lingerie asked if she was a belly dancer, it was a serendipitous meeting. "Ever since I was little I was obsessed with the Crusades and those Sinbad movies. Playing hopscotch I'd say, 'Please, merciful Allah, let it land on square eleven.' All my favorite rock songs sounded like Arabic music—'Venus in Furs' or 'Paint It Black,' all the Jajouka Stones' music. I was wearing crazy Indian clothes, coin belts, and bindis before Gwen Stefani was even out of grade school!"

The prescient girl who recognized Pleasant's inner sultan-teaser was a belly dancer herself. "I started stalking her at parties. Everyone thought we were locked in the bedroom doing drugs, but she'd be showing me hip figure eights. People would bang on the door, 'Can I have some?'"

I ask Pleasant if she felt belly dancing was her "calling," already knowing the answer because I've seen her dance. "*Completely*! I could do it immediately, and I *looked* like a belly dancer—I have dark eyes, I'm curvy. I started dancing at thirty-two just for fun, and within six months people were *paying* me, saying, 'You're the best belly dancer I've ever seen!' Anytime I danced I had a huge smile on my face. I've been doing it for fourteen years now—I'm forty-six. Who starts a dance career at the age of thirty-two?"

In 1997, one of Pleasant's writing assignments brought an old fair-haired boy into her workplace: she interviewed Iggy Pop for *Request* magazine. They were discussing a book project Iggy was considering when things got romantic.

"I'm being Miss Professional, and since I had two books out he was asking me about publishers. He wanted to write a book called *52 Girls*, because there are fifty-two weeks in a year and fifty-two cards in a deck. All of a sudden he starts kissing me. And we kissed for a pretty long time." Iggy wanted to take Pleasant to see Metallica that night, but she declined because she had to work. When he found out Pleasant was a belly dancer, Iggy flipped. "'Arabic music has so much soul,' he said. 'It has so much *passion*. I wanna come see you!'"

Pleasant neglected to tell Iggy about the very strict dress code, so of course he arrived in classic shredded Iggy regalia. "I hear this commotion at the door but didn't see what it was because we were in the middle of a number." Balancing a sword on her head, Pleasant spotted Iggy's platinum locks. "He was the only person with white hair in the whole place. Later, the leader of the troupe screams, 'Oh my fucking God, Pleasant. What is *Iggy Pop* doing in here? I *know* this has to be your fault!'"

Afterward, Pleasant had a glass of wine at Iggy's hotel, and he wanted her to spend the night. "I said no because I had a boyfriend. He was also living with someone so I just didn't feel right about it. He walked me to the car and kissed me goodbye. My thing with Iggy spanned, like, two *decades*."

Princess Farhana got another kind of satisfaction when one of her long-ago rock gods came to see her dance not once, but twice. "It was slow that night—only one party with a reservation and they kept calling, saying they were gonna be late. My boss knew I had a lot of friends in bands and he said, 'Chili Pepper Red Hot came here!' We were talking about music, and because he's Tunisian, I told him about how the Stones were into the whole Marrakesh Jajouka thing; ex*pound*ing on it." After waiting another twenty minutes, Pleasant's boss told her she might as well go to her next dance job. "I was backstage getting ready and got a phone call from my boss. 'Oh, my God, I cannot believe it. Michael Jagger, he is at the restaurant right now!' and I say, 'Shut *up*! Oh, my God, you're serious!' I was going to dance for the man I'd been crazy about since I was *four*. Mick Jagger has been a constant in my life, like the Empire State Building. I thought 'What could I possibly give back to someone who has given *me* so many hours of pleasure?'"

Even though she was quaking inside, Pleasant must have pleased Sir Jagger, because he beamed, his dimples prominently on display, then politely tipped her a hundred dollars. She admits saving the bill for six months, until she "was pretty sure the DNA had worn off."

Pleasant Gehman, aka Princess Farhana, "Flower of the Desert," is at the tip-top of her field, delighting rapt audiences with her dancing almost every night of the week. She's currently happily ensconced in a long-term relationship with a talented artist, James Packard. Walking back to our cars in the baking SoCal sunbeams, Pleasant is indignant when I mention that despite its seven letters, groupie is still considered a four-letter word.

"I've always loved behind-the-scenes people, but groupies were the most glamorous. I compared them to artists' models in the '20s because I knew about Man Ray and Kiki, his muse. Groupies were the complement to rock stars. When they walked into a room, everyone would gasp. They were beautiful, smart, well versed, and could handle any situation. They were the seventeenth-century definition of a courtesan: intelligent, well-spoken, *worldly* women who were looked up to—and just let everybody eat cake. My mother said, 'Why do you wanna be a *groupie* and not the star?' A groupie *is* a star! There were groupies who were film stars and music stars. Marianne Faithfull was a groupie. Pat Smear was a groupie for Queen, Darby Crash was a boy groupie, and they went on to become stars. Angie Bowie was every goddamned bit as important as *David* Bowie. She was the person who had songs written about her. Angie's art was just to *exist*. Her husband wrote great songs, but Angie was the belle of the ball. And that's a huge talent in itself. Being a groupie doesn't mean you're backstage doing something sleazy. Being a groupie is like worshipping at the church of rock and roll—and you're the high priestess."

Bebe Buell

A Chat Regarding the Infamous G Word

There have been a scant handful of groupie books published by the muses of rock. The first, I believe, was Jenny Fabian's *Groupie*, in 1969, which lightly disguises flings she had all over London with Pink Floyd, the Nice, and the Animals. In 1993 Angela Bowie told tales on the Thin White Duke with bitter aplomb in *Backstage Passes,* and the same year the late Cyrinda Foxe-Tyler alternately savaged and adored her rock hubby in *Dream On: Livin' on the Edge with Steven Tyler and Aerosmith.* Marianne Faithfull bravely showed how low she could go and still be the coolest chick who ever held a ciggie or a Stone in 1994's *Faithfull.* Cynthia Plaster Caster is currently working on her spectacular art-*cum*-sex memoir, Catherine James has just sold her bio to St. Martin's Press, and my own rollicking contribution, *I'm with the Band*, has been republished and is selling briskly, I'm delighted to say.

The most recently published fresh groupie tome was 2001's *Rebel Heart* by Bebe Buell. Our books are frequently referred to in the same hot breath, and if you take a look at Amazon's listing for *Band*, you may find a suggestion that you purchase *Rebel Heart* as well. It's a small groupie world, after all!

Bebe has had issues with the G word for years, so I felt it was appropriate to include her highly educated opinion on the subject.

Pamela: I want to get a few words from you about the word "groupie." I know you prefer "muse."

Bebe: But if you say that, you get misunderstood. Because the word muse immediately sounds narcissistic if you use it about yourself. But I think it's OK to acknowledge that there's a difference.

Pamela: It all depends on who is using the word.

Bebe: I suppose if Picasso said, "She's my muse," it would have a lot more impact. Perhaps one of his many mistresses, whose initials he had to hide in his paintings so he could pay tribute to her without his wife finding out. If she said, "I was the muse for that painting," society would immediately ostracize her.

Pamela: But you have publicly said that you prefer that word to the G word.

Bebe: Muse is a much more beautiful word. It just sounds nicer. It's a lot more romantic. I'm going to read you something I wrote. It's one paragraph, and it kind of sums it up.

"As far as the groupie tag, I don't believe the word means now what it did in the '60s and '70s. Much like other misused terms, such as punk and grunge, the term groupie is used to describe almost anyone associated with musicians today. Because of that, I have disassociated myself with the label. The innocence that once surrounded the word has been replaced by an almost "anything goes" mentality. I'm sure it is an insult to girls like Pamela Des Barres, Cynthia Plaster Caster, and the GTO's—who coined it—to be lumped in the same category as women who sleep with anyone associated with a band or crew. That is not what a groupie is, in the old-fashioned sense. . . . The music was, and is, the most important thing to a true groupie of days

Credit: Bebe Buell
private archive

gone past. The modern sense of the term, I find degrading and false. It gets my back up."

Pamela: I suppose a lot of people perceive the word as a slur.

Bebe: Or a mud wrestling harpie on meth!

Pamela: But I met these girls called the Beatle BandAides and the Rock N' Dolls. They go around in troupes and are claiming the word again.

Bebe: If they can clean it up and get people appreciating real art again, I would love that. I'm sick and tired of it being associated with scantily clad girls with no eyebrows and silicone breasts.

Pamela: The first time I heard the word, it must've been about 1968, and it wasn't negative. It was just a word.

Bebe: It was cool! I remember seeing you in *Rolling Stone* when I was in high school. The photographs seemed very glamorous. You didn't look at them and go, "Eeewww, those whores!"

It was very rock and roll. And there was the importance of being "eye candy." But also the social scene that girls could bring to a band. You took them shopping, introduced them to people that had power—much like Mick Jagger was introduced to English society by Marianne Faithfull. There was a certain aura about what girls like you did. And then it just went a little cuckoo.

Pamela: I'm very friendly with Lori Mattix now, but it happened right around the early '70s, when the baby girls started putting on those tiny little hot pants . . .

Bebe: . . . and started having sex when they were fourteen! To me, that was weird, because I didn't have sex until I was eighteen.

Pamela: Yeah, I was nineteen.

Bebe: We were positively prehistoric! I can't even imagine having sex at fourteen.

Pamela: I had my Barbie dolls all in a row.

Bebe: Going out with Todd [Rundgren], I got introduced to the whole scene very quickly. Of course, if you have the chance to live that rock and roll lifestyle, it's wonderful.

Pamela: My friend, Cassandra Peterson—Elvira—was a big groupie! She loves what she did and happily claims it.

Bebe: I heard that she and Todd had a [conspiratorial whisper] "sexual romp." I think it's fabulous. Everyone should fuck Todd.

Pamela: She said that when she was backstage, the word groupie was like "roadie" or "road manager." She would proudly say, "I'm a groupie," and people would say, "Ooooooh . . ."

Bebe: I'm not upset about the actual word. I would be an idiot to say that I never hung around a rock band, didn't date a rock star, or marry one, or see a lot of music in my life. Because it's who I am, that's part of me. But I'm not going to let somebody call me stupid, judgmental names for it either. What's the equivalent today? "I'm a stripper!" "I'm a porn star!" Aaahhh! Everybody's a little bit of a groupie anyway. We're all fans of something. The musicians don't get any credit for choosing us, wanting to be with us. Doesn't that mean we

Bebe wrapped
around Todd
Rundgren.
Credit: Bebe Buell
private archive

have to be pretty damn fucking special and smart? That we weren't throwaways, one-night stands, discards? We were girls they sought out and wanted to be around and whose energy they needed. Everybody sitting in the audience, appreciating a band, should thank the girls backstage! The real heart and soul of a moving concert is like an organism. Certain flowers aren't going to grow if they don't have their shit in place.

Pamela: You're saying almost the same thing that Lexa Vonn from the Plastics said. She's a Marilyn Manson groupie.

Bebe: I can see how somebody would be into Marilyn Manson. He's one of my favorite rock stars, by far.

Pamela: She says, "Manson taught me that art is not just a song or a painting. Art is you, the essence of your being."

Bebe: That's pretty awesome. We're living in a society where half the culture thinks it's a cool term—associated with a time in rock culture that was glamorous and innocent. Then there are people who associate it with sluts, blow jobs, and roadies.

Pamela: That's why I'm writing this book. I'm bound to get some heavy shit for it.

Bebe: I say, polish up that skin right now, girl! My book came out five years ago, and I'm finding it's split down the middle. People either love it, or they don't like it at all. And I think that's great. I'm going to quote Marilyn Manson because I think he's a genius! He said that all the best art is either loved or hated—there is no in between. I have found that to be true. So, I'm pleased.

Pamela: Another thing Lexa said is, "I believe music comes from God, or whatever is up there, the higher power source. Musicians channel that source, and when they look at you with those eyes, it's like being with God."

Bebe: That's very well said. It almost has the ring of George Sand. It's like she's talking about Liszt or Chopin. I agree with her completely. If you can't see that, you're not a groupie.

Pamela: It's such a drag how tarnished the word has become.

Bebe: I've been looking at industry forums, the Velvet Rope, and somebody started this thread "Groupies, Groupies, Groupies." I purposely have not posted, but I've watched it. This is another way the word is viewed, and why I hate it now. And God bless her, she might love animals and keep a beautiful garden, but Miss Connie doesn't help things either.

Pamela: But she's the real thing, and she loves the music.

Bebe: Well, she has had a song written about her, and certainly never hurt anybody, that's for sure. I have to read this last post to you. Somebody writes, "I suppose, being some rock star's receptacle for semen is not a great career choice. Groupies, take note." See? That's how some people view it.

Pamela: Unfortunately, yes, and those people are usually jealous in some way.

Bebe: That's possible. But notice that girls considered the crème de la crème of the groupie crop—every single one of them, you included—has had a career. I have a career, so have Pattie Boyd and Jane Asher. They have substance. There's a reason these guys wanted to be with Linda McCartney or Patti D'Arbanville. They are strong, beautiful, independent women, who are very connected and make their men look fantastic!

Pamela: Yes, it seems even goofy-looking musicians get the glorious chicks.

Bebe: Power is an aphrodisiac. There's something incredibly sexy about a normal, geeky guy, strapping on a guitar and becoming Roy Orbison. I've always adored men like Arthur Miller, so it doesn't surprise me that I was attracted to brainy guys—Rick Nielsen, Elvis Costello, Todd Rundgren. In his own way, Stiv Bators was a brilliant creature. Physically, he was unique. And it was also kind of interesting to date an alien, you know? He was one of the best boyfriends I ever had. And I miss him.

Pamela: You have no regrets, correct?

With Marilyn
Manson.
Credit: Bebe Buell
private archive

Bebe: I can't say that completely, because of course I do. I did a lot of stupid things when I was young that I'd do entirely differently. I would have liked more children, so that does encompass some regrets. It's not like I didn't have my chances. But now I have a grandson, so I get to feel that connection. It's a real trip, holding my daughter in my arms while she holds her baby. I can't even tell you how overwhelming that is.

Pamela: I'm happy for you. So I assume it's all been worth it?

Bebe: Yes. I remember turning up backstage at a Cheap Trick show and watching Rick Nielsen's face light up. It's a beautiful thing. They look at you and go, "Oh my God, you're here! We're gonna play so fucking great tonight!" They want to know that their girls are there. And we're going to tell them the truth when they get off stage: "You suck" or "You were brilliant" or "The bass player's overplaying" or "It was mixed horribly." We know our shit! There was only a handful of It Girls who got treated like rock stars and maintained that status.

Pamela: And it's still going on in dressing rooms and tour buses all over the world.

Bebe: Yeah, but you have to try to educate people. Feminism isn't a bad thing once it's properly explained. But Gloria Steinem had to keep fighting, she kept saying, "Listen, this is what I mean. This is what I'm trying to tell you. Women can do anything." Either we've got to take back the word groupie, we've got to come up with another one, or we've got to educate people as to what it actually means.

Pamela: That's what I'm hoping to do.

Patti and Lisa

Dangerous but Worth the Risk

When I put the word out on my Web site that I'm scouting hot-blooded music muses, one of the most intriguing responses I receive is a twenty-page chronicle entitled, "Story of an Eighties Groupie." Here are a few samples:

We go to his hotel, where we talk the night away. When it's finally time to go to bed, he asks, "Has anyone ever made love to you before?" I laugh, thinking, "Does he think I'm a virgin after Robbin?" Then I realize by the look on his face, he means LOVE, not sex . . . and he did make love to me. He had a guitar player's skillful fingers and played me all night long . . .

Though my feelings for Taime were deep, I didn't have much time to mourn the loss. Because shortly after our breakup, Lee Rocker of the Stray Cats came into the Rainbow and took a shine to me. He had blue eyes, black eyeliner, and dark hair combed into a ducktail. He wasn't tall, but he was strong, especially his arms, from playing stand-up bass . . .

As I'm lying on his chest, I glance over at the Medusa tattoo on his arm. The same tattoo I'd seen on MTV, him running his hand over it seductively in "Dancin' with

Myself." *As I run my hand seductively over it, I suddenly realize, this is BILLY IDOL. Billy Idol's in my bed! I ask him, "So, what's it like to be Billy Idol?" And he says, "They want the lip, I give 'em the lip." Then he gives me his sexy, trademark sneer . . .*

Patti Johnsen, the eloquent author of these lusty memories, has just arrived in Los Angeles from Denver, where she lives happily with her hubby and two young daughters. She's in town for a few days visiting Lisa Nichols, her former groupie soul sister. Patti worked at the notorious Rainbow Bar & Grill on the Strip from 1985 to 1993, where she had her pick of rock's big-haired boy beauties. Lisa left her dinky hometown of New London, North Carolina, and moved to Hollywood in 1989, after years of dallying with rockers down South. She is now a special education teacher and lives in Santa Monica with her twenty-year-old daughter. Patti is a pleased-as-punch, bubbly blonde. Lisa's once platinum-frosted locks are long gone, and her demure demeanor almost disguises her mile-wide wild streak. Between the two of them, Patti and Lisa have covered a whole lot of tempestuous rock and roll terrain. These feisty women are proud of their many rock conquests and have come to my pad to relay their sexy tales. They have much to say, so I'm just going to let them say it.

Pamela: How did you two become addicted to rock and roll? And what made you want to step into that world?

Lisa: The Bay City Rollers were my first crush. And the Monkees reruns, my God! I had it bad for Davy Jones. I remember Elvis dying and being sad about it because I didn't know him. Even at nine I knew I was supposed to. My first up close taste was a Rick Springfield show at an amusement park. I threw a stuffed animal onstage, and was ecstatic for days thinking he might actually have that teddy bear.

Patti: My parents loved rock and roll. When I was little, I knew all the words to "In-A-Gadda-Da-Vida." In 1981, when I was seventeen, I got my heart broken by the first boy I truly

loved. Like a bad after-school special, I caught this evil girl
with her arms around my boyfriend, and she said, "What's
the matter, Patti, did you lose somethin'?" My heart broke
into a million pieces. Then I saw Van Halen in concert and
was mesmerized. The next day at school, a freckled-faced girl
told me she followed them to their hotel and met David Lee
Roth. I decided my life had new purpose, and I took my million pieces and went in search of Van Halen. I followed them
to Chicago and met PK, the head of Van Halen merchandis-
ing. He said, "Find the company that made the bootleg VH
necklace you're wearing, and I'll give you a backstage pass." I
went straight to the shop where I bought it and got the company's info. I also announced to everyone that I would be
working for Van Halen someday. I didn't believe in miracles.
I just knew I wouldn't stop trying until I did.

Pamela: That's an interesting angle. Why did you want to work
for them?

Patti: I wanted to be a rock and roll gypsy on the road with
them, and part of their world. I knew Van Halen wouldn't
magically pluck me out of obscurity and ask me to work for
them. I just thought, "I don't care how long it takes."

Pamela: So it worked! Excellent!

Patti: I went to Cleveland, found PK, and delivered the bootleg
info. He was shocked to see me, but impressed, and I pushed
for a job doing *anything*. The merch crew travels with the
band, staying with them at the Hyatts and Hiltons in every
city, and PK took me with him to Cincinatti. But, before I
was hired, he called me to his room and said, "Take off all
your clothes." Shocked, I asked, "Do I have to?" He said,
"No, but you don't have to work for Van Halen either." It was
an easy decision. I thought, "All I have to do to work for Van
Halen is have sex with you?" My clothes hit the floor. It was
awkward at first, but I really grew to love PK. He was rich,
powerful, and he was good to me. He was also twice my age.
When we finished, I thought, "What'd I get myself into?"
Then he shook my hand and smiled: "Welcome to the organi-
zation." I smiled back, realizing I was right where I belonged.

And this seventeen-year-old girl from Battle Creek, Michigan, had just been hired by Van Halen.

Pamela: Lisa, how did your groupiedom begin?

Lisa: It stemmed from my desire to get away from the small, suffocating town I grew up in. I lost my mom when I was thirteen. That town held nothing but death, loss, and sadness for me. And I was about to find my way out. I went to a Loverboy concert and saw girls from my school with passes. I thought, "Please! Those girls aren't so great." The next band I saw was Autograph, and I asked the singer, Steve Plunkett, to sign my bra. That was my first experience. I realized, "This is my ticket out of this town." I ended up sleeping with him. My first rock star. And I even spent the night.

Patti: Yeah, I never got the boot, either.

Pamela: Certainly never happened to me, dolls. So how long did you hang with Van Halen, Patti?

Patti: From 1981 to '84 I saw Van Halen play thirty-eight times. Once, on that first tour, David Lee Roth saw me waiting in a

Patti in the late '80s.   Credit: Patti Johnsen

crowd for the hotel elevator. He said, "Going up, beautiful?" I literally looked behind me to see who he was talking to. My heart was racing, because I knew the "road rules": sleep with Dave, and you're off the tour, *period*. Besides, I was with PK. But how could I refuse Diamond Dave? So I went to his room, and he strutted around, tanned and shirtless, showing off his achingly beautiful body. I was nervously talking a million miles a minute. "I work with PK, and I love working for you." He was teasing me, bending over to pack, giving me the perfect view of his perfect ass. I said, "I wish I had some coke to offer you." He said, "Why, you want a toot?" and pulled out a sandwich bag half full of coke. He used his long pinky fingernail as a coke spoon, and gave me a blast for each nostril. I'd never done cocaine *that* good before. In a low, sexy voice, Dave said, "Penny for yer thoughts, beautiful." By now I had no inhibitions, and I said, "You are fucking gorgeous." He laughed, "You have a beautiful little body yourself, honey." Then he kissed me. It was so surreal, my fantasy coming true. He said, "I'm going to take a shower, would you like to join me?" Suddenly, it was the saddest moment of my life. I said, "I want to take a shower with you more than anything in this world. But I *don't* want to get fired." So I left. Within the hour, everyone knew I'd been in David's room. Their manager grilled me about what went on. I told him the truth, and PK defended me, but it didn't matter. I said no to David Lee Roth and got fired anyway. I went home, finished high school, and never told anyone what I'd accomplished. I learned discretion on the road, and the accomplishment meant more to me than bragging about it. I'd become a part of something bigger and more wonderful than I ever dreamed, and no high school heartbreaker could ever take it away from me. My relationship with PK continued for three tours. Then in 1984 I saw him again after my devastating breakup with guitar god Yngwie Malmsteen. I'd moved to L.A. to live with Yngwie and thought I'd found my true love. But five months later he dumped me. I halfheartedly considered suicide, then remembered Van Halen was on tour.

Lisa with Michael Kelly Smith of Britny Fox and Cinderella, 1988.
Credit: Lisa Nichols

It took me three days to get from Burbank to Providence, Rhode Island, on a Greyhound bus. When I arrived, I told PK my sad story. He said, "Tell that guy to get a real fucking name. You don't need him, you've got Van Halen." And rock and roll saved me again. [Big sigh] To this day, the smell of a tour bus or diesel fuel is an aphrodisiac.

Lisa: Once I learned how to do it, my first major tour was Mötley Crüe and Guns N' Roses. I met a security guard named Skunk, obviously due to his breath. He liked me and let me in. Pure luck. I sat on the bus and partied with Guns N' Roses. No sex, just hanging out. The guitarist, Izzy Stradlin, said, "Call me. My alias is Mr. Jewel. I'll put you on the list for the next show." I told him I was moving to L.A. someday, and he said, "Well, if you ever do, here's my number." That was the real beginning. I took it from there. And I rarely spent just one night with anyone, except for Def Leppard's drummer, Rick Allen.

Pamela: Wow! That must have been a unique experience!

Lisa: I went to the show and was invited back to their hotel for a party. It was getting late, so Rick Allen got us a room for the night. I really wanted Ric Savage, but he went to bed early, asking me to join him when we were done partying. Since I didn't have his room number, Rick tried to find it for me. We went to his room in search of the band's room list, but once we got there, we didn't even look for it. It was a wonderful night, and Rick was very attentive to me. With one strong arm, he easily got on top and was just so beautiful. I think his accident and recovery made him even more gorgeous. Another unique experience was with Dave Mustaine of Megadeth. I knew their manager, so my friend and I got a room in the same hotel. She wanted Dave, but the poor girl was overweight. He wasn't even going to look at her.

Pamela: Oh God, the cruel facts of life.

Lisa: Exactly. Dave Mustaine could get any girl he wanted, and he was clearly interested in me. So my friend hatched a plan. She said, "Go to his room, get him all worked up, and say you have to leave. Then I'll come in, and he'll do *me*!" It was really sad. Inside of ten minutes, he and I were done and went back downstairs. I told my friend he couldn't get it up and never told her what really happened. The sex was good, probably because it was quick! He was powerful, just threw me down and took me. That's always good. I wasn't really into sex back then. I tolerated it because I so desperately wanted to be with them. Sex was the price I had to pay and I gladly paid it, all night long, again and again. Rock stars are so beautiful. But even if they weren't, my motto's always been, "He's a rock star, ain't he?"

Patti: Amen! I really enjoyed the sex, but I couldn't tell you if I came or not.

Lisa: I'm sure I didn't.

Patti: The sex was love, or as close to it as you were going to get with a rock star. I was giving them my love. I just packaged it in fishnets and high heels!

Lisa: I used the smaller bands to perfect my groupie skills. If I could just give them head, I was totally into that. The sex was all right, but what made me enjoy it was who I was with. And ultimately, that they were with me. Rock stars made me realize how special I was. And I made my rounds on that '88 tour. I was with the guitar player of Savatage, who later died in a car crash. Then I was with a roadie from Dio. And according to my journal, Ken Fox, the guitar player from Jason and the Scorchers, was the best sex I'd ever had. I remember him taking the spurs on his cowboy boots and running them up and down my body.

Pamela: That reminds me when Chris Hillman told me he was going to "curry me like a fine mare." Those cowboys, eh? Luckily, you enjoyed sex, Patti. Does anyone stand out, so to speak?

Patti: On the Invasion of Your Privacy tour, I met Ratt's guitar player, Robbin "King" Crosby, in the hotel lobby. Looking up at him, I said, "Wow, you're huge! How tall are you?" In a deep voice, he said, "6'7". What about you?" I said, "5'2". That's like, a foot and a half between us." He looked down at his considerable bulge, smiled wickedly, and said, "Yeah, about a foot and a half." I laughed and said, "So that's why they call you King!" I had other preferences in the band, but thankfully they didn't pan out and at the end of the night Robbin said, "Are you coming, or what?" Well, the answer was yes, and apparently, all night long! He was an excellent lover, ridiculously good. You know how sometimes they go down on you and it gets to be too much? "Yes, yes, yes! OK, that's enough!" Well, when it got to be too intense, I tried to stop him, but he just gripped my thighs harder and sent me into another earth-shattering climax. He was a real throw-you-down-and-take-you lover with a *huge* dick. He was a beautiful man, with a wild mane of blond hair. He was so big, and I was just a little thing, but together we were a perfect fit. The best part was when he held me in his arms. I'd lie on his broad, hairy chest all night long. But he had terrible insomnia.

Patti in 1987.
Credit: Patti Johnsen

Pamela: So many of them do. Keith Moon, God love him, would
wake up every hour shouting incoherent babble, and I had to
soothe his weary soul.

Patti: Robbin would stay awake and hold me all night while I
slept. I think he just didn't want to be alone. Later, I went to
Chattanooga to see him again, and we spent another night
making love and talking for hours. Again, I offered to leave
so he could sleep, but he insisted I stay. I sometimes think of
how terribly lonely he seemed. He was big and strong, but
AIDS reared its ugly head and took Robbin's life in 2002.
The official cause of death was a massive overdose of heroin,
but that was just King going out on his own terms. AIDS
was taking his life, and drugs had taken his soul. Despite all
the makeup and big hair, the glam metal world was quite a
hetero, macho scene. The guys would say, "I might be wear-

ing lipstick, but I can still kick your ass." AIDS wasn't even on the radar for them. And I never once used a condom until 1987. And even then it was hit and miss. But after I was with Billy Idol, I got better about it.

Lisa: I only used condoms when *they* wanted to. If they had one, we'd use it.

Pamela: So let's hear about Mr. Rebel Yell, Patti.

Patti: I met Billy at the Rainbow. I was standing at the top of the stairs to the loft—the Lair of the Hollywood Vampires. From my vantage point I could see a perfect microcosm of '80s rockers: "There's one who looks like Nikki, one who looks like Vince, and *that* guy thinks he's Billy Idol." Then I looked again. "Holy shit, that is Billy Idol!" I flew down the stairs, skidded to a stop in front of him, presented my ample cleavage for his perusal, and with obvious innuendo, I asked, "Can I get you anything?" He understood my offer, and with a sexy smile, said, "Yeah, a Jack and Coke." I brought his drink, saying, "It's on me," but he handed me a twenty and said, "Rock 'n' roll paid for it, din'nit?" Then I asked if he'd like to smoke a joint with me after work. He smiled broadly and said, "Yeah, I would!"

Pamela: So you were a *forward* groupie?

Patti: You have to be forward in L.A. There's too much competition!

Lisa: Out here, maybe, but back home I was kind of quiet.

Patti: So, after the fastest last call and clean up in the history of waitressing, I left the Rainbow with Billy. My bosses and father figures all nodded approvingly, always proud when one of their girls scored a rock star. Billy put his arm around me and went to catch a cab. We walked past Taime Downe, my very first lover in Hollywood, and he smiled as if to say, "You're gonna have a good time tonight!" He was right.

Pamela: Several girls have told me Taime stories. There must be something about him . . .

Patti: Taime was so gorgeous, like a sleazy Marilyn Monroe with a cock. He had that raunchy, '80s glam rocker scent: testosterone mixed with Aquanet and Max Factor. Ah, the intoxicating smell of a man wearing makeup. Anyway, minutes after Billy and I got to my apartment, I was getting rug burns from making out on my living room floor. He's so sexy and his body is absolutely perfect. Billy takes the wheel and he *knows* how to drive. I finally came up for air, long enough to suggest that we go to bed. He's intensely sexual and knew exactly what I wanted. And I discovered how kinky he was when he asked me to put things up his bum! I'm game for anything that gives pleasure. Just because I don't accept rear deliveries doesn't mean I won't play with you in *your* backyard. The "sex toys" he found to use were everyday items around my bedroom. My hairbrush got a turn up his ass, then my stiletto heel. As I saw him looking around, I couldn't help but think, "Please tell me I put the broom away!" This was as kinky as I'd ever been, but he was so fun and sweet about it. He'd stop every once in a while, look in my eyes, and ask, "It's a bit wild, yeah? But it's OK?" And I said, "Yeah, it's fine. I'm having fun!" He'd keep stopping and checking in with me, "It's just a laugh, in'it?" It *was* a laugh, *and* it was incredibly satisfying sex.

Pamela: Did you see him again?

Patti: Yeah, a few times. One night, I was home listening to his music. The phone rang, I picked it up, and a familiar, sexy voice said, "Hey, Patti, it's Billy." I said, "Sorry about the loud music. I was just getting my Billy Idol fix." In his thick, Cockney accent, he said, "How would you like the real thing?" Yes, please! That was a *great* rock star moment. Next thing I knew, I was in a cab flying to the Sunset Marquis. We spent another wild night, making love on every available surface, with only Billy's imagination to guide us. And his imagination was endless. He even requested a golden shower! I can remember one perfect moment. His rock hard body was on top of mine, and I could feel him inside me, slow and steady, rockin' "the cradle of love." I glanced over his shoulder and his new video was playing on TV. I laid back down and looked up at Billy. The real thing is so much more fun.

Pamela: Do you think regular sex bores him? Does it have to be kinky?

Patti: Kinky is in the eye of the beholder, I guess. But after being with him, I heard a rumor he had AIDS. He was a promiscuous rock star, was known to use heroin, and liked things up the bum. That's about as high risk as you can get. I took the test and I was fine, and obviously so was he. Still, after being paralyzed with fear waiting for test results, and with logic only a groupie would understand, I conjured up all sorts of creative ways to have safe sex with Billy, not using a condom. Luckily, Billy was so wild, anywhere I wanted his bodily fluids was fine with him. Like, "Hey, we could do a money shot on my tits!" I managed to have fairly safe sex, and didn't have to utter the one word that I never wanted to say to a rock star again . . . *"No."*

Pamela: Money shot, hmm? I've never heard that term before.

Lisa: I met the guys in Britny Fox a few times and hooked up with Michael Kelly Smith. We spent some great evenings together—always on the bus—never in his hotel room. Fine by me. Tour buses are way sexier than a cheap-ass Holiday

Lisa with Rudy Sarzo of Whitesnake.
Credit: Lisa Nichols

Inn. He was the first guy to ever enjoy a "money shot" with me. And he gave me his hairdresser's name so I could get hair extensions like his when I got to L.A.

Pamela: How thoughtful. Did you dolls ever get your hearts broken by a rock star?

Lisa: I stopped sleeping with rock stars for a long time, because I fell in love with Elwood, a roadie for Aerosmith. I met him while lobby loitering, pretending to make a phone call, and he bought it. He gave me a key to the bus and my own laminated pass. We had a long-term relationship. He was the love of my life. It still breaks my heart that we didn't make it. I had tons of other heartbreak because I always got my hopes up. Like with C.J. Snare from Firehouse. I was devastated when I found out he was married. I wanted to be "rescued" from my life and thought only a boy could do that for me. I didn't realize I was already rescuing myself.

Patti: I was madly in love with Taime.

Pamela: It's amazing how many girls have been with Taime Downe. And they still adore him!

Patti: Taime's a great guy. He's really down-to-earth and doesn't lead you on. And believe me, Taime knows what he's doing. He'd throw me down and fuck me like "the whore that I am!" But ultimately I realized I was the only one who was being exclusive. When I asked him about it, he seemed sad, like he didn't want to hurt me. Then he said quite honestly, "I never said you were my girlfriend." I realized, "You're right, you didn't." It's actually the sweetest breakup I've ever had, and the way it ended allowed us to stay friends. Even after we stopped sleeping together, he'd sing my praises and occasionally announce that I gave great head. I'm a groupie, so I'm proud of that. Practice makes perfect! My husband's sexual history is shorter than mine, and he never got a lot of oral sex. I always tell him, "It's so sad that you don't even know how good I am at this." He slyly says, "Oh, yes, I do."

Pamela: Was there anybody you craved like that, Lisa?

Lisa: I wanted Vivian Campbell in Whitesnake badly. Nearly had him too. He invited me to the bus and we made out.

Then he changed his mind and decided to call his wife. What a good boy. I also wanted Sebastian Bach, the gorgeous singer for Skid Row, but the guitar player, Snake, hit on me, and I wound up with him for several more shows. I was with two guys from Tesla one night. I met Tommy Skeoch briefly before their show. When I saw him afterward, bold, brave me, said, "I really want to fuck you." And he took me up on my offer. What fun we had in the dressing room that night! When we finished, we went out to talk with the rest of the band. That's when Tommy got the great idea of doing it again, and he asked Frank Hannon to join us. That was fun. I thought, "This will make a great story for the grandkids."

Pamela: Was that your only "sharing" experience?

Lisa: I'm not quite sure. One night, I was with Skid Row and wanted to get my nose pierced. Rachel Bolan, who's famous for his nose rings, said, "I'll do it." I proceeded to get trashed because I knew it would hurt. We didn't have any ice, so he poured Jack Daniel's on my nose, saying, "This will numb it." Then he stuck me with a safety pin. I screamed, so he repierced it with an earring. We were hanging out, watching TV in the room he shared with Snake. The next thing I knew, it was morning. I woke up in Snake's bed with a roadie

Patti with Taime Downe in 2005, twenty years after their first night together.
Credit: Patti Johnsen

standing over me, saying, "It's time to go." I have no memory of that night, but there *was* a video camera lying on the floor. Perhaps my dreams of starring in a rock video were realized. It's a shame I passed out and missed it. That's one of those yucky groupie stories, which explains why I didn't usually get so wrecked.

Pamela: Is that your only questionable groupie experience?

Lisa: The first time I met Warrant, Eric Turner was being sweet while trying to get in my pants. I didn't stay with him that night, but we did have a long talk. Then I saw him again and we had a *great* time. When he fell asleep, I went looking for my friend, and found her talking to the lead singer, Jani Lane. He proceeded to pounce on me in a big way. Well, not a *big* way, by the feel of things. He asked me to walk him to his room. Halfway there, he pulled out his dick (yes, I was right about it) and told me to suck it. He was gross and I knew if I slept with him, my dreams of Eric falling in love with me would never happen.

Pamela: Do you stay in touch with any of your rock amours?

Lisa: I'm still close with Michael Lardie, the keyboard player from Great White—and I have friends I stay in contact with—mostly roadies. I always left things friendly, so they all seem genuinely happy to see me again.

Patti: I've stayed in touch with Taime and a few other free spirits. But, unfortunately, a lot of their girlfriends don't believe in "old friends" like me.

Pamela: It seems you girls often hooked up with roadies.

Patti: Roadies are right in the center of the decadence, like pirates. When Aerosmith played the Forum in '89, we didn't have tickets, but we were sitting on the roadies' tour bus. Somebody said, "If you don't have tickets, why are you here?" I said, "The circus is in town! Just because we're not in the Big Top doesn't mean we can't play in the sawdust."

Pamela: One of the unfortunate clichés in groupiedom is having to do "favors" to get backstage. Did you ever?

Lisa: I rarely had to go that direction.

Patti: It was only twice for me. I always thought, "I don't want to shake the hand of my idol with the same hand that jacked off his drum tech."

Pamela: A wonderful groupie rule! Did you ever do a favor to get a pass, then not get one?

Lisa: No, never!

Patti: No, there is honor among thieves. Never did I do something and not get my pass. And visa versa. If I promised something for a pass, I delivered. I'd rather be a slut than a cock tease.

Pamela: With all the trauma and drama involved, why was it so important to be with the band?

Patti: They asked me that on VH1's *When Metal Ruled the World*. It's that feeling, "They want to be with me." How could I continue to be crushed because my high school boyfriend didn't want me when David Lee Roth *did*?

Lisa: Exactly. And there was something about being the outcast in high school. I'd go to shows and be standing at the light board and see those bitches who'd been horrible to me. And I thought, "I'm not a rock star, but I'll be with one tonight!"

Patti: And these rock stars always wanted a repeat performance. If I showed up in the next town, even with all new girls to choose from, they wanted *me* again. I know some people find it sad that we found validation in rock stars and sex. But being a groupie taught me never to settle for less. I can't imagine what my life would be like without my groupie experiences. I'd probably still be in Battle Creek, divorced from the first loser that gave me attention.

Pamela: How does your husband feel about your colorful past, Patti?

Patti: By the time I met my husband in 1990, I wanted to be loved, not in spite of who I was, but *because* of it. I learned the I-can-do-anything-I set-my-mind-to mantra by being a groupie, and all of my dreams came true. That same determination is how I finally found the man I'd been looking for. My husband knows everything about my groupie days. He's a musician, he's proud of me, and he *gets* it. I am the sum of all my parts. I'm a wife, a mother, *and* a groupie, and I'm proud of it all.

Lisa: Recently I was hanging out with some middle-aged "mean girls," and they ripped into me, saying, "You're just a groupie!" and I thought, "As a matter of fact, yes, I am."

Patti: Like it's a dirty word! I'm thinking, "Fuck you. You wish you were with the band." But I don't usually tell my stories with this much detail. I might say, Taime and I both appreciated the fact that I enjoyed going "Downe."

Pamela: I have to ask, how would you feel about your daughters being groupies?

Patti: If that's the path they choose, I hope they have the time of their lives, because I sure did. I'd only worry about them having safe sex.

Lisa: I agree. Whoever my daughter is with, I just hope she's safe.

Patti: I was in the Rainbow one night, talking about being a groupie. This woman butted in, and said, "Don't *lower* yourself." I responded by saying, "Listen, unless you've never left a bar with someone you just met, you have nothing to say to me. There's no difference between us except this: tonight you'll leave here with someone you just met, climb into a Pinto, pick up a six-pack, and head to a Motel 6, where you'll spend the night with a stranger. I will, however, leave here with a *rock star* I just met, climb into a limo, drink champagne, and head to the Hyatt, where I'll spend the night with a stranger that I've seen on MTV. Which one of us has the better deal?" As Steven Tyler said, "We give it out and the groupies give it back." Once, I was standing by a backstage door in all my groupie regalia, when some woman sneered, "What are you supposed to be?" And I said, "I'm the reason they picked up a guitar in the first place."

Miss B

Come as You Are

I have long been fascinated with rebellious types, from Mozart to Walt Whitman, from Elvis to Eminem. I honor them for not being able to keep their candor, fury, and naked truth under wraps, even when it hurts like mad.

So where have all the outraged rock stars gone? Real rock stars are supposed to upend tables, point fingers, and shake drumsticks at the flimsy, insidious status quo. I believe the last rock star that wreaked such havoc in the world was the late Kurt Cobain. Like Dylan, he was able to put into words what was lurking within the hearts and minds of his disillusioned fans. For better or worse, he single-handedly altered rock fashion forever, but what he contributed musically and sociologically far outweighs the plethora of flannel-wearing wannabes that moaned and wept in his wake. He was a multitalented, desperately angst-ridden genius, and he pointed out small-minded hypocrisy and the shameless sellout of his pissed-off generation. Nirvana altered music the way the Sex Pistols had a decade earlier, and it was a welcome slap in the face. Kurt unwittingly became eerily close to what he was railing against, which I feel added to his reasons for leaving us all behind. I met him once when I interviewed Courtney Love at their messy house in damp, gray Seattle, and his torment was a palpable thing that filled the room.

In my search for open-hearted groupies, Lexa from the Plastics suggested I meet a certain sensual, edgy brunette who's been making her name as a singer in Hollywood. "Miss B," as she wants to be called for this chapter, also spent several nights with Kurt Cobain just as he donned his rusty grunge crown.

She doesn't make any pretense about the difficult and shady turns her life has sometimes taken, but she's feeling more optimistic these days. She e-mailed me some bombshell photos of herself—heavily darkened, come-hither brown eyes, extra low-cut black lace accenting her voluptuous curves—so I am surprised by her initial shyness when I arrive for our interview. She has just moved into a charming deco apartment in West Hollywood and there is nothing on the walls except a poster for Gus Van Sant's film *Last Days* with Michael Pitt uncannily channeling Kurt Cobain. While we chat, Miss B focuses on three absurdly cute baby kittens that take turns purring in our laps.

It turns out that she was introduced to the dizzying world of rock and roll at thirteen by an old friend of mine, Steppenwolf guitarist Michael Monarch. "It was very exciting for me," she says, intently stroking her jet-black kitty, "especially because I don't come from normalcy. I come from a broken home. I was a foster child, so I was really looking for something that would tie me in to people I could hang out with." Her relationship with Monarch was purely platonic, but the fact that she felt included gave her some much-craved self-assurance. "The music scene became a family that I could fit into *perfectly*. It seems like anybody can fit into some kind of genre of music, so I found a welcome home right away."

With almost no parental nurturing or attention, Miss B made her way to the Sunset Strip, seeking counsel from unlikely rockers. "I was just finding my way, not even looking for that kind of scene. But I've always loved music. I really didn't have an identity. I'm almost a Jane Doe because I didn't know who my father was, so it made me feel special to be involved with well-known people. I became very attached to guys who were famous, and believe it or not, I was finding my identity through them. It helped me move forward in life and made me think, 'If I can be with *this* person, that means that I am worthy of just about anything.'"

Today Miss B is a member of two local rock bands, playing bass for Krell, a metal band she describes as "Marilyn Manson meets Black Sabbath," and fronting a tribute cover band that mainly focuses on Jefferson Airplane anthems. She's been writing for local Hollywood papers for ten years. She had a small recurring role on HBO's *Deadwood*. She also admits to being a longtime groupie but wishes the word hadn't become so besmirched. "I've had people label me, 'Oh, you're such a groupie,' and I laugh and say, 'You wish *you* were!' Rock stars *marry* their groupies—Sid and Nancy, Kurt and Courtney. I mean, what is a groupie anyway? Somebody who enjoys music and wants to be around it. I don't like when it's used in a derogatory sense because *everybody* wants to get backstage. I was at a show recently and my friend asked, 'How do we get back there?' I said, '*I'll* get back there.' I just walked right in and she *hated* me for it. I was like, 'Sorry, but I'm good at this.' I also wanna say that from a musician's standpoint, most people in bands are groupies as well because they like to be with other groups. You could say that about half the world is made up of groupies, you know?"

Couldn't agree more.

Miss B's late teens and early twenties were drastic and dangerous, and she freely admits she never believed she'd make it to thirty, a momentous mark she passed five years ago. "I wanted to live the ultimate rock 'n' roll life. The rough stuff kicked in when I was eighteen or nineteen. I don't know if I planned it like that, but I was living the life, and I was around it 24-7."

One of her earliest conquests was the ubiquitous Taime Downe of Faster Pussycat. I have spoken to many girls who described encounters with Taime that range from the sublime to the scandalous to the pitiful. Miss B and Taime recently reconnected and it seems she still has the hots for the rocker/DJ/Strip fixture. "I was into the notoriety of Faster Pussycat and Taime took a liking to me. We started hanging out a lot and becoming friends, then I went to his house and we had sex. He had a doll next to his bed; a woman, but she was decapitated so there was just the torso, and not even both arms, but it was all dressed up. Taime is an incredible lover. And he's also a creative, interesting person, very intelligent."

Hanging out on the wicked Strip in the mid-'80s, Miss B easily hooked up with various hard rockers. "There've been quite a few," she admits candidly. "I was with a couple of guys in Pretty Boy Floyd, Jeff Pilson from Dokken, and I had a brief sexual encounter with Lemmy from Motörhead. He's definitely a weird one. He's probably the oldest guy I've been with; he's been around since the Jimi Hendrix days."

She may have been wild, but Miss B makes it clear that she's never been into kinkiness or group sex. "I'm not the kind of groupie who's a home wrecker. I didn't steal anyone's boyfriend, and I prided myself on that. I've never had threesomes; I've never had more than a twosome in my life. I've seen certain things going on with other people, but never participated. The only rock stars I knew that were into really crazy stuff were Guns N' Roses, because I saw them having orgies. I was at Slash's house one time, with Duff, and I saw Slash and Ron Jeremy in bed with some porn stars. But I don't mess with that. I'm not into that whole thing." She did, however, wind up sharing the sack a few times with their enigmatic frontman, Axl Rose. "Axl was more of a friend that became like, you know, a lover. He was sensuous and very good. He's an interesting person, but he's shorter than the kind of guy I usually like. That was his dilemma—he was *real* short, but trying to be all manly. Axl had short-man syndrome, I think, so he overpowered people. I guess that's partially because when he was young on the farm in Indiana he had a mean stepfather who abused him. He's withdrawn and more of a pot smoker and a drinker than a drug-taker."

I saw GNR open for the Stones in the middle of their rock peak and was taken with Axl whooping it up, slip-sliding back and forth in his bicycle shorts, slinging his long, flaming hair in every direction. Sadly, I have heard that Axl is a bad-tempered scalliwag who regularly beat up his wives and girlfriends. "He didn't flip out on me because I didn't give him a chance. I know he's done awful things to women, but I didn't get attached to him in that way. Besides, he's doing better now. We were more like friends and didn't sleep together that often. Even when we *had* sex, there were all these people in the other room. He knew my past so he was very nurturing with me. Contrary to most people's beliefs, every time I was with him, he was trying to calm *me* down. Usually it's him flipping out on other people, but I was freaking out and he was sweet, saying, 'C'mon, calm down!' I will always consider him a friend."

Since I know Miss B is still friendly with Axl, I ask if she's heard *Chinese Democracy*, the infamous album he slaved over for over eight years.

"He was actually gonna use my voice on one of the tracks, but they never released the album. It's techno, and the record companies didn't believe in it. It's like Ozzy all of a sudden going techno, because Axl was *such* a metalhead."

So what happened? Why did he suddenly alter his music and himself so radically with techno beats and those crazy braided hair extensions? He now seems like an impersonator trying to copycat Axl Rose in his prime. "I know he's had a lot of surgery," Miss B says. "He wants to look young again. I think he's trying to look like a hip-hop guy and it's just not working." Like so many reclusive rockers, Axl seems to have lost touch. "Oh, yes, he's a *hermit*, definitely. Anything he does, he does with the few people that surround him. He has a South American maid that lives in his house in Malibu, and she's protective over Axl." Sadly, Axl's life sounds like it's become a rock and roll *Sunset Boulevard* with Axl Rose as Norma Desmond. "Yeah," Miss B agrees, "except that his housekeeper looks like tattooed Barbie from Brazil."

During the late '80s, Miss B was slowly sucked into the dismal, thriving hard drug scene in Hollywood. She was spending a lot of time among heroin users, and a quiet, slim blonde from Seattle soon became her constant copping companion. "I used to hang around a lot of people doing that kind of drug, and Kurt Cobain and I met in those circles. He became a friend. I was always pretty easygoing; people warm up to me. It began by him giving me rides places, taking me to buy drugs. I remember he used to compliment me a lot—I hadn't had any of that growing up, so I *really* liked that about him."

There was an underground buzz about Nirvana's first album, *Bleach*, already a pre-grunge classic, and they were playing small clubs around town. Miss B says that surprisingly, Kurt's dream was to move his band to sunny California. "He wanted to be out of the Seattle thing. Even though he had affection for Washington, he wanted to make it in California. I think growing up in Aberdeen helped nourish his misery, because he took that dismal outlook with him—it didn't change when he was in L.A. Still, he wanted the California dream and he was gonna live it, he was gonna make his music, and he wanted make it *here*. He was very intelligent. He was well read and into philosophy, but the drugs probably sidetracked him."

Kurt was a junkie, and even though speed and coke were Miss B's drugs of choice, they soon started "palling around." "I had done heroin—the snorting kind. I hadn't done the injecting kind. A lot of people around me were injecting dope. I was drugged out and so was he. I was usually going in a faster-paced mode, and he was slower-paced, but he was always friendly, a very nice and gentle person. He complimented me on my looks *and* my personality because he was into people's personalities more than what they looked like. Maybe that's why I got to liking him." Miss B laughs. "And we shared the same interest in music—we both liked the Lemonheads. Those days must have been like the late '60s all over again—people were just going out and doing *whatever* during that time. We spent about a month or two together, and I kept in contact with him. I was living in Hollywood and he would stay with me, then I'd go over to his motel. At the time there was a motel across from the Roxy, but they tore it down." When I tell her that Jim Morrison stayed at that same little motel when he was fighting with his girlfriend Pamela, she shakes her head. "It figures they'd live in the same place. Anyway, I'd pick Kurt up and we'd do certain errands."

These "certain" errands were mainly of an illegal nature, but spending so much time together created an intimacy between the two young misfits. "He was a real sweetheart; a little skinny, but attractive, small-boned, and not as tall as I usually go for, but he was hot looking. A lot of our relationship consisted of going to get dope, coming back, and doing it. We just became friendly in that way. I never had great self-esteem, and Kurt had the same problem. He was the most kindhearted rock star I've been with, definitely. It's funny because both of us were the same way. I don't know who was the more outgoing of the two—probably me, because he was so shy. I never understood why, but he had the same problem I had: self-loathing. I can't say I feel like that today because I like myself now. But I still have this scary other side that Kurt had all over. He didn't feel worthy of anything, you know? That's why I think when he became famous he couldn't handle it. It was overwhelming, and he didn't feel deserving of it, and that's really tragic."

I certainly agree that Kurt seemed to be the most obviously tortured artist since Vincent Van Gogh chopped off his earlobe and sent it to a hooker. "He was almost Gothic. If he'd had black hair, he would have been a Goth guy. He had deep trouble and chronic pain," Miss B continues. "There were problems with his stomach—bleeding ulcers—and he would get very ill. But what he complained of was not only physical. He had mental pain."

I know the heroin use must have assuaged some of Kurt's discomfort, but didn't Miss B worry that he might accidentally die from an overdose?

"Yes," she says quietly, "and he was always tragic, as are most of the men I've been with. From what I've heard, Jim Morrison was like that, too. They all have a common theme: a kind of death wish. So I knew from the early stages that something could go wrong. He was a suicide junkie—if you knew him, you would know that. Most people in rock 'n' roll have it to some degree. They're different from the rest of us; they're a different breed."

I comment that at least Kurt's desire to express himself overcame his anguish long enough for him to create some of the most profoundly influential music in rock history.

"Yeah, well, most artists, actors, or musicians, a lot of them are shy people but they come out of their shells during their music and their acting."

Somewhere along the line, the kindred tortured souls started spending nights together. "I don't even know how it happened, but it did, and Kurt was an excellent, tender lover," Miss B sighs deeply before providing some pretty potent insight into Kurt Cobain. "Basically, he was into cross-dressing."

Wow. Well, I suppose it does make sense. When he wasn't wearing flannel, Kurt showed up on stage in long skirts and smeared glam makeup, seemingly quite comfortable flaunting his androgyny. Since she has claimed to be fairly square sexually, how did Miss B respond to Kurt's particular quirk? "I don't know. He *did* ask me about it before he dressed up. 'If I show you this, are you gonna be OK with it?' And I was like 'I'm fine . . . *whatever*.' He wore pantyhose with cut-out parts in certain areas, high heels, dresses, wigs, makeup: the whole thing. Strangely enough the sex was very regular, nothing out of the ordinary. There was never another person involved. The only oddity was that he dressed up a lot—that was his specialty, that's what he liked. Kurt knew his masculinity and his femininity. They were mixed together and he was all right with that."

I ask Miss B where Kurt got the various ladies' garments. "He had some of his own women's clothes made for him," she says. "And he was the kind of person who would go into your closet. He was a Dumpster diver, too, and he got stuff out of the trash. I can attest to that because I saw it with my own eyes. He would pick random places around the Hollywood area, then he'd bring a bundle of women's clothes to my house along with wigs and makeup and jewelry. I don't know where he got the wigs. He would also wear my things. I was glammy back then, very into makeup and clothes. I was stylish—probably more so than I am now. I had Lip Service skull and crossbone pants, everything that was cool, and Kurt was creative with the outfits, too."

About the same time Kurt went back to Seattle, Miss B moved to Florida to tidy up her act. "I was only twenty years old, and

I left L.A. so I wouldn't be wrecked. I was *so* far into the scene and so messed up on dope."

Kurt and Miss B spoke on the phone occasionally until Courtney Love came barreling into the picture. "We didn't stay in touch after the thing with Courtney started; I played a small part in his life, and I don't want Courtney coming up to me going, 'I'm gonna kick your butt.' She's an outspoken, strong person, and I understand why he was attracted to her. I think she's really cool, and I don't feel she's at all responsible for Kurt's death, and I hate people who say she is. I was very saddened when I heard he had killed himself. But I wasn't shocked; I saw it coming. He used to try to find ways to hurt himself. I don't think he understood the impact he would make or even *dreamed* that he'd make the impact he did."

Miss B and I play with the kittens, who've just roused from their naps, and we bemoan the sorrows of drug addiction. "But drugs also spawned the creativity that *is* Nirvana," she claims. "Because he probably couldn't have expressed what was going on inside him, or even gotten up on a stage without them."

When she returned from her healing stint in Florida, Miss B made the acquaintance of another of Seattle's finest, Pearl Jam's Eddie Vedder. They wound up at the infamous Riot House for a night of frolicking. Mr. Vedder has always seemed so low-profile and untouchable. How the heck did she make *that* happen? "I went backstage at his concert and met him," she says simply. "I have a knack. I just *do* it—I can't really describe how I do it. I ended up knowing so many people, and I kind of worked it. It probably had something to do with the way I was dressing: really provocative with my boobs hanging out, tight T-shirts and Lip Service pants. But I was still grungy. I worked my sexiness. At one point I went to the Billboard Awards and interviewed George Harrison—not many people can say *that*. I really worked the fact that I wrote for a rock magazine. I was young and pretty and used it to my advantage. Yeah, I had a good time with Eddie, but his personality wasn't as interesting as Kurt's."

Soon after her very close encounter with Pearl Jam's sensitive wailer, Miss B met a roadie for Slayer, fell in love, and settled into a fairly normal rock relationship that lasted eight years. They even made it legal, but she came to realize that wedded bliss wasn't what she hoped it would be. "My marriage broke up, but we stayed good friends. I went right back into the old rock-star routine. I hooked up with Taime again and my old habits. I ended up liking Taime too much. I wanted to be his girlfriend."

From what I've heard, Taime Downe cannot be tamed or tied down. "Oh, I think he could be," Miss B protests. "He's had long-term girlfriends. But I pushed the issue. I was into him and called him all the time. I could have done the same thing with Kurt, had Kurt been around longer."

What is it about Taime that evokes such passionate fervor in Miss B? "I think he's made an amazing impact on the L.A. scene. He's done a lot musically. Taime's a fabulous front man, so I think he will go down in history—not like Nirvana, of course, but his band, Faster Pussycat, has a huge cult following. I love his version of 'You're So Vain' and the cover of 'These Boots Are Made for Walkin'.' And he's got a lot of great *original* material."

I put a halt to the Taime tirade by asking Miss B what she's been listening to lately, *besides* Taime Downe. "Nowadays I listen to gothic music, metal, classic rock. I try to have a mix, you know? I've been spending some quality time with Matthew Robert from this great industrial band, New Rising Son. They even sampled my voice on their new record."

I peel a kitten off my lap and ask Miss B how she sees her future. "My only goals are to keep doing my acting, music, and art. I'm living for that right now. If it turns out that I should get married and have ten children, well, then, it turns out that way. If it turns out that I'm dead before forty, then it turns out like that. It's not that I don't like living; I do. It's just the way I live, I know I can't go on this way forever. Sometimes I go to goth clubs and people are like, 'You can become one of us.' And I say, 'If you think you can make me immortal with your vampire teeth, go right ahead, but I don't think it's gonna happen.' I was wearing a T-shirt the other day that said 'Outlaw'; I'm definitely a rebel. I really am the epitome of somebody who is living for the moment."

Pleather

The Male Groupie

"I saw an old TV show where Dick Cavett was interviewing Janis Joplin, and he asked if she had male groupies. She said, 'Not nearly enough,' and I felt strangely validated." So begins my first fascinating chat with Mr. Ian Wagner, more flamboyantly known as "Pleather." Our initial meeting takes place at the swell old Hollywood landmark, the Farmers Market on Fairfax Avenue. I've been frequenting this classic hotspot for decades, enjoying many tasty turkey burgers and crab salad platters with the likes of Ron and Russell Mael from Sparks, my ex-husband Michael, and our boy, Nick. Today I've suggested lunch at the Gumbo Pot. As I peruse the yummy Cajun menu, I suggest my guests try the scrumptious oyster po'boy.

The slim, seemingly shy Pleather has brought along Drama, the disarming, outspoken platinum blonde bass player in the all-doll, straightedge (no drugs, no booze) band Switchblade Kittens. When I ask Pleather how he got such a unique nickname, he can't seem to remember. Drama certainly can: "It was the *pants*. He has this pair of pleather pants that are extremely form-fitting and you see his endowments very clearly." Aha.

But thirty-two-year-old Pleather insists that despite his renowned proportions, he's never been a show-off. "I'm not that

Credit: Ian Wagner

type, but what the hey, it's worked wonders for me. I had never considered myself a groupie until Drama informed me of that fact. I was just living my life, then I went through a couple of her band members, or they went through *me*. I started telling Drama all my stories and she said, 'You are a groupie.' And I said, 'OK, I guess I am.' I never thought of the term as having a negative connotation, and now I'm proud of it. People don't understand how much it's about the music. I'm not just turned on by a woman playing an instrument; it's the empathy I have with the musician. I want to get close to the creativity. That's all."

There doesn't seem to be any difference between Pleather's adoring attitude toward his musical heroes and any of the female groupies I've interviewed. Can a man be a muse? Why the heck not?

"I grew up downstairs from Johnette Napolitano from Concrete Blonde. When I was eleven or twelve, her little sister was my babysitter. She was a musician, too—a typical '80s, stoner, burnout chick. I was a bit advanced for my age, and nature took its course. After that experience, I started chasing it. The only women I've ever been attracted to are musicians. Ever. I've never been attracted to normal people. Never. I've tried it, but there's always something missing."

I tell Pleather that I've given it the royal try as well, but always come back to the man on the pedestal, er, the stage—perhaps because my daddy was bigger than life and seemingly unreachable.

"My relationship with my mother has completely formed and determined my life," Pleather says. "I was homeschooled, so we were always together and extremely close. She taught me how to play guitar, told me what books to read. She made me stay up late to watch great movies. She exposed me to everything about life and art. I had a strange grown-upness about me. I was reading by the time I was two. When I was six, I played guitar constantly. By the time I was eight, I could hang out with my parents' friends and talk on an intellectual level. My dad always worked, provided, did the dad thing. He was a drummer in two or three bands. So almost every night, he would go off and play. When I was ten, my parents formed a punk band, so I went to all their practices. This was '81 and still pretty groundbreaking. My mother plays guitar, bass, and keyboards, so from an early age I found myself relating to female musicians."

And which female band initiated Pleather into the mysteries of love? "The first all-girl band I had a real experience with was the Pandoras. They started as a garage band, then went into metal. I was fifteen. They were in their late twenties, and all too willing to have a plaything in their midst. Things got really crazy; they were very free and open—let's just say that. They were not shy and would engage in couplings anytime—wherever and whenever was fine. They would do each other while you did them, get another guy over, two in one, every permutation possible. I went on tour with them and was kind of their toy."

"On more than one occasion he coupled with the entire band," Drama adds.

"Yeah, that happened," Pleather concedes. "It's for the record."

"He's rock and roll's best-kept secret," Drama continues. "People don't realize that he is the greatest feminist, and if you're gonna have a Band-Aid you might as well have Pleather around. Sure, you can have sex on the tour bus, but what matters about Pleather is that he's the most intelligent male I've ever met. *And* he wears pink hot pants! But some female musicians are afraid of him, because he's known as THE male groupie." I can't tell if Pleather is pleased by this handy little factoid or a tad embarrassed.

"Growing up, I was too young to realize that female rockers were a novelty. I came of age when the Runaways, Joan Jett, Patti Smith, and Heart came out. After the Pandoras, I moved on to Pleasant Gehman's band, the Screamin' Sirens. I think Pleasant got a kick out of treating men the way she'd been treated. I got a sense that she was playing a role; she was so much smarter than

Drama.
Credit: Switchblade Kittens

the people she followed around. I always thought she was better than Darby Crash and had a lot more to say."

I assume that due to his reputation, Pleather usually didn't have much trouble corralling the most coveted rock chicks.

"His *reputation* is that he has the biggest dick in rock and roll," Drama purrs.

"Don't believe the hype," Pleather counters.

I'll bet a lot of Pleather's partners have been equally impressed with his musical knowledge and appreciation. "I've studied the history of music, and I think all the stuff men had to say ended with punk rock, and that's where women started. Anything meaningful to be said in rock music today is being said by women. I've always been chasing that; I want to be at the center of where it happens. In 1990, there was no band with more of a buzz than L7. You'd walk into a club they were playing, and it felt like the world was gonna explode. They really had something to say. They came onstage and it was ultimate power. I had my longest association with them. I was their support system for several years, but it became a traumatic experience because my emotions were played with. I went back and forth between three members of the band. And I really loved all of them simultaneously, *loved* them more than anything. I would still be with any member of L7. An unfortunate, unprotected accident occurred— one of them got pregnant. That was my cue to be ushered out of that situation because they are like a coven. They talk about each other behind their backs, but when something comes into their world, they just close ranks. They wouldn't return my phone calls. They'd just walk past me. It was heartbreaking because I considered them my family—sisters, lovers, *everything.* So I said, 'That's it, from now on I'm gonna be celibate. I'm not getting emotionally involved.'"

He didn't lose his heart, but Pleather soon wound up catering to another troubled rock waif, Inger Lorre from the Nymphs, who is mainly remembered for getting pissy with her A&R man. Her album was in the can for too long, and in what would soon become legendary in naughty rock behavior, she climbed up on the unfortunate fellow's desk and urinated all over it. "I'd bring

Credit: Ian Wagner

Inger to Perry Farrell's house to score heroin and help her shoot up, which I know was beyond the call of duty. She was so talented, but in such physical, spiritual, and mental pain. Heroin was the only thing taking her away from that. We'd watch *Drugstore Cowboy* five times in a row. One afternoon, I woke up and her breathing was strangely slow, and I couldn't wake her up. I knew there was a short amount of time before she'd be dead, so I had to do the ice cube method up her bum. I ended up saving her life that day. That relationship lasted about six months, but it was obvious there was no saving her. She was one of those people that you had to do what she did, so I was doing heroin with her. But I wouldn't take as much and was somehow able to keep my faculties."

Did Pleather feel like it was his duty to accommodate and encourage the women in his life? "Of course. Jennifer Finch from L7 introduced me to Courtney Love and I immediately recognized that she was on another level; she was a poet. She would open for L7 and I'd have to coach her before and after every show. She'd say, 'I'm just not as good as L7.' I'd tell her, 'You don't understand, you're gonna be huge, you're the next Patti Smith or Madonna. You're gonna be an icon!' When I knew her she was humble, and I think she's carried that through. I spent time with her when she was on the outs with her guitar player, Eric. They had an on-and-off relationship and he didn't care what she did because he knew he couldn't control her. He worshipped her too. But she put herself down. She gave it up to men. She doesn't believe she's as talented as she is, and she let Kurt, Billy Corgan, Trent Reznor influence her too much. All she needs to do is follow her artistic instincts. I did wind up with Courtney, but it was more of a friendship/love thing. I thought she was great, and I slept with her, but it was all in fun. I hate to say it, but she was pretty normal in bed. She wasn't wild. I don't know, maybe I'm wild, but she was nothing in comparison to the Pandoras—real Hollywood sleaze all the way. But I have nothing bad to say about Courtney. I think she was the bee's knees.

"Later, two of the Pandoras went on to form the Muffs, a band that destroyed themselves because of their egos. I was with Kim Shattuck for a while. What everybody thinks about Courtney was true about Kim; she'd completely destroy everyone around her for her own ego. No human feelings, just a robot."

Despite promises he made to himself about keeping his emotions in check, Pleather careened down the rock and roll rabbit hole again in 1992. "I fell in love completely with Carla Bozulich, the lead singer of the Geraldine Fibbers. I love brains and creative spirit. She was everything I'd ever looked for and I'm still looking for—the love of my life without a doubt. So, Carla and I started out as friends, and it turned out to be the longest courtship I ever had. I chased her, which I wasn't used to doing. She was a tortured genius, totally screwed up, just the way I like 'em. She needed lots of help, and I like helping."

"He likes 'em cra-*zee*," Drama chimes in.

"I just wanted to facilitate, so she didn't have to deal with the world. I wanted to remove anything placed between her and her creativity. I worshipped the ground she walked on. I kept the circus rolling, and for a while it worked." The ill-fated romance lasted just over two years before Carla found someone else. "That was the worst," Pleather moans. "I've dealt with deaths in the family, and it wasn't anywhere near the amount of pain I experienced losing Carla. That was the only time I found myself standing on the overpass with one foot on and one foot dangling. I went into a three-year hermetic time—no sex, no relationships. I worked as a clerk in a bookstore, I read my books and started writing. I didn't even go out."

For cathartic reasons, Pleather started writing a book, *I'm with the Girl Band*. "I was going to check with you, to see if it would be all right," Pleather insists. I assure him that I'd be first in line to buy it.

From the time he was fifteen, and during his rocky relationships, Pleather played guitar in several local bands. "Yeah, I always had my own bands while I followed everyone else, but I never put any value on my music. For me it was all about *them*. But after my hermetic period, I said, 'OK, this is it, I'm focusing on other people too much, I'm gonna do my own thing.'" But when he put an ad in the paper, seeking "female friendly" musicians, he wound up being the only guy in his new group. "I had that band, Roller Girl, for a few years and fell in love with Rosanna the drummer, which pretty much destroyed my life again." Pleather sighs. "She was also in a goth band, and I became their aide, did everything for them. Then she joined Switchblade Kittens, and I met Drama. That was three years ago."

"He ended up breaking up with that drummer, then he *married* our next drummer. In fact, he's dated, lived with, or married all of our drummers," Drama adds. When I inquire as to how many drummers the Switchblade Kittens have gone through, Drama's answer cracks me up. "Seventeen! Seventeen psycho drummer girls that Pleather has tried to save."

"You're kidding me, right?" I marvel, "This is beginning to sound like *Spinal Tap*!" Pleather laughs heartily, "Yes! They spontaneously combust and then it's over! Seriously, taking care of a drummer *is* a full time job. Here's the fundamental difference I see between male and female groupies: all the women I've known just want to be talked to. They want someone to listen. I've always been empathetic. I like to listen and I like to help. I don't think most men put much stock in that. In a lot of ways, I think they just want to use women."

"You can be a successful woman in rock and don't have to resort to getting back at men," Drama says, "and some women have done that to Pleather."

"That's exactly what has happened," he agrees. "But I still refuse to hold it against any of them. Anyway, when I go out these days, I'm just there to be who *I* am. I'm there to be seen and make an impression—to be *fabulous*."

Drama digs into her purse and hands me a pastel pink Switch-blade Kittens CD. She tells me the one they're working on now is going to be even better. "Pleather is my confidence in the studio," she adds, gently patting his hand.

"That's what I live for," he says. "That's why I do what I do. It's natural for me. I just have to be where the creativity is."

Credit: Ian Wagner

A few weeks later, on a gray, rainy day, Pleather and I meet up for another heart-to-heart at a coffee shop in my old Reseda neighborhood. I haven't been here in years, and sadly, it looks like any other bland corner in the Valley. But Pleather certainly stands out in his tight black ensemble, cute leather cap, and splendid woolly scarf that accents his high cheekbones. After a hug, he tells me he's glad we're alone this time. "It's not that I didn't tell you the truth last time, but Drama was there. It was probably good for you to see me like that, because that's how I am when I'm with a musician I admire. I ended up letting her tell my story."

Pleather gallantly buys me a vanilla latte and we sit by the window and listen to the pitter-pat of the rain. "I was walking here, thinking of what I wanted to say. I've always had my own bands, but I only ever wanted to be the guitar player in Blondie, or Bjorn in Abba. I want to be the person helping the goddess-female-artist-singer. What I realized when I read your book, and all the ten thousand times I reread it, is that there's a positive and a negative to the whole experience. Being so profoundly influenced by my mother from an early age, it's simply innate for me to have empathy. I've subconsciously set up my entire life to take the traditionally feminine role in relationships. When I say feminine, I mean the person who is seen as *weaker* to the outside world, but is really the one making things happen. Women make the world go 'round, but the men take the credit." Pleather continues, "To me, the real revolution of the '70s wasn't punk—it was women taking a more powerful role. Punk was just a restatement of traditional values. The real shift was the female phenomenon, but I was too young to realize it. I would turn the television on, and see *Wonder Woman* and *Charlie's Angels*, all these women with guns. It was like, 'Yeah! This rules!' I have all the *Wonder Woman* seasons on DVD. I was watching an episode with Drama recently, and she paused Wonder Woman in action. She was trying to talk to me, and I said, 'I can't talk.' I had to turn around and face the other way. Wonder Woman still has this profound effect on me. It's insane! I had a fundamentally warped perception of women from early age. I was very influenced by pop culture, and that's when the women's movement really became mainstream. It wasn't so much the manifesto, bra-burning thing. It's more like when it reaches the pop mainstream, that's when the revolution really happens. I had to be a part of it and be plugged into the ultimate center." Pleather laughs. "That's a pretty sexual metaphor; I didn't mean it quite that way. There's just something ultimately greater. If you're not one of those people thinking, '*I'm* larger than life,' then you want to be with a person who *is* larger than life. The first time I laid eyes on Courtney, I knew she was a genius. There was something in her, the same thing I recognized when I saw Dylan or Patti Smith. People like that have an aura about them. There's such a glow."

What, besides his God-given, majestic physical endowment, made the goddesses flock to Ian "Pleather" Wagner?

"I have a saving complex, and I tend to go for the ones who are the most screwed up. A friend of mine said, 'If Squeaky Fromme and Donna Reed were standing next to each other, you would go for Squeaky.' And I said, 'Yeah, exactly.' I just want to help, I want to fix, and I want to be the shoulder. With Courtney, I saw someone with a lot of hurt; genuine, honest female energy; rage; and knowledge. She just needed to be told how great she was. At that time, there was no one telling her she was great. No one. Every single musician I knew would say, 'I can't believe you go see Hole. They are the worst band I've ever seen.' This was in the beginning, when they used my friend's house as their practice space. At the time, L7 were going to be the next big thing, the big revolution band—female rockers doin' it. Courtney was opening for them, and I had to give her confidence to go on. Every time she played a show, I would be there. It got ridiculous. One club was so broken-down, they only had one mic stand. Halfway through the show, the stand broke, and Courtney said, 'Well, I guess the show's over.' I said, 'No, let me hold it,' and I held the thing up. I was trying to rock out and hold the mic stand for her at the same time. How metaphoric can you get?" He laughs, "No, that's *beyond* metaphor; it's too literal."

So, what's the secret? How did he go from holding her mic stand to getting in her panties?

"There's a lot of truth in certain caricatures, the way women and men relate to each other. Women primarily just want to be listened to and empathized with. They want to be rough, tough, and in control at certain times and not in control other times. I've always had a sixth sense about knowing the right time to be the listener—to be the girlfriend, basically, and exactly when to shift back into the male role. I think the success I've had with women is because of that. They aren't used to having a guy put his own ego under. It's a rare thing for women to experience. It has to do with finding a sympathetic soul. It's like souls in transit. You may be on a different path, but it's OK as long as you have that one experience, that *one* night. The best time I had with Courtney was just kissing. We were sitting in front of a club, cars were passing by, everyone was inside getting drunk, and for ten minutes, being alone with her, kissing and making out." I can tell by his dreamy look that Pleather is enjoying this particular sense memory.

"That feeling is what I've been chasing ever since. That was probably the most romantic moment, the sweetest experience I've ever had." Pleather pauses and smiles, "I guess that's kind of sad."

I understand completely. He had a tender moment with his icon, and it's become one of those extremely rare snapshot memories.

"Actually, I've had very few sexual experiences that didn't also have a lot to do with sharing emotions. Women's emotions are very close to the surface, and when you tap into that, it all comes pouring out. Female musicians have a lot of hurt they need to express. And if you show some interest, they're more than willing to share their emotions, their souls, and their bodies with you."

It sounds to me that even though Pleather has had his heart destroyed a time or three, the torture and tribulation has been worth it. "Oh yeah, that's the main thing I want to say. No matter how badly I got treated—and I did get badly treated by a lot of them—there isn't a single woman that I hold anything against. We're all just trying to do the best we can and make our own

Credit: Ian Wagner

lives work. It was an honor for me to be around them for the short amount of time I was. It was my pleasure. I would give any one of them my last two dollars."

Before we open our umbrellas and head out into the Reseda rain, Pleather surprises me. "I've joined the Switchblade Kittens," he announces proudly. "I'm cowriting and coproducing their album, which is turning out great. And that's so fulfilling, I can't even say. I'm also codirecting their documentary. There's a lot of stuff going on with that band. They're like a multimedia, crazy circus."

I have to ask. Is he dating the drummer?

"No, no, no," he laughs, reassuring me. "I'm going to try to separate business and pleasure for once in my life. And I'm discovering that the grass isn't really always greener over there. We tend to put more value on other people's stories than our own. We value the mad, visionary genius, artistic people. We're fascinated by them and think, 'Oh my God, where does she get those ideas?' Of course, I'm still enthralled with that and always will be. And I make no apologies whatsoever for chasing my dream. But hopefully, the natural balance starts to happen and you begin to value your own story and realize your own worth." Pleather pauses for a moment, looking into the dark winter sky, then smiles at me, "But I still love Lynda Carter. If I saw her, I would just . . . I would . . . I would just fall down dead. All I've been looking for, *ever*, is Wonder Woman with a guitar!"

Lexa Vonn and the Plastics

User Friendly

I grabbed the latest copy of L.A.'s local *Rock City News* to read about myself when another brazen headline suddenly became more interesting. "The secret to my SeXcess! The True Meaning of Groupie-ism," written by Lexa Vonn, the same journalist who had interviewed me. I eagerly perused her instructive missive.

> The word "groupie" has often been attached to many grave misconceptions over the years. The average person usually envisions a sexually immoral girl who sleeps around with famous people in order to satisfy a deeper need for notoriety or other form of self-gain. However, the former definition more describes what I refer to as a "star fucker." A true groupie defined by my own experiences, as well as the original groupie jet set of the 1960s, portrays a much deeper version of the meaning. Being a real groupie is a talent on its own, and not one that can be performed by just anyone. Sex, while an important part of the groupie experience, is only one facet of the whole picture. A true groupie has a deep connection and understanding of both music and the dimension in which

musicians exist when they are performing. Rock and roll is a ritual and groupies are the high priestesses. . . . After all, what would a concert be without anyone there to hear it?

Good question, doll.

Miss Lexa is a founding member of the Plastics, a quartet of flashy groupie publicist-promoters, and their impudent photograph adorned the cover of the zine *Rock City News*. I recalled my recent snappy chat with the flame-haired, ivory-skinned Lexa and knew I had to investigate her escapades and those of her playmates-in-crime.

It does me proud that Lexa and the Plastics do such a smashing job of decorating rock and roll events here in Hollywood. Especially since she insists that my all-girl group, the GTO's, helped inspire their inventive brand of merrymaking. Not only are these voluptuous show-offs proud to be called groupies, they are also successful business babes who use their savvy to get bands seen and heard. Their Web site, www.myspace.com/backstage_plastics, offers various types of assistance to up-and-coming rock stars:

- *photoshoots, product endorsement, modeling*
- *host, MC your event, show, or party*
- *go-go dancing and burlesque for shows*

Lexa has invited me to her 1920s heart-of-Hollywood apartment, and as she brews tea in her Sex Pistols T-shirt, miniskirt, and combat boots, I wander around enjoying the lineup of vintage lunchboxes, rock 'n' roll action figures, and Gothic dolls that adorn the walls. Her furniture is covered in tapestries and fur, and the coffee table has been converted to an altar, littered with candles, incense burners, daggers, crystals, oils, flowers, and framed photos of Lexa with Marilyn Manson. A homemade collage featuring Kurt Cobain and Jesus Christ hangs in the kitchen next to the fridge, which is plastered with concert and club flyers. After Lexa shows me the trashy treasures in

Credit: Lexa Vonn

her frock-filled closet, I'm ready for an engrossing peek into her imagination.

Lexa Nicoletti felt strangely out of place as far back as she can remember. Her artistic parents were considered peculiar in their conservative hometown of Andover, Massachusetts. "It was upper middle class—very white, very rich—and I was the *total* black sheep," Lexa says as she pours an herbal tea concoction. "There were blonde Christian cheerleaders, then there was me— the girl raised in a pagan household. I never knew what church was. My mother was a painter and my father was a chiropractor who ran his own practice. They were never around. I had three older sisters and the youngest is always neglected, which is how I got away with so much. My father was a dark character. He was cold and uninvolved but claimed to be a high wizard. Both he and my mother claimed they could heal people with energy, but I suf- fered from bad bladder infections for years and was never treated, even though I complained. I also suffered insomnia, paralyzing night terrors, episodes of disassociation, and severe depression. I had no family structure and didn't have a family at school either. But I knew there was something else out there. MTV had just started, and I was addicted. I was reading music magazines and thought, 'This is the world I wanna be in.'"

Once again, the saving grace of rock and roll gave the odd girl out a reason to thrive. Lexa's first mad crush was Poison's C. C. DeVille. "Pirate Radio used to broadcast from L.A. on Saturday nights and you could call the special guest rock stars. Every week I would dial until I got through. One night I got Poison's Bret Michaels on the phone and my question was 'How do I meet you in person?' He didn't know I was fourteen and told me, 'When we get to your town, come to sound check about three or four o'clock. Talk to the road crew, tell them you want a

Original Plastics lineup: Jenni Jayde, Staci Paige, Lexa Vonn, and Sandra Starr.
Credit: Lexa Vonn

backstage pass, and they'll forward you to the head of security.'" Lexa got the skinny straight from the rockers' mouth! "Yeah," she laughs. "That was my first time being backstage. It was cool, there was free beer, and I got my autographs. After that, my life depended on the next show. When I knew a band was coming, I'd go on a diet, buy new clothes, get my nails done . . . it was like going to the prom every time."

As she traversed venues along the Eastern seaboard, young Lexa sensed right away that she shared something special with the performers. "I had a real psychic connection with the guys in the band. That's why I always go directly to the front row. As soon as the band hits the stage, it's magnetism. The singer will almost always start singing to me, stare at me, and communicate with me."

Even though I know the answer, I ask Lexa how that kind of heightened communion feels. "It feels like sex—that is my sex, my religious experience—like being on drugs. But I never use drugs at shows. I don't want to alter the experience."

Why were musicians able to move her in such a profound way? "Looking back, some of it was because my father was absent. I always knew something was wrong with me, emotionally and physically, but our issues were swept under the rug. At sixteen, I told my mother I believed my father had sexually abused me. She insisted it couldn't be true and instead of sending me to a psychiatrist, she sent me to her psychic—who told me I was right. But I never spoke of it again to my mother. I remember reading an interview with Axl Rose about how his father sexually abused him. As a teenager I thought if I could find a rock star who'd been through something like I had, they'd understand me and protect me. The attention I got from musicians filled a void and validated me. But it's the *music*, mostly, that drives me. I believe music comes from *God*, or whatever is up there: the higher power source. Musicians channel that source, and when they look at you with those eyes, it's like being with God. You're communicating with a medium that has God inside them at that moment."

After leaving home at eighteen, Lexa got to California via the Misfits and hasn't looked back. She was so jazzed at their gig in

Boston that she jumped onstage, got handed a microphone, and sang a song with the band.

"After the show I hit it off with the drummer. I told him I was backpacking around the country and didn't live anywhere. And he said, 'Here's our tour schedule. If we're ever in the same place, come hang out with us.' About a week later, I hitchhiked to California. I always had groupie assistants accompany me, but this time I brought a *traveling* groupie, and we met up with the Misfits in San Diego. After the show, the drummer and me went on our first date, skinny-dipping under the moon, then came back and had a threesome with my girlfriend on a private beach."

Isn't that every drummer's dream? "Yeah, I was experimenting with my bisexuality, and we became a threesome for awhile. We had so much fun the Misfits said, 'You guys are too cute to be living on the streets. Come on tour. You've got permanent passes, you're family now.' He went on to a side project, Graves, and they have a song about me called 'Ophelia,' which is one of my nicknames. I saw him on and off for four years."

Lexa moved with her girlfriend to San Francisco after the Misfits tour, but soon felt adrift. "The tour ended, I didn't have a car or money, I was completely estranged from my parents, and my relationship wasn't working out. Then one day I took a lot of acid and had a spiritual experience listening to Marilyn Manson's *Antichrist Superstar*. An entity came to me and said, 'Don't kill yourself. You're meant to do something else. Go find Manson and go on tour.' I had met him a few times in high school, when he was starting out, playing clubs. Back then, he was very accessible and I had *that* connection with him instantly. The first time he hit the stage, he came right over to me and gave me his water bottle, teasing me. He pulled down the bass player's underwear and started jerking him off right in front of me—so there was some sort of instant connection between us. I was just seventeen at the time. I thought, 'This man is interesting.'"

Lexa's remembrances of her early interaction with Marilyn Manson are sharp and clear. Each glance, word, and touch held complex, esoteric meaning. "We were hooked up with passes for

Current Plastics line up: Alexxa Hex, Lexa Vonn, and Jenni Jayde.

Credit: Lexa Vonn collection

Manson's Fourth of July Grotesque Burlesque show in Vegas. I had been doing pinup modeling for a couple of months and was excited about my new glamorous lingerie image. I had this see-through beaded gown and wanted to make sure I looked fabulous, so I didn't eat all day. It was over 100 degrees, and I had gotten a body wrap at the spa and was totally dehydrated. I was in the front row, and Manson threw me his fancy expensive stage hat, and I felt so cool. Backstage, I was pounding back free drinks and got plastered *really* fast. Manson invited us to a party at the hotel where they had half a floor rented, and I sat on the bed with him, wearing a bra and panties and the hat he had given me. We were staring at each other, and he said, 'Shut up, Lexa. Stop laughing.' I was like, 'I didn't say anything!' And he said, 'But you're *thinking* it.'"

When Lexa left home for good, the bad memories came more often. "Finally, during one of my suicide kicks, I downed a bunch of acid, put on the newly released *Antichrist Superstar*

With Marilyn Manson.
Credit: Lexa Vonn collection

album, and the whole memory of childhood abuse came back. I had a religious experience under the influence of music and hallucinogenics. It was as if I'd been unhooked from the matrix and was in a make-believe land where all the lies of humanity were exposed. I could hear this voice faintly coming from the music, guiding me through the experience, protecting me, showing me the truth about why I was so fucked up, letting me know it wasn't my fault. Within two weeks I joined Manson on tour with nothing to my name but a backpack of clothes, a tarot card deck, and a journal."

Lexa needed to explain to Manson how his music spoke to her and started writing letters to him. "I wanted to know if he had intentionally put subliminal messages in the music to induce this meditational state. He was impressed. I'd been doing a great deal of speed, coke, heroin, and acid. I quit everything cold turkey when I began following the tour. The withdrawal combined with the intensity of the show left me in a paranoid and highly aware state. He was oddly interested and took me seriously."

Because of her unusual connection to Manson, Lexa eventually moved to Hollywood, started her own band, Ophelia Rising, and got into the music publicity biz through Manson's former guitar player. She also started doing extra work. "I was cast as a groupie in *Almost Famous* and *Rock Star*, and one of my gigs was Manson's 'Coma White' video. I hadn't seen him in over a year and was nervous, but he spotted me quickly and beelined for me. We were like a mirror image of each other. We'd look into each other's eyes and giggle at the same time, then awkward silence. There was weird energy between us. I was on the set for two days and *had* to see him again. I went unannounced backstage to the L.A. show, and when Manson saw me, it was like 'whoa.' I had just had a terrible fight with my most recent boyfriend, and the next thing I knew I was driving to Texas for the Manson tour."

It seemed whenever Lexa was breaking up with another rock scoundrel, Manson was there. "I didn't know if he thought I was just a weird acid freak, but in Houston he said, 'I want you to come to the hotel tonight. We're having a little party.' Five times he said, 'Promise me you'll be there.' Even though their time together was usually brief, Manson always went out of his way to make Lexa feel included. One strange night, she was among a cadre of girls ushered into his inner sanctum. "Manson was at the height of his fame, his album was number one, and there was a lot of security because he got death threats. It was surreal, like going to see the *president*. We were shuffled into this hotel suite, and it was the most bizarre scene I've ever witnessed. Twiggy Ramirez was sitting in the corner drooling on himself, the keyboard player was rocking back and forth, and the other guitar player was hitting on this skanky groupie who had told me earlier how she fucked their drummer, and *now* she was gonna fuck the guitar player. There was so much going through my head: the insecurity about things I'd said to Manson years before, the guards in the room watching us like Secret Service men. I wondered, 'Is Manson trying to sleep with me? What the hell is this shit?' I watched movies with him all night, but could barely speak. He didn't either. Finally I asked, 'How're you doin'?' He didn't answer me verbally, but I could hear him telepathically. He just nodded, and I said, 'Another day, huh?' There was this in-another-dimension glowing energy; too much for me to handle. I wondered, 'Is he fucking with my head or does he wanna hang out with me? Does he want me to make a move?' But I certainly wasn't going to touch him! Maybe if he'd acted like other rock stars I'd hung out with, being a jackass, hyper and funny, it would have been easier to make a move. But he's so quiet and introspective, I was completely freaked out."

But Lexa *wanted* Manson to make a move, didn't she? "Not on that tour. I was still nervous with him, but I did start falling in love. I didn't know if he liked me *that* way, or if he was being fatherly. He had one of those cult followings and thought of his fans as his children. He forbade the roadies from talking to me because he saw me as his child or because he was *jealous*. I don't know which. He treated me like a *lady* and not like a whore. He has my loyalty for life, because most guys, including my father, have never cared for me like that. Most big rock stars hang out and have fun, but want to have sex as quickly as possible. And here was this guy who spent the night with me and didn't even touch me."

An encounter with Manson's guitarist, John 5, left Lexa perplexed. After a gig, John whispered in her ear. "He said, 'Let's you and me hang out when Manson leaves.' I was thinking, 'Why *after* Manson leaves?' I walked John to his car and suddenly he grabbed my hand and put it down his pants, and I thought, 'Whoa. You know the rules with me. Ooh, big cock, too! This is scandalous.' So I pulled away. I thought he was cute, but I had too much respect for Manson to go there. He saw me as innocent, even though I wasn't, and I didn't want him to see me as a slut. We had always been platonic, but I felt very loyal. That whole camp is so strange—for all I knew, it was some sort of test."

Despite all the drama, Lexa and Marilyn Manson have spent some rare quality time together through the years. "Once we were all fucked up at his house, and he took out his camera and got intricately involved with photography. He did a photo shoot of me wearing his underwear in the pool and filmed it, too. I believe I truly am a muse to him. He uses me as inspiration in his work, and that's much more than sex. Sex would be great too, and I'd love to be with him, but sex comes and goes and loses its passion. Art is immortal."

What is it about Manson's music that has kept her fascinated for so long? "Manson gives a lot of hints in his songs. If you follow along and research each subject, you'll get an education. It's all there: philosophies, religions, magic, political history, lies in the media, conspiracy theories. After a while you figure out the fabric of the matrix we live in. He was following me following him, taking notes on my progress figuring him out. When I'd figured out enough, he gave me the wink-wink handshake, and the door to the chocolate factory opened. That was my goal: I wanted to crack the mystery."

Perhaps the reason Manson and Lexa have been friends for so long is because they *haven't* slept together. "That's what *his* take is. We agree there is an attraction, but why ruin a perfectly good

John 5 (guitarist for Marilyn Manson, Rob Zombie) with Lexa, Sandra Starr, and friend.

Credit: Lexa Vonn collection

relationship? I'm a permanent fixture even though it's tortuous. I'd give up every man in the world for him. I've had sex with a handful of rock stars, and nobody has ever touched me the way he does. It's difficult for anyone to get in my pants now. I'm hard to impress after being intimate with Manson on a psychological level. I wind up comparing them to him."

At least her passion for Manson hasn't stopped Lexa from giving rock romance a chance. "Ben Graves from the Murderdolls was interested in me, but he was intimidating, and had overpowering energy. I'm 5′2″ and he stands 6′6″. We got hot and heavy one night, and I backed out from going all the way because I was dating the keyboard player for London After Midnight and didn't want to fully cheat on him. Ben had some of the best pickup lines ever. When I asked, 'Why me?' in a dark and dramatic, perfectly scripted way, he said, 'Because I like to exist somewhere between a dream and reality, and you seem like someone I could do that with.' Just the way he said things got your juices running. One night at this Goth fetish club, Bar Sinister, he introduced me to his new band member, Joey Jordison, who was also the drummer in Slipknot. I didn't realize that because they wear masks on stage, but he let me know right away. There were a million girls, but he took to me from the get-go. He said, 'I've got cocaine back at the hotel, why don't you come up?' At the time I was doing a lot of coke and was initially more interested in the coke than in Joey." Joey soon began begging Lexa to be his girlfriend. "He came across very genuine. I wasn't super-smitten, but I was single and thought I'd give him a chance. I soon discovered he liked me to talk dirty. I'd worked at a phone sex office and had my routine down. He was eating it up, my scenarios were getting weirder and kinkier, and I wondered how far I could push the limits. I finally told him, 'What I really want is to put you in a dress, smear red lipstick all over your mouth, and bend you over like the bitch you are.' I expected him to say 'Dude, that's not cool,' but his response was 'I *have* a dress.' I love any kind of fantasy play, and my ears perked up. He told me to close my eyes, and he transformed into a cute girl. I liked seeing this heavy metal drummer, who hit the shit so hard, jump into bed in a little black minidress."

When Lexa showed up at a Murderdolls gig in San Diego, Joey sang a different off-key tune. It turned out he had girls in various cities and wanted Lexa to be his L.A. woman. "When he told me, I was tripping on mushrooms and thought, 'This sucks in a million different ways.' I tried to maintain coolness while frying, but inside I was humiliated. I can deal with any situation as long as you're honest about it." Her pal Ben Graves commiserated, and they wound up all lovey-dovey again. "I was tripping, so everything clicked into place, and I realized I was chasing after an asshole who lied to me, meanwhile my true friend Ben was telling me he loved me."

Lexa says she "melted" and when Ben got home from tour they began sleeping together. But when Joey found out, he coaxed Lexa away. "He found me with Ben and out came the amazing apology. Here was this big rock star, and I'd rather be with his 'hired help' as he referred to Ben." Lexa relented and went back to Joey, but it was a disaster. "It was all about his ego. I stupidly gave Joey another chance, which was the worst mistake. I was only with him a couple nights. I still feel horribly guilty about it. I think I was actually in love with Ben but was on drugs and didn't know how to handle the situation. He took me back but was bitter from then on. I tried to repent, but Ben was also aware of my situation with Manson and that made him not want to take the relationship further."

Not long ago, Lexa had a fling with Monster Magnet's androgynous guitarist, Ed Mundell. "I was Ed's L.A. girlfriend. When he was here he didn't see anyone else. I really like the experience of being with a guy in drag. Ed *loved* me to dress him up like a girl and take pictures. He couldn't get enough. He said, 'Oh, I look *just* like Gwyneth Paltrow.' Putting makeup on guys is foreplay for me. There's something about a cock underneath a dress. Ed and I genuinely liked each other. He told me there was a part of him he shared with me that he didn't share with anyone else in the world." Lexa sighs, "But it's hard for me to date anybody because I wind up comparing them to Manson.

Ed Mundell playing
dress up at Lexa's
Hollywood apartment.
Credit: Lexa Vonn collection

I don't think I'll fall in love with anyone unless they're on that
same level. His shoes are really hard to fill."

There has been so much speculation about Manson's eccentric-
ity. Does Lexa feel it's warranted? "He's not your average, normal
person, but we don't sacrifice goats or anything. He's a character,
an artist, but he's no weirder than I am. We all love those androgynous rocker boys, but if they don't have the art to back it up, it
doesn't mean anything. I'm very flattered and honored that he lets
me in on his projects, his ambitions, what he's pursuing in the
future. It's like being the chosen fan, the one inside, knowing all
the secrets, seeing everything before it happens. If you're a halfway decent girl, anybody wants to fuck you, it's not that hard
to accomplish. [Manson] trusts me and respects my opinion, and
that's a lot more flattering than just fucking. It's weird because
I was so attracted to rock stars, even as a small child. I suffered

through so much trauma and kept myself alive by fixating on this mythical rock star who would one day reach out and bring me through the TV screen into his imaginary rock star world. And the most ironic thing is . . . Manson did just that!"

For an entire decade, Lexa has had sporadic encounters with Marilyn Manson and his crew while having romantic relationships and creating an entertaining life for herself. As we await the rest of the Plastics, Lexa says matter-of-factly, "I didn't see him for a while, and during that time he met Dita Von Teese. I got engaged to a singer from a band called Fetish, and shortly after I got engaged, he got engaged to her. I was only engaged for a year, then we broke up. Manson got married."

The doorbell chimes and the rest of Lexa's decked-out team arrives in high spirits. Sandra has on a Pink Floyd baby-T and Gothic platform sandals. Staci wears a strategically torn tank top with multireams of necklaces and scarves, while Jenni is head-to-toe in shiny black vinyl, tattered fishnets, and giant knee-high Demonia boots from last night's revelry. We quickly get into a rollicking chatterfest about the extreme highs and lows of groupiedom.

It all begins with Faster Pussycat's ubiquitous Taime Downe. What a surprise.

Pamela: C'mon, which one of you hooked up with Taime?

Staci: I was out in Hollywood one night and he was calling my phone, "Hey, you wanna come over and check out my place?"

Lexa: You wanna come over and sit on my face? I mean check out my place?

Staci: So I go his house, we hook up for a good two minutes, then he just watches TV. I'm like, "I can't deal with this, I'm going to sleep!" Taime has done way too much cocaine and has a difficult time getting an erection.

Lexa: I don't think he'll verify that.

Staci: I was expecting us to have sex, but it was just me going down on him and him going down on me and that was it. And it only lasts about two minutes until he comes.

Pamela: Well, someone like Taime who's probably had sex with five thousand women . . . I'm surprised he still wants to do it.

Sandra: He's a horn dog! I've kissed him a couple of times. He's actually a good kisser, big lips.

Staci: He's a good kisser but with all the cocaine he's done, his penis isn't very big.

Lexa: I heard it *used* to be.

Pamela: What? Cocaine can change penis size?

Lexa: Oh, yeah . . . I've seen it happen to people.

Pamela: Have you been with any of those big-hair guys?

Staci: Steve Summers from Pretty Boy Floyd. He was playing with Dokken, and after the show he grabbed me by the arm, dragged me backstage, locked the door, and said, 'I just love your tits. They're so big I want to come on them.' I'm like, 'OK.' And he starts jacking off, staring at my boobs. It was pretty hot.

Pamela: A regular fellow couldn't get away with that.

Lexa: If a typical lawyer came up to you in a bar and said, 'I really like your tits. You wanna go to the bathroom so I can jerk off?' you'd probably call security.

Sandra: In the music industry, you've been looked at and prodded and touched so much that your assets aren't seen in the traditional way. I'm used to going out and having people ask to touch my tits or my ass, and I'm comfortable with it. It's just like someone asking to shake my hand.

Pamela: Some people might view that as a low self-esteem issue.

Lexa: I think that's a misconception. It might be considered low self-esteem if you did it for acceptance or approval. Some women, including us, are more open and honest about sexuality. Women want sex too and don't need to be freaked out by it. It's not low self-esteem; it's having *more* self-esteem.

Sandra: It's flattering that someone thinks a part of my body is so beautiful that they want to touch it. As long as it's not done in a disrespectful way, what's the harm?

Jenni: A while back I happened to meet and hook up with a very hot former member of Guns N' Roses who was phenomenal in bed.

Lexa: I guess he would be after fucking ten thousand chicks.

Jenni: He was the kind of guy that would hold your face: passionate, caring, and gentle, a sweetheart.

Pamela: How many times did you see him?

Jenni: About eight times. I flew out to visit him on tour, and he had this great Jacuzzi in his room and we took baths together.

Pamela: Were you in love?

Jenni: Totally, he broke my heart!

Pamela: How did it start?

Jenni: I met him at a club where he was playing, and we really clicked. He seemed sad, and we started talking and exchanged numbers. It kept getting better as time went on—until he told me he couldn't concentrate on his work because he couldn't stop thinking about me. He said, 'I wake up and all I think about is how I'm going to see you next and it's not good for me, I have other things to take care of.' I was unhappy about that.

Sandra: It's fun to mess around with rockers, but I let them know where I stand. When it comes to sex, I don't want to take anything home with me that I didn't have when I arrived. And it's less complicated if you just fool around because you leave your options open in case you want to hook up with someone else in the band. It doesn't cause as much drama as going all the way with them.

Staci: Sandra has newfound love for a guitar tech she met last night.

Lexa: One of our rules is that we *don't* engage in sexual relations with anyone in the road crew.

Sandra: But he's sooo cute!

Pamela: You have other groupie rules of etiquette, right?

Sandra: One word of advice to a girl dating a rock star: when they get back from the road, make sure they get tested for

STDs. If you don't get an STD, you'll get some other girl's yeast infection. Make sure you get that boy tested before you sleep with him!

Lexa: Another rule is not to have sex in a tour bus. That's for the low-rate girls.

Sandra: Lexa taught me the groupie rules. I'd broken a few when she gave me the list. I'd already been on the Dope tour bus with one of the guys from Twisted Method, the opening band.

Lexa: A real groupie gets invited to the hotel.

Sandra: Unless they don't have a hotel that night.

Lexa: Yeah, if you've already had sex repeatedly in hotel rooms, and it's an ongoing relationship, it's OK to hook up on the bus. I've never done it, though. You'll get invited to the hotel if you're worth it.

Sandra: The first time I hooked up with Ben from Twisted Method was in a hotel room. We spent a week in hotels on the first tour, but on the second tour they weren't getting hotels. So I had sex on the bus quite a few times. It's good when they kick everyone else off the bus so you can have complete privacy.

Lexa: Isn't that what the back of the bus is for?

Sandra: He wanted the whole bus. We had sex in his bunk, the band member's bunks, the couch, the driver's seat. People should be careful 'cause groupies can make band members do horrible things. The first time Ben and I had sex on the tour bus, I was mad at the guitarist, Andy, 'cause he was being a real jerk. So after we were done and needed something to clean up with, I said, 'Why don't you get one of Andy's beanies!' So Ben grabs one of his beanies, flips it inside out, cleans me off with it, and throws it back on Andy's bunk. The next morning we walk in and Andy's wearing that beanie!

Pamela: Yikes! What do guys think of the actresses, porn stars, and models who have taken the place of the real groupies in recent years?

Jenni: It sucks for those of us who don't have connections.

Lexa: I've seen some celeb-type girlfriends at concerts and they don't even know the words to the songs. I think a lot of those girls do it to up their status and don't really understand what it's like to be emotionally involved in someone's music.

Sandra: It's a trend now: rock stars and porn stars go together. They even did a VH1 show about it.

Lexa: One of the things we're trying to do is turn the groupie into a celebrity once again, give us status so musicians date us publicly. They're all dating us, they're just not publicizing it.

Pamela: It's not being written about because you're not Winona Ryder.

Lexa: That's sad because a lot of musicians are in relationships with girls who don't treat them well. They stay with them because of celebrity pressure instead of being with someone who loves them for *them*.

Sandra: If you have to change someone, you really didn't like them to begin with.

Lexa: A real groupie will only sleep with someone whose music they admire. It's giving something back—engaging in a ritual with somebody you have feelings for through their art. The Plastics don't just go to shows; we are *part* of the show. That's why we dress up; we're performing as well. And how boring for the band without us there!

Jenni: For the word "groupie" to stop being used negatively, it needs to become more elite. I was at C. C. DeVille's house last night with his current girlfriend. Everyone was calling her a groupie, but she was the epitome of everything bad. She was controlling and threw out all C. C.'s alcohol. She asked me questions like she thought I was dumb. I'm not ignorant; I'm working on my Ph.D. right now. Everyone who hangs out with musicians isn't necessarily a groupie.

Lexa: There's a big difference between a star fucker and a groupie. Star fuckers are there to get something for themselves. A groupie is there to say, 'Thank you, I got your message. I loved it, and I'm here to honor you.'

It's when your eyes connect, and you don't have to say anything, you both feel it and break into a smile. The magic moment when you get them in that same frame of mind with you, when you simultaneously exist in that dimension of art. It's like sexual euphoria.

Pamela: What started the rocker obsession for you guys?

Sandra: For me it was Marilyn Manson. Seeing that show made me want to be a part of it, to look like that and be in that environment.

Staci: For me it was watching Keri Kelli with L.A. Guns. It was one of the first shows where I met and hung out with the band. Just watching him I thought, "I want that! I want a musician. *That's* what's been missing from my life."

Lexa: But you have to accept that they are always going to be with other people, whether it's sexual or emotional.

Jenni: I'm what you call polyamorous, I suppose. It's hard when you get into a serious relationship with a musician because a lot of them can't handle commitment, and I get jealous.

Sandra: It's not about them being able to stay faithful, it's about me being able to stay faithful. I couldn't be in a committed relationship and not stray. There are too many musicians that I think are amazing. I couldn't keep my hands off them! Every time I see a tour bus, I get giddy wondering who's on it.

Jenni: We're all hopeless.

Lexa: And probably damned to be single forever.

Pamela: Any particular instrument you go for?

Sandra: Drummers tend to flock to me.

Lexa: Drummers are a scary breed. They have the most issues.

Jenni: I love bass players!

Lexa: I tend to end up with drummers or singers. Polar opposites. But whoever I'm with in the band, the singer always tries to steal me away.

Pamela: Why do you think that is?

Sandra: Lead singer complex.

Lexa: Singers often write the lyrics, so they research interesting topics. I research a lot of alternative subjects as well, so I think they like that I can hold a decent conversation. Whereas other guys in the band might not care as long as the girl is hot.

Sandra: Is that why drummers flock to me?

Lexa: Yes, they need someone to indulge their mommy issues and their sick fetishes!

Sandra: I think what's different about the four of us is that we're on the level. We won't put up with any shit. If you don't treat us well, we won't stick around.

Lexa: It's different when you're a famous groupie. As we get more notoriety it's becoming a status symbol for smaller bands to be seen with us. I've gotten laid so many times by people who think I've slept with Manson—even though I've never confirmed the rumors. Mystery is sexy. Never confirm or deny anything.

Sandra: We get recognized at shows a lot. Bands dedicate songs to us and give us shout-outs.

Jenni: Yeah, I'll never forget the time we were walking into a show with our laminates and this random guy whispered to his friend, "Oh my God, the Plastics!"

Pamela: That's a wonderful feeling, isn't it? So, Lexa, how would you sum up the influence Marilyn Manson has had on your life?

Lexa: Manson made me. He has inspired almost everything I've done. I owe my survival to him. Everything out there that needs to be cracked, he's cracked it. All I had was my brain, and those clues hooked me. He played with my mind, and it was almost like turning in my homework. He still drops clues to see if I can figure 'em out, but now I do it back to him. It's very exciting, waiting for the puzzles. I've almost created a religion around Manson, and now I have a little following of fans that are also cracking the codes. These young kids come to me with the work they're doing and we listen to the music and talk it over. I've become the high priestess of Mansonism. He taught me that art is not just a song or a painting; art is *you*. Art is the essence of your being, anything you create. That's what the Plastics are: living, breathing performance art."

Sarah Madison

Miss You in a Heartbeat

Even in the drop-dead of winter, with the promise of snow squalls swirling 'round my head, I'm happy to leave the sunny shores of California and board a plane to the freezing Midwest. I've been e-mailing back and forth with a couple of lively groupies residing in Minneapolis and have decided to meet up with them. It's quite a trek, but I sincerely enjoy tromping around all-America, meeting new dolls after my own heart. Landing at the Minneapolis–St. Paul airport, I burrow into my huge faux-fur coat, rent a little Toyota, check into a Holiday Inn Express, and call Sarah Madison, a savvy-sounding cutie in her early twenties. She suggests we meet at a nearby seafood joint in the same gigantic mall where she works at the local Hooters.

Sarah has sent me photos of herself, nonchalantly posing next to wild-eyed rocker dudes from Tantric, Sevendust, and Marilyn Manson's band, so I recognize her right away. She is tall and willowy with long, straight platinum hair and a knowing green-eyed gaze. After a hug, we scooch into a booth, order a couple of exotic tropical drinks, and I find out pretty quickly that she's not too thrilled with the G word. "I *hate* that word. But sometimes I think 'Band Aid' is okay. But any sort of label implies that the only reason I'm friends with these people, or attracted to them, is because they're famous. When you work for a music magazine, you don't meet a lot of people outside the rock and roll community. Until I moved here, I was writing feature stories, doing CD reviews in Madison, Wisconsin, for *Maximum Ink* music magazine—'All Access with Sarah.' Who knew that kids genuinely want to know what kind of beer Nickelback drinks? Yep, Corona." Sarah laughs.

Even though she professes to understand on-the-road rocker mentality, it wasn't too long ago that Sarah's heart got crushed by one of those tantalizing, careless boys. "It happened in December. I had already thought about talking to you, but didn't want to name names. After that experience, I changed my mind. I realized that these people don't give a damn about me. So why am I giving a damn about protecting their reputations?"

How did the ravishing daughter of a "big-shot lawyer," who graduated top of her class, wind up backstage? "For my sixteenth birthday, I got *Vault: Greatest Hits 1980–1995* and *Adrenalize* by Def Leppard, and *boom!* I never turned back. My first real concert was Def Leppard. After the show I told my girlfriend, 'Oh my God, during this one part in this one song, Joe Elliott totally looked right at me!' It's funny to think that was such a big deal back then."

Although Sarah didn't meet her heroes that night, she was bewitched by real live rock and roll. "When I started going to concerts I couldn't help but notice the chick on the side of the stage. She looks great, she's drinking her beer, she's just happy to be there. I thought it would be so cool to be *that* girl. My roommate and I went to see *Almost Famous*, and there's this scene at the Hyatt House, Penny Lane is walking around and everybody knows her. I thought, 'God, that's cool.' In the rock world, or in *any* world, it feels good to be the person that people want to talk to. We met the band Oleander when they played in Madison. They were in Milwaukee the next night and invited us down. We were in the back drinking with them until the moment they went on. They were on stage before we were even out of the dressing room. We came out and three girls were looking at us like, 'You lucky bitches,' and I thought, 'Wow, I've made it. I'm the chick I used to be jealous of.'"

Sarah's sexy wholesomeness often attracted the attention of roadies scanning for tasty morsels. "We were still in high school. I never walked up to roadies, going, 'Hey, can I flash you for a pass?' But, remember, I was at heavy metal shows. First of all, it's 75 percent men. Secondly, 90 percent of the girls weigh three hundred pounds and wear Korn T-shirts from 1995. It was by default that we stood out. I always wanted to be up front. There's kind of a rush about making eye contact. You listen to this music every single day, nonstop, in your bedroom, and the people who made that music are looking right at you. It's not so much them as people, it's what they've created. After that, I was trying to be the cool rocker chick. The first time I got my confidence, I was in the front row at a Slipknot concert because I've *got* to be there. A roadie came over and said, 'You, come back here.' So I watched from the side of the stage. If I wanted to meet or hang out with somebody, I wouldn't go up and start gushing about how great they were. I'd say, 'I really liked the show. Can I buy you a drink?' If they were talking to somebody, I'd say, 'I'll be over there. Come on over when you want that drink.' They love that."

Sarah had an adoring high school boyfriend but says she was afraid to get close to him. "I think that's what I liked about musicians—you're able to have great closeness for, like, a day. It's perfect. You're boyfriend and girlfriend, completely in love, for a day. Then they leave. You have all the good stuff and none of the bad. It's fun and games until you try to get serious. That's when you get hurt."

I remark that most of the groupies I know feel differently. A night or two with their idols simply isn't enough. "I've always been pretty realistic about it. Early on there were a few people who fooled me. I thought, 'Oh, he really likes me!' But I knew deep down exactly what was going on. Still, sometimes I'd lie in bed thinking, 'Wouldn't it be cool if *this* would happen?' But most of these guys have wives or girlfriends at home. Why would I want to be attached to a guy who's cheating on his girlfriend?"

With Jeff Labar of Cinderella.
Credit: Sarah Madison

Didn't she have pangs of guilt? "It's not like they're going to fall in love and not want to be with their wives anymore. I'm not going to hurt their relationships."

No matter how much I plead, Sarah won't divulge the name of her first rock amour. "I'll tell you the second one I hooked up with: John 5, the guitar player from Marilyn Manson. It was a tour bus experience, *quite* the experience, too. It wasn't like we had this big thing going on, but he's an awesome guy. To this day, I have a lot of love for him. But I was actually at the show to see Buckcherry that night. I worked my way up to the front, and some guy on the other side of the barricade had a video camera. I smiled at him, and he said, 'I don't want you to flash or anything, just say hi to the camera.' An hour later he saw me and said, 'I showed Manson and John your tape. They really want to meet you.' I thought, 'How brilliant! They sent a guy out with a video camera.' That is *so* rock and roll. I was

new to the rock world and kind of scared of Manson, but I went
to the meeting place along with thirty other girls. They took us
to this room, and all these girls were saying, 'Do you have any
beer? God, why is there no *beer*?' I'm not high maintenance, and
I think John liked that about me. Finally they pointed at me, and
three girls in bikinis. We got to the bus and I didn't know what
to do. I was friggin' nineteen years old! Manson was sitting there
with Twiggy and John, and I was just awed. But I took a deep
breath and thought, 'These people are no better than me. We're
all human.' I walked up and said, 'What's up? I'm Sarah,' and he
said, 'I'm Manson.' I said hi to Twiggy and sat down and started
talking to John. I wasn't flirting; we were just laughing at the
bikini chicks because Manson was saying, 'Why don't you do
this to him, and *that* to him.' And they were like, 'OK!' After
that display, the girls were kicked off the bus, and I was thinking, 'Wow, it really *is* like VH1!' John and I were attracted to
each other, and it was just that simple. We had a great time. I saw
him a couple weeks later at Ozzfest. In the meantime I'd started
dating this other guy, Glen Sobel, who was also on the tour. He
played drums for Beautiful Creatures."

Aha. Rock star number three appears. "I saw him as much as
you see somebody who's on the road with Ozzfest. We did the
whole talk-on-the-phone thing. Glen was a great guy and we
were legitimately seeing each other—but the tour ended, and due
to sheer geography, we didn't see each other for years. But we're
still good friends. Then it was the beginning of the end." Sarah
sighs dramatically. "Lajon Witherspoon of Sevendust, the first
one to completely fool me. Until then, I'd had great experiences.
But I know Lajon now, and he's probably *the* biggest player in
the game. The girls enabled him to be that way. The first time
we met at a concert, I knew who he was because he's the only
black man in hard rock. He was signing autographs, so I handed
him my ticket stub to sign. He said, 'You've got to hang out
with me tonight. Do you have a pass? Come with me right now,'
and he whisked me backstage. God, he plays the game so well.
We got to the bus and he introduced me to his band. A security
guard brought me to the side of the stage and put me right by

the speaker. When you're not used to this, you're thinking, 'Oh my God, I'm loving life!' The singer in the band was saying, 'I want her right here—close to me.' He was getting ready to go on and the tour manager said, 'You can't wear those pants without a belt; hop up and down three times.' He did, and half his ass was hanging out. I was wearing this shiny, sparkly belt, so I gave it to him and he wore it onstage. I was thinking, 'That's my belt!' He said, 'I'm glad I've got this because now you have to see me afterward.' He kept coming over to me during the show, and my heart was all aflutter."

Sarah got tipsy, but only made out with Lajon that night, and he promised to invite her to the next local gig. "The day comes around, and I don't seem to have a phone call. But I still went to see what was going on. We were hanging out after the show and my best friend said, 'Turn around.' I said, 'No, I'm not going to,' and she said, 'Just turn around.' So I swung around and there's Lajon, turning on the charm again: 'Come here, I'm so sorry.'

With Lajon Witherspoon.
Credit: Sarah Madison

His excuse was that 9/11 happened, and everybody's head was in a different place. That was the first night we hooked up. It was quick tour bus lovin', and he was going to call me again, right? Nothing. We go to Chicago to see them, and I'm so angry, thinking, 'God, I hate him, I hate him,' but of course there I am at the show."

Lajon apologized again, telling Sarah he had tried to reach her at Hooters. "We're not supposed to get personal calls, so the girl just hung up on him and I never got the message. That was the only time Lajon and I spent the whole night together because they had a hotel. It was absolutely perfect. That night he was extraordinary."

In my groupie prime, not many bands used tour buses, and I comment that intimacy on the road must be much more difficult these days. "Yeah, but most musicians are used to getting it all the time. I should cut Lajon some slack because a lot of the time we hooked up, the bus was full, so we were in the bathroom. There really isn't good lovin' to be had in the friggin' tour bus bathroom. But that night in the hotel was *very* good. It was December and he asked me what I wanted for Christmas. At least I had one night that made me very happy. Of course, the next night they played Milwaukee, and after our great night, did he even call me to put me on the list? No. We got on the list through somebody else. I went up to Morgan Rose, the drummer, and said, 'Where the fuck's Lajon?' and he said, 'Oh, he went to bed already.' I said, 'Sure he did.' The next time I saw him, I said, 'Fuck you, Lajon. How dare you send your drummer to do your dirty work!' I walked into the women's bathroom at the House of Blues and he was sitting there with four chicks. He said, 'Hey everybody, this is Sarah. The one I've been talking about.' I'm like, 'Yeah, right.' I wish I could say I didn't see him anymore after that. But I saw him tons more times. He even came to my place."

Sarah was learning that you can't count on rock guys for the long haul, but decided she could still have some fun. "I think they look for confidence more than anything, and if you happen to have good facial features to back it up, so be it. But having

With Jason
"Gong" Jones of
Drowning Pool.
Credit: Sarah Madison

some dude on the cover of *Rolling Stone* wanting to hang out with you doesn't hurt your confidence one little bit. My friend and I will be standing in a group of twenty girls, and they'll know. 'These two? They'll be fine.' They like it if you've done it before, because you know what's appropriate and what isn't. Like not to take a crap on the bus, and not to put your toilet paper in the toilet." That's a frightening thought. Hmm. Where *does* one put their toilet paper on the tour bus? So, who came along to take Sarah's mind off Lajon?

"There were a lot of couple-of-week flings. Jeff Labar, the guitarist from Cinderella. We hit it off within five seconds and had a blast. We always made each other laugh. We were perfectly compatible—as compatible as you're going to be on the Poison summer tour. Then there was Jason 'Gong' Jones, lead singer from Drowning Pool—he was cool. He pursued me a little bit, but I said, 'Honey, you've got an album coming out in a few months. You're about to go huge. I'm not even going to pretend we could have any sort of a relationship.'"

Sarah was diligent, sticking to her keeping-it-fun rule until one of the rockers treated her a little too well. "I'd been seeing this guy from Dope, Sloane 'Mosey' Jentry, just casually. When he quit the band, I remained friends with the rest of the guys, then they got Brix, his replacement. You're supposed to stick to one dude per band, but I made an exception because Brix was phenomenal. He treated me really well. He took me out to dinner, then we got to the show and he handed me, like, thirty dollars and said, 'Here, this should buy you drinks until I'm ready to hang out.' We were seeing each other a lot and I started to feel guilty because he was married. As far as his wife knew, he was just 'wham, bam, thank you, ma'am,' on the road. But if she'd known he was taking me out to dinner . . .'"

Dope was playing Madison, and as far as Sarah knew, all was still groovy between her and Brix. "After the show, I'm waitin', waitin', waitin'. Finally, he came out and I said, 'What the fuck is going on?' He said, 'Let's go talk about it. I've been thinking, and I just don't think we're compatible anymore.' I said, 'That's obviously a blatant lie.' If he'd said, 'I think you have an ugly vagina and I never want to see it again,' I would've been way less offended than if he tried to BS me. Like, was he watching *Sex and the City* last night for bad breakup lines? We certainly didn't seem to be incompatible two weeks earlier when we were getting it on. So that was the end of that. I text messaged him a week later, 'When you're ready to tell me the truth, I'm ready to listen.' He left me a voice mail, 'I'm so glad you called. I really want to talk to you.' Then I saw their drum tech at Hooters and he said, 'Hey, Brix wants your number. He wants to apologize,' but I haven't heard a word from him. But he made me realize they're all the same. Even when they give you the impression that they're good people, they're all the goddamn same. That's when I decided to do this interview."

It sounds to me like Sarah may have finally had it with rock stars, especially married ones. "For right now I have," she agrees.

"It was part of my life and I had a blast. But I'm just tired of it. I need something real, and you aren't going to find it *there*. But I know the second I say, 'Oh no, I'll never date another musician,' some dude on a national tour will sweep me off my feet. I truly feel I've lived my life with no regrets. If ever I think, 'Should I, or shouldn't I?' I always *do*. How many times have you looked back and thought, 'God, if I had only done *that*.'"

Yes, I recall the exact moment Jimi Hendrix beckoned to me, and I wimped out on him. Of course, I was a semi-inexperienced seventeen-year-old virgin at the time. Noel Redding, the adorable, scrawny, pale-faced bass player seemed like a safer bet.

"I still dream, because I have more in common with musicians than with accountants," Sarah continues. "It's really the look more than anything else. I like the piercings and the tattoos. I like the funky hair. Everybody's got their top five guys they'd like to sleep with. It's not a pipe dream to me. I think, 'This could *maybe* happen.' Joe Perry is my number one. Then Lenny Kravitz was my number two until I heard he doesn't smell that good. But I'm like, 'I'll plug my nose, just bring me that man and his PA!'"

Does Sarah ever imagine herself twenty years from now, all cozy with her funky, tattooed rock guy? "You've got to look at the facial features," she says with a knowing smile. "Because he may look pretty hot now with all that hair, but you have to imagine that schnoz on your kid!"

After dinner, we cruise over to Sarah's condo, an immaculate, airy place, to look through her copious rock scrapbooks. She opens a chilled bottle of white wine and pours us a glass. "This is me with Jeff from Cinderella, thirty seconds after we met . . . here's Jason from Drowning Pool . . . these are the feathers from Ozzfest that Ozzy blew up at the end . . . here's Glen from Beautiful Creatures . . . ahh, look at Tommy Lee! I have never been so starstruck in my life. He was trying to talk to us and we just kept stuttering. He finally said, 'All right, nice meeting you guys' and started to walk away. My friend was going, 'P-p-picture!' If Tommy Lee wanted to have some kids, I'd be more than happy to oblige. Oh, these are the guys from Nickelback. I didn't hook up with any of them. But I *did* kiss Nick. Oh, this is a great shot, because right when I moved to Madison, we went to see Tantric and took a picture with the singer, Hugo Ferreira. We walked back saying, 'Oh, he's so dreamy.' Then two years later I hooked up with him. I'd been hanging out with their drummer, Matt Taul, the night before. We were chillin', and he got me into the show. I was looking for him and I asked Hugo, 'Where's Matt?' and he said, 'Just go on the bus.' I refused, because you look like an idiot when you do that. So he said, 'Come with me.' It was Matt and Hugo and me, and they were watching porn. I said, sarcastically, 'Dude. *This* is really fun.' I had a fling with Hugo on the bus that night, and the next day we went to Chicago. We had a blast because we actually got a hotel that night. Hugo is phenomenal, and he smells good in the morning. He's that guy right there," she says, pointing to another shot of the haughty bad boy. "If I was going to be unrealistic and wanted one of them to change and be *the guy*, it'd definitely be him."

I've noticed that all the younger groupies call sleeping together "hooking up." "Right," Sarah says. "To me, the term 'hooking up' puts less weight, less pressure on it. It goes in order as it gets more relationship-y. You've got 'hooking up,' then 'sleeping together,' 'having sex,' then 'making love.'"

Where do blow jobs come in, I wonder? "I'm not sure. I guess that could be called hooking up. But I very rarely do that. I'm like, 'Uh-uh, dude!'" I'm astounded. Not even when she's crazy about someone? "No, at that point, I've already got 'em," Sarah declares, "so why do I need to impress them anymore? I see no pleasure in that whatsoever."

I ask Sarah if she scans groupie message boards on the Internet. "I'm not going to post anything, but you bet your ass I read the message boards, especially Metal Sludge. I'm sure you've heard of this girl who goes by Rikki Sixx? Let's just say that when she got to be 'Sludgette of the Month,' she probably pissed herself from excitement. She's talked about how she's in love with Taime Downe and had hung out with him, like, thirty times. Then suddenly she announced on the message board, 'I BLEW TAIME.' I was thinking, 'Taime does *not* want people to know that.' Have you seen the sex tape of Kid Rock and Scott Stapp? As if you couldn't hate Scott Stapp any more. They show him sitting back, saying stuff like, 'It's good to be the king . . . this is my third one today.' Where was that girl's self-respect? I mean, go ahead, sleep with him. But to allow herself to be filmed sucking him off while he says such degrading things. Like I said, I don't really do that a whole lot."

I tell Sarah that Miss Tina, the other girl I'm meeting here in Minneapolis, is proud of her oral abilities and loves to climb aboard the bus to show her appreciation. "But when she leaves, they're probably going to talk a lot of shit about her," Sarah says, sipping her wine. "When I leave, at best, they'll say nice things, and at worst, they'll say nothing."

Tina King

In So Deep

M iss Tina King is persistent. She has called several times, making sure I have the right directions to her house on the other side of town. When I pull up and park in the crunchy snow, Tina is waiting for me on the porch, smiling brightly. She's just a little over five feet tall, with short pixie blonde hair and impish dimples, and she looks like she's about to burst with bliss.

Tina has inundated me with e-mails about her exploits, and of all the girls I've come across, she is the most effervescent and excited at the prospect of sharing her experiences. "Oh, I just can't believe you're here!" she exclaims, hugging me tightly and ushering me into the small wooden house she shares with her mother, Debbie, and her four-year-old daughter, Amber. Debbie welcomes me with a wide grin. Little Amber has been diagnosed with Autism Spectrum Disorder, and although she frolics happily with her toys, she doesn't interact much with me.

Before I arrived in Minneapolis, Tina and I discussed my desire to plunder antique malls and thrift stores to hunt for buried treasure. So the first thing we plan to do on this bitterly cold afternoon is rummage around Goodwill and Salvation Army stores together. While Tina gets ready to go, I notice an eight-by-ten of her with Kid Rock hanging over the big television set.

Debbie motions me toward her and whispers in my ear. "Tina gave Kid Rock a B-L-O-W-J-O-B," she says proudly, spelling out the letters, then looking over at Amber. "She can't spell, but you can't be too careful." For the first time in years, I am actually speechless. Debbie doesn't seem to notice and pulls out Tina's high school newspaper, *The Bluffer*, dated November 4, 1988. She points to a small article: "Time Will Tell—Imagine a world famous professor invented a machine that can answer any question about the future. Tina King: Will I ever reign as a groupie queen and be featured on the cover of *Rolling Stone*?" She then shows me an assignment Tina wrote for English class that describes Richie Sambora's guitar playing: "Magician's fingers produce auras of tone to mesmerize the fans . . ." I am struck by how wonderfully OK Debbie is with her daughter's, shall we say, *achievements,* and I'm filled with admiration for this open-minded mama.

While we gadabout antique shops, I ask Tina how her mother came to be so accepting. "She got divorced when I was fourteen and never remarried. We'd go to concerts and meet rock stars together. I'd take her backstage. We liked the same kind of music, and the same musicians. At first, I'd say, 'Hey, guys, this is Debbie.' But if it was a band I hung out with more than once, I'd finally say, 'Guys, this is my mom.' They'd say, 'Oh, that's really cool.' But since Amber was born, Mom mostly stays home with her."

Tina's remarkably sunny disposition belies a difficult beginning, as well as laser-focused determination. She already has a master of arts in human development and is close to getting a master's degree in social work. The job she hopes to land is quite unique. "I would like to work at a veterinarian hospital so I could hold a grief and support group for people who've lost a pet or recently found out their pets have a terminal illness. That combines my two big loves of animals and people in one setting."

Pretty incredible for a girl who says she came from a family that was "dirt poor." "I was four when my parents divorced. My mom married a traveling salesman when I was seven and was gone a lot, so my grandma raised me. I was pretty slick at keeping things hidden from my grandma. I'd sneak off and party. Where I grew up, if you weren't rich, no one paid you any attention, so I didn't get any boyfriends. I was really smart, but I was a stoner. I hung out with potheads but made good grades. Later on, my mom was a single parent on welfare and food stamps. She worked in a bar for $2 an hour and didn't make enough to make ends meet, so we both moved in with my grandparents and uncle. The five of us shared a one-bedroom house. My mom and I grew up as friends. We loved Dokken—all the '80s hair bands, we just loved 'em. They were great showmen. I thought glam rock guys wearing makeup, spandex, and big hair were really sexy. I started followed them around, and knew that between two and four, they were at sound check. So I'd go hang out by the buses. I'd dress sexy and flamboyant, and it always caught their attention. I'd say, 'Hey!' and they'd send their tour manager out to get me. A lot of times, security would try to prevent me from going to the bus: 'Stay back behind the yellow line. The police tape says do not cross.' But the rock stars would always say, 'She's with us.'"

We're cruising through the local Goodwill, and Tina holds up a pair of black patent leather Mary Janes. "These will look so cute on Amber," she says delightedly. After checking out with our swag, we stop for a cup of joe and some rock reminiscing. Her first big crush was Jon Bon Jovi, but she couldn't get near him. "It was like getting through a vault trying to meet the guy," Tina says. "My first sexual experience with a rock star was Tommy Skeoch, the guitarist for Tesla. It was awful, very methodic, no foreplay—he just pulled my clothes down. We were in the very back of his tour bus, and he didn't use a condom, or even kiss me. It lasted ten minutes. It was horrible."

Not surprisingly, Tina was disappointed and her crush on Tommy was instantly over.

"Each month, the editor of *Metal Edge* magazine would ask a bunch of rock stars the same question. This particular question was, 'What really worries you about being a rock star?' Tommy's answer was, 'All the numerous women I've slept with, without

With Phil Lewis, singer for L.A. Guns, March 2006.
Credit: Tina King

protection.' When I read that, a chill went down my spine. So I wrote him this long letter, and sent it in care of the record label. I ran into him about two months later. I got a backstage pass and was mingling with fans, talking to the other guys in the band. Suddenly, Tommy walked right over to me and said, 'I got your letter.' He looked at me like he could see into the very essence of my soul. But I didn't say a word, I just left."

I ask Tina why she kept going backstage after such a horrible first experience. "It's an addiction. Some people skydive, but I'd be afraid my parachute wouldn't open. Meeting a rock star and engaging in some sort of intimate, sexual act is such a thrill because it makes me feel special. Like I'm among the chosen ones. When I was a baby, my mom rocked me on the front porch, listening to '70s music. So I grew up loving the guys who play that music. It touches my heart. It touches my soul, and I want a piece of that person. I want to take a piece from them and put it into myself. It doesn't get more intertwining than a sexual act. After it happens, I see them on TV or in the magazines, and I think, 'I had a piece of that. I was with that person.' My dream has always been to marry a rock star. I never cared what my career would be. I just wanted to be a rock star wife or girlfriend. That's been my goal since I was a child."

But how would she feel about her rock honey hooking up with the likes of *her* out on the road? "I understand it goes with the territory. But I'd be the one they'd be with the majority of the time. I don't care about the wealth or being in the limelight. Just having them as my private rock star, to sing to me at three in the morning. Rock stars are a different breed: free-spirited gypsies that march to the beats of their own inner drums. There aren't many musicians in my small town, so I got away to hang with the bands. It was the best vacation ever and an escape from my own shitty life. I heard it in the halls and it was taped to my locker, 'You're a slut groupie.' I dealt with that all through high school and it sucked. So when I finally met the band and had the laminate and saw those same bitches who called me a slut, I could show them, 'Now look who's the slut, bitches?' They wanted to meet the bands so they'd try to brownnose me, 'Oh, Tina! How've you been?' I don't think so. Ha ha ha. Payback's a motherfucker, isn't it? Revenge is sweet medicine. I know that wasn't very nice, but they weren't nice to me either."

Tina's husband of eleven years wasn't a rock star but was certainly a different breed. "He was a pilot from Norway, and unlike all the guys in my little town—very Norwegian looking, almost white hair, tall, thin, with a dimple in his chin. I was almost twenty-one when I married him, because he was different. But being a groupie was one thing I was *not* giving up, and he hated it. Anytime a band was coming to our area, he'd stress out for a whole week. My second sexual rock star experience was Bill Leverty, the bass player for Firehouse. I gave him a blow job and didn't finish. He said, 'Oh, jeez, don't do this to me.' He was ready to get blue balls. I said, 'I can't. I'm married. I gotta go. Good-bye!' As I was running off the bus, he yelled, 'You've already cheated, you might as well finish!' I felt awful. It's sad to

With Bob Ritchie,
aka Kid Rock.
Credit: Tina King

say, but it was still fun. He's hot! I told my husband because I'm an open soul. I cheated on him once more with the guitar player for Survivor. I went back to his hotel room after the show and we swam and had sex. I didn't tell my husband about that one until a week later."

Tina went to shows and partied with band members, but stayed true until her marriage finally fell apart. "After my divorce, the '80s bands were coming back around, playing small clubs. So the next one was five years ago, Phil Lewis, the singer for L.A. Guns. A lot of groupies call him 'Philthy' Lewis, so he gets around. But I think I actually fell in love with him. The first time I gave him a blow job on the bus. The next time we had sex. He's a very good lover, and it wasn't just sleazy sex. He cared about *me*. The concert was phenomenal. I was front row center, and at the very end of the show, he looked at me and said, 'Thanks, Tina,' then bent down on one knee and gave me a big kiss, in front of everybody. I was thinking, 'Oh my God, it doesn't get any better! This just isn't going to happen, ever again.' We did things that were different from the other rock stars' sex acts. For example, he met my mom. Then a few months later, he came over to my house and took a shower. I just knew he lived in a fancy area of L.A. and had a mansion and fancy sports cars. I was so embarrassed because the tile had fallen off in part of my bathroom, but I didn't want to say no because he needed a shower. He had met my mom before, so they were chatting, and I called my friend Angie, who was taking me to the show in her yellow Volkswagen. I said, 'Somebody else is here and he needs a ride too.' She asked, 'Who is he?' and I said, 'Phil Lewis.' She got there and was all starry-eyed. On the way to the show, we had the sunroof open. It was surreal because we grew up listening to him, and I never thought I'd be having sex with him seventeen years later. Not once, not twice, but *four* times. After that show, we got on the tour bus and had sex in one of the little bunk beds. It reminded me of the Japanese hotel cubicles I'd seen in movies, but it was actually quite comfy. It was small quarters, but it worked. There was a curtain, so we had privacy. And we weren't

With Phil Lewis.
Credit: Tina King

getting loud. We were respectful because we were cognizant of everybody else on the bus. Once I spent the weekend with him. I took off work and went to the Super 8. There were three tour buses in the parking lot and I didn't know which one was theirs. So I stayed in my little red Ford Aspire, thinking, 'I'll just wait until some rock star gets off the bus.' It was Tracii Guns, the former guitarist for L.A. Guns. He's now with Brides of Destruction. He had seen me numerous times, hanging out with Phil. I said, 'Tracii, would you tell Phil to call Tina? This is my room number, 301.' I checked into the same hotel, the same floor, too. So Phil came to my room, we took a bath with candles, and it was so romantic. We sat there and talked about personal stuff going on in our lives. He told me he wrote that song 'Crazy' about his ex-wife who had mental problems. It's a wonderful song because part of the lyrics go, 'Don't call me crazy.' We fooled around in the bathtub, but that didn't go so well, because it's hard for guys have orgasms in bathtubs. At least that's what I've found in my experience. So he put the candles beside the bed on the nightstand. I gave him a blow job and when we were having sex, the tip of the pillowcase touched the candle flame and caught fire. I couldn't think, I couldn't move, but he was really quick-acting. He pounded the pillow on the carpet and the fire finally went out, but there was this huge hole with no carpet at all. I said, 'Oh, shit. I'm going to have to pay property damages.' But Phil put the table over the burned part, so I totally got out of that one. A few hours later he asked me to come to his room, and Brent Muscat of Faster Pussycat was there. They were hungry, so we went to Perkins. And that was really cool, because I was out to breakfast with two big popular rock stars. Everyone was staring and a lot people kept coming to the table. I was so nervous, I couldn't eat. It's weird: I could have the sex, because that's second nature, but here I was sitting with two rock stars I had idolized when I was younger and just didn't know what to say. Basically, I listened to them talk and just drank my pop. We went back to the hotel room, and Phil suggested a threesome. I felt a little awkward because I really liked him. I wondered if I should do it because what if he lost respect for me? At the same time, I was excited and thrilled by the idea. So I just went for it, and it was OK. Brent was shy, and that surprised me. He acted like a schoolboy, not quite sure what he was doing. Phil was more aggressive. I gave Brent a blow job, then Phil and I kissed for a while. Brent and I started to have sex, but I stopped so we didn't go all the way. Then Phil and I had sex, and Brent just walked away and did his own thing. They'd been good friends for years, and it didn't seem like it was uncomfortable for them. I don't think it was the first time they'd had a threesome. I even I wondered if they were bisexual. I saw a video camera and worried that he'd set it up to record. I still strongly suspect there's a video out there of us. I'd like to get my hands on it and destroy it—or actually, keep it! The next day, when I told Phil I was leaving, he told me he wanted to talk to me. He said, 'I think you're a really special girl and I don't want you to get your heart broken. I can't give you what you need.'"

Tina continued to hang out with the band whenever they came through town, and finally one night, it seemed Phil had a change of heart. "He said, 'Do you want to get together after the show?' But that never happened because at the end of the night, I ended up giving a blow job to Ronnie Munro, the singer of Metal Church. Then Stephen Pearcy's drummer was being flirty, and said, 'You're gorgeous. You want to hang out?' So we ended up getting in my minivan and I gave him a blow job too."

But why was she with two other guys when she could have been with her fave? "I don't know," Tina shrugs. "I wanted something strange and different. I guess I wanted to add more notches to my belt. Hey, I might as well have all of them. I thought it was cool because I got one from each band. Except the one I wanted the most."

But wasn't she worried that Phil would find out? "No, because I didn't tell those guys my name. I don't think the opening bands would tell the headliners because they compete for the same ladies' attention. It's competitive in that aspect, like a turf thing."

The next night, Tina invites me to one of her favorite strip mall rock clubs, where we boogaloo to a '70s cover band, shaking our booties like disco fools. She tells me about Amber's father, a local dark-haired musician with whom she had a short romance. Luckily, they remain friendly, and he sees Amber frequently. Afterward we drive around until we find an open IHOP so we can finish our chat. A proud vegetarian, Tina orders a middle-of-the-night grilled cheese, while I dig into an obnoxious, gooey plate of whipped cream–slathered pancakes.

Since she gives head so often, I assume that Tina sincerely enjoys performing oral sex. "It's a power thing," she admits readily, "especially if the guy really enjoys it. If he climaxes quickly, I get this rush. Musicians have had lots of it, and if you're able to excite them, you think, 'Wow, I'm pretty good at this. I rock!' I like discovering who is easy and who isn't. If it's more difficult, it's a challenge."

Has there ever been a time when she couldn't get her conquest off, I wonder? "No. I do the deep throat technique because I don't have a gag reflex. I swallow if they ask. Otherwise, I don't,

With Brent Muscat and Taime Downe of Faster Pussycat.
Credit: Tina King

because it's bitter and salty and kind of yucky. Usually, I wait until the very last second, then move my face. Or I let them come on my breasts. That's a real rush for some guys. Of course, with Kid Rock, it was all over my face."

Hooray, we've finally come to the infamous Kid Rock story. "The second week of August 2000, I took my friend to his show for her thirtieth birthday. We were in the fifth row, and his tour manager kept staring at me, so I flirted back. He came over to us and said, 'You ladies sit up here. Kid Rock only wants to look at beautiful women in the front row.' We could almost touch him, and he looked right at me, so I flashed him. He seemed to like that because shortly thereafter, we got all-access passes. We went backstage after the show, and it was a wonderful spread. When Kid Rock arrived, we took pictures with him, and I whispered in his ear, 'Do you wanna have a threesome?' He said, 'No, thank you, but it's really sweet of you to ask.' There were all these gorgeous strippers flirting with him. I knew he could have his pick of the litter, but I kept making eyes. Then I took my beer bottle and simulated fellatio. It went *all* the way down, completely, until the bottle didn't show. I could tell by the way he watched me that he was getting turned on."

Kid Rock was mighty intrigued and had his roadie invite Tina to pay him a visit at the back of the bus. "I thought I might be meeting a roadie or the guitar player, and I was really nervous. I went in and Kid Rock was there alone. He said, 'You can shut the door.' He was standing there with just a white towel wrapped around his waist, moisture on his chest and stomach, his hair wet, and he was so sexy. I said, 'Are we going to have sex?' He said, 'No, I saw you with that beer bottle, and I want to find out if you're as good as you seem to be.' So I gave him a blow job, and he said, 'Can I come on your face?' I told him, 'Sure, you can do whatever you want.' He got a towel and wiped me off, dabbing at my face. He said sweetly, 'Are you OK?' I said, 'Yeah, everything's fine,' and he said, 'Well, thank you . . . bye,' and I left. He has a beautiful one," she says with hushed reverence, "and it's extremely clean. I couldn't believe what had just happened! I told Lisa, and she was jumping up and down, saying, 'That's so awesome! I'm so happy for you!' We got in her SUV and just drove around for an hour. I sucked Kid Rock's cock! That was my Mount Everest, because of all of 'em, he's the most well known worldwide. His new CD just came out yesterday, and I got my tickets for his show in April. I have tenth row. But I'm going to find an empty seat closer to the railing. I have to be in the first four rows on the floor or the first row on the side of the stage. I want them to see me and make eye contact. If I'm twelve rows back, there's no way they're going to see me. Unless I do what I did at the Keith Urban show, which is stand up on my seat and flash them. But they don't always see that. You may have to flash them a few times before they see you. I'm spoiled, because once you get front row center, there's no going back. That's the Big Kahuna."

Tina's hardly touched her grilled cheese and seems suddenly somber. "After I've spent time with a band and the show is over, I get After-Show Depression. When everything is going on, the music, the excitement, it touches my very essence. And then they leave and I feel empty afterward."

Does she feel her *real* life is boring? "My daughter enriches my life so much, but if it weren't for her, I'd be pretty dragged down by the same old routine of school, work, and internship. When you're with a band, for that moment in time, you're sharing something incredibly special. You're intimate and close—you get a piece of them, and they get a piece of your soul."

I pay for the mediocre food and walk out into the pre-dawn, arm-in-arm with Tina. "I'm really psyched right now because there are three good concerts coming up in the next couple of months," she says joyously. "Kid Rock, L.A. Guns, and INXS! When I first saw the new INXS singer, JD Fortune, my heart melted and I was weak in the knees. He's not just good looking; he is breathtaking. I've had crushes on rock stars, but never this bad. I feel like I know him, and the fact that he's a vegetarian is very rare. Amber even knows who he is now and loves his song, 'Pretty Vegas.' It's the cutest thing, when I play his video, she says, 'JD! JD!' and points at him saying, 'Dada.' I say, 'No, that's not Dada, sweetie. JD is a lot cuter than Dada.'"

I've been back home for a few weeks when I get an e-mail from Tina, laden with animated happy faces, saying that she needs to talk to me. Debbie answers the phone and tells me that Tina is out shoveling snow, so I take the opportunity to ask how she feels about her daughter's groupie experiences. "It's OK with me. If that's what she wants to do, more power to her," Debbie says. Then speaking quietly, Debbie adds, "Did Tina tell you that she gave JD Fortune a blow job? She sure did. She said, 'Come here, JD,' then whispered in his ear, 'How would you like a blow job?' and the manager took her on the tour bus."

Another dream came true for Miss Tina King.

I congratulate Tina on her most recent conquest, and she is giddy with delight. "Never in my wildest dreams did I imagine it would happen. Kid Rock is the most famous one I've been with, and I didn't think lightning would strike twice! It was even better because I really didn't have a crush on Kid Rock, though I thought he was hot. But following JD's story every week on TV? It felt like I knew him already."

Tina found out when INXS would be at her local radio station and lay in wait in the lobby. "Then, BOOM, there he was, wearing his 'I Love PETA' T-shirt," she squeals. "I've met forty or fifty bands over the years, since first meeting Whitesnake in '85. I've never been starstruck, I just call them by their names and treat them like human beings. Of course, some want to be worshipped. They want the big brouhaha, because it's an ego trip for them. So with JD, I gave him this great big hug and lifted him off the ground. He's 6'2" and weighs about 145 pounds. He laughed and said 'OK, OK!' then I put him down and said, 'Somebody please take our picture!' While we were getting our photo taken, I reached back and grabbed JD's ass. He started laughing and said, 'Oh my God, she just grabbed my ass!'"

After the "phenomenal" concert, Tina took her place by the bus. "I was the only one there because I left after the first encore. I knew I had to be right there so I could get to him, pronto. Here came JD and I yelled, 'JD, JD! I have a flower for you!' Everybody was pulling him this way and that, like a ping-pong ball getting tossed around. As he was about to get on the bus, I said,

'JD, hurry! I've got to tell you something.' He came right over, leaned in to me and I whispered, 'Do you want a blow job?' He gave me a big smile and said, 'Yes!' I was speechless, thinking, 'He's just trying to be nice because he's a sweet guy, and I'm sure he gets asked this all the time. OK, stay calm, stay calm. Breathe, count to ten.' One minute later, the tour manager grabbed me by the arm and put me on the bus. It was surreal. Ever since I first laid eyes on him in episode one, I wanted to give him a blow job, and now it was happening! I walked by the backup singers and said, 'Hey, ladies, great show!' JD was at the very back of the bus, exactly like Kid Rock. There was an assistant pulling down the blinds, emptying cigarette butts, then she walked out and closed the door. JD said, 'Did you really mean what you said out there?' 'Hell, yeah, I meant it. Let's do it!' He looked like a kid in a candy store and a little bit nervous. I pushed him down onto the couch. He seemed to be thinking, 'She's assertive. I'm liking this.' Then, of course, he pulled his pants down and I started sucking his dick, but it wasn't getting hard. I was thinking, 'I've given a lot of blow jobs and I've never had any complaints. Am I getting rusty?' So I mentioned it to him, 'Honey, it's not getting hard, you're going to have to help me out here.' He said, 'Well, baby, I just got done performing for two hours, you know.' I'd never heard that if somebody gives a really physical, emotional performance, it could cause him not to get a hard-on. I was thinking, 'I'm just rusty and he's obviously had a lot of excellent blow jobs.' So he helped me out by masturbating while I was sucking his dick. Then he said, 'This isn't a good position for me.' He stood up and turned me around, real assertively, pulled my pants down and started fingering me. I wanted to have sex, but didn't ask because I was so nervous. Then he said, 'I want to look at your beautiful tits.' I took off my hoodie and was bare chested. He played with my titties and sucked on them, then I went back to giving him the blow job. I said, 'Do you want to give me a facial?' He said, 'Yeah!' So that's what happened. He came all over my face. There was tons of come, too. It was on both cheeks, my chin, everywhere except my eyes. Then, he said, 'Oh, that was *hot*!' I asked for a towel and he started wiping my face, really gingerly, so daintily and sweetly, and *so* considerate. He stood up and put his clothes back on, and said, 'Oh, damn, that was hot. Your tits are beautiful.' I said, 'Thank you,' then he said, 'Let me walk you out,' and like a dumb ass, what did I do? I just took off. I was so freaked out, I didn't say goodbye or anything. I'm so upset with myself, because I wanted to ask questions that aren't on any of his Web sites. I wanted to know when he became a vegetarian and why. He's a member of PETA, which I've been a member of since 1990. But I didn't get to tell him any of that. I wanted to find out how it feels to suddenly be extremely famous: from being homeless, living in his car, to *this*. I wanted to talk to him as a human being. I wanted to know what makes 'Jason' tick, what touches his heart and soul, but I didn't get any of that. I got the sexual part, but it left me wanting more. I'm wondering what he's thinking of me. He probably thinks I just used him, or that I do this all the time. If I'd stayed and talked to him, I could've said, 'Hey, you want to go to a vegetarian restaurant and talk?' INXS is touring Canada for two months, and I'm all ready to go. I told my mom, 'Just so you know, we're going to Canada.' She's not gung ho about it. She said, 'Amber and I have to go with you.' They're more than welcome to come, of course, but they're not going to the concert with me."

A few days later I got another e-mail from Tina.

Attached in my email you will find some video footage of JD performing fellatio on his mike stand in Minneapolis, the very night I "Tasted IT" & it sure "Tasted SWEET!" I want seconds!

Love,
Tina (aka Penny Lane)
(aka Mrs. Fortune)

Amanda Milius

Let Me Stand Next to Your Flower

R obert Plant had just dazzled the upscale crowd at the Santa Barbara Bowl and was weaving his way through the in-crowders gathered backstage to pay him homage. I was nibbling melon balls with Catherine James, while we grabbed our one-on-two moment with the veteran rock lord. As we reminisced and reveled in our long friendship, I noticed a tall, wide-eyed brunette watching us, agog with delight. When Robert turned to greet another well-wisher, she approached and nervously asked me to sign her vintage leather bag. "Sign next to Robert's auto-graph," she gushed. "I can't believe I'm meeting Robert Plant and Pamela Des Barres in the same night!" She had read *I'm with the Band* and compared her recent adventures to my own long-ago romps. We got into a lively conversation and I instantly recognized a music-crazed kindred spirit in Amanda Milius.

When I learned that the twenty-three-year-old groupie (and proud of it) had joyously discovered Gram Parsons through my books, I suggested she come to my boyfriend Mike Stinson's upcoming gig, as he is cut from the same hand-embroidered, honky-tonk cloth. She arrived decked out in a pioneer-girl dress very reminiscent of my purple gingham Burrito sister square-dance frock. It was my birthday, and we danced all night to

Credit: Pamela Des Barres

Mike's true country tunes. As she bopped and swayed, Amanda's glowing face seemed lit from within.

It's been such a pleasure coming across a doll after my own heart. And even though most of her conquests aren't household names (yet), her adoration for her unsung heroes is all-consuming and very familiar.

Like many self-proclaimed outcasts, her love for classic rock and roll saved Amanda's sanity and self-worth throughout her sad, disturbing childhood. Raised in stately SoCal mansions, mainly by a Guatemalan housekeeper, Amanda was neglected and barely tolerated by her reclusive, egomaniacal mother. Her daddy, screenwriter John Milius, enthralled the public with films such as *Apocalypse Now*, *Clear and Present Danger*, and most recently, the HBO miniseries *Rome*. Unfortunately, he fled the family's Bel-Air digs when Amanda was still in the womb, dumping her mother for a bit player in his film *Red Dawn*, whom he later married. These days, Amanda has made wary peace with her dad, declaring that their relationship is "friendly" rather than "parental."

A year ago, Amanda returned from a long stay in New York, where she completed her student films and philosophy thesis at Eugene Lang College. One of her many goals is to make "'70s era–inspired psychedelic road movies, westerns, and California noir." While in Manhattan, she spent several months as a live-in rock gal pal, alongside Sune Wagner from the Danish band the Raveonettes. She was also a constant and integral part of the vibrant alt-country bluegrass scene and had some unforgettable, swoony nights with one of her heroes, Greg Garing, a downtown Nashville legend (now playing guitar with Hank Williams III). While photographing bands for a music festival, she met her current beau, Richie Eaton, singer/guitar player for the upstart loud and rowdy Anaheim band the Willowz.

Amanda wears her long, dark hair parted evenly down the middle, and very little makeup, preferring the unfettered, au naturel look to blatant eye-catching dazzle. Her scrubbed clean innocence, however, neatly belies the holy terror she regularly morphs into. Amanda admittedly teeters on the edge, drinks a lot of liquor, and brazenly acts out at clubs. She dresses like she's on her way to a love-in and is on a constant search for vintage boutique hippie garb. She speaks quickly and energetically, as if there might not be enough time to share all her antics before dashing off to one more show. We somehow fit our conversation in between gigs and parties and her oddball odd jobs.

"I remember crawling around my parents' big stone house. It's kinda sad—I was alone a lot," Amanda tells me. "I didn't see my dad much until I was seven, and we finally started talking when I was thirteen. We're more like buddies; he thinks I'm a total fuckup but he likes it because *he* was a total fuckup. I think he enjoys that I'm the only child of his getting arrested repeatedly and kicked out of schools."

The first memory of her stepmother still sends a prolonged shiver down Amanda's spine. "She's the banshee on the hill. I try not to think about her ghoulish, white, screaming face. In my childhood mind she represented a primordial sense of evil. I remember going to Dad's house when I was four and she told me if I made any noise, the witches upstairs were going to *eat* me. I have two half brothers, but I grew up with my mom. Her name is Celia Kay and she was in *Island of the Blue Dolphins*. But more frequently it was just me and my housekeeper, Mema. My first word was 'agua,' Spanish for 'water.' I'm still close with her. I don't care what my parents think of me. Mema's the only person I'm afraid of disappointing. She instilled the only morals I have. She's very nunlike and wanted me to be nunlike, but it didn't happen."

Amanda says that her "teenage problems" actually began when she was in grade school. "Things went sour with my mom so early. I made a conscious decision at about eight: 'These people are crazy. If I'm going to grow up to be the person I want to be, I'm never going to depend on anybody or be afraid of anything.'"

She remembers blanking out to the Doors, leaving grief and chaos behind. "My mom and I fought viciously and I was in a constant state of unrest. Anything that blocked out the sound of the world was important to me. I had the swimming pool

Amanda and me.
Credit: Pamela Des Barres

and I had my Walkman. I'd stay underwater as long as I could because it was silent down there. I'd press the Walkman against my ear and lose myself in the Doors, the Rolling Stones, Guns N' Roses, Led Zeppelin."

With so much time unattended and unrestricted, imaginative Amanda turned her first boyfriend into her own living, breathing rock star. "Matt was older than me and the embodiment of Jim Morrison because he wrote poems and played music that sounded like the Doors. I glorified the past and still do, so modern musicians have never intimidated me. I was aware that they were just people I could hang out with. The greats were gods, but it was easy to talk to mortals. Since I didn't have anything to say to anyone at high school, it seemed artists, musicians, and general L.A. weirdos were the only people I made sense with."

One of the most horrendous conflicts with her mother began when she spotted muddy footprints on Amanda's windowsill the night she lost her virginity. "But I never regretted sleeping with Matt for a second. He wrote the most beautiful poetry and love songs. He was a perfect teenage dream and such a bad boy. I loved him, but he got me really into drugs."

By using a fake ID, or charming the doormen, Amanda started haunting the Whisky, the Troubadour, and the Roxy. "I told stories up the wazoo about leaving my wallet at my grandmother's house. I just wanted to be on the Sunset Strip. It didn't matter who was playing, I wanted to be near the music."

Excerpts from Amanda's diaries convey her desolate state of mind:

11-20-96
Got in another fight with my mom and she sat there like a dumb bitch while one of her boyfriends screamed at me, threw stuff and hit me. I hate her so much I wanna kill them both. I'm so full of sadness and anger I'm going to end up killing myself if I stay here. Dad won't call me back. He is in Texas shooting a movie. I want to die. I'm not crazy.

4-12-97
Kara's Flowers played at the Alligator Lounge tonight.
They think they are the Beatles. They light candles and
sing like it's the '60s. I don't feel awkward at these places.
I feel better in bars than in real life. [Kara's Flowers went
on to become Maroon Five.]

4-15-97
I was reading the encyclopedia of serial killers under the
bleachers at assembly and this boy said it was a terrible
thing for a young girl to read. Whatever. There is so
much I want to do. I want to figure out what my writing style is before it is tainted by the Brentwood English
department. They are robots. I don't care if I never get
a good grade or have any friends, I will never be boring
and normal like them.

9-4-97
I hate 9th grade. I got stoned and went to the Whisky.
Some drunk guy tried to dance with me and asked for
my number. If he calls I'm going to tell him I'm a
lesbian.

9-22-97
I met a guy named Matt and I love him. He is Jim Morrison I think. He doesn't live anywhere and he's 19, rides
a dirtbike, wears a leather jacket, and smells like beer and
cigarettes. I had to sneak out and it was really foggy and
I saw him standing under the streetlight.

12-5-97
I just got back from the KROQ Christmas show. Jane's
Addiction was really great. Art Alexakis from Everclear
asked if I wanted to go back to the dressing rooms and I
got freaked and told him I was 14. He was shocked but
left me alone. Marilyn Manson invited us to go to a party
with him in his limo!! (what kind of party would *that*

Credit: Amanda Milius

be?!) but Lisa was too nervous. I'm so pissed we didn't go. I will never *not* do something because of my parents.

1-29-98
Being 15 is amazing. Last night I snuck out to see Matt and the moment I saw him I knew I would love him forever and he would never be mine. I don't care. He makes meth in a bathtub and sells it for a living. I don't mind. I want him to be the first person I have sex with. He makes me a different person, more like a god. He's like a god.

1-30-98
I had sex with Matt last night and I'm so glad I did. We went driving on Sunset and he bought some acid at a 7-11. Then I snuck him in my window and we had sex. The

only light was coming from my stereo. "Light My Fire" was playing. I wish I could have crawled into his brain.

7-30-98
Life is getting intense. I'm going to boarding school in the fall. I saw Ringo Starr at the Roxy last night. I called Matt and a girl answered and said he was in jail.

9-24-98
Boarding school fucking sucks, it's fucking cold. I took acid and called my mom and the phone was dialing itself and I couldn't stop laughing. My mother is an idiot. My roommate had a bad trip and almost got us caught. A senior girl talked her out of it, she's an old hippie. She likes the Grateful Dead.

11-7-98
I had some meth sent from CA and everybody loves it. Now I have a ton of money to buy acid in town. I stole my dad's credit card numbers and have accounts at all the stores. I'm gonna save money and run away back to L.A.

Acid notes:
Bacchus is lying on top of me.
Ray Manzarek was an asshole.
The inside of your lungs are basically the same as trees.
Slash is my Dad. I'm reborn in guitars.

Along with venting in her diary, live music temporarily freed Amanda from her hazardous predicament. "I was standing at the front of the stage like I was worshipping at an altar. I felt it intensely at fourteen. I think young girls feel music in a way nobody else does. It made me feel part of something. I've always felt I'm living in a postapocalyptic musical world. Meeting Robert was the coolest moment, and that night was *epic* for me, but why couldn't I have seen Led Zeppelin when they were Led *Zep-*

pelin? If only I'd been born earlier—I would have been right there with you. I wish the word 'groupie' still meant something more than just girls who have sex with guys in bands. I always thought it *did* mean something more: an appreciation and love for music."

Along with a pack of girls from school, Amanda went to the Roxy and finally made her first rock star acquaintance. "Some boys from our grade formed a ridiculous high school punk band. When they got offstage, *another* band came on, and their singer was a cross between Kurt Cobain and Mick Jagger. He was all dripping wet with long black hair—and I was like, '*Oh, my God!*'"

The girls with Amanda were content to sigh over this skinny treat, but when they decided to leave, Amanda stayed put. "They said, 'We can't leave you here! How are you gonna get home?' and I'm like, 'I'll figure it out—go away!' I went up to the singer and said, 'I think you're beautiful and I'd like to smoke a cigarette with you.' I didn't even smoke cigarettes at the time! He's like, '*OK.*' I don't even remember his name, but I know he was English. It was the first time I was backstage at the Roxy, and while we were sitting on this nasty couch making out, I thought, 'This isn't very glamorous!'"

When the Roxy closed, Amanda dragged the rocker to a place she considers "magical." "We walked around the Beverly Hills Hotel like we were big *somebodies*. We sat in the little enclaves, kissing, and someone finally said, 'What are you doing? You need to leave!' I must have been drunk because I said, 'Don't you know who you're talking to? This is Mick Jagger!'" When the singer gallantly offered to drive Amanda home, she was suddenly embarrassed. "I didn't want him to take me to Bel-Air because it made me seem square."

This taste of rock glory fanned Amanda's pubescent fire, and she began spending more time at the clubs.

"Everything revolved around getting away from my house. Mema sure didn't like it. 'I found a beer under your bed, Amanda. You smell like a boy's cigarette!'" Beer and cigarettes were the least of it. "I was taking far too much acid for someone my age.

I'll bet I took more LSD than my parents and their friends combined during the entire '60s and '70s. I'd drop it and go to math class. I was a mess!"

Amanda demanded that I watch Ondi Timoner's outrageous rock doc *DIG!*, about the rivalry between the lead singers for the Dandy Warhols and the Brian Jonestown Massacre, before regaling me with her Anton A. Newcombe tales. "You'll be entranced with him," she insists, "but at the same time it's clear that he's an asshole."

Anton is the hell-bent front man for Jonestown and I *did* watch *DIG!*, alternately enthralled and repulsed, seeing this obviously brilliant maniac systematically destroying himself and his band—over and over again. But I could also see the attraction.

"A lot of bands are coming up now because of *DIG!* Brian Jonestown, the Warlocks, the Black Rebel Motorcycle Club . . . and Anton Newcombe inspired all of it. When I was fifteen, my mom started going out of town, and I had this awesome house

With Anton Newcombe.   Credit: Amanda Milius

at my fingertips. I'd take a lot of drugs and throw giant parties; the most outrageous and insane people would show up at my house—musicians, artists, photographers, designers, writers, every L.A. band in the scene, and all the weirdos that came with them. It was very throwback to the '60s and '70s. The music was vintage, the vibe was classic; it just didn't feel like the present. One night my mom came home during a chaotic party. People were saying, 'Amanda, we're out of margaritas! Hey, somebody's throwing up in your living room!' I was trashed and couldn't handle all these yahoos with my mom home, so I laid out in the middle of my swimming pool, looking up at the stars. Anton came up to me and I could see in his eyes that he was completely E'd-out. He said, 'Amanda, listen. I wanted to meet your mom and get to know her. I've been in her room for two hours and we've been talking while she showed me your baby pictures. I think the problem between you two is that she misses you since you're not in the house much anymore.' I said, 'You're insane, Anton. You were talking to my *mom*?' And he's like, 'I'm trying to make things better for you, honey. People listen to me.' I was like, 'Who *is* this guy?' I got to know him around town, and he's like Charles Manson, but in a good way. He has an army of girls and he's the most intense person I've ever met."

Amanda somehow graduated from her ultra-chic west side high school. "I was smart but hardly ever went to class. I was the only person to get arrested on the Brentwood School campus. According to the report, it was for assault and battery, but all charges were dropped."

This unfortunate crisis occurred because Amanda's mother attempted to stop her from driving to see Matt in the desert. "She took the keys to my car, so I took the keys to her car and hid it up the street. She called the police and told them I'd stolen the car and accused me of assaulting her. Meanwhile I was the one with bruises all over my face and arms." When she arrived at school Monday, the headmaster took Amanda to his office, where the cops were waiting for her. "I thought I was about to get busted for selling cocaine and LSD on school grounds and was freaking because I had all this coke in my purse." She convinced the authorities to let her get her backpack and tossed the cocaine into some handy bushes before being taken to juvenile hall and booked. "My coppers totally liked me and let me wear sunglasses in my mug shot. I was in solitary for eleven hours before my dad came and got me out. I found the coke in the bushes the next day."

After graduation, Amanda fled to New York and enrolled in Eugene Lang College. During summer vacations, the parties continued in Bel-Air.

Royal Trux was Amanda's intro into the exemplary world of indie rock. "They are my favorite band of all time—a husband and wife team. Jennifer Herrema was my idol and she stayed at my house for a couple of months. We were off the hook! I was like, 'Mom, this is my friend from college!' She was the most important musician of the '90s." When I admit I've never heard the band, Amanda launches into an aficionado's tirade. "Nobody's heard of the bands I really care about. You know the Jon Spencer Blues Explosion? OK, then there's Pussy Galore, Jon Spencer's band with Neil Hagerty, and Neil was in the band with Jennifer, Royal Trux. They are the cornerstone of the whole indie rock map."

While attending classes during the day, Amanda frequented the Baggot Inn, an Irish pub that hosted a weekly bluegrass night. She had long been a country fan, but bluegrass gave her a new thrill, especially local singer/songwriter Greg Garing. She met him after following Merle Haggard around on tour for two weeks and was in a romantic country state of mind. "I've never been so moved by music before. There isn't a person who comes in contact with Greg, man or woman, who isn't in love with him. He's tragic and dark and mysterious—like he's from an ancient era. He played with Bill Monroe when he was seventeen, and Bill said that bluegrass music was made for Greg's voice."

She became a regular on the scene and slowly built a flirty friendship with Greg. "By the end of the night, it would be just the two of us; we'd wander to another late-night bar and talk and talk." She was painfully attracted to him, but wary when he started calling her in the middle of the night. "I thought, 'What business do I have with this guy? He's nothing but trouble.' There were always ten million girls around him, randomly coming out of the woodwork. Greg's life is so romantic, he seems fictional; the perfect man to fall in love with when you know you can't have him. One night the whole audience was gathered around him, and I walked in the door wearing my weird hippie wizard outfit. When he saw me, he stopped playing and pulled out a chair next to him. I thought, 'Well, I'm certainly not gonna go unnoticed!' I sat there with him staring at me—so intense and insane."

Amanda eventually spent a few memorable days with Mr. Garing. "I decided to leave New York the summer of 2004. Greg was breaking up with his girlfriend, and one night he said, 'I need someone to talk to.' So I went over and we watched television, cuddling under blankets on the floor, holding each other. We were about to kiss and I thought, 'What's *this* gonna be like?' I won't forget that kiss for the rest of my life. He said, 'I've been waiting to do this for a long time.' It was the kiss to end all kisses. Those three days were strange and awesome; he was in a sad place and it was almost too emotional to be sexual. Van Morrison's version of 'It's All Over Now, Baby Blue' kept playing in my head. For some reason, that Dylan song epitomized the entire experience."

Amanda was leaving for Los Angeles, and Greg walked her out to hail a cab. As a parting gift, Greg had given Amanda a holy relic to remember him by: his banjo pick. "I tied it on a ribbon around my neck and he said, 'I'm giving it to you, but you have to bring it back to me.' He finally said, 'Well, I guess this is good-bye.' I was trying to keep it together. After he kissed me, I walked down the street, sobbing. I hadn't cried in seven years. I didn't take that pick off all summer, and I didn't let anybody touch it."

Upon her return to Manhattan that fall, Amanda attended a party for her friends in the Warlocks. "I don't know what I was drinking, but apparently I threw a bottle at an ex-boyfriend and tried to get him kicked out of the party. Sune Wagner was the person next to me absorbing my tirade. I left my phone in a cab and the next day he called my cell so many times that the cab driver answered it. Sune arranged to get my phone, then met me at one of my classes. I was like, 'Who are you again?' He came into the picture during a crisis-filled time and did his best to sweep me off my feet, which he totally did. He was sweet and attentive and treated me like a queen; he was just gaga over me. Also, he was romantic and wrote me love notes. The surprise was, oops, he's a great musician in a great band! But I wasn't his groupie because I hadn't even heard of the Raveonettes."

Amanda moved into Sune's apartment, and when she wasn't in class, they spent time in upstate New York with Sune's record producer. She went to all of the Raveonettes' shows, but felt like she was standing around wearing a sign that said "girlfriend." The bliss slowly turned into frustration and boredom.

"He was never bad to me, but he turned out to be an awful boyfriend. He'd say something one week and the next week, he'd act completely different. I think he had a vision of what his needs were. At that time he thought he needed a *girlfriend*, and I fell into that role. He didn't know me at all. The qualities he said he liked about me were traits I'd never even considered, like how sweet and maternal I was, and how I'd be a good mom. That's not the way to describe the drunk girl throwing bottles at her ex, waking up in strange people's houses. And he didn't take me seriously as a person not connected to *him*. I had my own aspirations aside from standing around at his shows. He forgot my shoot dates for my student films, but I was expected to remember every European tour date for three months. We did go to Hawaii for ten days, but it was depressing at times because I knew he'd be away on tour for the next six months. We had fun driving around the island and drinking piña coladas. We went surfing, which he thought he'd be good at because he'd been in a surf rock band."

The rocky relationship lasted almost nine months before completely fizzling. "I don't know what happened to the person I met. He'd go on tour for a month and be happy to get back, or come home so crazy and mean that he'd kick me out of the apartment. Two days later he'd call and say, 'Where are you? I miss you.' But then he wouldn't even talk to me. I didn't know how he felt one day to the next. It became too draining. The Raveonettes were on tour when my friend called from Dallas, inviting me to Willie Nelson's July 4th picnic. I didn't know if Sune would even want me at the apartment when he got home. I finished editing my student film and booked a ticket to Dallas. He finally called when I was at the airport and I told him I was moving out." Amanda sighs, adding that she and Sune are now friends. "The Raveonettes have this song about groupies called 'Love in a Trash Can.' If that song is about me, I'm gonna kill him. But I seriously doubt that it is."

The following spring, Amanda encountered an old acquaintance. "I knew Brian Jonestown was playing the Bowery Ballroom, and even though I didn't have a ticket, I thought, 'I'm just gonna do it!' She arrived a bit late, expecting the band to already be onstage. "People were lined up around the block, and I was talking to some friends from L.A. and who shows up, but *Anton*, and he's *wasted*. Of course, he's *always* wasted. He said, 'Oh, my God. You're here! Don't you look nice tonight?' He's being this charming little dude, saying, 'You have beautiful eyes! You've really grown up, haven't you?' He introduced me to some biker guys, telling me they knew my dad, and I was like, 'I don't need Hells Angels friends right now.' They were fucking scary dudes. Anton got down on his knees and kissed the guy's boots and said, 'There, that's how much I love you.' This giant biker didn't know how to respond."

Just then, a security guard reminded Anton that his fans had waited forty-five minutes, and it was high time he got on stage. When Amanda told him she didn't have a ticket and couldn't get in, Anton said, 'Oh, I think you *will*.' He pulled me *through* the audience—girls are throwing themselves at him. Yeah, I felt special when he took me onstage, sat me on an amp, and said, 'There, now you're in,' then picked up his guitar and started playing."

Amanda was sitting in the prime groupie dream spot: atop the rock star's amplifier in full view of the rampaging fans. "The show went on forever and by the end I was just a puddle of psychedelic feedback."

Jonestown Massacre played so long that night, the venue pulled the plug. "Nobody would touch Anton because he's bonkers, but they yanked the rest of 'em off the stage. Of course the girl sitting on the amp didn't need to be there either. When they cleared the audience, I realized Anton had vanished."

That week Amanda kept hearing the usual rumors about Anton's dangerous misbehavior. "Apparently bad shit had been happening. He got kicked in the head at a bar and had a concussion. He tried to set somebody on fire. He was drunk here and got in a fight there. I thought, 'Sounds to me like he's being Anton.'"

Amanda's dad has cozy cabins sprinkled hither and yon, so before heading home to L.A. she invited some friends to join her in the screenwriter's upstate paradise for a couple days. They, in turn, told Anton about the secret hideaway, and two hours after her pals left, Amanda's phone rang. "It was a 213 number and I thought, 'Who the hell?' It was Anton. 'I heard you're leaving soon, darling, so give me a call. I'd like to hang out before I go back to my girlfriend.' All of Anton's girlfriends look like they've seen a ghost for six months running. So, I called back and said, 'You're obviously not doing so well in the city—I think you need a vacation.' I picked him up at the train station at midnight. I was the only person on the platform . . . pretty romantic, right? It's cold up there, but he was wearing just a blue silk shirt and layers of necklaces. Businessmen dashed off the train and he said, 'What's the problem, guys? You can't face the truth?' Obviously he had gotten into a fight on the train. He said, 'Tell me you've got something to drink at the cabin,' and I said, 'Of course I do. Come on.' He thought it was beautiful up there. We hiked around, went to graveyards, and stayed up all night long. The guy only sleeps two hours a day. We bought these lifelike target dummies and shot at them across the meadow, pretending they turned into zombies coming to kill us."

With so much private time together, didn't they feel the temptation to get entangled?

Amanda and her
fiance, Richie.
Credit: Amanda Milius

"I can't lie, I'd been attracted to him the whole time. One night he was sitting in the kitchen while I cut up limes for our drinks. I had a pile of them and held one out to him, like, 'Here, you want a *lime?*' He leaned over, kissed me on the mouth, and put the lime in his drink. I snatched the entire pile of limes from the table and looked at him as if to say, 'If that's what I get for one lime slice, what do I get for all of these?' He grabbed me and we started ferociously making out. We lost our minds and went to some kind of primal realm. It was intense and crazy, like a Dionysian ritual."

The impromptu madness in the wilderness ran its course, and Amanda drove Anton to his girlfriend's house in New York, which suited her fine. "He's a cross between Manson and Jesus and every influential person combined with a bratty rock star. To me he's like an older, spiritual mentor presence." She smiles. "We were only ever friends—with a little bit of primal thrown in."

After over four years in college, Amanda took a year off, dating, traveling, and throwing several more outrageous bashes in Bel-Air. One of her flings was with Year Long Disaster's guitarist, Daniel Davies, son of Kinks legend Dave Davies. "We drank like there was no tomorrow and wound up in Jacuzzis all over town. Daniel and I got involved romantically, in one Jacuzzi or another. Their drummer's dad was one of Led Zeppelin's producers, and when I arrived at the studio with a giant bottle of whiskey, he said, 'In all my days I never met a bird who came with her own bottle. Good girl!' We all had a good time until two of them told me they were checking into a rehab clinic. I was surprised that my favorite cohorts were taking the dry road, but I wanted them to do well. It had become extreme. The week before, we busted up my car because we drank too much opium poppy tea and were blasting AC/DC along Laurel Canyon. Daniel had a scar from the bad sunburn he got when he passed out in my mom's pool. We're still great friends. The band has done much better without all the drinking. I think they'd like to see me do the same, but so far that hasn't happened."

Perhaps Amanda's most extreme days and nights are behind her. A few months ago, during a trip to Manhattan, she says she finally "met her match."

"I got trashed and wound up at the Willowz show at two thirty in the morning. A good friend of mine owns a record label and I was checking out bands, but I couldn't see two feet in front of me. You could have told me Elvis was on stage and I would have said 'That's cool.' I thought the singer, Richie, looked like Neil Hagerty from Royal Trux. I was talking to his drummer, and he stepped between us, saying, 'Hi, I'm Richie.' Since I was taking pictures of the bands, he asked me for my 'contact info.' Now we joke that we can tell our kids, 'When Daddy met Mommy he asked for her *contact info*.' When he tried to kiss me at the bar, I almost got hit by a drink his ex-girlfriend bass player threw at us. We ended up making out on the street, then drove all over Manhattan looking for a hotel room. We practically had sex in the cab, but finally wound up at my apartment. We hooked up that night and have been psyched on each other ever since. I knew the next day that he was going to be my boyfriend for a really long time. He is the best, most versatile guy in bed; he has so many personalities. He can seriously have sex for five hours and it's never boring."

Lucky Amanda and tireless Richie are now engaged and just got an apartment in Silver Lake that they share with the Siamese kitty he bought for her twenty-third birthday. Amanda had almost given up on getting involved with another musician who might be away on the road for months. "Luckily I met Richie, and he renewed my faith in being in love—regardless of the circumstances. But we do have a hard time. When he's away, he freaks out, imagining I'm hanging out with other guys, which I'm not. And I've gotten into my share of fights with his ex and other random girls. The band is his life, and I have my own life, and sometimes it's difficult to make them fit together. We love each other and don't want to lose what we have due to the circumstances of our lifestyle. I've never been with someone so intelligent, creative, and inspiring. He makes me want to do great things. He played me a song from the new record and I said, 'Richie, you just made the most perfect song of the last thirty years. It's a good thing we're engaged, because if I didn't know you and heard this song, I'd have to go out and find the man who wrote it and marry him.'"

Static Beth

Size Queen of the Stars

Ms. Static Beth of Boston, Massachusetts, began her journey to infamy in July 2003, when she became Sludgette of the Month at www.metalsludge.com. Fascinated by the penis chart, she began indulging her obsession by creating what she calls a "visual version" of the chart, by compiling naked photos of rock stars showing off their finest assets. If you want to take a gander at Beth's growing collection, go to www.staticbeth.com, click on "Photos," then "Naughty," and peruse the list. There's Asses ("There's so much ass on this website that the page had to be split in two"), Balls and Pubes (from Chris Cornell's "Ball Sack" to Slash's pubes), Famous Cocks, and Unsigned Cock.

Beth has just announced that she is now accepting photos from unsigned bands. As she says on her Web site,

I have decided to give some unsigned bands exposure (no pun intended) on my website. For those who have been living under a rock for the past few years, my website features cocks of famous musicians, actors, and athletes . . . until now. I was inspired the other day when I was sent a cock from an aspiring musician that I talk to regularly. His picture was hotter than hell. So I thought to myself,

*there must be other hotties in unsigned bands looking
for instant fame like this guy does. Metal Sludge exposes
unsigned bands by giving them the opportunity to answer
ten questions, and I will be just plain exposing them.*

*I do have a criteria for submissions that must be fol-
lowed in order to have a picture posted.*

Rules:
1. You must be in a band. If you aren't a struggling musician, I don't want to look at your cock.
2. Band members are the only people allowed to submit
a picture. Pictures from disgruntled ex girlfriends, ex-
wives, or fans are not allowed
3. The band member has to be at least eighteen years of
age.
4. The band must have a Web site for verification and
promotion.
5. The band member must be considered nice looking by
the general public. Just because your mom says you're
cute doesn't mean you really are. Anyone that looks
like George Costanza or former WWE wrestler King
Kong Bundy need not apply.
6. The penis must be erect in the picture. No one wants
to look at your floppy dick.

*Pictures will be published under the discretion of Static-
Beth.com. I have a keen eye for fakes, so Photoshopped
penises are not accepted.*

Since my Web site (www.pameladesbarres.com) is listed
among her links, I contact Static Beth to ask a few pertinent
questions and thoroughly enjoy her sardonic sense of humor.

Pamela: What made you decide to create this very informative
chart?
Beth: I used to have my own tiny Web page with pictures from
Playgirl. I thought, "I'll just scan the pictures and put them

Credit: Static Beth

up. It'll be cute." It started catching on. People began sending me random naked pictures of celebrities, so I bought my own domain.

Pamela: Do you mind being called a groupie?

Beth: I *do* have groupie boots in my closet. They haven't been out for a while.

Pamela: How did groupiedom begin for you?

Beth: Oh my God, anything for Guns N' Roses! I sent Axl a birthday card every year. I'm sick. I'm very sick. Every time I go out to L.A., I drive up his hill. I even stole his newspaper! It was in the driveway, and I thought, "I've got to grab *something* of his!"

Pamela: Do you have flings and relationships with rock guys?

Beth: Yes, I do. And most of my male friends are in bands. I love the lifestyle. I'm a normal girl. Only one boss knows what I do at night and a couple of coworkers. By day, I work for a news agency. Then I hang out with these guys by night. They go from city to city, they're on TV, they're in videos and all over the Internet. I try not to get too starstruck. It gives them big heads. Now it's weird because with me, they're like, "Ooh, it's Penis Girl! Static Beth!" Either they love me or they run away from me. "Oh no, you're the dick girl."

Pamela: You're renowned. How do you feel about that?

Beth: I'm not sure, but it's more amusing to me than anything.

Pamela: Do you consider yourself a size queen?

Beth: Yeah, I do. Although I think some men are intimidated by it: "If I have a small one, I sure don't want to go with her."

Pamela: Many of the guys on your site aren't that huge.

Beth: The huge ones are the exception. Not everybody looks like Tommy Lee. Phil Varone's is long, it has girth, and it's pierced. That bad boy would probably split me in half, but I enjoy looking at it. Some of them are really bad, like the Marilyn Manson ones. I'm like, "Poor guy. Poor Dita."

Pamela: Well, he's not hard in the photo.

Beth: I know people who've been with him, and it doesn't get much bigger than that.

Pamela: There aren't that many famous groupies anymore, and that's sad. I love your Web site, and how you're carrying on the groupie tradition in such an interesting way.

Beth: Thank you! Now with the Internet, everybody knows who's been with everybody. It was better when you were doing your thing. Now all the guys can trade stories. I'll tell you a quick one of mine. I used to hook up with the drummer from Slipknot, Joey Jordison. He's the most famous one I've been with . . . a Grammy Award winner. It started out great, but this other groupie girl ran her mouth and said I talked about him on message boards, which I never did. She also told him that he was on my Web site, which he wasn't, and he completely turned on me.

Pamela: Apparently he likes to dress up like a little girl with smeared lipstick and dresses.

Beth: He also likes to wet the bed. I don't know if she told you that. He's a big bed wetter. He's *so* strange. He likes to throw up on stage. It makes him feel better. He wears a dress and looks just like a little boy, naked. I call him the Forehead because he has the biggest forehead I've ever seen in my entire life!

Pamela: Do you have a happier groupie tale you could share?

Beth: I have a better one. This is with Racci Shay who was in Dope. I went up to him at the show and handed him my

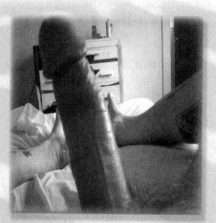

Dirt, the bass player for Society1, sent Beth this picture of his cock for her birthday present.
Credit: Static Beth

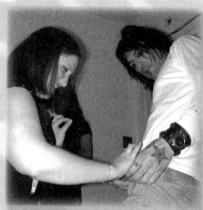

Beth inspecting Phil Varone, formerly of Skid Row, Prunella Scales, and Saigon Kick.
Credit: Static Beth

business card. He looked at me and said, "You're Static Beth? Oh my God, I was just talking about you!" They were on tour with Mushroomhead, and he and Mushroomhead's guitar player, Bronson, were looking at their cocks on my site before the show. He said, "I am so excited to meet you. There's something I have to show you," and he whipped out his cock, put a match in the tip of it, lit it on fire, and said, "I've been dying to show you this!"

Pamela: Please tell me you had a camera.

Beth: Oh, the pictures are on my Web site! He said, "Blow out the candle." I blew it out, and we were inseparable for the rest of the night. He was my biggest fan and so proud to hang out with me. He introduced me to everybody, "This is Static Beth. My cock's on her Web site!"

Pamela: Did most of them already know about Static Beth?

Beth: Oh, they knew. It was funny. Racci said, "Bronson wants to see you." We were going to get on Mushroomhead's bus, but got stopped by their roadie, who said, "You can't go on there. Bronson's girlfriend is on the bus, and she doesn't like the pictures on your site." I thought, "I've been *cock blocked*!" I wasn't allowed on Mushroomhead's bus. It sucks because she should be proud of him! Anyway, Racci and I were hanging out, drinkin', and he said, "Do you wanna go to the bathroom? I've gotta pee." So I went with him, and he said, "Will you hold it?" I aimed his cock for him, so he could pee in the urinal, and he said, "Hey, you're pretty good." Later on, we were hanging out, taking regular stupid band pictures. All of a sudden, Racci pulled down my shirt—in the middle of the venue with everybody standing around—and started kissing my boobs. Then he asked if I wanted to go to the back room, and I said, 'OK.' He showed me the trick with the match again and asked, "Do you want to blow me?" and I said, "Why not?" So we went into the boiler room. It was dusty, stinky, and disgusting. So I went down and did my stuff, and in the middle of it, he said, "Do you want to fuck?" Very casual, like "Do you want a piece of gum?" And I said, "All right. Do you have a condom?" and he said, "Oh, sure. I'm a Boy Scout," and I said, "Excellent!" We were having sex in the boiler room, and the floor was made out of bricks. All of a sudden he started laughing. I said, "What?" and he said, "My foot's stuck in the bricks! Give me one second," and he finally got his foot untangled. I grabbed onto something, and my hand was all covered in soot. When it was all over, we came out of there, completely covered in dirt. It was so funny. And so strange. The whole night was very random.

Pamela: Would he have been your first choice in the band?

Beth: Yeah, because he did that flaming thing with his penis. I thought, "I love this guy. He's so cute." It was a very good time. I didn't expect anything. Sometimes I think, "Oh, I like you so much," but it was none of that. It was just, "OK, we're done." He got his drink and left, and I went home happy.

Pamela: So oftentimes, like many groupies, your feelings get tangled up?

Beth: Oh, yeah. I've been hurt many, many times. So that was a good experience for me because there were, like, no strings

With Racci Shay,
formerly Dope's
drummer.
Credit: Static Beth

attached. Actually, I think it was exciting for him—he was with *Static Beth*.

Pamela: He was your groupie.

Beth: He was! He was my little fan.

Pamela: Have you been compared to Cynthia Plaster Caster?

Beth: Yes. I love her Web site. I'm sure you've seen it, with the sperm squirting?

Pamela: It's incredible. I think you're performing a service with your Web site too. People are so uptight, and what you're doing is refreshing. You're reminding people that it's just a dick, for God's sake!

Beth: There isn't any other site like it, unless you want to look at gay porn. There really isn't anything out there for women who are into the music scene.

Pamela: And it's obvious the rock guys like to be seen on your Web site. That's why it's so successful!

Epilogue

Cameron Crowe

Almost Famous

"The chicks are great. But what it all comes down to is that thing. The indefinable thing when people catch something from your music." —JEFF BEBE

"I'm not a . . . groupie. Groupies sleep with rock stars 'cause they wanna be near someone famous. We're here because of the music. We are Band Aids. We inspire the music." —PENNY LANE

When you spend intimate time with a band, especially on the road, there's an uncommon camaraderie and trust that develops. So even though my romance with Jimmy Page was history, I was still quite warm with the rest of Zeppelin and saw them whenever they careened into Hollywood and took the town hostage. It was 1973 and Robert Plant had invited me to visit him at the Riot House on the Strip. We had always been flirty but never quite got romantic and maintained (still do) an invaluable connection and a uniquely similar point of view.

When I flounced into his suite, Robert was winding up a rare interview with a sweet-faced kid who seemed particularly thrilled to meet me. Actually, Cameron Crowe has much better recall about that afternoon than I do. Perhaps because it was his first gig writing for *Rolling Stone*, and he was interviewing *Led Zeppelin*. Apparently Robert had been enlightening Cameron about the significance of the GTO's and other girls on the scene. Here's what actually made it into the article that day:

"It's a shame to see these young chicks bungle their lives away in a flurry and rush to compete with what was in the old days the good-time relationships we had with the GTO's and people like that. When it came to looning, they could give us as much of a looning as we could give them."

Decades later, Cameron Crowe created the silver screen groupie Penny Lane and her group of rock-loving Band Aids for his 2000 film, *Almost Famous*. I was invited to a preview when it was released and saw many similarities between the shimmering blonde sweetheart portrayed by Kate Hudson and the devoted Miss Pamela. There was one glaring exception: although I agonized and mourned lost rock love on occasion, I wouldn't have tried to off myself over *any* rock star.

When I met Kate, she threw her arms around me and told me she read *I'm with the Band* for inspiration and that old photos of me had adorned her dressing room walls during filming. It seemed like art imitating life imitating art imitating life, watching her cuddle and coo with her rock husband, Chris Robinson from the Black Crowes.

Several of the girls I interviewed have told me how deeply Penny Lane and her band of merry Band Aids inspired and validated them, so I've decided to ask my friend Cameron just how he developed this consummate character. He's invited me to have lunch with him at Paramount Studios, where he's working on a new script.

I love going to movie studios. As I parade through the old lot on my way to Cameron's office, I'm sure I can feel showbiz ghosts tugging on my velvet Betsey Johnson minidress. Vinyl Films is in the Bob Hope building, where black-and-white classic rock photos line every wall. I spot one of Jimmy Page that looks eerily familiar. I'm sure the same one hung on *my* wall over thirty years ago.

Cameron is a heavyweight director nowadays, but his first love is rock and roll. He even snagged his own rock goddess when he married Heart's Nancy Wilson ten years ago. Friendly

With Kate Hudson as Penny Lane in *Almost Famous.*

Credit: Neal Preston, © Dreamworks

and boyish, Cameron greets me with a big hug. Our sumptuous lunch has been delivered and we retire to his private office, where I ask my first question: who is Penny Lane?

"I saw the Penny Lane character more as a *group* of people," Cameron says. "More than anything else, she represented a *feeling.* Penny Lane was the person who hosted the arrival of that great indefinable *it*, asking, 'Do you have everything you need?' I auditioned actresses by saying, 'Don't do the dialogue. I'm going to play some music, 'People's Parties' by Joni Mitchell or Zeppelin's 'That's the Way,' and this is the music you hear in your head as you go around this imaginary dressing room, making sure everybody has what they need.' There were a few actresses who got it and many who didn't.

"When I first met you at the Continental Hyatt, Robert and Jimmy had been talking about you and how important the GTO's were. So when you showed up and were so nice and appreciative of the same things I loved as a fan, it was like, 'Here's royalty.'

You were a rock star in your own way, but so approachable and so much about loving the music. And you cannot discount the fact that they set the tone about how to view you. Pennie Lane in Portland was another person who treated me like a mascot and had a group of girls around her she called Band Aids. She had a blow job club, which was, 'We don't sleep with the guys. We only give 'em blow jobs. That way we have mystery, yet we're still serving the cause.'"

It sounds as if Cameron had respect for the dolls he met while interviewing musicians on the road. "I did admire groupies. Some of the guys mistreated them and that always hurt to watch. I dug them because they were friendly to me. My mom skipped me grades, and the girls at school were very cruel about me being younger. Later on, when I met musicians I'd written about over the years, the coin of the currency seemed to be, 'Have you spoken to so-and-so? How's Michelle?' They wouldn't even ask about the guys in their own band. They'd ask, 'Have you spoken to *her*?' It would be the girl who'd been there when I was interviewing them."

He had long wanted to tell his tale of traveling with the bands, but it took the massive success of *Jerry Maguire* to convince the moguls to let Cameron make his very personal movie. "I think they assumed that the next thing I did might be more overtly commercial, but I truly believed that the story *could* be universal—because it was about a family."

For some people, the term "groupie" has become synonymous with "whore" or "gold digger." The girls I've met love the Penny Lane character because she expresses the qualities of groupiedom they relate to—purity and love of music. They see her as the real thing. *Almost Famous* has certainly struck a major chord with groupies, and it's done well on DVD, but it flopped at the box office. "That's OK," Cameron insists. "When you tell me how it's captured a feeling for real people—the groupies and rockers—that's why I did it. To capture that amazing feeling."

Cameron seems surprised when I tell him that many modern groupies call themselves Band Aids. "If that term empowers someone, whether she calls herself a groupie—which to me doesn't have a stigma—or a Band Aid, then fire any arrow you want at the movie, and I'll regard it with amusement. I love that the opportunity wasn't missed to create a hero of the muse."

I understand why the Penny character insisted she had "retired." I felt the same way when the pubescent upstart groupies descended on the scene. "I remember reading about that in your first book," Cameron says. "The newer wave of groupies who had sharp teeth, and a 'GI Jills at war' thing going on. They didn't love the music as much as the spotlight and the trappings. And they were tough with each other."

Since I've been talking to groupies who are hanging out with bands right now, Cameron is curious, "Is there still the ethic of the blow job being safer than having actual intercourse sex?" I remember how differently Tina and Sarah felt about giving head and tell Cameron it still seems to be an individual choice. "One of them *wouldn't* give a blow job and the other one, that's *all* she'd do!"

In between my *Almost Famous* inquiries, Cameron and I have been reminiscing about old Hollywood friends, like the late Michele Myer who once said, "We know our limits—and there are none." We also speak fondly of our favorite male groupie, Rodney Bingenheimer.

When I ask if he liked the documentary *Mayor of the Sunset Strip*, Cameron shakes his head, "I never got Rodney's love of music in that film. I get it from your books. I get it from an Al Green documentary, just Al sitting in a studio with a guitar, telling stories. But in that solemn portrait of a lonely man being used by the girlfriend? Sure, it's true, but what about the joy? To me, Rodney's not somebody to be used to inspire sympathy. He's a hero for not trying to get money for all the bands he broke. He's a *hero*. He never took the stupid job and tried to capitalize on what he'd done. He did it out of true fandom. And that's the spirit of Penny Lane. She's not in a crumpled heap by the side of the road. She's more *rock* than the band, and that was always the point. There's a scene in the director's cut of *Almost*

Famous where Billy Crudup talks about, 'When you get a little bit of success, your career becomes about maintaining the lifestyle.' So many of those guys trail off into the world of lifestyle maintenance. And who's left knowing what it's truly about?"

I know the answer: "The girl on the side of the stage!" Cameron smiles, "Exactly. *That* girl. She is still there. And she'll always be there. I wanted the whole movie to be about that feeling, and the celebration of that feeling. The girl off to the side of the stage is the keeper of the flame."

> *"I need to see you face to face because I'm never as good as when you're there, and I can see myself the way you look at me."*
>
> —Russell Hammond to Penny Lane
> in *Almost Famous*

Me, Amanda, Miss Mercy, Gail, and Lori, 2006.

Cherry Vanilla, Lexa, me, Miss Mercy, and Cassandra, 2006.

Index